Office VBA:

Macros You Can Use Today

Office VBA: Macros You Can Use Today

Authors: Juan Pablo González, Cindy Meister, Suat Ozgur, Bill Dilworth, Nico Altink and Anne Troy.

Publisher: Bill Jelen

Project Manager: Anne Troy

Art Director: Scott Pierson

Technical Editor and PrePress: Linda DeLonais

Cover Design: Shannon Mattiza, 6'4 Productions

Published by: Holy Macro! Books, 13386 Judy, Uniontown OH 44685

Distributed by: Independent Publishers Group

ISBN: 1-932802-06-1

LCCN: 2005921880

First Printing: December 2005. Printed in USA

Table of Contents

Foreword .... a

About the Authors and Contributors c

Juan Pablo González c
Cindy Meister .... d
Suat Ozgur .... d
Bill Dilworth .... e
Nico Altink .... e
Contributors .... f

Introduction 1

What is VBA? 1
Save Time 1
Take Advantage of UserForms 1
Develop User-defined Functions 2
Enjoy Security 2

How to Use This Book 3

Using the Procedures 3
Understanding Code Comments 3
Inserting Paragraph Returns in Code 4
Using Menu Commands 4
Identifying Procedure Components 4
Using Sample Files 5
Backup Your Files! 5
Version Compatibility 5

Introducing the Visual Basic Editor 7

Accessing Visual Basic Editor (VBE) 8
Touring the VBE Toolbar 9
Setting VBE Options 11
Using Project Explorer 12
Understanding VBA Project 13
Working with Modules 14
Using the Main Code Window 16
Protecting Your Projects 18

Excel Procedures 19

Printing All Files 19
Saving a Workbook as Today's Date 21
Highlighting Duplicates Within a Range 23

Sorting Worksheets 25
Generating a Unique List 27
Using AutoFilter on a Protected Sheet 30
Deleting Rows Based on Criteria 31
Checking Whether or Not a File Exists 35
Removing Hyperlinks 36
Applying SUM / COUNT by Color 37
Using More Than Three Conditional Formats 40
Providing a Calendar to Choose Dates for Input 42
Restricting Text Box Entry to Numbers 45
Running a Macro When a Cell Changes 47
Forcing the Use of a Custom Print Procedure 49
Restricting the User to a Portion of the Worksheet 50
Copying a Workbook with Macros Removed 52
Inserting Empty Rows in a Range 54
Creating a Custom Toolbar 56
Creating a Table of Contents of a Workbook 60
Changing the Case of Text 62
Creating a Photo Album 64
Deleting the Empty Rows in a Range 67
Creating a List of Files That Reside in a Directory 69
Forcing the User to Enable Macros 73
Finding and Replacing a String in All Open Workbooks 75
Converting Data to a Tabular Format 76
AutoNumbering Invoices and Other Workbooks 79
Comparing Columns Using Various Criteria 80
Deleting the Contents of Unlocked Cells 83
Hiding All Standard Toolbars Except Your Own 85
Creating a PPT Presentation from a Pivot Chart 88
Saving a Backup Copy of a Workbook 93
Importing Your Contacts from Outlook 96
E-mailing from Excel with Outlook 99
Printing a UserForm 102
Importing and Formatting a Text File 105
Extracting Numbers from a Text String 109
Finding and Deleting Erroneously Named Ranges 111
Logging Actions When a Cell Changes 113
Synchronizing Page Fields of Pivot Tables 116

Word Procedures 119

Applying Your Favorite Bullet/Number Format 119
Finding and Replacing in Multiple Documents 122
Highlighting a Selection 126
Highlighting a Selection in Word 2002/XP 127
Removing All Highlighting 129
Inserting AutoText with No Formatting 130
Updating All Fields 131
Setting Hyperlinks on Index Entries 132
Displaying a Number in Millions as Text 138
Copying Nested Field Codes as Text 141
Converting AutoNumbered Text into Normal Text 144
Reverse Numbering 144
Tables: Changing the Tab Direction 146
Tables: Suppressing New Rows When Tabbing 148
Tables: Formatting Numbers in a Selection 149
Tables: Copying Formulas 151
Using Calendar Wizard 157
  Formatting Your Calendar 163
Inserting a Picture with Caption 164
  Making Changes 168
Associating a Picture with a Page 170
Forms: Suppressing New Paragraphs in Form Fields 175
Forms: Formatting Text Input in Form Fields 178
  Changing Other Types of Formatting 182
Forms: Inserting a New Table Row 183
Forms: Deleting a Table Row 189
Forms: Placing a Picture in a Protected Form 193
Mail Merge: Using a Relative Path for Data Source 195
Mail Merge: Displaying the Mail Merge Interface 198
Mail Merge: Creating a User-Friendly List of Fields 200
Mail Merge: Making Placecards Using WordArt 203
Mail Merge: Creating a One-to-Many List 205
Mail Merge: Merging with a Chart 215
Transferring a Selection to a New Document 225
Splitting a Document into Multiple Files 230
Creating a Folder Tree Menu 236
Changing Custom Dictionaries On-the-Fly 245
Formatting Spelling Errors for Printing 249

Entering Data Easily Using a Custom Dialog Box 254
Creating a Bookmark from a Selection 260
Making Bookmarks Visible 264
Forcing the User to Enable Macros 265
Generating the Document Using VBA 265
Using Forms Protection 267
Macros in Files Opened by Code 267

Outlook Procedures 269
Creating Control Buttons 269
Saving E-mail Attachments in a Specified Folder 271
Creating a Contacts Database 274
Sending a Web Page as the Body of an E-mail Message 279
Sending a Message Individually to Multiple Recipients 282
Sending Daily Attachments to Certain Recipients 287
Creating Reminders Automatically 290
Creating Task Items Automatically in Outlook 294
Special: Outlook Security 300
Auto Replying to Selected E-mail Messages 301
Remote Control with Outlook E-mail Message 302

PowerPoint Procedures 305
Inserting a Predefined Number of Slides 305
Manipulating AutoShapes 306
Grabbing All Text 308
Moving Shapes and Graphics During Presentation 310
Making a Random Jump to Another Slide 313
Random Madness 315
Sending Word Outline to Notes Section of PowerPoint 316
Wrapping Text to the Next Slide 319
Saving the Show Point 321
Personalizing a Presentation 322
Creating a New Presentation 324

Access Procedures 327
Splitting Names 327
Designing Consistent Forms 331
Triggering a New Form Based on a Subform Selection 334
Selecting and Filtering with Cascading Combo Boxes 337
E-mailing a Selection 342
Making a Rolodex-type Selection Listbox 346

Validating Data 350
Moving Rows Between Listboxes 353
Moving Rows in Listboxes 355
Creating a Dynamic Crosstab Report 357
Generating Periodic Reports 359
Creating Controlled Numbers 361
Making a Wizard with Tabbed Control 363

Combined Procedures 367

Transferring Charts From Excel to PowerPoint 367
Saving Word Form Data to an Excel Spreadsheet 368
Filling a Word Combo Box with Data from Excel 371
Transferring Data from E-mail Attachments to Excel 378
Creating Word Labels from an Excel Recipient List 382
Creating Custom Mail Merge Using Data in Excel Worksheet 389
Using Calendar Control for Office Applications 391

Appendix A 403

Opening and Using the Visual Basic Editor 403
Locating the Code Object 404
Inserting a Module 406
Inserting a UserForm 407
Opening Worksheet Objects (Excel) 410
Opening ThisWorkbook Object (Excel) 412
Opening ThisDocument Objects (Word) 412
Opening ThisOutlookSession Objects (Outlook) 413
Opening Slide Objects (Powerpoint) 414
Access Objects 415

Appendix B 417

Running a macro 417
Running a Macro Automatically 417
Running a Macro Manually 417
Running a Macro from a Toolbar Button 418
Running a Macro Using Shortcut Keys 419

Index 421

Foreword

A simple macro language appeared in version 3 of VisiCalc. When Lotus 1-2-3 introduced the keystroke macro recorder, accountants everywhere began developing arcane little macros to automate the daily task of importing and formatting sales data in their spreadsheets. When Excel 5 shipped with a new macro language called VBA in 1993, the world changed. Using VBA, it became possible for every one of the 400 million users of Microsoft Office to develop great looking and powerful applications.

The message board at MrExcel.com hosts over 30,000 questions per year and over a third of these questions are posed by people who have questions about VBA in Excel. Clearly – there are very many people using VBA around the world. However – the typical VBA coder is someone is not necessarily a programmer. You will have someone who is very good at a certain Office application – perhaps I would go so far as to call him or her a guru with a particular application. Soon, our coder has mastered every aspect of the application and starts to explore the macro recorder and then get in to writing VBA macros to automate the use of that application.

However – it is rare to find someone who is a guru in both Excel and PowerPoint. Either you work somewhere where you process lots of data or somewhere where you design a lot of presentations and your expertise in one app or another allows you to climb the learning curve for that VBA app.

At MrExcel Consulting, I prefer to write applications for Excel, but occasionally a client needs Excel to interface with PowerPoint or Word and things generally come to a halt. We know Excel VBA inside and out. We know the gotchas and the peculiarities that don't quite work. But, when we need to tread in the PowerPoint VBA object model, we are rookies.

The idea for this book was to gather together VBA experts from each of the Microsoft Office applications and to have them all design really cool applications for their individual application. The goal is for an expert in Excel VBA to be able to pick up the book and learn from example how things are done in PowerPoint or Word or Access or Outlook. There are many books on the bookstore shelves that address VBA for one particular Office app or another – my goal with this book is that you can comfortably write useful macros in all of your Office apps.

Bill Jelen
co-author of VBA & Macros for Microsoft Excel

This page intentionally left blank.

About the Authors and Contributors

We have asked some of the greatest, most respected developers from all over the world to provide you with the most commonly asked for VBA routines, and to demystify those routines for you.

Juan Pablo González

Excel Development Author

Juan Pablo was born in Bogotá, Colombia. He started programming in Basic and then ventured for a while with Q–Basic and Pascal. But it wasn't until the spreadsheet battle between Lotus, Quattro Pro, and Excel that he started to build small applications to solve simple problems.

While he attended Pontificia Universidad Javeriana for his major in Industrial Engineering, Juan Pablo developed several applications—all of which were based in Microsoft Excel—to deal with issues that are found on a daily basis in different areas of any organization, such as customer service, marketing, and accounting.

In 2001, working as an analyst for an Insurance company, he began browsing the message board at www.MrExcel.com, where he realized the potential of Microsoft Excel—something very few people seem to grasp. After winning with an entry he submitted to MrExcel's "Challenge of the Month", he began working as a part-time consultant, creating Excel-based applications for clients around the globe.

He works now as a full-time developer and software architect for Dealerware, LLC, a software company based in Illinois. Their main product is F & I Menu Wizard (www.FIMenuWizard.com), a very impressive Excel-based application used by automobile dealerships. JP (as his friends call him) lives in Carbondale, Illinois, and continues to offer free peer-to-peer support at the www.MrExcel.com message board as well as the Microsoft public newsgroups. These contributions have earned him Microsoft's Excel Most Valuable Professional (MVP) Award. JP can be reached at JuanPablo@MrExcel.com.

Cindy Meister

Word Development Author

Cindy has a BS in Agronomy and practical experience in various business fields, which provide a diverse background for her consulting work as INTERSolutions. She provides training, but specializes in Word automation, particularly when linking Word with other Office applications.

Cindy is a regular author for the German magazine "Inside Word". She occasionally contributes articles to "Microsoft Office and Visual Basic for Applications Developer", Pinnacle Publishing's "Smart Access", and Logical Expression's "Computer Companion".

To get away from the computer, Cindy makes bobbin lace, rides horseback, and reads science fiction novels.

Suat Ozgur

Outlook Development Author

Mehmet (Suat) Ozgur is a Licensed Civil Engineer with a Master's degree in Mechanics from Yildiz Technical University.

Suat began coding with GWBasic to save time on his school projects, which required mostly algorithms for numerical analysis. His first PC was an IBM PS/2, given to him by his Uncle, who also encouraged him to take an English language course that would change his life.

Suat worked through school as packing designer (CAD) during university years, and met with database logic while building packages. He found he enjoyed working with databases and decided to focus on database programming. He figures the database is "everything. If you have data, then you have a reason to create an application to manage this data."

Under the moniker "smozgur", Suat has contributed to many technical forums, including Experts-Exchange, TheOfficeExperts, MrExcel, and VBAExpress. In attempting to answer questions, he was forced to look up many things, and ended up learning ASP, PHP, and HTML coding as a result.

Suat has been working as a MrExcel programming consultant for more than three years. He is very happily married and has no idea how he could exist without his wife, Muge. They live in Istanbul, Turkey. He can be reached at Suat@MrExcel.com.

Bill Dilworth

PowerPoint Development Author

"Cutting-edge", when Bill was in high school, was two Teletype machines with an acoustic modem link to the University of Delaware's mainframe. Anyone remember yellow punch tape? Bill's done a number of things over the years, including installation of stage counter-weight and curtains systems, being a maintenance crew member of the Dickinson Theater Pipe Organ, lighting of same, club bouncer, pinball machine mechanic, vending machine mechanic, data entry, hospital orderly, providing lighting and set design/construction for some very small stage productions, and even a few classes in the behind-the-proscenium-arch stuff. He was able to learn from these varied experiences the core basics of theater and presentation, message and media, players and costume.

Bill changed over to Ophthalmology, becoming a technician more than 15 years ago, where he continues to learn about people and communication. He has learned how to be understood by scared, nervous or bored people and to translate medical jargon into 'people' language. He is currently managing the Ocular Imaging Center of the Eye & Ear Institute of Pittsburgh.

Bill picked up PowerPoint as a sideline while doing occasional presentations at work and helping co-workers solve their computer problems. He really began to focus on PowerPoint when his wife volunteered him for the post of Tech Team Leader at their church, where he designs and presents PowerPoint supplements for the worship services and sermons.

Nico Altink

Access Development Author

Nico began programming in the early seventies at the "Verkeers academie" (Traffic Academy) where they had a PDP-11 with a card reader. Thus, his first programs had to be punched on an IBM punching machine. Creating a program in such a way was an elaborate task. Imagine what happened when someone dropped the punched cards on the ground!

Having been a mainframe programmer for almost five years, Nico stepped through technical design, functional design and finally, information analysis. However, in the 80s with the introduction of the home computer and out of curiosity, Nico bought a Commodore 64. He told his wife it came in handy for making shopping lists but later had to admit it was just a hobby. As a matter of fact, Nico is still fascinated by that machine because it turned out to be a "real" computer with sound and graphics and it even forced him to learn the Assembler language (Basic was way too slow for a lot of tasks he had in mind). After an upgrade to the Amiga 2000, Nico had to buy an IBM PC. All the customers he worked for were switching from the IBM 3090 monitors to PCs, and it would look strange to the company, family, and neighbors if a computer expert had no knowledge of such a "simple" thing as a PC.

When asked by a neighbor to develop a database system, Nico took the challenge. The neighbor owned Microsoft Office 95 with Microsoft Access, making the choice of database programs obvious. The database has grown to its current size of over 250 forms, 60 tables and countless queries created both in the query editor and in VBA code.

Working as an information analyst, Nico began to use Microsoft Access to make his job easier. The first thing he normally does when he gets some data is to import it into Access and run some basic queries to assess the quality of the data and reveal any possible problems with it. Using the right-click popup menu to filter and sort has become his standard method of investigating "raw" data.

Nowadays, Nico is often found helping people in the Microsoft Access topic area of www.experts-exchange.com, because for him there's no such thing as dividing knowledge, but only knowledge multiplication. Helping others to understand the way Microsoft Access works and the cooperation with the other Microsoft Access experts expands Nico's knowledge; he believes this book shows some of the fruits of this knowledge multiplication.

Contributors

Ken Puls of Nanaimo, British Columbia, Canada, provided technical review of the contents, and wrote the Appendix.

Anne Troy of Quakertown, Pennsylvania, developed the idea for this book, managed it as a project, and edited its content.

Jacob Hilderbrand of www.VBAExpress.com has generously allowed us to use a revised version of their Lesson 1 of VBA Programming and Certification to provide you with an understanding of Visual Basic for Applications.

TJ Brandt of www.Brandtrock.com consulting assisted in writing of non-procedural portions of the book, and organizing and editing portions.

The following persons for their small, but not insignificant, contributions: Rich Shields, John Skewes, Carlos Fernando Paleo da Rocha, and Tony Jollans.

Introduction

We have created a basic book for users of all of the Office applications, rather than focusing on any one application or going into great detail.

This is not a manual to teach you Visual Basic for Applications (VBA); it is an introduction to show you what VBA can do for you. It provides over 100 programming examples for real-life situations. The average user may find 10 or more macros that they can begin using instantly, while others may find that they can implement half the macros in this book within a few days.

What is VBA?

VBA is Visual Basic for Applications. Visual Basic (VB) is a programming language that has long been used to create custom applications. VBA is a mini-version of VB that Microsoft includes with each application of the Microsoft Office products. Why pay someone to custom-program a spreadsheet application when you can use VBA in Microsoft Excel for a fraction of the cost? Many people grumble and groan over the limitations of these applications until they learn that VBA can provide for their specific needs.

Here are just a few of the reasons to use VBA.

Save Time

Macros perform repetitive tasks. If you spend 20 minutes each day formatting data to report the previous day's earnings, then a macro can format that spreadsheet for you with the click of a button. If you run and print the same three mail merges every day, then this task can be reduced to a button-click that runs a macro to do it for you.

Take Advantage of UserForms

VBA can provide UserForms. If you have ever used a wizard in a software application, then you have used a UserForm. If you have ever entered data into pre-defined boxes, then you have used a UserForm. UserForms enable us to provide an easy user interface, to restrict entry of data to valid values, and to allow the application to work behind the scenes.

Develop User-defined Functions

When the function you need to perform isn't built-in, VBA provides a method to create any function you need. These are called user-defined functions, or UDFs. Many of the procedures contained herein use a function to perform their task.

Enjoy Security

Have you ever wanted to keep your users from seeing that data on your payroll worksheet? Have you ever wanted to ensure that they can add only certain information to that contract document? If so, then VBA is for you.

How to Use This Book

This book is not set up like most technical books. We have attempted to organize it so that someone reasonably familiar with an application can go to the chapter for that application, start reading, and begin using the automation procedures within a few minutes. However, if you've never heard of macros, procedures, or VBA before, then you may want to first continue reading the materials here in the front chapters to get more comfortable before you start using the sample codes.

Once you've become familiar with the contents, go right to the chapter for your favorite application, find a macro or procedure you can use, and start using it by following the instructions provided with it.

Using the Procedures

Experts who have a great deal of knowledge in particular applications provided the procedures for this book. The macros simply need to be copied to the appropriate places, which are indicated with each macro. If any modifications are required, these are also listed with the macros provided.

Understanding Code Comments

The code is heavily commented so that you can understand what it does. Any line of code that is preceded by an apostrophe (') turns the font green in your Visual Basic Editor window and is ignored when the code is run; hence, we call it "commented code".

When code is written to provide multiple outcomes, there are instructions to "uncomment" a portion of the code—to remove the apostrophe from the beginning of the line or to "comment" a portion of the code—to add an apostrophe to the beginning of the line.

Many of the applications herein use more than one procedure. When this occurs, we have separated the procedures by a commented line of asterisks for reference purposes only, as follows:

```
' * * * * *
```

Tip: There is no need to use these separations in your own code, but it may help you to read it more easily.

Int

Inserting Paragraph Returns in Code

The code in this book has been enhanced with visible paragraph returns. If you manually type the code into the module (see Opening and Using the Visual Basic Editor on page 403), you should only hit the Enter key when you see a paragraph return symbol. This scheme enabled us to present the code from the experts without modifying it for this book. (Of course, we used a macro to add the paragraph returns to the code text!)

This is the paragraph return symbol; it is actually called a "pilcrow": ¶

Note: Be sure, when manually typing code from this manual, to *hit Enter only when you see a pilcrow* (¶).

Using Menu Commands

The steps to follow using menu commands are written using the following format:

```
Insert | Module
```

This example means that you should choose Insert from the menu at the top of the window and then choose Module from the Insert dropdown menu.

Identifying Procedure Components

Each procedure described has some or all of the following components, depending on whether they apply for that procedure:

- Descriptive title
- Brief description
- Name of the example file, if any
- Screenshot(s) of the example file, if any
- Scenario for its use
- Location in which code should be stored
- Code
- Information about customizing the code, if possible
- Notes and cautions about using the code, if any

Using Sample Files

The sample files that contain the procedures are available for download at www.MrExcel.com/officevba/index.html.

Simply download the ZIP file, extract the files to a location on your PC, and work with them there.

The code in the sample files may differ slightly from the code in the book because we have formatted the code in the book to be slightly more standardized from one expert's code to the next.

Backup Your Files!

You may want to try running the code in a sample file before you try using the code in your own file(s).

Note: Always create a copy of your own file for safekeeping prior to manipulating it with any of the procedures herein. We can't be responsible if your file becomes unusable as a result of using the code.

Version Compatibility

The procedures in this book are intended to work in the Office 2003 version of the applications; however, most of them work in versions 97 and up, or are commented with information on how to edit the code for earlier versions.

Int

Introducing the Visual Basic Editor

Understanding a concept begins with defining unfamiliar terms. The terminology required to understand Visual Basic for Applications (VBA) is fairly straightforward and is introduced throughout the book. In order to start learning, you need to become familiar with the following terms:

Term	Description
Code	This term is generally used to refer to the text of the program language.
Visual Basic for Applications (VBA)	The programming language used to write programs in Microsoft Office applications.
Visual Basic Editor (VBE)	The environment (or window) in which VBA code is written.
Procedures	Entities that perform a task and in which the code is written; also called macros. Think of them as containers for code.
Modules	A container for Procedures. A Module can hold many Procedures or just one.
Projects	A container for modules. All of the VBA code in any single workbook, document, database, presentation, or Outlook item is called a project.
Comments/ Commented Code	This is a part of the code that is preceded by special characters so that it is seen as text and will not run. Placing an apostrophe as the first character of the line “tells” VBA that this line is a comment. Good coders heavily comment their code so that it can be more easily edited when necessary.
Add-ins	When a Microsoft Office program opens, any installed add-ins also open. Add-ins are special programs that extend the built-in features of the program in some way. Thus, there are sometimes more objects open within the application environment than you might think. Not all of these objects have a visible presence in the standard interface, but they are all at least partially exposed in the programming environment.

Accessing Visual Basic Editor (VBE)

The VBE (the programming environment) can be accessed from any of the Microsoft Office programs by opening the program and then either pressing Tools | Macro | Visual Basic Editor from the Menu or using the keyboard shortcut: Alt+F11. Clicking the right mouse button on some objects in the Microsoft Office programs gives the option to View Code; others have the Visual Basic Editor as an option on the drop-down menu. Any of the methods mentioned can be used to open the VBE.

For consistency, we use the VBE for Microsoft Excel to illustrate the functionality of the VBE in this book. When one of the other applications varies from the way Excel uses the VBE, we note this exception.

When the VBE opens, it pops up in a new window. An example for Excel is shown in Figure 1.

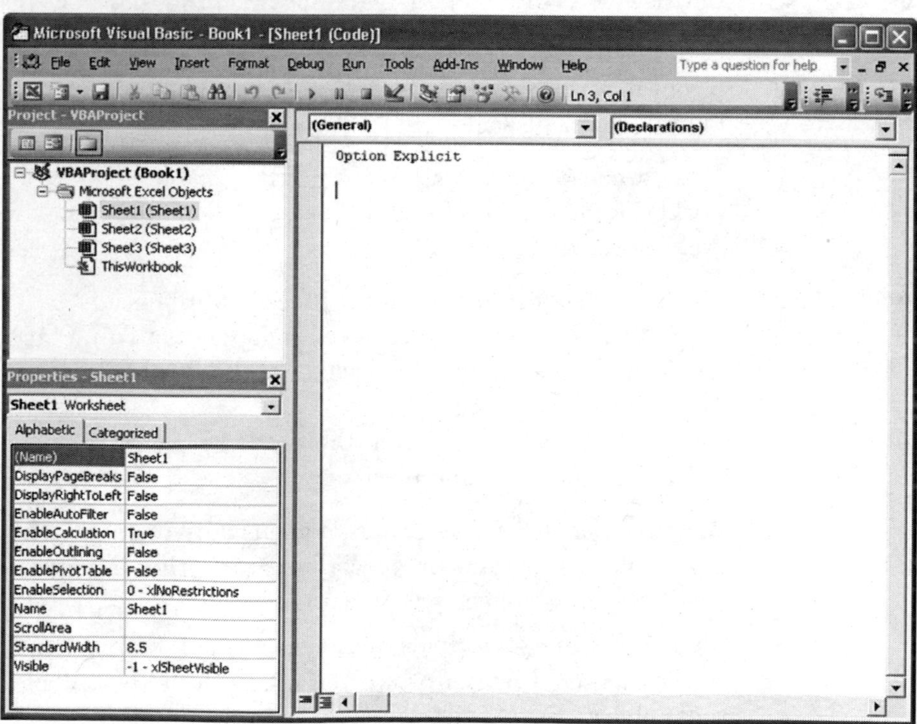

Figure 1 –Microsoft Excel Visual Basic Editor

The VBE window is just like any other window. It has a Title bar, a Menu bar, and a Tool bar, and likely contains some familiar options or icons, and some that you might not have seen before. The main body of the VBE window consists of one or more sub-windows.

Each individual Office program launches its own VBE. When running multiple programs, multiple VBE windows can be open at the same time without interfering with each other. The coding in any window is relevant only to the program that launched it.

Touring the VBE Toolbar

Figure 2 depicts the Excel VBE Menu bar and Standard toolbar, collectively called the Visual Basic Editor toolbar in this book. You can perform various tasks from this toolbar when using or writing code.

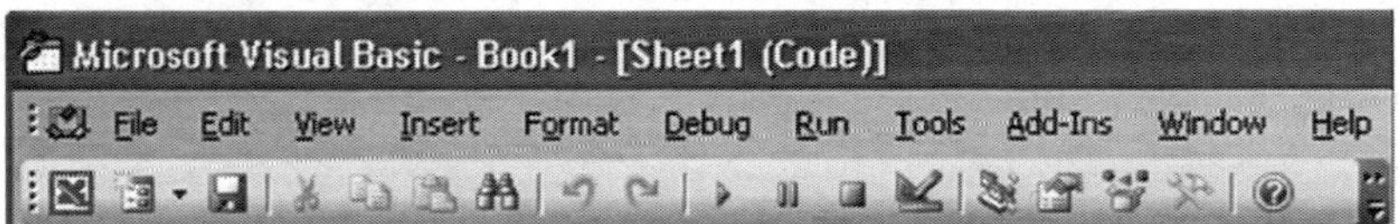

Figure 2 – The VBE Toolbar

Some of the buttons available on the VBE toolbar are described in the table below.

Icon	Name	Description
	View Microsoft Office	Switch focus from the VBE back to the Office application associated with the VBE. The icon for the program that "belongs" to the VBE resides in the first position on the left of the VBE toolbar. The Excel icon is illustrated here.
	Insert	Select the drop-down arrow to see choices to insert a new UserForm, Module, Class module, or Procedure. The UserForm option is not in the drop-down list in Access.

Icon	Name	Description
	Run	Press this button to run a procedure.
	Break	Press this button to put code in Break mode and stop it from running.
	Reset	When code is in Break mode, press this button to reset the code to its normal status.
	Design Mode	Press this button to temporarily disable any code from running while working on a project, such as when editing a command button; also used to create UserForms.
	Project Explorer Window	Display the Project Explorer window.
	Properties Window	Display the Properties Window.
	View Code	View the code for the selected module.

Setting VBE Options

The VBE has a set of options that allow for customizing the interface to individual user preferences. From the VBE Toolbar, select Tools | Options to display the Option dialog shown in Figure 3.

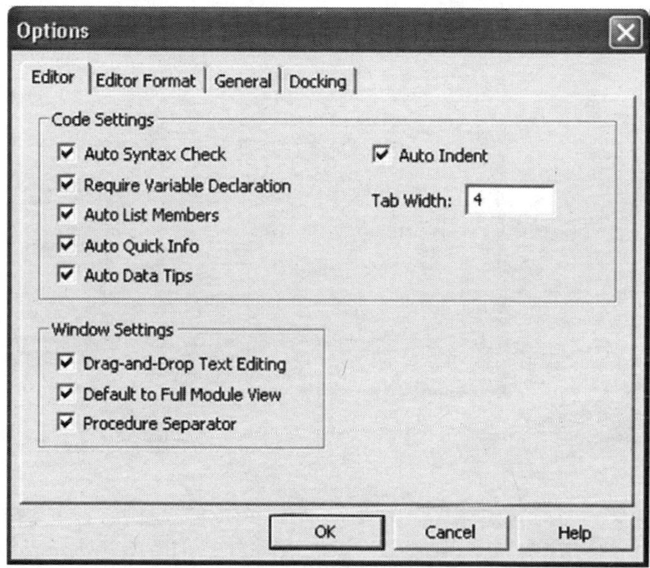

Figure 3 – The VBE Options Menu

The Options Dialog in the VBE affords users the opportunity to modify the way the VBE looks and behaves. From the Editor tab, make sure that all the checkboxes are checked. While the individual settings are not covered in detail in this book, we do recommend checking the box for Require Variable Declaration. It is not checked by default, but it is good programming practice to enable this option.

Tip: For those interested, more detail and online VBA Training can be found online at www.VBAExpress.com, as well as other websites.

Using Project Explorer

To navigate within the various elements in the programming environment, there is one very useful window: the Project Explorer. By default, it is located at the top-left of the VBE; it is shown in Figure 4.

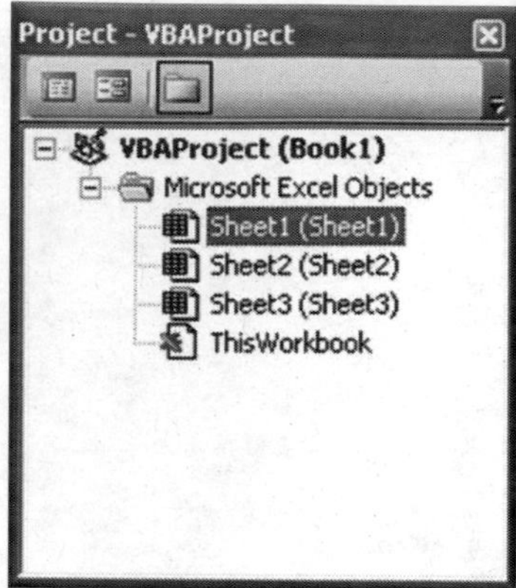

Figure 4 – The Project Explorer Window

The Project Explorer window should be visible by default. If it is not, or if you accidentally close it, it can be shown by any of the following methods:

1. Select View | Project Explorer from the VBE Toolbar.
2. Click the Project Explorer icon on the VBE Toolbar.
3. Use the Ctrl+R keyboard shortcut.

The Project Explorer is much like any other Windows Explorer interface. It shows a hierarchy of objects from which to choose. Branches to expand and/or choose elements to view in detail in one of the other panes are shown with the familiar + or –.

Understanding VBA Project

The first item in the Project Explorer (see Figure 4) is called VBAProject(Book1). Book1 is simply the name of the Excel workbook being used in the screen capture. When the workbook is saved, the name changes to the name and file extension of the workbook. For example, if the workbook were saved as MyWorkbook.xls, then the Project Explorer window would also change to display VBAProject(MyWorkbook.xls). If multiple workbooks are open, each one is listed in the Project Explorer alphabetically, as well as any loaded Add-ins. For simplicity, we assume that just one workbook is open at this time.

Word displays the Normal project as open in the VBE if a document is open. It loads when Word is launched. The file name of the Normal project is normal.dot and it is Word's default template; it is always in use when Word is in use, much like an Add-in.

The first item within the VBAProject is Microsoft Excel Objects. As with Windows Explorer, any of the items with a plus (+) or a minus (–) can be expanded or retracted by double-clicking on the name or by single-clicking the + or –.

These are some of the primary differences in the user interface between the five applications:

Application	Differences
Excel	Lists every worksheet that is in the workbook within the Microsoft Excel Objects group. ThisWorkbook is listed as well. In the macro examples, the specialized code that can be placed in these sections is illustrated.
Word	Lists Microsoft Word Objects where ThisDocument is listed. It operates in a similar fashion to ThisWorkbook.
Microsoft Outlook	Lists Microsoft Outlook Objects where ThisOutlookSession is listed. It operates in a similar fashion to ThisWorkbook, also.
Microsoft Access	Lists no Microsoft Access Objects group. There is no ThisDatabase object.
Microsoft PowerPoint	Does not list an Objects group. There is no ThisPresentation object, which has long frustrated those trying to learn how to use VBA with PowerPoint.

Working with Modules

VBA has several places in which to store code, but the vast majority of code is stored in Standard modules, regardless of the application. Before a module can be used, it must first be added to the project. From the VBE Toolbar, select Insert | Module as shown in Figure 5. Alternatively, press the down arrow on the Insert button and select Module.

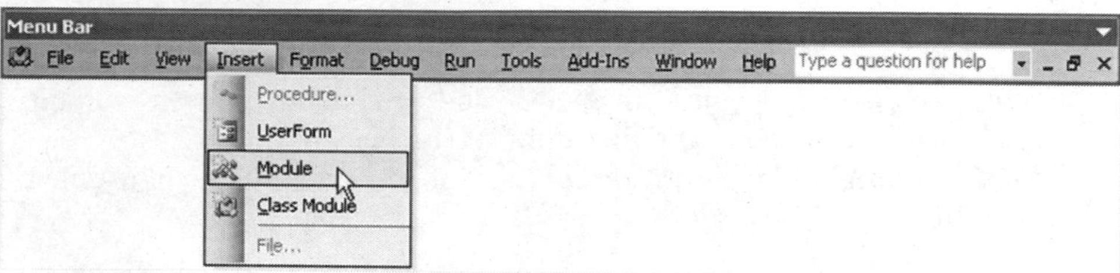

Figure 5 – Inserting a Module

The only limitation to the number of modules an Office file can have is the limitation imposed by the amount of the computer's memory. Each module can have one or many procedures. Writing a project using modules to group similar procedures together helps keep your project better organized.

In this book, the word "module" is used to indicate a Standard module, though the word "Standard" is rarely used to describe it; it's just called a "module". Class modules can also be used in VBA Projects; these are referred to as Class modules in this text.

In our next graphic, the project is expanded to display the contents. Double-click to hide the contents. Click on the Toggle Folders button to display the projects as folders, as shown in Figure 6.

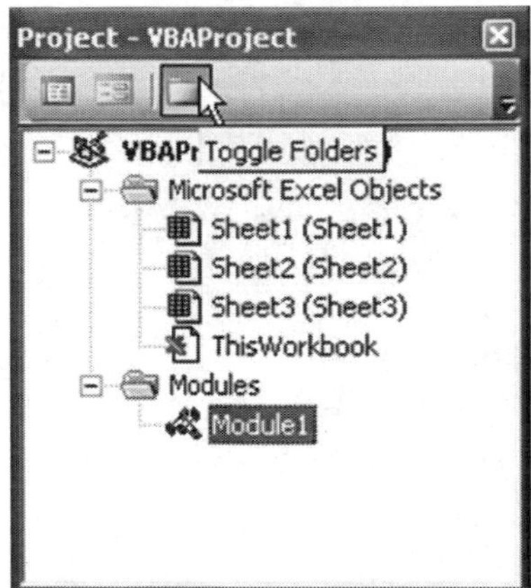

Figure 6 – Toggle Folders View

Once the module is inserted, be sure to give it a meaningful name. If you leave the name as Module1, when the project is revised later there will be no immediate clue as to the content of that module. Applying meaningful, descriptive names to modules makes troubleshooting or retooling much easier.

To rename a module, first make sure that the Properties window is visible. By default, it is located at the lower-left of the VBE, and is shown in Figure 7.

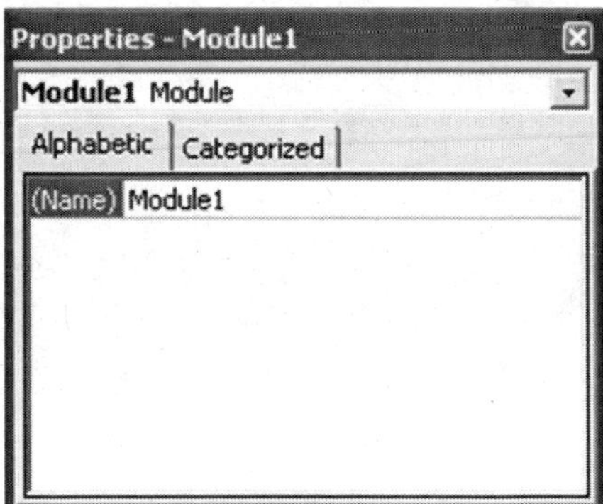

Figure 7 – The Properties Window

The Properties window should be visible by default. If it is not, it can be shown by any of following methods:

1. Select View | Properties Window from the VBE Toolbar.

2. Click the Properties Window button on the VBE Toolbar.
3. Use the shortcut key, F4.

Change the name of the module by typing the desired name into the Name field. The name must start with a letter, cannot be more than 31 characters long, and cannot contain any spaces. Also, most symbols cannot be used. For the illustration in the next section, we renamed the module from Module1 to MyCodeModule. When the name in the Properties window is changed, the Project Explorer is automatically updated with the new name.

Using the Main Code Window

Now that we have gone through the objects that can appear in the Project Explorer, it is time to see the actual window where code for modules is displayed, edited, and debugged.

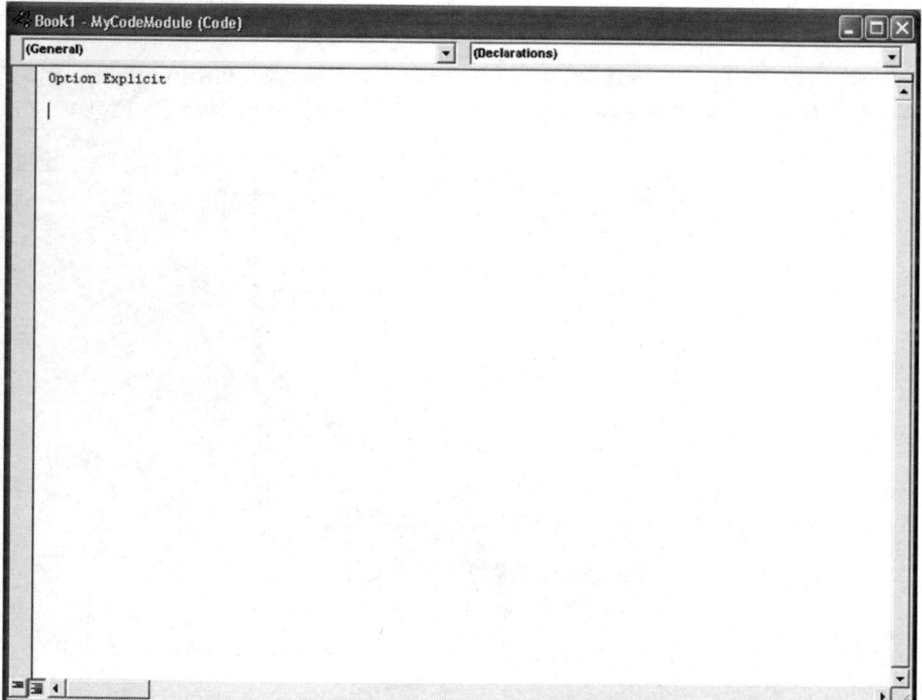

Figure 8 – Main Code Window

To work with an existing module, first select it by clicking on its Name in the Project Explorer. You can then open it using any of the following methods:

- Double-click it.
- Click the View Code button from the Project Explorer.
- Select View | Code from the VBE Toolbar.
- Use the shortcut key, F7.

At the top of the Main Code window, you will see two drop-downs. The drop-down on the left lists various objects within the module. The drop-down on the right lists the different procedures within the module. Refer to Figure 9 and Figure 10.

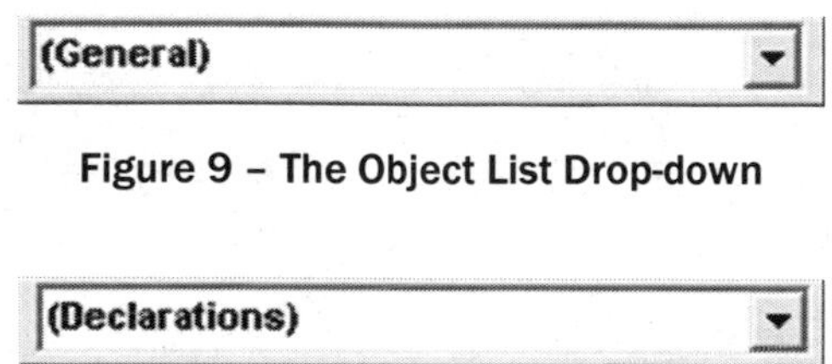

Figure 9 – The Object List Drop-down

Figure 10 – The Event/Procedure List Drop-down

When you write multiple procedures, you can use these drop-downs to navigate directly to the start of any procedure. Think of them as menus for the module.

There are three windows in the VBE that we will not discuss: the Immediate window, the Watch window, and the Locals window. These windows are used in specific instances, and are not necessary to operate the macros in this book.

Protecting Your Projects

Int

You can protect a VBA project so the user cannot show the worksheets directly from the Visual Basic Editor. To do so, go to Tools | VBA Project Properties.... The dialog that launches has a Protect tab. On this tab, check the box to Lock project for viewing; then press Enter and confirm the password to be used.

Note: Be sure to write the password down so you don't forget it!

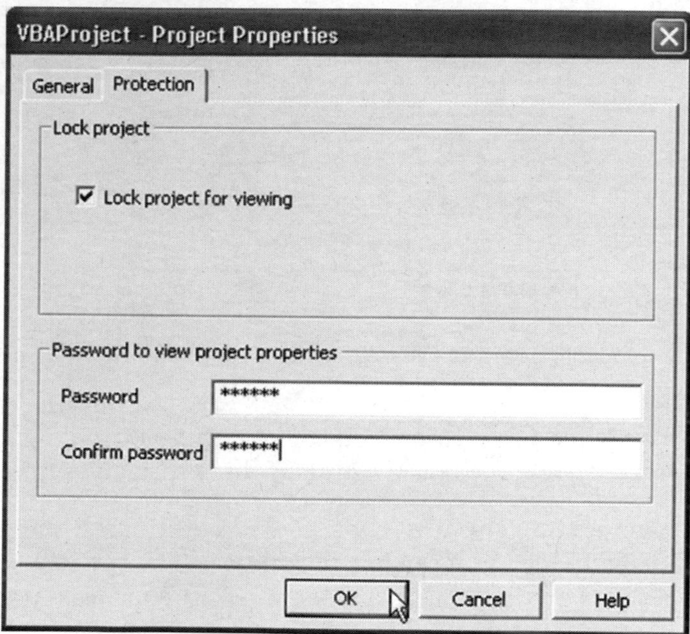

Figure 11 – The Project Protection Screen

Excel Procedures

By Juan Pablo González

Printing All Files

Use this procedure to print all the available workbooks within a directory without having to open and print each one separately.

Exl

Example file:
E001.xls

> **Scenario:** This macro is useful when there is a list of files (for instance, sales reports from different regions or statistics from all the departments in the company) within a folder and/or its subfolders, and printing them out quickly is desired.

View the Appendix to learn about storing this procedure in a Standard module.

```
Option Explicit¶
' * * * * *¶
Sub PrintAllFiles()¶
    'This macro will print all files in a specific directory¶
'Variable declarations¶
'Variable containing the name where Excel will search¶
  Dim Folder As String¶
'Workbook for each document¶
 Dim File As Workbook ¶
'Counter¶
  Dim Counter As Long¶
'Decides if Excel needs to look in subfolders¶
  Dim LookInSubFolders As Boolean¶
'Store old calculation method¶
  Dim OldCalculation As Long¶
  'Change the following variables¶
  'set the folder programatically¶
  Folder = "C:\"¶
  'set the folder via user input¶
  Folder = Range("B1").Value¶
  'set the subfolder search programatically¶
  LookInSubFolders = False¶
  'set the subfolder search via user input¶
  LookInSubFolders = Range("B2").Value¶
  'Turn off various settings to speed up the code¶
```

Exl

```
    'Screen Updating¶
    Application.ScreenUpdating = False¶
    'Calculation¶
    'Store current calculation method in variable¶
    OldCalculation = Application.Calculation¶
    'Set calculation to manual¶
    Application.Calculation = xlCalculationManual¶
    'Alerts¶
    Application.DisplayAlerts = False¶
    'Events¶
    Application.EnableEvents = False¶
  'Use Excel's built-in search engine¶
    With Application.FileSearch¶
      .NewSearch¶
      'Feed the parameters¶
      .LookIn = Folder¶
      .SearchSubFolders = LookInSubFolders¶
      'Look only for Excel workbooks¶
      .FileType = msoFileTypeExcelWorkbooks¶
      'Execute the search, return number files found if any¶
      If .Execute() > 0 Then¶
        'Loop through each file¶
        For Counter = 1 To .FoundFiles.Count()¶
          'Open the file, using the "File" workbook as the variable¶
          Set File = Workbooks.Open(Filename:=.FoundFiles(Counter), _¶
              UpdateLinks:=False, ReadOnly:=True)¶
          'Print to the default printer¶
          'Print only one copy (change the 1 as needed)¶
          File.PrintOut Copies:=1¶
          'Close the workbook, without saving changes¶
          File.Close SaveChanges:=False¶
          'Next file¶
        Next Counter¶
      Else¶
        'No files found, notify the user¶
        MsgBox "No files found", vbCritical¶
      End If¶
    End With¶
    'Restore settings¶
    'Events¶
    Application.EnableEvents = True¶
    'Alerts¶
    Application.DisplayAlerts = True¶
    'Calculation¶
    Application.Calculation = OldCalculation¶
    'Screen Updating¶
    Application.ScreenUpdating = True¶
End Sub¶
```

You can change the information in the 'Change the following variables' section by changing the path in which to look for the files and setting the

LookInSubFolders to True or False, depending on whether the subfolders should also be searched.

Saving a Workbook as Today's Date

This macro saves the workbook using today's date as the base name.

Example file:
E002.xls

> **Scenario:** This macro automates the creation of period reports that can be easily identified by the file name.

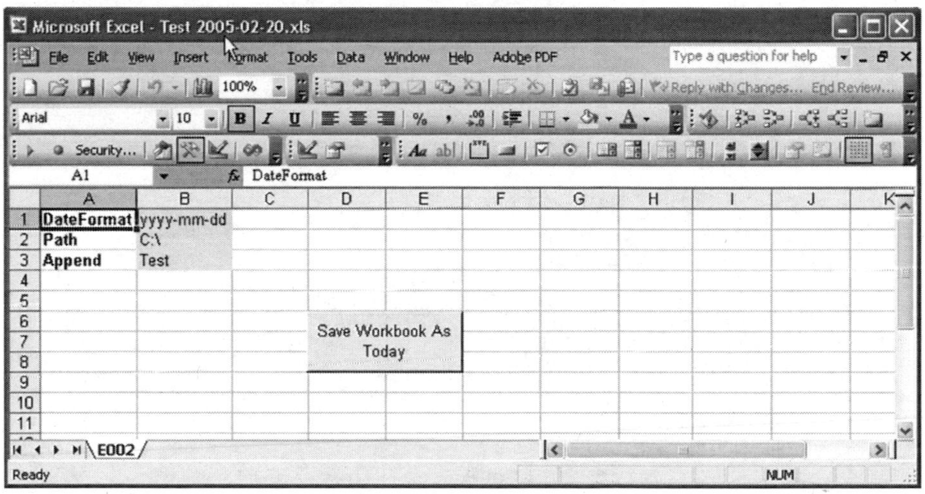

Figure 12 – Saving a Workbook Named as Today's Date

> View the Appendix to learn about storing this procedure in a Standard module or in ThisWorkbook.

```
Option Explicit¶
' * * * * *¶
Sub SaveWorkbookAsToday()¶
  'This macro saves the current (active) workbook with today's date¶
  'variable declaration¶
'The format to be used for the file name¶
  Dim DateFormat As String¶
'The path to be used to save the file (if empty, current path of
workbook is used)¶
```

Exl

```
  Dim Path As String¶
'Any text to be appended to the file name¶
  Dim Append As String¶
  'Change the following variables¶
  'Do not use "\" or "/" as a date separator¶
  DateFormat = "yyyy-mm-dd"¶
  DateFormat = Range("B1").Value¶
  Path = ""¶
  'Path = "C:\My Documents"¶
  Path = Range("B2").Value¶
  Append = ""¶
  'Append = "Report "¶
  Append = Range("B3").Value¶
  'Make sure a valid date format is used¶
  If DateFormat Like "[\/]" Then¶
    MsgBox "Illegal date format used", vbCritical¶
  Else¶
    'Assign today's date¶
    DateFormat = Format$(Date, DateFormat)¶
    'Add text to the filename?¶
    DateFormat = Append & DateFormat¶
    'Is there a path assigned?¶
    If Len(Path) = 0 Then¶
      'Use the current directory¶
      Path = CurDir()¶
    End If¶
    'Create the full name for the file¶
    'Make sure there's a folder separator at the end¶
    If Right$(Path, Len(Application.PathSeparator)) <> _¶
      Application.PathSeparator Then¶
        Path = Path & Application.PathSeparator¶
    End If¶
    'Append the date¶
    Path = Path & DateFormat¶
    'Try to save the active workbook with that name¶
    On Error Resume Next¶
    ActiveWorkbook.SaveAs Path¶
    'See if an error occurs¶
    If Err.Number <> 0 Then¶
      MsgBox "The following error occured:" & vbNewLine & _¶
          "Error: " & Err.Number & ", " & Err.Description, vbCritical¶
    End If¶
  End If¶
End Sub¶
```

In the 'Change the following variables' section, there are three variables that you can change:

- **Path:** where the file will be saved
- **DateFormat:** the format to use for the file name

- **Append:** in case adding something to the file name of the workbook (such as 'Sales for') is desired

Tip: See Excel's Help topic, 'About number formats', to see examples on formatting dates.

As the code is written, these three variables are entered into cells B1, B2, and B3. The location of the input cells can be changed as long as you reflect that change in the code. The user then can change the values of those input cells but doesn't need to change any of the VBA code. So, you could write this code in your workbook and let others use it without ever entering the VBE.

Highlighting Duplicates Within a Range

Use this procedure to highlight any duplicate entries that appear within a contiguous range (not only a column).

Scenario: This macro enables the user to visually highlight any duplicates entries within a range of cells. It is particularly useful when consolidating information from accounts or when trying to pinpoint items that appear more than once in a long list.

Example file:
E003.xls

	A	B
1	**Customer Name**	
2	Aaron	
3	Erin	
4	Cody	
5	Michelle	
6	Shirley	
7	Mary	
8	Anna	
9	Erin	
10	Michelle	
11	Kaytlin	
12	Rachel	
13	Anna	

Figure 13 – Highlighting Duplicates

Exl

View the Appendix to learn how to store this procedure in a Standard module.

```
Option Explicit¶
' * * * * *¶
Sub HighlightDuplicates()¶
'Highlights any duplicate entries that appear within a contiguous range
(not only a column)¶
  'Variable declarations¶
  Dim Rng As Range¶
  Dim Formula As String¶
  'Check if a worksheet is selected¶
  If TypeName(ActiveSheet) <> "Worksheet" Then¶
    MsgBox "There must be at least one worksheet visible", _¶
        vbCritical¶
    Exit Sub¶
  End If¶
  'Change the following variables¶
  'use the following line for a constant range - change as required¶
  Set Rng = Range("A1:A13")¶
  'Comment out the line above (add an apostrophe at left)¶
  'and remove the apostrophe on the line below to use the¶
  'selected range¶
'  Set Rng = ActiveWindow.RangeSelection¶
  'Can only do on contigous ranges¶
  If Rng.Areas.Count > 1 Then¶
    MsgBox "Unable to work on non contiguous cells", vbCritical¶
  Else¶
    'Delete any conditional formats¶
    Rng.FormatConditions.Delete¶
    'Create the formula¶
    Formula = "=COUNTIF(" & Rng.Address(True, True, xlR1C1) & ","¶
    If Rng.Columns.Count > 1 Then¶
      Formula = Formula & ActiveCell.Address(False, False, _¶
          xlR1C1) & ")>1"¶
    Else¶
      Formula = Formula & ActiveCell.Address(False, True, _¶
          xlR1C1) & ")>1"¶
    End If¶
    'Make sure that the correct position is used¶
    Formula = Application.ConvertFormula(Formula, xlR1C1, xlA1, , _¶
        Range("A1"))¶
    'Add the new condition¶
    With Rng.FormatConditions.Add(xlExpression, , Formula)¶
      .Interior.ColorIndex = 38    'Light red¶
    End With¶
  End If¶
End Sub¶
```

This macro has only two variables. As it is written, it works only on the range A1:A13. Change the range A1:A13 to your desired range. Or, you can change it to work on a range selected by the user. The Interior.ColorIndex = 38 can be set to a different color by changing the 38 to a different number.

Note: This macro erases any conditional formats on the range that gets checked.

Sorting Worksheets

With this procedure, you can sort the worksheets of the current workbook—all or just the selected ones—in ascending or descending order, according to their names.

Scenario: There are situations in which a workbook might contain quite a few worksheets, making it very hard to find a specific one. Sorting them alphabetically might alleviate the problem. Another example might be a workbook that contains one sheet for each employee in the company. This workbook would be much easier to use if its sheets were sorted alphabetically.

Example file:
E004.xls

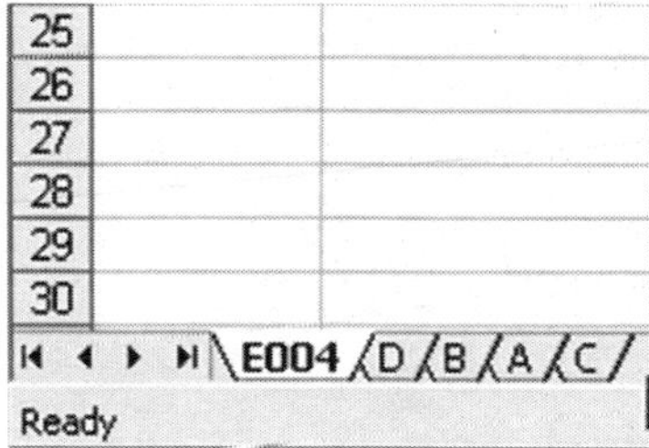

Figure 14 – Worksheets Unsorted

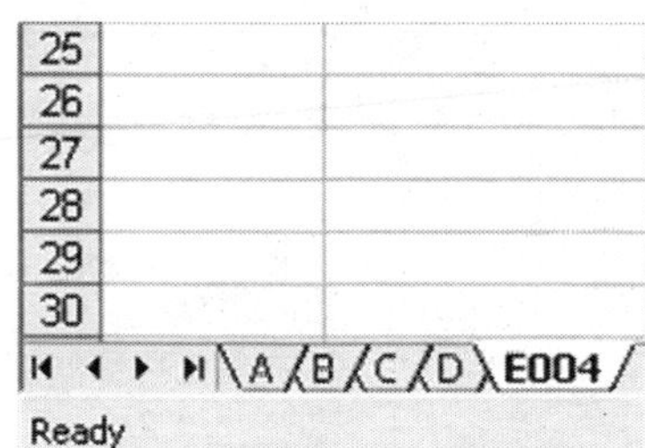

Figure 15 – Worksheets Sorted

Exl

View the Appendix to learn how to store this procedure in a Standard module.

```
Option Explicit¶
' * * * * *¶
Sub SortSheets()¶
  'Variable declarations¶
  Dim FirstSheet As Long, LastSheet As Long, Counter As Long¶
  Dim i As Long, j As Long¶
  Dim Ascending As Boolean¶
  Dim ActiveWS As Object¶
  'Change this variable if descending order is wanted¶
  'sets order programatically¶
  Ascending = True¶
  'sets order via user input in worksheet¶
  Ascending = Range("B1").Value¶
  'Make sure a workbook is open¶
  If ActiveWorkbook Is Nothing Then¶
    MsgBox "This macro must be run on a visible workbook", _¶
        vbCritical¶
    Exit Sub¶
  End If¶
  'Number of sheets that are selected¶
  Counter = ActiveWindow.SelectedSheets.Count¶
  If Counter = 1 Then¶
    FirstSheet = 1¶
    LastSheet = ActiveWorkbook.Sheets.Count¶
  Else¶
    FirstSheet = ActiveWindow.SelectedSheets(1).Index¶
    LastSheet = ActiveWindow.SelectedSheets(Counter).Index¶
    If LastSheet - FirstSheet + 1 <> Counter Then¶
      MsgBox Prompt:="This requires contiguous sheets to run", _¶
              Buttons:=vbCritical¶
      Exit Sub¶
    End If¶
  End If¶
  'Turn off screen updating¶
  Application.ScreenUpdating = False¶
  Set ActiveWS = ActiveSheet¶
  'Do what is called a “bubble sort” routine¶
  For i = FirstSheet To LastSheet - 1¶
    For j = i + 1 To LastSheet¶
      If Ascending Then¶
        'Check both names¶
        If LCase$(ActiveWorkbook.Sheets(i).Name) > _¶
          LCase$(ActiveWorkbook.Sheets(j).Name) Then¶
          'Need to move it¶
          ActiveWorkbook.Sheets( _¶
              j).Move Before:=ActiveWorkbook.Sheets(i)¶
        End If¶
```

```
      Else¶
        'Check both names¶
        If LCase$(ActiveWorkbook.Sheets(i).Name) < _¶
          LCase$(ActiveWorkbook.Sheets(j).Name) Then¶
          'Need to move it¶
          ActiveWorkbook.Sheets(j).Move _¶
            Before:=ActiveWorkbook.Sheets(i)¶
        End If¶
      End If¶
    Next j¶
  Next i¶
  ActiveWS.Activate¶
  'Restore screen updating¶
  Application.ScreenUpdating = True¶
End Sub¶
```


There is one variable that can be changed in this workbook: change the sort order from ascending to descending depending on your needs. To do this, change the Ascending variable from True to False. This can be done via cell B1 of the example file.

Tip: The macro will still work if the user selects only some of the sheets to sort, as long as they are next to one another (contiguous).

Generating a Unique List

Using a given range, this macro creates a subset containing only the unique records within it.

Scenario: Whenever there is a database or a list of records, such as inventory parts, customer information, employee information, or account numbers, obtaining a unique list to perform analysis of the data is often required.

Example file:
E005.xls

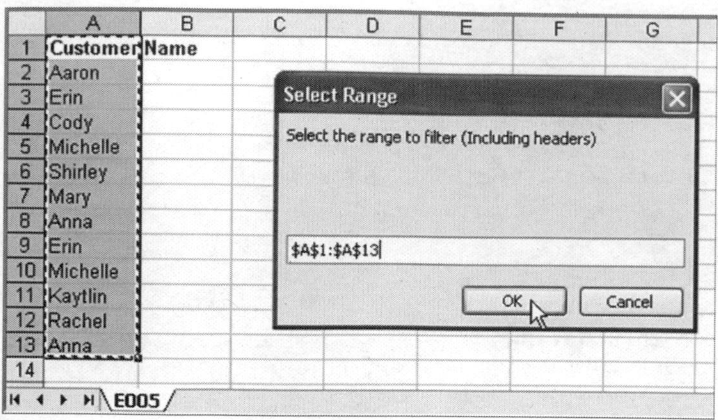

Figure 16 – Selecting a Range for a Unique List

	A	B	C	D	E	F	G
1	Customer	Name					
2	Aaron						
3	Erin						
4	Cody						
5	Michelle						
6	Shirley						
7	Mary						
8	Anna						
9	Kaytlin						
10	Rachel						
11							
12							
13							
14							

E005 Sheet1

Figure 17 – Unique List Created

View the Appendix to learn how to store this procedure in a Standard module.

```
Option Explicit¶
' * * * * *¶
Sub GenerateUniqueList()¶
  'Variable declarations¶
'Range to be used¶
  Dim Rng As Range¶
'New worksheet holding the data¶
  Dim WS As Worksheet¶
  'Change the following variables¶
  'Three options exist(all must include headers)¶
```

```
  '1. Have a hardcoded range¶
  'Set Rng = Range("A1:C100")¶
  '2. Use the current selection¶
  'Set Rng = ActiveWindow.RangeSelection¶
  '3. Ask the user for a range¶
  On Error Resume Next¶
  Set Rng = Application.InputBox( _¶
      Prompt:="Select the range to filter (Including headers)", _¶
      Title:="Select Range", Type:=8)¶
  On Error GoTo 0¶
  'Make sure a valid range is used¶
  If Rng Is Nothing Then¶
    Exit Sub¶
  End If¶
  'Create the new worksheet after the selected one¶
  Set WS = Rng.Worksheet.Parent.Worksheets.Add( _¶
      After:=Rng.Worksheet)¶
  'Filter the items (Use Advanced Filter for this)¶
  Rng.AdvancedFilter Action:=xlFilterCopy, _¶
      CopyToRange:=WS.Range("A1"), Unique:=True¶
End Sub¶
```


There is one variable that can be changed in the 'Change the following variables' section: the range. Inside the code there are three examples of how to set this variable:

1. Use a predefined range.
2. Use the currently selected range.
3. Ask the user to input a range (this is the option enabled in the code as written).

To enable one of the other two, place an apostrophe in front of the code lines for the one currently in use, and then remove the apostrophe in front of the code line for the option desired.

Using AutoFilter on a Protected Sheet

This macro enables you to use worksheet protection, while still allowing the end user to use the AutoFilter and/or Outline capabilities.

Scenario: Prior to Excel 2002 (XP), it was not possible to protect a sheet AND still be able to use the AutoFilter. The same problem applies to using Outline, which is still not possible in Excel 2003. This procedure provides for these capabilities.

Example file:
E006.xls

View the Appendix to learn how to store this procedure in a Standard module.

```
Option Explicit¶
' * * * * *¶
Sub EnableAutoFilter()¶
  'Variable declaration¶
'Worksheet to enable Autofilter¶
  Dim WS As Worksheet¶
'Password to protect the sheet (optional)¶
  Dim Pwd As String¶
  'Change the following two variables accordingly¶
  'Set the password to nothing¶
  'Pwd = ""¶
  'Set the password programatically¶
  'Pwd = "YourPassword"¶
  'Set the password via user input¶
  Pwd = Range("F1").Value¶
  'Hard code the worksheet reference¶
  'Set WS = ThisWorkbook.Worksheets("Sheet1")¶
  'Set the worksheet to the active sheet at the time¶
  'the macro is started¶
  Set WS = ActiveSheet¶
  With WS¶
    .Protect Password:=Pwd, Contents:=True, _¶
        UserInterfaceOnly:=True¶
    .EnableAutoFilter = True¶
    'To enable outline uncomment the following line¶
    '.EnableOutlining = True¶
  End With¶
End Sub¶
```

```
' * * * * *¶
Sub Auto_Open()¶
  'Enable when the workbook is opened¶
  EnableAutoFilter¶
End Sub¶
```

In this macro, the password used to protect the sheet (Pwd) can be changed. The worksheet in which it is run can also be changed in the code. The line to uncomment if using Outlines is indicated in the code as well. If you plan to leave the worksheet protected, it's a good idea to call this macro from the Workbook_Open event of the workbook, to make sure that the users have AutoFilter and/or Outline available each time they use the workbook.

Deleting Rows Based on Criteria

With this macro, you can delete all the records (rows) that meet certain criteria; for example, column A equals 0.

Scenario: When handling big files with a lot of records, finding a way to delete all the rows that match a given condition can be a cumbersome process. This macro is designed to facilitate this task, by setting a column and a condition to match in order to delete the rows.

Example file:
E007.xls

View the Appendix to learn how to store this procedure in a Standard module.

Exl

	A	B	C	D	E	F
1	Games played	Team	Games won			
2	0	Team A	0			
3	0	Team B	0			
4	1	Team C	1			
5	2	Team D	0			
6	1	Team E	0			
7	2	Team F	1			
8	2	Team G	0			
9	0	Team H	0			
10	2	Team I	1			
11	2	Team J	0			
12	2	Team K	1			
13	0	Team L	0			
14	2	Team M	0			
15	1	Team N	0			
16	0	Team O	1			
17	2	Team P	0			
18	1	Team Q	0			
19	2	Team R	1			
20	2	Team S	0			
21						
22						
23	Conditions					
24	WhichColumn	1				
25	TheCondition	0				
26						

E007

Figure 18 – Selecting Conditions

	A	B	C	D	E	F
1	Games played	Team	Games won			
2	1	Team C	1			
3	2	Team D	0			
4	1	Team E	0			
5	2	Team F	1			
6	2	Team G	0			
7	2	Team I	1			
8	2	Team J	0			
9	2	Team K	1			
10	2	Team M	0			
11	1	Team N	0			
12	2	Team P	0			
13	1	Team Q	0			
14	2	Team R	1			
15	2	Team S	0			
16						
17						
18	Conditions					
19	WhichColumn	1				
20	TheCondition	0				
21						

E007

Figure 19 – Conditional Rows Deleted

```
Option Explicit¶
' * * * * *¶
Sub DeleteRows()¶
  'Variable declarations¶
'The range to be used¶
  Dim Rng As Range¶
'The column with the condition¶
  Dim WhichColumn As Long¶
'The condition to be matched¶
  Dim TheCondition As Variant¶
  'Change the following variables as desired¶
  'Set the range by hard coding¶
  Set Rng = Range("A1:C20")¶
  'Uncomment the next line if you want to use the selected¶
  'range as the variable¶
  'Set Rng = ActiveWindow.RangeSelection¶
  'Hard coded variable definition¶
'First column of the range has the condition¶
  WhichColumn = 1 ¶
  'Set variable via user input¶
  'WhichColumn = Range("B24").Value¶
  'Hard coded variable definitions¶
  TheCondition = 0     'Delete rows where the cell equals 0¶
  'TheCondition = ">0"  'Delete rows where the cell is greater than 0¶
  'TheCondition = ""     'Delete rows where the cell is empty¶
  'Set variable via user input¶
  'TheCondition = Range("B25").Value¶
  'Turn off screen updating¶
  Application.ScreenUpdating = False¶
  'In order to use autofilter, make sure it is not already used¶
  If Rng.Worksheet.AutoFilterMode = True Then¶
    Rng.Worksheet.AutoFilterMode = False¶
  End If¶
  'Filter the Rng¶
  Rng.AutoFilter Field:=WhichColumn, Criteria1:=TheCondition¶
  'Look for visible rows in Rng (start from row 2 of Rng, not row 1)¶
  With Rng¶
    'turn off errors in case there are no visible cells¶
    On Error Resume Next¶
    .Offset(1).Resize(.Rows.Count - 1).SpecialCells( _¶
        xlCellTypeVisible).Delete Shift:=xlShiftUp¶
    On Error GoTo 0¶
    'Turn off autofilter again¶
    .Worksheet.AutoFilterMode = False¶
  End With¶
  'Restore screen updating¶
  Application.ScreenUpdating = True¶
End Sub¶
```

Exl

There are three variables that can be changed in this code:

- **Rng** The range that will be used in the code. Uncomment the line (remove the apostrophe) to use the selection if that is what is desired.
- **WhichColumn** The column that will be checked for the condition. 1 equals the first column in the range, 2 the second, etc. This can be either hard-coded or input on the sheet by the user. The example file is set to use hard-coded values. Uncomment the line (remove the apostrophe) to use the user input. Comment out the hard-coded line (add an apostrophe to the left).
- **TheCondition** The condition that the cells must meet to delete the rows. This can be either hard-coded or input on the sheet by the user. The example file is set to use one of three hard-coded values. Uncomment the appropriate line (remove the apostrophe) to use the other hard-coded values or the user input method. Comment out the hard-coded line (add an apostrophe to the left).

Note: This macro removes any previous filters that may exist on the worksheet.

Checking Whether or Not a File Exists

This macro demonstrates how to check if a file exists in a path.

Example file:
E008.xls

Scenario: When running a macro, it may be necessary to access different files stored in the user's computer. However, if one of those files is missing, the macro is likely to fail. This example shows how to check if a file exists in order to display an error message and cancel or exit the macro in a user-friendly manner.

View the Appendix to learn how to store this procedure in a Standard module.

```
Option Explicit¶
' * * * * *¶
Function FileExists(sFullName As String) As Boolean¶
  FileExists = Len(Dir(PathName:=sFullName)) > 0¶
End Function¶
' * * * * *¶
Sub TestFileExists()¶
  'Variable Declaration¶
'Variable for search path¶
  Dim Path As String¶
'Variable to test existence¶
  Dim Exists As Boolean¶
  'Change the following variables¶
  'Set variable via hard coding¶
  'Path = "C:\My file.txt"¶
  'Set variable via user input¶
  Path = Range("B1").Value¶
  Exists = FileExists(Path)¶
  If Exists Then¶
    MsgBox "The file exists"¶
  Else¶
    MsgBox "The file doesn't exist"¶
  End If¶
End Sub¶
```

In the macro TestFileExists, you can change the Path variable to point to the file name that is to be verified. The example file is set to use the user input method for the Path variable. Comment out the user input line (by adding an apostrophe to the left) and uncomment out the hard-coded line (remove the apostrophe at the left), if that is desired.

Exl

Removing Hyperlinks

These three procedures help the user remove all hyperlinks within a specific range, within a worksheet, or within an entire workbook.

Scenario: When data copied from the web is pasted into Excel, the hyperlinks are usually pasted along with it. Sometimes this is useful, but most of the time the hyperlinks get in the way. There is not a direct way to remove the hyperlinks from a range any larger than a single cell, which would be a painful and slow task if many cells needed hyperlinks removed. This macro provides an alternative for this missing tool in Excel.

Example file:
E009.xls

View the Appendix to learn how to store this procedure in a Standard module.

```
Option Explicit¶
' * * * * *¶
Sub RemoveHyperlinksBook()¶
  'Variable declarations¶
'Include charts, too¶
  Dim WS As Object¶
  Dim WB As Workbook¶
  'Change the following variables¶
  'To apply to a particular book¶
  'Set WB = Workbooks("MyBook.xls")¶
  'To apply to the active book¶
  Set WB = ActiveWorkbook¶
  For Each WS In WB.Sheets¶
    WS.Hyperlinks.Delete¶
  Next WS¶
End Sub¶
```

```
' * * * * *¶
Sub RemoveHyperlinksSheet()¶
  Dim WS As Object¶
  'Change the following variables¶
  'Apply to a particular sheet¶
  'Set WS = ActiveWorkbook.Sheets("Sheet1")¶
  'Use the current active sheet¶
  Set WS = ActiveSheet¶
  WS.Hyperlinks.Delete¶
End Sub¶
' * * * * *¶
Sub RemoveHyperlinksRange()¶
  Dim Rng As Range¶
  'Change the following variables¶
  'Apply to a particular range¶
  'Set Rng = Range("A1:E20")¶
  'Use the current selection¶
  Set Rng = ActiveWindow.RangeSelection¶
  Rng.Hyperlinks.Delete¶
End Sub¶
```


There is one procedure for each of the workbook objects, worksheet objects, and range objects. In each of the procedures, one variable can be changed: the object that will have hyperlinks removed. By default, all three will use the active object.

Applying SUM / COUNT by Color

The built-in SUMIF and COUNTIF worksheet functions act on cells that meet a condition. Ordinarily, the background color cannot be used as a condition. This procedure allows such an action.

Example file:
E010.xls

Scenario: There are situations when certain fields ought to be emphasized—such as an 'Urgent' field. Colors are often used to show the information for each record: Red = Very Urgent; Yellow = Be on Guard; Green = Ok.

The problem is that there is no easy way to interact with this data, such as how to count how many are urgent, or how to count the dollar values of past-due orders that are marked Urgent (red).

These two functions work exactly like SUMIF and COUNTIF, but use the criteria cell's background color instead of the cell's value.

Follow these steps:

1. To first determine the color you would like to use, fill cell A1 (in a blank workbook) with the desired color.

2. Place the function shown on the following page in a standard module.

	A	B	C	D	E	F	G
1	Field 1	Field 2			COUNT	SUM	SUM
2	6	1			1	2	5
3	5	2			3	10	11
4	4	3			2	9	5
5	3	4					
6	2	5					
7	1	6					
8							

Figure 20 – Sum/Count by Color

View the Appendix to learn how to store this procedure in a Standard module.

```
Function GetColor(Rng As Range) As Long¶
    GetColor = Rng(1).Interior.Color¶
End Function
```

3. Go back to the application interface, and type the following in cell B1:

   `=GetColor(A1)`

   This provides you with the color number to use in the VBA code below.

```
Option Explicit¶
' * * * * *¶
Function CountIfColor(ByVal Range As Range, _¶
    ByVal criteriaColor As Range) As Variant¶
  'Variable declaration¶
  Dim Rng As Range¶
  'Make it volatile - automatic calculation¶
  Application.Volatile True¶
  'Validations, only one area¶
  If Range.Areas.Count > 1 Then¶
    CountIfColor = CVErr(xlErrValue)¶
  End If¶
```

```
'Limit the range to the used range¶
  'Intersect method takes cells common to both Range and¶
  'Range.Worksheet.UsedRange¶
  Set Range = Intersect(Range, Range.Worksheet.UsedRange)¶
  'Only use the first cell of criteriaColor¶
  Set criteriaColor = criteriaColor(1)¶
  For Each Rng In Range.Cells¶
    If Rng.Interior.Color = criteriaColor.Interior.Color Then¶
      CountIfColor = CountIfColor + 1¶
    End If¶
  Next Rng¶
End Function¶
' * * * * *¶
Function SumIfColor(ByVal Range As Range, _¶
    ByVal criteriaColor As Range, _¶
    Optional ByVal sum_range As Range) As Variant¶
  'Variable declaration¶
  Dim i As Long¶
  'Make it volatile¶
  Application.Volatile True¶
  'Validations, only one area¶
  If Range.Areas.Count > 1 Then¶
    SumIfColor = CVErr(xlErrValue)¶
  End If¶
  'Limit the range to the used range¶
  'Intersect method takes cells common to both Range and¶
  'Range.Worksheet.UsedRange¶
  Set Range = Intersect(Range, Range.Worksheet.UsedRange)¶
  'Check for a valid range to sum¶
  If sum_range Is Nothing Then Set sum_range = Range¶
  'Only use the first cell of criteriaColor¶
  Set criteriaColor = criteriaColor(1)¶
  'Loop through each cell in range¶
  For i = 1 To Range.Count¶
    If Range(i).Interior.Color = criteriaColor.Interior.Color Then¶
      SumIfColor = Application.Sum(SumIfColor, sum_range(i))¶
      If IsError(SumIfColor) Then Exit Function¶
    End If¶
  Next i¶
End Function¶
```

4. To count or sum using the font color instead of the cell's fill color, change the code wherever it says Interior to Font.

5. Type the function(s) into a cell, following the same syntax as these two examples:

```
=COUNTIFCOLOR(RangeToCheck, CellWithColor)
=SUMIFCOLOR(RangeToCheck, CellWithColor, RangeToSum)
```

Similar to the SUMIF worksheet function, the third argument is optional. See the file for examples.

Note: These functions do not count colors if they have been applied using conditional formatting. For those, use the condition behind the conditional format to do the COUNT/SUM.

Also, these functions do not update when you change the format of a cell, for that, you must update the worksheet/workbook by pressing F9 or Ctrl+Alt+F9 to force a full recalculation.

Using More Than Three Conditional Formats

With this procedure, you can overcome the limitation of using only three conditional formats.

Scenario: Users often want more than three conditional formats, but the Format→Conditional Formatting option only provides for three. Using VBA, however, allows you to overcome this limitation and to create as many conditions as necessary. For example, you may be evaluating credit scores, coloring them in bands of 50 points, going from bright red to bright blue, to give an indicator of how reliable a potential customer may be. Now you can use as many colors as you like.

Example file:
E011.xls

This example assumes the following different sales levels and provides conditional formatting, as follows:

- $0 – $15,000 = dark blue
- $15,001 – $25,000 = blue
- $25,001 – $35,000 = light blue
- $35,001 – $50,000 = light red
- $50,001 – $75,000 = red
- $75,001 and more = dark red

This macro is called from the Worksheet_Change event. It passes through those cells that have changed to see if they need to be formatted.

View the Appendix to learn how to store this procedure in a Standard module.


```
Option Explicit¶
' * * * * *¶
Sub ConditionalFormat(ByVal Target As Range)¶
  'Variable declarations¶
'Range used for the loop¶
  Dim Cll As Range¶
  'First, check if the range that was received is¶
  'between the one that is needed, use A1:A100¶
  Set Target = Intersect(Target, Target.Worksheet.Range("A1:A100"))¶
  If Target Is Nothing Then¶
    'The cells that changed are not in the range, exit¶
    Exit Sub¶
Else¶
    'Loop through the cells (in case more than one changed)¶
    'only check cells that have numbers in them in this case¶
    If Target.Count = 1 Then¶
      If Not IsNumeric(Target) Then¶
        Set Target = Nothing¶
      End If¶
    Else¶
      On Error Resume Next¶
      Set Target = Target.SpecialCells(xlCellTypeConstants, _¶
          xlNumbers)¶
      On Error GoTo 0¶
    End If¶
    If Target Is Nothing Then¶
      'Don't have any numbers, exit¶
      Exit Sub¶
    End If¶
    For Each Cll In Target.Cells¶
      'Use Select Case to figure out where the value of¶
      'the cell falls¶
      'Change the following variables¶
      Select Case Cll.Value¶
      Case 0 To 15000¶
        Cll.Interior.Color = 8388608¶
      Case 15000 To 25000¶
        Cll.Interior.Color = 16711680¶
      Case 25000 To 35000¶
        Cll.Interior.Color = 16764057¶
      Case 35000 To 50000¶
        Cll.Interior.Color = 13408767¶
      Case 50000 To 75000¶
        Cll.Interior.Color = 255¶
```

```
      Case Is > 75000¶
        Cll.Interior.Color = 128¶
      End Select¶
    Next Cll¶
  End If¶
End Sub¶
```

View the Appendix to learn how to store the following procedure in a Worksheet module.


```
Option Explicit¶
' * * * * *¶
Private Sub Worksheet_Change(ByVal Target As Range)¶
  ConditionalFormat Target¶
End Sub¶
```

This procedure has two main items that can be changed:

- The range to which it applies; currently, it is hard-coded to work for cells A1:A100.
- The conditions and the formats to be applied. The 'Change the following variables' section of the code is where the conditional format is created and applied. Changing colors and borders in this section of the code affects the cells in the workbook.

These macros run automatically as long as macros are enabled in the workbook.

Providing a Calendar to Choose Dates for Input

Use this procedure to facilitate the entry of dates by displaying a calendar with which the user can interact.

Scenario: Ensuring that users enter dates correctly is not always an easy task in Excel. This example shows how to program the double-click event on certain cells. The user can double-click the cell and actually choose a date instead of having to type it. This approach reduces errors, especially if the workbook is going to be used in different countries.

Example file:
E012.xls

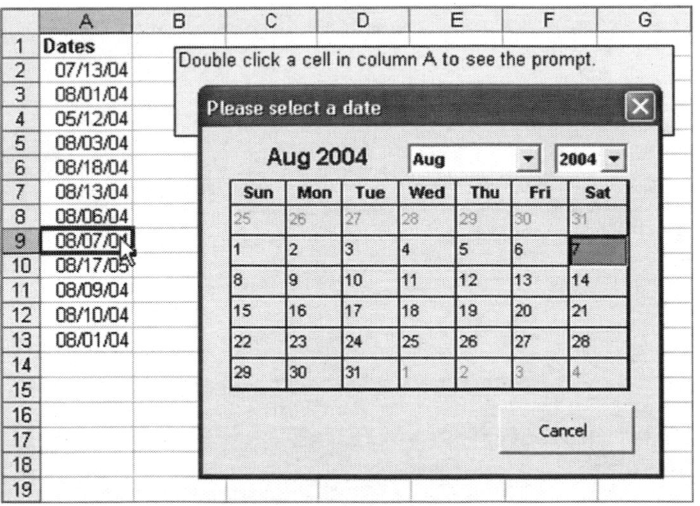

Figure 21 –Calendar Form

View the Appendix to learn how to store this procedure in a Standard module.

```
Option Explicit¶
' * * * * *¶
Sub DisplayCalendar(Optional ByVal Target As Range)¶
  'Variable declaration¶
'calendar form¶
  Dim fmC As fmCalendar¶
  Dim Cll As Range¶
  'Was a range received?¶
  If Target Is Nothing Then¶
    'Use the active cell¶
    On Error GoTo err_h¶
    Set Target = ActiveCell¶
  End If¶
  'Ask for one date for each cell¶
  For Each Cll In Target.Cells¶
    Set fmC = New fmCalendar¶
    fmC.Display Cll¶
    Select Case TypeName(fmC.GetChoice)¶
    Case "Boolean"¶
      'do nothing, user pressed "Cancel"¶
    Case "Date"¶
      'assign the new date to the cell¶
      Application.EnableEvents = False¶
      Cll.Value = fmC.GetChoice¶
      Application.EnableEvents = True¶
```

```
    End Select¶
  Next Cll¶
  Exit Sub¶
'error handler - errors jump to this location and the procedure ends¶
err_h:¶
End Sub¶
```

View the Appendix to learn how to store this procedure in a Worksheet module.

Exl

```
Option Explicit¶
' * * * * *¶
Private Sub Worksheet_BeforeDoubleClick(ByVal Target As Range, _¶
    Cancel As Boolean)¶
  'Ask for a date for any cell in column A¶
  Dim Cll As Range¶
  If Intersect(Target, Range("A:A")) Is Nothing Then¶
    Exit Sub¶
    'Range ("A:A") restricts the macro to column A. This can¶
    'be changed to whatever range is desired.¶
  End If¶
  For Each Cll In Intersect(Target, Me.Range("A:A"))¶
    DisplayCalendar Cll¶
    Cancel = True¶
  Next Cll¶
End Sub¶
```

Place the following code in the UserForm ‘fmCalendar’. The example file has the form with the code already in it. This form has a calendar control and a command button.

View the Appendix to learn how to store this procedure in a UserForm.

```
Option Explicit¶
Private mChoice As Variant  'Holds the choice of the user¶
' * * * * *¶
Private Sub BCancel_Click()¶
'User cancelled¶
  mChoice = False¶
  Me.Hide¶
End Sub¶
' * * * * *¶
Private Sub Calendar1_Click()¶
  mChoice = Calendar1.Value¶
  Me.Hide¶
End Sub¶
```

```
' * * * * *¶
Public Sub Display(ByVal Target As Range)¶
  'Make sure that only one cell was received¶
  Set Target = Target(1)¶
  If IsDate(Target.Value) Then¶
    mChoice = Target.Value¶
  Else¶
    mChoice = Date¶
  End If¶
  Calendar1.Value = CDate(mChoice)¶
  Me.Show¶
End Sub¶
' * * * * *¶
Public Property Get GetChoice() As Variant¶
  GetChoice = mChoice¶
End Property¶
```


Notes: The procedure uses the BeforeDoubleClick event of a worksheet module to display the UserForm.

This procedure is designed to operate only in column A. This restriction can be changed to limit the functionality to whatever cells are required.

In the Example file, the macro runs when a cell in column A is double-clicked, but the macro can also be called from a button.

The calendar control used in the UserForm requires a reference to be set in the VBE. There are examples of VBA-only calendar controls that perform in the same manner at www.vbaexpress.com and www.brandtrock.com.

Restricting Text Box Entry to Numbers

This procedure shows you how to ensure that a UserForm text box accepts only a numeric entry.

Scenario: For an application that uses a UserForm—say a loan calculator—some code is required to make sure that the user enters only actual numbers in the textboxes. This reduces errors. The example shows how to control the input from the source, meaning at the same time that the user is entering the data into the textbox.

Example file:
E013.xls

View the Appendix to learn how to store this procedure in a Standard module.

```
Option Explicit¶
' * * * * *¶
Sub AcceptOnlyNumbers()¶
  fmNumbers.Show¶
End Sub¶
```

Exl

Note: The following code goes in a UserForm, which is named fmNumbers in our example file.

Drag the following controls from the control toolbox onto the blank area of the UserForm: a label, a text box, and a command button. Position these on the form as desired.

View the Appendix to learn how to store this procedure in a UserForm.

```
Option Explicit¶
' * * * * *¶
Private Sub CommandButton1_Click()¶
    Unload Me¶
End Sub¶
' * * * * *¶
Private Sub TextBox1_KeyPress( _¶
    ByVal KeyAscii As MSForms.ReturnInteger)¶
  Select Case KeyAscii¶
  Case 48 To 57¶
    'Numbers 0 to 9, ok¶
  Case Asc(Application.International(xlDecimalSeparator))¶
    'Decimal separator. Check if there is more than one¶
    If InStr(1, TextBox1.Value, _¶
        Application.International(xlDecimalSeparator), 1) > 0 Then¶
      'Cancel the key¶
      KeyAscii = 0¶
    End If¶
  Case Else¶
    'Cancel the key¶
    KeyAscii = 0¶
  End Select¶
End Sub¶
```

This sample requires only that the code in the UserForm works—specifically, the code in the KeyPress event of the text box.

The code in the Standard module is used to display the UserForm. This procedure has been assigned to a button in the example file for easy use.

The UserForm includes one text box, which is the control that is attached to the code. To use this in another UserForm, copy the code from the KeyPress event to the respective events of other text box(es).

The macro in the sample file runs automatically.

Running a Macro When a Cell Changes

This procedure demonstrates how to run a macro when the value of one or more cells changes.

Scenario: Sometimes, you may want to run a macro whenever the value of a cell changes, for instance to bring up a dialog telling a user that the amount they've entered is over $10,000 and requires special consideration.

Example file:
E014.xls

A common but false approach to accomplish this is to create a formula, such as:

```
=IF(A1=10, "Macro1", "")
```

This does not work, of course. Macros cannot be run by writing a formula into a cell. This sample shows how to run a macro when the value of a cell changes, using the condition that if A1 equals 10, B1 does not equal 5 and C1 is greater than 10, as expressed on the following page:

```
A1 = 10, B1 <> 5 and C1 > 10
```

This procedure uses either the Calculate event or the Change event. The problem with the Calculate event is that it is triggered on each calculation, and could also be run several times, after A1 equals 10, because the condition is always true.

The use of the Change event requires the use of dependents (dependent cells), because when the formula is evaluated, A1 is the changing cell, not the cell with the formula.

In the code below, Union(Range("A1"), Range("B1"), Range("C1")) creates the range of interest. Intersect(Target,Union(Range("A1"), Range("B1"), Range("C1"))) checks to see if the current selection (Target) is in the range of interest.

View the Appendix to learn how to store this procedure in a Standard module.


```
Option Explicit¶
' * * * * *¶
Sub RunMacroOnChange(ByVal Target As Range)¶
  'First, check that the range is one of those three¶
  If Intersect(Target, Union(Range("A1"), Range("B1"), _¶
      Range("C1"))) Is Nothing Then¶
    Exit Sub¶
  End If¶
  'Ok, one of the cells has changed, evaluate the condition:¶
  'A1 = 1 and B1 <> 5 and C1 > 10¶
  If Range("A1").Value = 1 And Range("B1").Value <> 5 And _¶
    Range("C1").Value > 10 Then¶
    'It's true, so, call Macro1¶
    Macro1¶
  End If¶
End Sub¶
' * * * * *¶
Sub Macro1()¶
  MsgBox "It worked !"¶
End Sub¶
```

View the Appendix to learn how to store this procedure in a Worksheet module.

```
Option Explicit¶
' * * * * *¶
Private Sub Worksheet_Change(ByVal Target As Range)¶
  RunMacroOnChange Target¶
End Sub¶
```

The code in the standard module uses a condition to run the macro 'Macro1'. This condition should be adapted to the user's specific needs. The cells that are involved in the condition will need to be changed as well.

Forcing the Use of a Custom Print Procedure

This procedure illustrates how to limit the use of the built-in Print (or Save) commands, thus forcing the desired end result.

Scenario: This macro could be used to create an invoice when company policy dictates that each invoice must be printed three times—perhaps one copy for the customer, with proper formatting, and two copies for the company in black ink only and without the logo and fancy formatting to save on ink/toner. Making sure that the user prints it exactly right each time can be a difficult task, so customizing the print procedure is a lifesaver.

Example file:
E015.xls

Exl

The sample file shows how to block the built-in commands from the File menu and toolbars to force the use of a specific button, which does all the formatting needed and takes care of the printing.

View the Appendix to learn how to store this procedure in a Standard module.

```
Option Explicit¶
'Variable declaration¶
Public AllowPrint As Boolean
'Variable to check if the user pressed the right button¶
' * * * * *¶
Sub MyPrint()¶
  'Turn the AllowPrint variable on¶
  AllowPrint = True¶
  'Printing code goes here¶
  'Do all the stuff that is needed¶
  With Range("A1")¶
    .Font.Bold = True¶
    .Interior.ColorIndex = 36¶
    .Font.Size = 24¶
  End With¶
  'Do the custom print (2 copies, to the default printer)¶
  ActiveSheet.PrintOut Copies:=2¶
  'Turn off AllowPrint¶
  AllowPrint = False¶
End Sub¶
```

```
' * * * * *¶
Sub StandardPrint()¶
  'Standard print of the activesheet¶
  ActiveSheet.PrintOut¶
End Sub¶
```

View the Appendix to learn how to store this procedure in a ThisWorkbook module.

Exl

```
Option Explicit¶
' * * * * *¶
Private Sub Workbook_BeforePrint(Cancel As Boolean)¶
'Cancel the print if the macro didn't start it¶
  If Not AllowPrint Then¶
    Cancel = True¶
  End If¶
End Sub¶
```

The code in the standard module requires the AllowPrint variable. The two procedures are examples of how to use this technique. The rest of the code goes in the 'ThisWorkbook' module.

The 'MyPrint' procedure, which is called from a button in a template or workbook, must be customized to fit the user's specific needs. The 'StandardPrint' procedure is not needed by the macro.

Restricting the User to a Portion of the Worksheet

Use this procedure to restrict the user to a specific area of a worksheet.

Scenario: When using an important worksheet, protecting the data may not be enough. You may need to restrict the user from entering data or performing other tasks on the data.

Example file: E016.xls

Note: This worksheet does not need to be locked. The ScrollArea is not persistent—meaning that when the workbook is closed and reopened, it is reset. Therefore, make sure that this macro is called, at a minimum, when the workbook is opened or when the worksheet is activated.

Exl

View the Appendix to learn how to store this procedure in a Standard module.

```
Option Explicit¶
' * * * * *¶
Sub RestrictUser(WhichRange As Range)¶
  'WhichRange is the range that the user is allowed to use¶
  With WhichRange.Worksheet¶
    'Set the ScrollArea property, which is a string, not a Range¶
    'object equal to the address of the given range¶
    'Only one Area can be used, so, use the first one in case¶
    'more than 1 area was received.¶
    .ScrollArea = WhichRange.Areas(1).Address¶
  End With¶
End Sub¶
' * * * * *¶
Sub Auto_Open()¶
  'Call the RestrictUser macro when the workbook is opened¶
  RestrictUser Range("C6:I18")¶
End Sub¶
```

For added security, the macro could be called from the Worksheet_Activate, SelectionChange, or Change events by copying and pasting the code below into the sheet module of the sheet on which you want to limit the scroll area, and then removing the apostrophes from the beginning of each line.

View the Appendix to learn how to store any of these procedures in a Worksheet module.

```
'Private Sub Worksheet_Activate()¶
'     RestrictUser Range("C6:I18")¶
'End Sub¶
' * * * * *¶
'Private Sub Worksheet_Change(ByVal Target As Range)¶
'    RestrictUser Range("C6:I18")¶
'End Sub¶
' * * * * *¶
'Private Sub Worksheet_SelectionChange(ByVal Target As Range)¶
'    RestrictUser Range("C6:I18")¶
'End Sub¶
```

Notes: The range address in which the user is allowed to select should be changed as needed for each worksheet.

The event macros are commented out. If they are used, the code needs to be placed in the worksheet where the scroll area is to be limited, and the apostrophes need to be removed.

Copying a Workbook with Macros Removed

Exl

This macro shows how to make a copy of the active workbook with the VBA code removed, including the removal of UserForms and modules that may exist in them.

Scenario: You have a workbook with macros that you use to update the data and to create charts or other reports that must be sent to people outside of the company, but your company policy does not permit revealing how data was calculated. This macro creates a copy of the active workbook, but without all the macros. Any UserForms and modules that exist in the workbook are removed as well.

Example file:
E017.xls

When using the VBComponents collection of the VBProject object of the workbook, we loop through each item, and, depending on the type of the component, we either delete the contents or remove the item altogether.

View the Appendix to learn how to store this procedure in a Standard module.

```
Option Explicit¶
' * * * * *¶
Sub CopyWorkbookWithoutMacros()¶
  'Copies the active workbook and removes any macros that¶
  'variable declaration¶
  Dim Ans As Variant¶
  Dim WB As Workbook¶
  Dim VBC As Object¶
  'Ask the user for a place to save the current file¶
  Ans = Application.GetSaveAsFilename( _¶
      InitialFileName:="Copy of " & ThisWorkbook.Name, _¶
      FileFilter:="Microsoft Excel Workbook (*.xls),*.xls")¶
  If TypeName(Ans) = "Boolean" Then¶
    'User pressed Cancel, exit¶
    Exit Sub¶
  End If¶
  'Make sure access to the VBA Project exists¶
```

```
  '(Security setting in Excel XP and above)¶
  On Error Resume Next¶
  'This line fails if access does not exist¶
  Set VBC = ActiveWorkbook.VBProject.VBComponents(1)¶
  On Error GoTo err_h¶
  If VBC Is Nothing Then¶
    'Access denied, ask the user to turn it on¶
    MsgBox "Access to the VB Project is not allowed." & _¶
      vbNewLine & vbNewLine & _¶
      "To allow it, go to Tools | Macro, Security..., " & _¶
      "and check the 'Trust access to the Visual Basic Project'" & _¶
      " checkbox under the 'Trusted sources' tab", vbCritical¶
    Exit Sub¶
  End If¶
  'Release memory¶
  Set VBC = Nothing¶
  'Save the workbook with the filename that the user indicated¶
  ActiveWorkbook.SaveCopyAs Ans¶
  'Now open it (disable events just in case)¶
  Application.EnableEvents = False¶
  Set WB = Workbooks.Open(Ans)¶
  'Turn events back on¶
  Application.EnableEvents = True¶
  For Each VBC In WB.VBProject.VBComponents¶
    Select Case VBC.Type¶
    Case 1, 2, 3     'vbext_ct_StdModule, vbext_ct_ClassModule,¶
                     'vbext_ct_MSForm¶
      'Object is a standard module, class module or UserForm,¶
      'so remove it¶
      WB.VBProject.VBComponents.Remove VBC¶
    Case Else        'vbext_ct_ActiveXDesigner, vbext_ct_Document¶
      'everything else (Workbook or Sheet module), delete¶
      'its contents¶
      With VBC.CodeModule¶
      .DeleteLines 1, .CountOfLines¶
      End With¶
    End Select¶
  Next VBC¶
  'Save the Workbook¶
  WB.Save¶
  'Close it¶
  WB.Close SaveChanges:=False¶
  'Done !¶
  MsgBox Prompt:="Done !"¶
  Exit Sub¶
err_h:¶
  MsgBox "Error " & Err.Number & ", " & Err.Description, vbCritical¶
End Sub¶
```

Exl

Inserting Empty Rows in a Range

This procedure shows you how to insert a specified number of rows in the midst of a range.

Exl

Scenario: It is a common task when working with other applications to need to format the data in a specific way in order for the application to understand it. One of these specific formats is that each record of the data must be separated by one or more empty rows.

Example file:
E018.xls

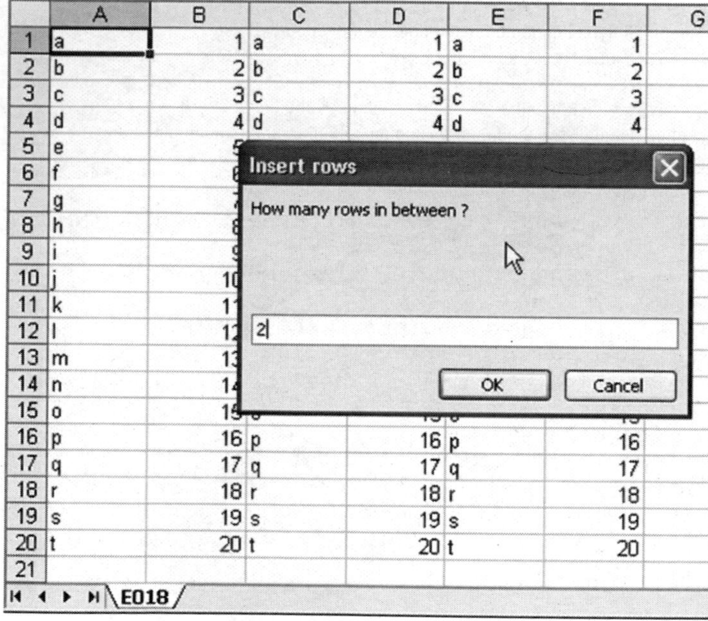

Figure 22 – Setting Number of Empty Rows to Insert

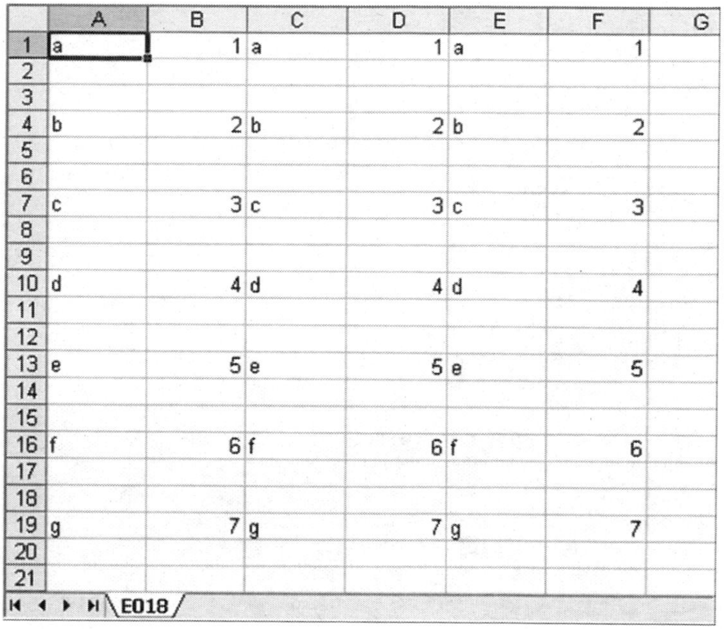

	A	B	C	D	E	F	G
1	a	1	a	1	a	1	
2							
3							
4	b	2	b	2	b	2	
5							
6							
7	c	3	c	3	c	3	
8							
9							
10	d	4	d	4	d	4	
11							
12							
13	e	5	e	5	e	5	
14							
15							
16	f	6	f	6	f	6	
17							
18							
19	g	7	g	7	g	7	
20							
21							

E018

Figure 23 – Empty Rows Inserted

View the Appendix to learn how to store this procedure in a Standard module.

```
Option Explicit¶
' * * * * *¶
Sub InsertBlankRows()¶
  'Variable declaration¶
  Dim NumRows As Long¶
  Dim StartRow As Long¶
  Dim EndRow As Long¶
  Dim i As Long¶
  Dim OldCalculation As Long¶
  'Ask for number of rows to insert (Force numbers)¶
  On Error Resume Next¶
  NumRows = Application.InputBox( _¶
      Prompt:="How many rows in between ?", Title:="Insert rows", _¶
      Type:=1)¶
  If NumRows <= 0 Then¶
    'Can not do this¶
    Exit Sub¶
  End If¶
  'Start in row 2¶
  StartRow = 2¶
```

```
    'Last row in column A¶
    EndRow = Cells(Rows.Count, 1).End(xlUp).Row¶
    'Turn off screen updating¶
    Application.ScreenUpdating = False¶
    'Store current calculation method in variable¶
    OldCalculation = Application.Calculation¶
    'Set calculation to manual¶
    Application.Calculation = xlCalculationManual¶
    'If an error happens, exit nicely¶
    On Error GoTo err_h¶
    'Loop through each row¶
    For i = EndRow To StartRow Step -1¶
      Cells(i, 1).EntireRow.Resize(NumRows).Insert¶
    Next i¶
err_h:¶
    'Restore calculation from variable¶
    Application.Calculation = OldCalculation¶
    'Turn on screen updating¶
    Application.ScreenUpdating = True¶
    'Does an error message need to display?¶
    If Err.Number <> 0 Then¶
      MsgBox "Error " & Err.Number & ", " & Err.Description, _¶
          vbCritical¶
    End If¶
End Sub¶
```


Creating a Custom Toolbar

With this procedure, you can create and customize toolbars to facilitate the use of a custom application.

Scenario: When developing an application in Excel, it is commonly necessary to give the user an interface with which to interact. Building a toolbar is an easy way to do that because it is familiar to them and gives the application a professional look, as well.

This sample shows the best practice for toolbar creation and use, which is to create the toolbar by code (or on-the-fly) instead of attaching a manually created toolbar, which often causes frustration.

Example file:
E019.xls

Figure 24 – Creating a Custom Toolbar

View the Appendix to learn how to store this procedure in a Standard module.

Exl

```
Option Explicit¶
' * * * * *¶
'Name of the toolbar¶
Private Const BarName As String = "My own toolbar"¶
'Unique identifier for the TextBox¶
Private Const BarTextBox As String = "MyBarTB"¶
'Unique identifier for the ComboBox¶
Private Const BarComboBox As String = "MyBarCB"¶
' * * * * *¶
Sub CreateToolbar()¶
  'Variable declaration¶
  'The toolbar¶
  Dim Bar As CommandBar¶
  'A button—the usual control¶
  Dim Button As CommandBarButton¶
  'A submenu on the toolbar¶
  Dim Submenu As CommandBarPopup¶
  'A textbox on the toolbar¶
  Dim TextBox As CommandBarControl¶
  'A combobox on the toolbar¶
  Dim ComboBox As CommandBarComboBox¶
  'First delete the bar if it already exists¶
  DeleteToolbar¶
  'Now, create the toolbar¶
  '(The position has the following options:¶
  ' msoBarLeft, msoBarTop, msoBarRight, msoBarBottom, msoBarFloating,¶
  ' msoBarPopup, msoBarMenuBar)¶
  Set Bar = Application.CommandBars.Add(Name:=BarName, _¶
      Position:=msoBarFloating)¶
  With Bar¶
    'Add one button¶
    Set Button = .Controls.Add(Type:=msoControlButton)¶
    'Change some properties¶
    With Button¶
      .FaceId = 33    'The icon¶
      .Caption = "Sample 1"¶
```

```
    'Show the icon and the text¶
      .Style = msoButtonIconAndCaption¶
      .OnAction = "SampleMacro1"¶
      .TooltipText = "This is the tool tip"¶
    End With¶
    'Add a submenu¶
    Set Submenu = .Controls.Add(Type:=msoControlPopup)¶
    'Change some properties¶
    With Submenu¶
      'Popups can't have an image associated¶
      .Caption = "My submenu"¶
      'Put a division before the control¶
      .BeginGroup = True¶
      'Now add a dummy button in there¶
      Set Button = .Controls.Add(Type:=msoControlButton)¶
      Button.Caption = "Dummy button"¶
      'Only display the text¶
      Button.Style = msoButtonCaption¶
      'Disable it¶
      Button.Enabled = False¶
    End With¶
    'Add the textbox¶
    Set TextBox = .Controls.Add(Type:=msoControlEdit)¶
    TextBox.BeginGroup = True¶
    TextBox.Text = "Sample text"¶
    TextBox.Tag = BarTextBox¶
    'Add a button to control the TextBox¶
    Set Button = .Controls.Add(Type:=msoControlButton)¶
    Button.Caption = "Show"¶
    Button.Style = msoButtonCaption¶
    Button.OnAction = "SampleMacro2"¶
    'Add the ComboBox¶
    Set ComboBox = .Controls.Add(Type:=msoControlDropdown)¶
    'Add items¶
    ComboBox.AddItem "Item 1"¶
    ComboBox.AddItem "Item 2"¶
    ComboBox.AddItem "Item 3"¶
    ComboBox.BeginGroup = True¶
    ComboBox.OnAction = "SampleMacro3"¶
    ComboBox.Tag = BarComboBox¶
    'Finally, make it visible¶
    .Visible = True¶
  End With¶
End Sub¶
' * * * * *¶
Sub DeleteToolbar()¶
  'Try to delete the bar, if it doesn't exist, ignore the error¶
  On Error Resume Next¶
  Application.CommandBars(BarName).Delete¶
End Sub¶
```

```
' * * * * *¶
Sub SampleMacro1()¶
  MsgBox "Clicked me !"¶
End Sub¶
' * * * * *¶
Sub SampleMacro2()¶
  On Error GoTo err_h¶
  With Application.CommandBars.FindControl(Tag:=BarTextBox)¶
    'Do something with this control¶
    MsgBox .Text¶
  End With¶
  Exit Sub¶
err_h:¶
End Sub¶
' * * * * *¶
Sub SampleMacro3()¶
  On Error GoTo err_h¶
  With Application.CommandBars.FindControl(Tag:=BarComboBox)¶
    'Do something with this control¶
    MsgBox .ListIndex¶
  End With¶
  Exit Sub¶
err_h:¶
End Sub¶
' * * * * *¶
Sub Auto_Open()¶
  'Create the toolbar when the workbook is opened¶
  CreateToolbar¶
End Sub¶
' * * * * *¶
Sub Auto_Close()¶
  'Delete the toolbar when the workbook is closed¶
  DeleteToolbar¶
End Sub¶
```

The 'CreateToolbar' procedure contains a sample of how to create a toolbar with buttons, submenus, text boxes, and drop-downs. Adapt this procedure to display and run whatever macros are appropriate to the menu being created.

The other procedures, 'DeleteToolbar', 'Auto_Open', and 'Auto_Close', can be left as they are.

Creating a Table of Contents of a Workbook

This macro creates an index or table of contents, with links that point to each worksheet in the workbook.

Exl

Scenario: Working with a workbook that contains many sheets can get cumbersome. It can be difficult to find or to activate a specific worksheet quickly.

This macro shows how to quickly create an index sheet, or 'Table of Contents', with hyperlinks that make it easier to navigate around multiple worksheets.

Example file:
E020.xls

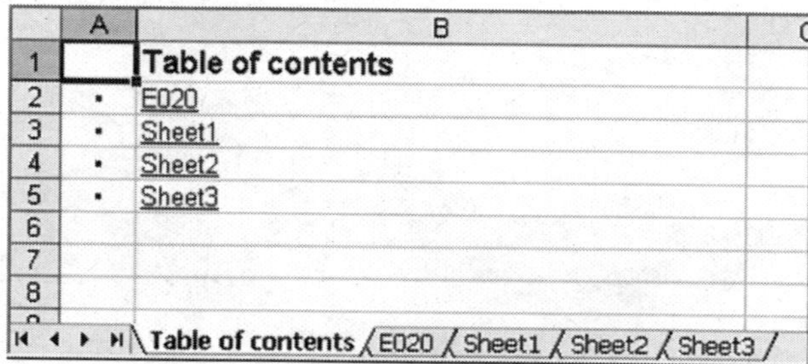

Figure 25 – Table of Contents with Links

View the Appendix to learn how to store this procedure in a Standard module.

```
Option Explicit¶
' * * * * *¶
Sub TableOfContents()¶
'Variable declaration¶
'Worksheet for the table of contents¶
  Dim WS As Worksheet¶
'Other worksheets within the workbook¶
  Dim Sht As Worksheet¶
'Worksheet that is currently active¶
  Dim CurrentSht As Object¶
  Dim Contents As String¶
  'Change the following variables¶
  Contents = "Table of contents"¶
```

```
  'See if a table of contents sheet already exists¶
  On Error Resume Next¶
  Set WS = ActiveWorkbook.Sheets(Contents)¶
  On Error GoTo 0¶
  'Turn off screen updating¶
  Application.ScreenUpdating = False¶
  If Not WS Is Nothing Then¶
  'Not WS Is Nothing is code for "Worksheet exists"¶
    'Ask if it should be overwritten¶
    If MsgBox( _¶
        Prompt:="Do you want to overwrite the current " & _¶
        Contents & " ?", _¶
        Buttons:=vbQuestion + vbYesNo) = vbNo Then¶
      Exit Sub¶
    End If¶
    WS.Activate¶
  Else¶
    'Add the sheet¶
    Set WS = ActiveWorkbook.Worksheets.Add( _¶
        Before:=ActiveWorkbook.Sheets(1))¶
    WS.Name = Contents¶
  End If¶
  'Format the sheet¶
  WS.Cells.Delete¶
  WS.Range("B1").Value = Contents¶
  WS.Range("B1").Font.Bold = True¶
  WS.Range("B1").Font.Size = 12¶
  WS.Range("A1").EntireColumn.ColumnWidth = 5¶
  WS.Range("A1").EntireColumn.HorizontalAlignment = xlCenter¶
  WS.Range("B1").EntireColumn.ColumnWidth = 45¶
  'Create the table¶
  For Each Sht In ActiveWorkbook.Worksheets¶
    If Not Sht Is WS Then¶
    'Not Sht Is WS is code for "the sheet is not WS"¶
      'Check all the worksheets except WS¶
      'Now, add the Sht reference to WS¶
      With WS.Cells(WS.Rows.Count, 2).End(xlUp).Offset(1)¶
        .Value = Sht.Name¶
        WS.Hyperlinks.Add Anchor:=.Item(1), Address:="", _¶
            SubAddress:="'" & Sht.Name & "'!A1"¶
        'Add a bullet in column A¶
        .Offset(, -1).Value = Chr$(149)¶
      End With¶
    End If¶
  Next Sht¶
  'Restore screen updating¶
  Application.ScreenUpdating = True¶
End Sub¶
```

Exl

Tip: In the 'Change the following variables' section, change the name of the Table of Contents sheet to whatever is required, such as "Index", "Dashboard", or "Home".

Changing the Case of Text

Exl

This procedure emulates Microsoft Word's functionality to change the case of text by looping between UPPERCASE, lowercase, Title Case and Sentence case.

Scenario: Excel lacks the functionality that exists in Microsoft Word to quickly change the case of text. This macro overcomes that by applying the same principle existing in Word. Simply select the cells that should change, run the macro, and it loops between upper case (SAMPLE CASE), lower case (sample case), title case (Sample Case) and sentence case (Sample case).

Example file:
E021.xls

View the Appendix to learn how to store this procedure in a Standard module.

```
Option Explicit¶
' * * * * *¶
Sub ChangeCase()¶
  'Variable declarations¶
  Dim Rng As Range¶
  Dim Cll As Range¶
  Dim Conversion As Long¶
  'To choose between¶
  'UPPERCASE¶
  'lowercase¶
  'Sentence case¶
  'Title Case¶
  'Get the strings within the selection¶
  With ActiveWindow.RangeSelection¶
    'Only one cell selected¶
    If .Count = 1 Then¶
      'Is it a text string?¶
      If Application.IsText(.Item(1)) Then¶
        'If it doesn't have a formula, use it¶
        If Not .HasFormula Then Set Rng = .Item(1)¶
```

```
      End If¶
    Else¶
      On Error Resume Next¶
      Set Rng = .SpecialCells(xlCellTypeConstants, xlTextValues)¶
      On Error GoTo 0¶
    End If¶
    If Rng Is Nothing Then¶
      MsgBox "No text was found in the current selection", _¶
          vbExclamation¶
      Exit Sub¶
    End If¶
  End With¶
  'Check the first cell in that range to see what must be done¶
  Select Case Rng(1).Value¶
  Case UCase$(Rng(1).Value)¶
  'Change to sentence case¶
    Conversion = 2¶
  Case UCase$(Left$(Rng(1).Value, 1)) & _¶
    LCase$(Mid$(Rng(1).Value, 2))¶
  'Change to lowercase¶
    Conversion = 3¶
  Case LCase$(Rng(1).Value)¶
    'Change it directly to Upper ?¶
    If UCase$(Left$(Rng(1).Value, 1)) & _¶
      LCase$(Mid$(Rng(1).Value, 2)) = _¶
      Application.Proper(Rng(1).Value) Then¶
      'Proper and Sentence are equal, change to Upper¶
      Conversion = 1¶
    Else¶
  'Change to proper case¶
      Conversion = 4¶
    End If¶
  Case Else¶
  'Change to uppercase¶
    Conversion = 1¶
  End Select¶
  'Turn off screen updating¶
  Application.ScreenUpdating = False¶
  'Change the cells, according to what needs to be done¶
  For Each Cll In Rng.Cells¶
    Select Case Conversion¶
    Case 1  'changes to UPPER CASE¶
      Cll.Value = UCase$(Cll.Value)¶
    Case 2  'changes to Sentence Case¶
      Cll.Value = UCase$(Left$(Cll.Value, 1)) & _¶
        LCase$(Mid$(Cll.Value, 2))¶
    Case 3  'changes to lower case¶
      Cll.Value = LCase$(Cll.Value)¶
    Case 4  'Changes to Proper Case¶
      Cll.Value = Application.Proper(Cll.Value)¶
    End Select¶
```

```
  Next Cll¶
  'Restore screen updating¶
  Application.ScreenUpdating = True¶
End Sub¶
```

This procedure operates on the current selection of cells.

Tip: The example file has the macro assigned to a button. Clicking the button cycles through the various case changes.

Creating a Photo Album

Using this macro, you can insert all the pictures in a given path and arrange them to simulate a photo album

Scenario: This procedure allows you to quickly create a sales brochure in Excel by inserting the pictures of products into a worksheet so your client can readily see the product with its specifications. It inserts all the pictures that reside in a given path/folder and places them in a single worksheet, emulating a photo album.

Example file:
E022.xls

View the Appendix to learn how to store this procedure in a Standard module.

```
Option Explicit¶
' * * * * *¶
Sub InsertPictures()¶
'Variable declaration¶
'Variable for each picture¶
  Dim Shp As Shape¶
'Counter¶
  Dim i As Long¶
'Folder in which to search¶
  Dim Folder As String¶
'Search in subfolders, too¶
  Dim LookInSubFolders As Boolean¶
'Column and row counters¶
  Dim Clm As Long, Rw As Long¶
'Worksheet in which to insert the images¶
  Dim Sht As Worksheet¶
```

Exl

```
  Dim Rng As Range¶
  Dim MaxClm As Long¶
  Dim Size As Long¶
  'Change the following variables¶
  'Hard code Folder value¶
  'Folder = "C:\"¶
  'Folder = "C:\My Documents\My Pictures"¶
  'Let the user input folder value¶
  Folder = Range("B1").Value¶
  'Hard code LookInSubFolders value¶
  'LookInSubFolders = False¶
  'User inputs LookInSubFolders value¶
  LookInSubFolders = Range("B2").Value¶
  'Hard Code MaxClm value¶
'Insert 4 pictures per row¶
  'MaxClm = 4¶
  'User inputs MaxClm value¶
  MaxClm = Range("B3").Value¶
  'Hard Code Size value¶
'Use 3 worksheet columns for each picture¶
  'Size = 3¶
  'User inputs Size value¶
  Size = Range("B4").Value¶
  'This macro will insert all the images from a folder, inserting¶
  'MaxClm pictures per row.¶
  'Turn off screen updating¶
  Application.ScreenUpdating = False¶
  'Insert a new workbook with one worksheet¶
  Set Sht = Workbooks.Add(xlWorksheet).Worksheets(1)¶
  Rw = 1¶
  With Application.FileSearch¶
    .NewSearch¶
    .LookIn = Folder¶
    .SearchSubFolders = LookInSubFolders¶
    .Filename = ".jpg"¶
    .Execute¶
    For i = 1 To .FoundFiles.Count¶
      Clm = Clm + 1¶
      If Clm > MaxClm Then¶
        Clm = 1¶
        Rw = Rw + Size * 3 + 1¶
      End If¶
      'Did Excel run out of rows ?¶
      If Rw >= Sht.Rows.Count - Size * 3 + 1 Then¶
        'Start over !¶
        Clm = 1¶
        Rw = 1¶
        Set Sht = ActiveWorkbook.Sheets.Add(After:=Sht)¶
      End If¶
      'Set the range where pictures will be inserted¶
      Set Rng = Sht.Cells(Rw, (Clm - 1) * (Size + 1) + 1)¶
```

```
      'Insert the picture (use a small size then resize it later)¶
      Set Shp = Sht.Shapes.AddPicture(.FoundFiles(i), False, _¶
          True, Rng.Left, Rng.Top, 10, 10)¶
      With Shp¶
        'Resize it to its original size¶
        .ScaleHeight 1#, msoTrue, msoScaleFromTopLeft¶
        .ScaleWidth 1#, msoTrue, msoScaleFromTopLeft¶
        'Make sure that when it is resized, it appears normally¶
        .LockAspectRatio = True¶
        'Move it to the specified range, just in case¶
        .Left = Rng.Left¶
        .Top = Rng.Top¶
        'Resize it¶
        .Width = Rng.Resize(, Size).Width¶
        'Does it need to be resized?¶
        If Shp.BottomRightCell.Row > Rng.Row + Size * 3 Then¶
          .ScaleHeight 1#, msoTrue, msoScaleFromTopLeft¶
          .ScaleWidth 1#, msoTrue, msoScaleFromTopLeft¶
          .Height = Rng.Resize(Size * 3).Height¶
          .Left = Rng.Left + Rng.Resize(, _¶
              Size).Width / 2 - .Width / 2¶
        End If¶
      End With¶
    Next i¶
  End With¶
  'Restore screen updating¶
  Application.ScreenUpdating = True¶
End Sub¶
```

In the 'Change the following variables' section, the following four variables can be changed:

- **Path:** The location of the pictures
- **LookInSubFolders:** Search in the subfolders as well (True or False)
- **MaxClm:** Number of pictures to insert per row
- **Size:** Width (in columns) of each picture

Deleting the Empty Rows in a Range

This macro deletes all the rows that are completely empty in a specific range.

Scenario: To analyze data correctly in Excel, it is recommended that the data be organized in a contiguous range. A contiguous range is one that is without "gaps" between the rows or the columns of data. That way, applying sorts, applying AutoFilters, creating pivot tables, or using subtotals can easily be done because Excel correctly recognizes the analyzed range.

Example file:
E023.xls

Exl

Tip: If this macro doesn't work on your selected range, perhaps the cells are not truly empty. To ensure blank cells are empty, select the cells and hit Edit→Clear→All, and save the file. Then try the macro again.

	A	B	C	D	E
1	Q 1	Q 2	Q 3	Q 4	Q 5
2	3		3	1	3
3	3	2	5	4	2
4	1	3	2		1
5		2		5	2
6	1	5	3	2	3
7	4		3	3	
8	4	3	1	5	5
9		3		5	
10	2	2	4	5	2
11	3	1	5		
12	4	4	1	2	3
13					
14	5	5	2	3	3
15				4	5
16	1	1	5	2	2
17					
18	3	2	2	4	3
19					
20	2	3	2	4	5
21					

E023

Figure 26 – Worksheet Before Running Macro

	A	B	C	D	E
1	Q 1	Q 2	Q 3	Q 4	Q 5
2	3		3	1	3
3	3	2	5	4	2
4	1	3	2		1
5		2		5	2
6	1	5	3	2	3
7	4		3	3	
8	4	3	1	5	5
9		3		5	
10	2	2	4	5	2
11	3	1	5		
12	4	4	1	2	3
13	5	5	2	3	3
14				4	5
15	1	1	5	2	2
16	3	2	2	4	3
17	2	3	2	4	5
18					
19					
20					
21					

E023

Figure 27 – Worksheet After Running Macro

Exl

View the Appendix to learn how to store this procedure in a Standard module.

```
Option Explicit¶
' * * * * *¶
Sub DeleteEmptyRows()¶
  'Variable declaration¶
  Dim Rng As Range¶
  Dim Rw As Range¶
  'Change the following variables¶
  'Hard coded range¶
  Set Rng = Range("A2:E20")¶
  'User inputs range by selecting it.¶
  'Set Rng = ActiveWindow.RangeSelection¶
  'Turn off screen updating¶
  Application.ScreenUpdating = False¶
  'Loop through each row¶
  For Each Rw In Rng.Rows¶
    'Is this row of data empty? (Use COUNTA() to check this)¶
    If Application.CountA(Rw) = 0 Then¶
      'Rw is empty¶
      Rw.Delete Shift:=xlShiftUp¶
    End If¶
```

```
    Next Rw¶
    'Restore screen updating¶
    Application.ScreenUpdating = True¶
End Sub¶
```

In the 'Change the following variables' section, the range that is processed can be defined and coded directly into the macro. By default, it uses the range that is currently selected.

Creating a List of Files That Reside in a Directory

Use this macro to create a list of all the files in a path (and its subfolders) and to include a number of properties about each of them.

Example file:
E024.xls

Scenario: Sometimes it is helpful to have a list of all the files within a directory (and subdirectories). For example, when the information stored on a server is going to be moved to a different server, to validate that all the files have been moved correctly and completely. This macro can serve that purpose.

It could also be used to verify the size of the different files in order to determine which ones are occupying more space than they should.

	A	B	C	D	E
1	**Full path**	**File name**	**Path**	**Size (kB)**	**Date created**
2	C:\COMLOG.txt	COMLOG.txt	C:\	0.00	Mar 15, 03
3	C:\devicetable.log	devicetable.log	C:\	29.97	May 19, 03
4	C:\temp.log	temp.log	C:\	1.19	Oct 23, 04
5	C:\Test 2005-02-19.xls	Test 2005-02-19.xls	C:\	23.00	Feb 19, 05
6	C:\test.log	test.log	C:\	3,127.37	Oct 23, 04
7	C:\test.txt	test.txt	C:\	13.53	May 19, 04
8					

Sheet1

Figure 28 – Directory Listing

View the Appendix to learn how to store this procedure in a Standard module.

```
Option Explicit¶
' * * * * *¶
Sub CreateFileList()¶
  'Variable declarations¶
'Counter¶
  Dim i As Long¶
'Folder in which to search¶
  Dim Folder As String¶
'Search in subfolders¶
  Dim LookInSubFolders As Boolean¶
'File¶
  Dim File As Object¶
'FileSystemObject¶
  Dim FSO As Object¶
'Store old calculation¶
  Dim OldCalculation As Long¶
  'Change the following variables¶
  'Hard code Folder value¶
  'Folder = "C:\"¶
  'Folder = "C:\My Documents\My Music"¶
  'User inputs Folder value¶
  Folder = Range("B1").Value¶
  'Hard code LookInSubFolders value¶
  'LookInSubFolders = False¶
  'User inputs LookInSubFolders value¶
  LookInSubFolders = Range("B2").Value¶
  'Turn off screen updating¶
  Application.ScreenUpdating = False¶
  'Store current calculation method in variable¶
  OldCalculation = Application.Calculation¶
  'Set calculation to Manual¶
  Application.Calculation = xlCalculationManual¶
  'New FileSystemObject¶
  Set FSO = CreateObject("Scripting.FileSystemObject")¶
  With Application.FileSearch¶
    .NewSearch¶
    .LookIn = Folder¶
    .SearchSubFolders = LookInSubFolders¶
    .FileType = msoFileTypeAllFiles¶
    .Execute¶
    'Does enough space exist for all the files?¶
    If i - 1 > Rows.Count Then¶
      MsgBox Prompt:="The search returned more results than can " & _¶
             "be displayed on a worksheet", _¶
             Buttons:=vbCritical¶
      'Exit nicely¶
      GoTo exiting¶
    End If¶
```

```
    'Add a new workbook with one sheet¶
    Workbooks.Add xlWorksheet¶
    'Put the headers¶
    With Range("A1").Resize(1, 5)¶
      .Value = Array("Full path", "File name", "Path", _¶
          "Size (kB)", "Date created")¶
      .Font.Bold = True¶
    End With¶
    'Loop through the found files¶
    For i = 1 To .FoundFiles.Count¶
      'clear File variable¶
      Set File = Nothing¶
      On Error Resume Next¶
      Set File = FSO.GetFile(.FoundFiles(i))¶
      On Error GoTo 0¶
      If Not File Is Nothing Then¶
      'Not File Is Nothing is code for "the file exists"¶
        With Cells(i + 1, 1)¶
          'Put the variables desired¶
           'Full path¶
          .Value = File.Path¶
           'Name only¶
          .Offset(, 1).Value = File.Name¶
           'Path¶
          .Offset(, 2).Value = File.ParentFolder¶
           'Size in KB¶
          .Offset(, 3).Value = File.Size / 1024¶
           'Date created¶
          .Offset(, 4).Value = File.DateCreated¶
          'Other available properties can be included by¶
          'removing the appostrophe in front of the line¶
          'that should be used.¶
          '.Offset(,5).Value = File.Attributes¶
          '.Offset(,6).Value = File.Datelastaccessed¶
          '.Offset(,7).Value = File.Datelastmodified¶
          '.Offset(,8).Value = File.Drive¶
          '.Offset(,9).Value = File.Shortname¶
          '.Offset(,10).Value = File.Shortpath¶
          '.Offset(,11).Value = File.Type¶
        End With¶
      End If¶
    Next i¶
  End With¶
  'Change the width of column A¶
  Range("A:A").EntireColumn.ColumnWidth = 50¶
  'Format column D (Size)¶
  Range("D:D").NumberFormat = "#,##0.00"¶
  'Format column E (Date)¶
  Range("E:E").NumberFormat = "mmm dd, yy"¶
```

```
   'Autofit columns B, D and E¶
   Range("B:B, D:E").EntireColumn.AutoFit¶
exiting:¶
   'Restore calculation¶
   Application.Calculation = OldCalculation¶
   'Restore screen updating¶
   Application.ScreenUpdating = True¶
End Sub¶
```

Exl

In the 'Change the following variables' section, you can change these two variables:

- **Path:** The location of the files
- **LookInSubFolders:** Search in the subfolders as well (True or False)

You can change the properties of the files that are displayed in the worksheet as well. Within the macro, there is a small list of available properties. To include any of the listed properties, simply remove the apostrophe in front of the code for that property line to include it in the data.

Also, be sure to change the “5” in the following line of code to reflect the number of properties being returned:

```
With Range("A1").Resize(1, 5)¶
```

The array also must have the additional headers added to the list after the “Date created”. Separate the headers with commas.

```
.Value = Array("Full path", "File name", "Path", _¶
    "Size (kB)", "Date created")¶
```

Forcing the User to Enable Macros

This procedure provides a workaround to force users to enable macros in order to use the workbook successfully.

Scenario: Because of the virus risk that exists in VBA macros, Microsoft created a security model for the Office applications that enables users to disable them as a preventative measure. This affects all applications that rely on macros to function properly and frustrates developers who need to have macros enabled for the workbook to work successfully.

This macro uses a workaround to disable worksheets in the workbook and displays a message warning the user that macros need to be enabled to use the workbook successfully.

Example file:
E025.xls

Exl

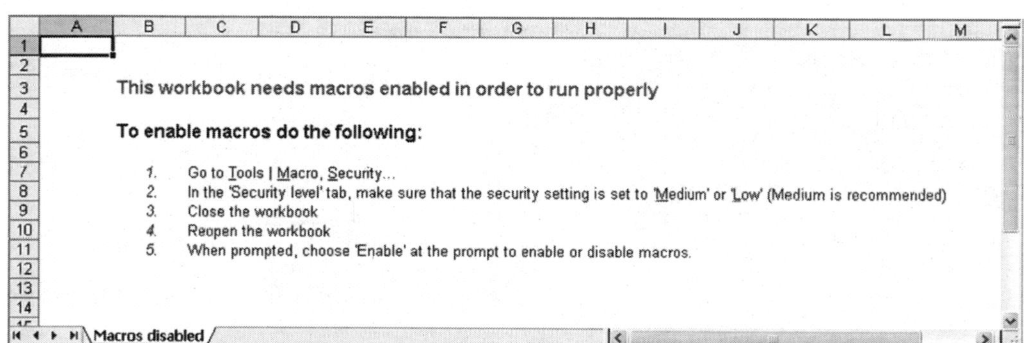

Figure 29 – Instructing the User to Enable Macros

View the Appendix to learn how to store this procedure in a Standard module.

```
Option Explicit¶
' * * * * *¶
Sub ForceMacros()¶
  'Variable declarations¶
  Dim DummySheet As Worksheet¶
  Dim OtherSheet As Object     'All sheet types¶
  On Error Resume Next¶
  Set DummySheet = ThisWorkbook.Worksheets("Macros disabled")¶
```

```
  If DummySheet Is Nothing Then¶
    MsgBox "Unable to find dummy sheet", vbCritical¶
    Exit Sub¶
  End If¶
  'Turn off screen updating¶
  Application.ScreenUpdating = False¶
  For Each OtherSheet In ThisWorkbook.Sheets¶
    OtherSheet.Visible = xlSheetVisible¶
  Next OtherSheet¶
  'Hide the Dummy sheet¶
  DummySheet.Visible = xlSheetVeryHidden¶
  'Mark the workbook as saved, because the user has not made any¶
  'changes yet¶
  ThisWorkbook.Saved = True¶
  'Restore screen updating¶
  Application.ScreenUpdating = True¶
End Sub¶
' * * * * *¶
Sub RunOnClose()¶
  'This macro hides all the "useful"¶
  'sheets, and displays the dummy sheet¶
  'Variable declaration¶
  Dim DummySheet As Worksheet¶
  Dim OtherSheet As Object    'All sheet types¶
  On Error Resume Next¶
  Set DummySheet = ThisWorkbook.Worksheets("Macros disabled")¶
  If DummySheet Is Nothing Then¶
    MsgBox "Unable to find dummy sheet", vbCritical¶
    Exit Sub¶
  End If¶
  'Turn off screen updating¶
  Application.ScreenUpdating = False¶
  'Show the Dummy sheet first, to avoid possible errors¶
  DummySheet.Visible = xlSheetVisible¶
  'Hide all except the dummy sheet¶
  For Each OtherSheet In ThisWorkbook.Sheets¶
    If Not OtherSheet Is DummySheet Then¶
      OtherSheet.Visible = xlSheetVeryHidden¶
    End If¶
  Next OtherSheet¶
  'Save the workbook¶
  ThisWorkbook.Save¶
End Sub¶
' * * * * *¶
Sub Auto_Open()¶
  'Run the ForceMacros macro when the workbook is opened¶
  ForceMacros¶
End Sub¶
```

```
' * * * * *¶
Sub Auto_Close()¶
  'Hide all the sheets except the dummy one.¶
  RunOnClose¶
End Sub¶
```

Tip: This macro requires a sheet called 'Macros Disabled', where a customized message to the user is displayed when the workbook is opened without macros enabled.

Exl

Finding and Replacing a String in All Open Workbooks

Use this macro to perform a quick Find and Replace on all open workbooks.

Scenario: Sometimes, due to a company name change, a text string must be changed in many workbooks. Making the change in all these workbooks one at a time can be a tedious and error-prone task. This macro solves the problem by doing a "global" Find and Replace on all workbooks that are open when the macro runs.

Example file:
E026.xls

View the Appendix to learn how to store this procedure in a Standard module.

```
Option Explicit¶
' * * * * *¶
Sub FindAndReplace()¶
  'Variable declaration¶
  Dim sFind As Variant¶
  Dim sReplace As Variant¶
  Dim Book As Workbook¶
  Dim WS As Worksheet¶
  'Ask for the text to find¶
  sFind = Application.InputBox(Prompt:="Enter the text to find:", _¶
      Title:="Find", Type:=2)¶
  'Did the user cancel?¶
  If TypeName(sFind) = "Boolean" Then Exit Sub¶
  If Len(sFind) = 0 Then Exit Sub¶
  'Ask for the replacement¶
  sReplace = Application.InputBox( _¶
      Prompt:="Enter the text to replace with:", Title:="Replace", _¶
      Type:=2)¶
```

```
    'Did the user cancel?¶
    If TypeName(sReplace) = "Boolean" Then Exit Sub¶
    'Turn off screen updating¶
    Application.ScreenUpdating = False¶
    'Loop through the workbooks¶
    For Each Book In Workbooks¶
      For Each WS In Book.Worksheets¶
        WS.Cells.Replace What:=CStr(sFind), _¶
            Replacement:=CStr(sReplace), LookAt:=xlPart, _¶
            SearchOrder:=xlByRows, MatchCase:=False¶
      Next WS¶
    Next Book¶
    'Restore screen updating¶
    Application.ScreenUpdating = True¶
End Sub¶
```


Tip: This macro requires no changing of variables because the variables are changed through an input box provided to the user.

Converting Data to a Tabular Format

With this macro, you can convert data into a format that helps utilize the built-in features of Excel.

Scenario: Inputting information and analyzing it are two very different things. What could be a good layout for data entry might be a bad one for analyzing data. A survey is a typical example, presented to the participant looking like this:

Example file:
E027.xls

	A	B	C	D	E	F	G
1	#	Survey	Question 1	Question 2	Question 3	Question 4	Question 5
2	1	ABC - 001	3	1	3	5	2
3	2	ABC - 002	2	1	4	3	4

Figure 30 – Great Data Layout for Data Entry

Scenario, continued: However, this layout does not allow you to compile and analyze the data efficiently with Excel. This macro converts the previous data into a more useful format that can be analyzed with Excel's built-in tools.

	M	N	O	P
1	#	**Survey**	**Question**	**Value**
2	1	ABC - 001	Question 1	3
3	1	ABC - 001	Question 2	1
4	1	ABC - 001	Question 3	3
5	1	ABC - 001	Question 4	5
6	1	ABC - 001	Question 5	2
7	2	ABC - 002	Question 1	2
8	2	ABC - 002	Question 2	1
9	2	ABC - 002	Question 3	4
10	2	ABC - 002	Question 4	3
11	2	ABC - 002	Question 5	4

Figure 31 – Great Data Layout for Data Analysis

View the Appendix to learn how to store this procedure in a Standard module.

```
Option Explicit¶
' * * * * *¶
Sub DataToTabular()¶
  'Variable declaration¶
  Dim RngOrig As Range¶
  Dim RngDest As Range¶
  Dim FixedColumnCount As Long¶
  Dim VarColumnCount As Long¶
  Dim i As Long¶
  On Error Resume Next¶
  'Ask for the data¶
  Set RngOrig = Application.InputBox( _¶
      Prompt:="Select the data to be converted " & _¶
      "(Inlcude the headers)", _¶
      Title:="Data", Type:=8)¶
  'Destination¶
  Set RngDest = Application.InputBox( _¶
      Prompt:="Where do you want the data " & _¶
      "(Select top left cell only)", _¶
      Title:="Destination", Type:=8)¶
```

```
  On Error GoTo 0¶
  'Did the user cancel?¶
  If RngOrig Is Nothing Or RngDest Is Nothing Then Exit Sub¶
  'Multiple selections in the origin? (can't do that...)¶
  If RngOrig.Areas.Count > 1 Then¶
    MsgBox "Please select only one range and try again", _¶
        vbCritical¶
    Exit Sub¶
  End If¶
  'Use only first cell of RngDest as the destination¶
  Set RngDest = RngDest(1)¶
  'Ask for the number of fixed columns (the variable will¶
  'be the difference)¶
  FixedColumnCount = CLng(Application.InputBox( _¶
      Prompt:="How many columns are fixed ?" & vbCrLf & _¶
      "Note that the macro assumes these columns go " & _¶
      "from left to right", Title:="Fixed columns", Type:=1))¶
  If FixedColumnCount < 1 Then Exit Sub¶
  VarColumnCount = RngOrig.Columns.Count - FixedColumnCount¶
  'Turn off screen updating¶
  Application.ScreenUpdating = False¶
  'Put the headers¶
  '  First, the fixed ones¶
  RngDest.Resize(1, _¶
      FixedColumnCount).Value = RngOrig(1).Resize(1, _¶
      FixedColumnCount).Value¶
  '  Next, two generic (Question and Value)¶
  RngDest.Offset(0, FixedColumnCount).Resize(1, _¶
      2).Value = Array("Question", "Value")¶
  'Ok, convert the data, loop through the RngOrig range¶
  On Error GoTo err_h                     'Trap errors¶
  For i = 1 To RngOrig.Rows.Count - 1     'Exclude the headers¶
    With RngDest.Offset(VarColumnCount * i - VarColumnCount + 1, _¶
        0).Resize(VarColumnCount, FixedColumnCount)¶
      'Place the fixed value, it will be repeated VarColumnCount times¶
      .Value = RngOrig.Offset(i).Resize(1, _¶
          FixedColumnCount).Value¶
      'Now, for the questions (Data needs to be transposed)¶
      .Offset(, FixedColumnCount).Resize(, _¶
          1).Value = Application.Transpose(RngOrig.Offset(0, _¶
          FixedColumnCount).Resize(1, VarColumnCount).Value)¶
      'Finally, the values¶
      .Offset(, FixedColumnCount + 1).Resize(, _¶
          1).Value = Application.Transpose(RngOrig.Offset(i, _¶
          FixedColumnCount).Resize(1, VarColumnCount).Value)¶
    End With¶
  Next i¶
err_h:¶
  If Err.Number <> 0 Then¶
    MsgBox "The following error occured: " & vbCrLf & "Error: " _¶
        & Err.Number & ", " & Err.Description, vbCritical¶
```

```
  End If¶
  'Restore screen updating¶
  Application.ScreenUpdating = True¶
End Sub¶
```

AutoNumbering Invoices and Other Workbooks

This macro shows how to create an AutoNumber field. It can be used across a network or on a single PC.

Scenario: When creating a template, such as one that can be used for an invoice or a survey, it is usually required that each workbook to have a unique number or 'key'.

Example file:
E028.xls

This sample shows how to AutoNumber workbooks and demonstrates how it can be used on a network where each individual, working from different PCs, gets a different, sequential number each time.

View the Appendix to learn how to store this procedure in a Standard module.

```
Option Explicit¶
' * * * * *¶
Type Template¶
  Number As Long¶
  DateStamp As Date¶
End Type¶
' * * * * *¶
Sub Autonumber()¶
  'Variable declaration¶
  Dim FilePath As String¶
  Dim File As Long¶
  Dim Counter As Long¶
  Dim Temp As Template¶
  Dim NewTemp As Template¶
  'Change the following variables¶
  FilePath = "\\Server\apps\Counter.txt"¶
  FilePath = "C:\Counter.dat"¶
  File = FreeFile()¶
```

Exl

```
  Do¶
    On Error Resume Next¶
    Open FilePath For Binary Lock Read Write As #File¶
  Loop Until Err.Number = 0¶
  'Loop through all the records in the file¶
  Do While Not EOF(File)¶
    'Get the record¶
    Get #File, , Temp¶
    'Is there information in it?¶
    If Temp.Number > 0 Then NewTemp = Temp¶
  Loop¶
  'Increase the number by one¶
  NewTemp.Number = NewTemp.Number + 1¶
  'Save the date¶
  NewTemp.DateStamp = Now()¶
  'Return the number to cell B1¶
  Range("B1").Value = NewTemp.Number¶
  'Store the number in the text file¶
  Put #File, , NewTemp¶
  'Close the file¶
  Close #File¶
End Sub¶
' * * * * *¶
Sub Auto_Open()¶
    'Call the macro when the workbook opens¶
    Autonumber¶
End Sub¶
```

Note: Change the FilePath variable to point to the folder and file in which the counter is to be stored.

Comparing Columns Using Various Criteria

This example includes code to highlight the entries that appear in one list but not in the other, to highlight the entries that are common to both lists, and to generate a unique list from both.

Scenario: Comparing data is one of the most common tasks for which people use Excel. If two files with inventory part numbers are received, you can find out which part numbers are missing from one list, or which part numbers appear in both lists, or create a list that contains all the part numbers without repetition.

Example file:
E029.xls

View the Appendix to learn how to store this procedure in a Standard module.

```
Option Explicit¶
' * * * * *¶
Sub CompareColumns()¶
  'Variable declaration¶
  Dim RngA As Range¶
  Dim RngB As Range¶
  Dim RngDest As Range¶
  Dim WhatToDo As Long¶
  'Continue if error occurs¶
  On Error Resume Next¶
  Set RngA = Application.InputBox( _¶
      Prompt:="Select the first column (Including the header)", _¶
      Title:="First column", Type:=8)¶
  Set RngB = Application.InputBox( _¶
      Prompt:="Select the second column (Including the header)", _¶
      Title:="Second column", Type:=8)¶
  On Error GoTo 0¶
  'Did the user cancel?¶
  If RngA Is Nothing Or RngB Is Nothing Then Exit Sub¶
  'Make sure only one column is in each range¶
  Set RngA = RngA.Columns(1)¶
  Set RngB = RngB.Columns(1)¶
  'Ask what to do¶
  WhatToDo = CLng(Application.InputBox( _¶
    Prompt:="- Enter '1' to highlight items that exist in 1 but " & _¶
      "not in 2." & vbCrLf & _¶
      "- Enter '2' to highlight items that appear in both columns." _¶
      & vbCrLf & _¶
      "- Enter '3' to extract a list of the unique items.", _¶
      Title:="Compare columns", _¶
      Type:=1))¶
  'Turn off screen updating¶
  Application.ScreenUpdating = False¶
  Select Case WhatToDo¶
  Case 1¶
    'Highlight in red the ones that are in A but not in B¶
    HighlightInANotInB RngA, RngB, RGB(255, 0, 0)¶
  Case 2¶
    'Highlight in blue the ones that are in A and are in B too¶
    HighlightInAandInB RngA, RngB, RGB(0, 0, 255)¶
  Case 3¶
    'Generate a unique list of both, and put it in column¶
    'user inputs¶
    'Continue if error occurs¶
    On Error Resume Next¶
    'Restore screen updating for the inputbox¶
    Application.ScreenUpdating = True¶
    Set RngDest = Application.InputBox( _¶
```

```
        Prompt:="Select the target cell", Title:="Unique list", _¶
        Type:=8)¶
    'Turn off screen updating¶
    Application.ScreenUpdating = False¶
    If Not RngDest Is Nothing Then¶
    'If Not RngDest Is Nothing is code for "RngDest indicated"¶
      UniqueList RngA, RngB, RngDest(1)¶
    End If¶
  End Select¶
  'Restore screen updating¶
  Application.ScreenUpdating = True¶
End Sub¶
' * * * * *¶
Sub HighlightInAandInB(ByVal Column1 As Range, _¶
    ByVal Column2 As Range, Color As Long)¶
  'Variable declaration¶
  Dim Cll As Range¶
  'Limit to the used range, to speed it up¶
  Set Column1 = Intersect(Column1, Column1.Worksheet.UsedRange)¶
  Set Column2 = Intersect(Column2, Column2.Worksheet.UsedRange)¶
  'Remove the header¶
  Set Column1 = Column1.Offset(1).Resize(Column1.Rows.Count - 1)¶
  Set Column2 = Column2.Offset(1).Resize(Column2.Rows.Count - 1)¶
  'Loop through the cells¶
  For Each Cll In Column1.Cells¶
    'Use the MATCH() function to see if the value is in there¶
    If IsNumeric(Application.Match(Cll.Value, Column2, 0)) Then¶
      'It is, so highlight it¶
      Cll.Interior.Color = Color¶
      'To delete the cell, use¶
      'Cll.Delete Shift:=xlShiftUp¶
    End If¶
  Next Cll¶
End Sub¶
' * * * * *¶
Sub HighlightInANotInB(ByVal Column1 As Range, _¶
    ByVal Column2 As Range, Color As Long)¶
  'Variable declaration¶
  Dim Cll As Range¶
  'Limit to the used range, to speed it up¶
  Set Column1 = Intersect(Column1, Column1.Worksheet.UsedRange)¶
  Set Column2 = Intersect(Column2, Column2.Worksheet.UsedRange)¶
  'Remove the header¶
  Set Column1 = Column1.Offset(1).Resize(Column1.Rows.Count - 1)¶
  Set Column2 = Column2.Offset(1).Resize(Column2.Rows.Count - 1)¶
  'Loop through the cells¶
  For Each Cll In Column1.Cells¶
    'Use the MATCH() function to see if the value is in there¶
    If IsError(Application.Match(Cll.Value, Column2, 0)) Then¶
      'Is not, so highlight it¶
      Cll.Interior.Color = Color¶
```

```
      'To delete the cell, use¶
      'Cll.Delete Shift:=xlShiftUp¶
    End If¶
  Next Cll¶
End Sub¶
' * * * * *¶
Sub UniqueList(ByVal Column1 As Range, ByVal Column2 As Range, _¶
    RngDest As Range)¶
  Dim WS As Worksheet¶
  'Use a temporary worksheet to use Advanced Filter on it¶
  Set WS = Workbooks.Add(xlWorksheet).Worksheets(1)¶
  'Put the first column¶
  WS.Range("A1").Resize(Column1.Rows.Count).Value = Column1.Value¶
  'Put the second column, skip one row, which is¶
  'the heading¶
  WS.Range("A1").Offset(Column1.Rows.Count).Resize( _¶
      Column2.Rows.Count - 1).Value = Column2.Offset(1).Resize( _¶
      Column2.Rows.Count - 1).Value¶
  'Now, use advanced filter and put the results directly in¶
  'the destination range¶
  WS.Range("A:A").AdvancedFilter Action:=xlFilterCopy, _¶
      CopyToRange:=RngDest, Unique:=True¶
  'Close the temp workbook without saving¶
  WS.Parent.Close SaveChanges:=False¶
End Sub¶
```

Exl

Deleting the Contents of Unlocked Cells

This macro illustrates how to delete only those cells that do not contain formulas and are unlocked, which means that they are entry cells.

Scenario: When using a workbook that has multiple sheets that all contain input (unlocked, so the user can enter data in them) and output cells (locked, so the user can only see the results and cannot change the formula inside them), you often need to clear only the input cells.

Suppose you take complaint calls and, using Excel, you fill out a form, print it, and don't save it because the printed copy is your only required record. Rather than using a template each time, or closing the file without saving, you can now put a command button on a worksheet that, when clicked, erases the data you entered, thus providing you with a new, blank form.

Example file:
E030.xls

Exl

View the Appendix to learn how to store this procedure in a Standard module.

```
Option Explicit¶
' * * * * *¶
Sub ClearUnlockedCells()¶
  'Variable declaration¶
  Dim Rng As Range, UnlockedRng As Range, Cll As Range¶
  Dim Sht As Worksheet¶
  'Turn off screen updating¶
  Application.ScreenUpdating = False¶
  'Loop through all the worksheets in the active workbook¶
  For Each Sht In ActiveWorkbook.Worksheets¶
    'Do it if the sheet is protected¶
    If Sht.ProtectContents Then¶
      On Error Resume Next¶
      'Delete the previous range¶
      Set Rng = Nothing¶
      Set UnlockedRng = Nothing¶
      'Get the used range in the worksheet¶
      Set Rng = Sht.UsedRange¶
      'Are there any?¶
      If Not Rng Is Nothing Then¶
        'See which cells are locked¶
        For Each Cll In Rng.Cells¶
          If Not Cll.HasFormula Then¶
            'check for formula in cell¶
              If Not Cll.Locked Then¶
                'check for locked cell¶
                  If UnlockedRng Is Nothing Then¶
                    Set UnlockedRng = Cll¶
                  Else¶
                Set UnlockedRng = Union(Cll, UnlockedRng)¶
              End If¶
            End If¶
          End If¶
        Next Cll¶
      End If¶
      'Clear it if something is there¶
      If Not UnlockedRng Is Nothing Then¶
        'Not UnlockedRng Is Nothing is code for "UnlockedRng¶
        'has something in it"¶
        UnlockedRng.ClearContents¶
      End If¶
    End If¶
  Next Sht¶
  'Restore screen updating¶
  Application.ScreenUpdating = True¶
End Sub¶
```

Hiding All Standard Toolbars Except Your Own

This procedure shows how to hide all the toolbars in Excel, displaying only a customized one, and thus forcing the user to use only those tools.

Scenario: To create a 'dictator application', that is, one that enables the user to use only the tools that the application provides, one of the first steps is to hide all of Excel's built-in toolbars.

Remember to follow the golden rule: If you customize a "dictator application", restore the user's application to its original setup when it quits.

Example file:
E031.xls

Exl

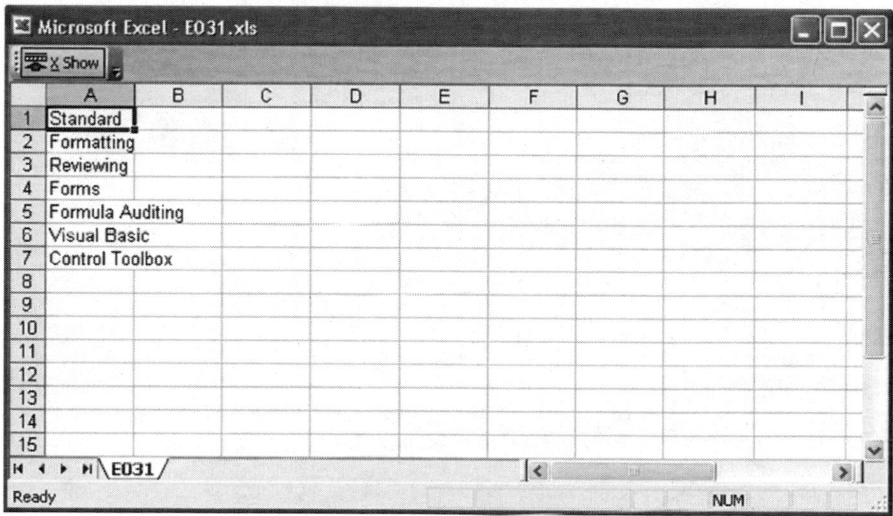

Figure 32 – Dictator Application

Exl

View the Appendix to learn how to store this procedure in a Standard module.

```
Option Explicit¶
' * * * * * *¶
Const BarName As String = "My Bar"¶
Const ControlTag As String = "HideControl"¶
' * * * * * *¶
Sub ShowHideToolbars()¶
  'Variable declaration¶
  Dim i As Long¶
  Dim Show As Boolean¶
  Dim Bar As CommandBar¶
  'Exit on error¶
  On Error GoTo err_h¶
  With Application.CommandBars.FindControl(Tag:=ControlTag)¶
    If .State = msoButtonUp Then¶
      'Hide them¶
      Show = False¶
      'Change the state of the button¶
      .State = msoButtonDown¶
      .Caption = "&X Show"¶
    Else¶
      'Show them¶
      Show = True¶
      'Change the state of the button¶
      .State = msoButtonUp¶
      .Caption = "&X Hide"¶
    End If¶
  End With¶
  'Sheet to store the information, can be hidden¶
  With ActiveSheet¶
    If Show Then¶
      'Loop through the entries that were saved, displaying them¶
      For i = 1 To .Cells(.Rows.Count, 1).End(xlUp).Row¶
        Application.CommandBars(.Cells(i, _¶
            1).Value).Visible = True¶
      Next i¶
      'Enable the Worksheet and Chart menu bar¶
      Application.CommandBars(1).Enabled = True¶
      Application.CommandBars(2).Enabled = True¶
      'Delete the entries¶
      .Range("A:A").ClearContents¶
      'Display the formula bar?¶
      Application.DisplayFormulaBar = True¶
    Else¶
      i = 0¶
```

```
      'Loop through the Toolbars and save the ones that are visible¶
      For Each Bar In Application.CommandBars¶
        If Bar.Type = msoBarTypeNormal Then¶
          If Not Bar.Name = BarName Then¶
            If Bar.Visible Then¶
              'Save the entry in the worksheet¶
              i = i + 1¶
              .Cells(i, 1).Value = Bar.Name¶
              Bar.Visible = False¶
            End If¶
          End If¶
        End If¶
      Next Bar¶
      'Disable the Worksheet and Chart menu bar¶
      Application.CommandBars(1).Enabled = False¶
      Application.CommandBars(2).Enabled = False¶
      'Hide the formula bar?¶
      Application.DisplayFormulaBar = False¶
    End If¶
  End With¶
  Exit Sub¶
err_h:¶
End Sub¶
' * * * * *¶
Sub CreateBar()¶
  'Custom toolbar here¶
  'Variable declaration¶
  Dim Bar As CommandBar¶
  Dim Ctl As CommandBarButton¶
  'Delete any previous bars¶
  DeleteBar¶
  Set Bar = Application.CommandBars.Add(Name:=BarName, _¶
      Position:=msoBarTop)¶
  With Bar¶
    'Add only one button¶
    With .Controls.Add(Type:=msoControlButton)¶
      .Caption = "&X Hide"¶
      .FaceId = 35¶
      .Style = msoButtonIconAndCaption¶
      'Set default to "not pressed"¶
      .State = msoButtonUp¶
      .OnAction = "ShowHideToolbars"¶
      .Tag = ControlTag¶
    End With¶
    .Visible = True¶
  End With¶
End Sub¶
```

```
' * * * * *¶
Sub DeleteBar()¶
  On Error Resume Next¶
  Application.CommandBars(BarName).Delete¶
End Sub¶
' * * * * *¶
Sub Auto_Open()¶
  'Create the bar when the workbook opens¶
  CreateBar¶
End Sub¶
' * * * * *¶
Sub Auto_Close()¶
  'Delete the bar when the workbook opens¶
  DeleteBar¶
End Sub¶
```


Tips: Customize the toolbar that remains visible by changing the 'CreateBar' procedure as desired.

You can call the macro by pressing a toolbar icon to show or hide the toolbars.

Creating a PPT Presentation from a Pivot Chart

This procedure demonstrates how to create a Microsoft PowerPoint presentation based on a Pivot Chart that includes one Page field.

Scenario: Pivot Charts are very useful tools, but distributing them becomes complicated. Usually, the people receiving them want only to see their respective piece of the chart. For example, you may want to create a PowerPoint presentation for each of the sales regions for the company that can be easily grasped by all the people involved (including supervisors).

Example file:
E032.xls

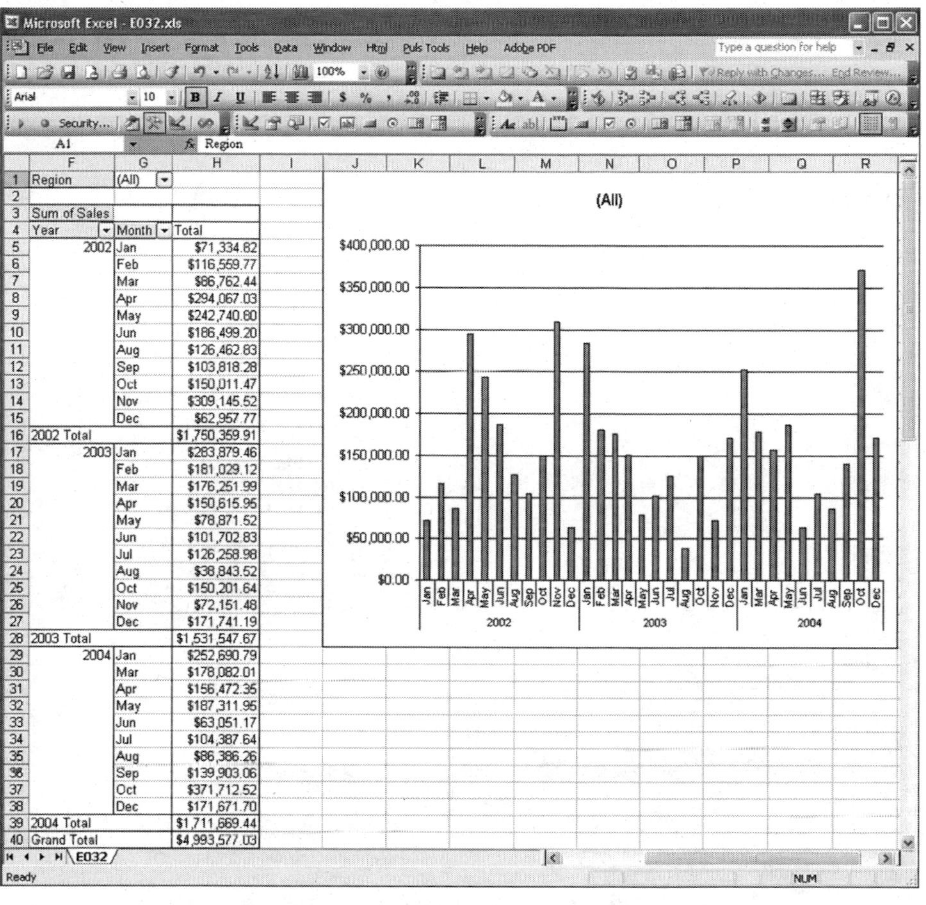

Figure 33 – Pivot Chart in Excel

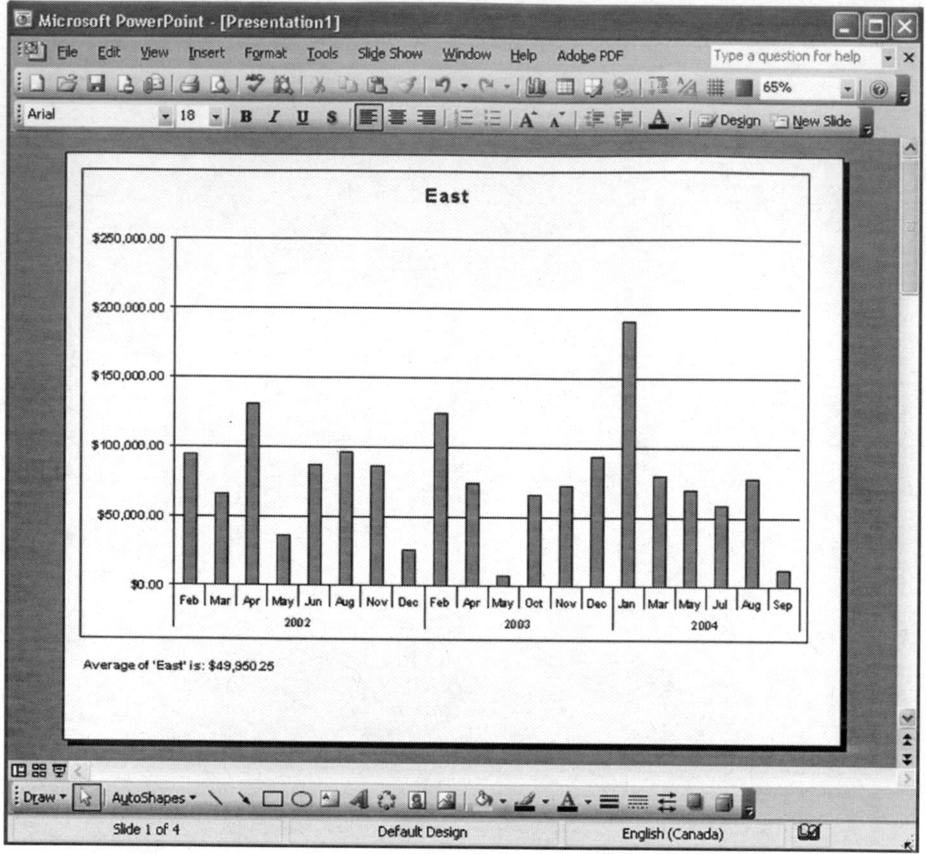

Figure 34 – Pivot Chart in PowerPoint

View the Appendix to learn how to store this procedure in a Standard module.

```
Option Explicit¶
' * * * * *¶
Sub CreatePPoint()¶
  'Variable declaration¶
  Dim pPoint As Object      'PowerPoint.Application¶
  Dim pPres As Object       'PowerPoint.Presentation¶
  Dim pSlide As Object      'PowerPoint.Slide¶
  Dim pShape As Object      'PowerPoint.ShapeRange¶
  Dim pAvg As Object        'PowerPoint.Shape¶
  Dim Cht As Chart¶
```

```
Dim Pivot As PivotTable¶
Dim PItem As PivotItem¶
Dim PivotData As Range¶
Dim Avg As Double¶
'Turn off screen updating¶
Application.ScreenUpdating = False¶
'Set a reference to the Pivot Chart¶
Set Cht = ActiveSheet.ChartObjects(1).Chart¶
'Set a reference to the PivotTable of the chart¶
Set Pivot = Cht.PivotLayout.PivotTable¶
'Set a reference to the database (using an Excel database)¶
Set PivotData = Range(Application.ConvertFormula( _¶
    Pivot.SourceData, xlR1C1, xlA1))¶
'Create a new PowerPoint presentation (and application)¶
'New PowerPoint.Application¶
Set pPoint = CreateObject("PowerPoint.Application")¶
Set pPres = pPoint.Presentations.Add¶
'Loop through each of the items of the page field¶
For Each PItem In Pivot.PageFields(1).PivotItems¶
  'Check for (All)¶
  If PItem.Caption <> "(All)" Then¶
    'Any slides yet ?¶
    Pivot.PageFields(1).CurrentPage = PItem.Caption¶
    If pPres.Slides.Count = 0 Then¶
      Set pSlide = pPres.Slides.Add(1, 12)    'ppLayoutBlank = 12¶
    Else¶
      Set pSlide = pPres.Slides.Add(pPres.Slides.Count + 1, _¶
          12)      'ppLayoutBlank¶
    End If¶
    'Copy an image of the chart¶
    Cht.CopyPicture Appearance:=xlPrinter, Format:=xlPicture¶
    'Paste it in PowerPoint¶
    Set pShape = pSlide.Shapes.Paste¶
    'Resize it¶
    With pShape¶
      .ScaleWidth 1, msoFalse, msoScaleFromTopLeft¶
      .ScaleHeight 0.94, msoFalse, msoScaleFromBottomRight¶
      .Left = 10¶
      .Top = 10¶
    End With¶
    'Create the average of this region¶
    Set pAvg = pSlide.Shapes.AddLabel( _¶
        Orientation:=msoTextOrientationHorizontal, _¶
        Left:=pShape.Left, Top:=pShape.Top + pShape.Height + 10, _¶
        Width:=pShape.Width, Height:=30)¶
    'Calculate the average¶
```

Exl

```
      With PivotData¶
        Avg = 0¶
        'calculate the total of elements first¶
        Avg = Application.CountIf(.Columns(1), PItem.Caption)¶
        'If some exist, calculate the average, if not, it's 0¶
        If Avg > 0 Then¶
          Avg = Application.SumIf(.Columns(1), PItem.Caption, _¶
              .Columns(4)) / Avg¶
        Else¶
          Avg = 0¶
        End If¶
      End With¶
      'Add the text¶
      With pAvg.TextFrame.TextRange¶
        .Text = "Average of '" & PItem.Caption & "' is: " & _¶
            Format$(Avg, "currency")¶
        .Font.Bold = True¶
        .Font.Size = 12¶
      End With¶
    End If¶
  Next PItem¶
  'Restore screen updating¶
  Application.ScreenUpdating = True¶
  'Activate and display PowerPoint¶
  pPoint.Visible = True¶
  pPoint.ActiveWindow.ViewType = 1    'ppViewSlide = 1¶
  pPoint.Activate¶
  'Destroy the variables¶
  Set pShape = Nothing¶
  Set pSlide = Nothing¶
  Set pPres = Nothing¶
  Set pPoint = Nothing¶
End Sub¶
```

This macro uses the pivot table in sample E032.xls. It should also work with a different pivot chart if you change the reference to it in the code and remove the code that creates the average of the field, unless it provides useful information.

Saving a Backup Copy of a Workbook

Using this procedure, you can create a backup of copy of your workbook in a different location (such as a server) each time you save it.

Scenario: When working with data, it is important to have procedures that allow the company or department to recover as painlessly and quickly as possible from a disaster. One common procedure is to do a backup of the information to a remote location—a server located in a different geographical spot—to diminish the chances of loss of data.

Example file:
E033.xls

Exl

View the Appendix to learn how to store this procedure in a Standard module.

```
Option Explicit¶
' * * * * *¶
Sub SaveBackup(Optional Book As Workbook)¶
  'Call this macro from the BeforeSave event of the workbook¶
  'Variable declaration¶
  Dim Path As String¶
  Dim FileNoExtension As String¶
  Dim Extension As String¶
  Dim TempFile As String¶
  Dim i As Long¶
  'Change the following variables¶
'Number of old versions to save¶
'If set to 0, no older version is kept¶
  Const History As Long = 3¶
  'Hard coded Path value¶
  'Path = "\\Server\apps\"¶
  'Path = "C:\"¶
  'User inputs Path variable¶
  Path = Range("B1").Value¶
  On Error GoTo err_h¶
  'If workbook isn't identified, assume the active workbook¶
  If Book Is Nothing Then¶
    Set Book = ActiveWorkbook¶
  End If¶
  'Does the folder exist?¶
  If Len(Dir$(PathName:=Path, Attributes:=vbDirectory)) = 0 Then¶
    MkDir Path¶
  End If¶
```

```
    'Make sure that there is a trailing backslash¶
    If Right$(Path, Len(Application.PathSeparator)) <> _¶
      Application.PathSeparator Then¶
      Path = Path & Application.PathSeparator¶
    End If¶
    If History <= 0 Then¶
      'Don't keep a history, overwrite if the file exists¶
      'Continue if error occurs¶
      On Error Resume Next¶
      SetAttr PathName:=Path & Book.Name, Attributes:=vbNormal¶
      On Error GoTo err_h¶
      Book.SaveCopyAs Path & Book.Name¶
      'Mark it as read only¶
      SetAttr PathName:=Path & Book.Name, Attributes:=vbReadOnly¶
    Else¶
      'Store versions on the path¶
      'First, get the name of the file without the extension¶
      Extension = GetExtension(Book.Name)¶
      FileNoExtension = Left$(Book.Name, _¶
          Len(Book.Name) - Len(Extension) - 1)¶
      'Delete the oldest version available¶
      'Continue if error occurs¶
      On Error Resume Next¶
      SetAttr PathName:=Path & FileNoExtension & "-" & Format$( _¶
          History, "000") & "." & Extension, Attributes:=vbNormal¶
      Kill PathName:=Path & FileNoExtension & "-" & Format$( _¶
          History, "000") & "." & Extension¶
      On Error GoTo err_h¶
      'Now rename any existing older versions¶
      For i = History - 1 To 1 Step -1¶
        'Name of the file being moved¶
        TempFile = Path & FileNoExtension & "-" & Format$(i, _¶
            "000") & "." & Extension¶
        'Does the file exist?¶
        If FileExists(TempFile) Then¶
          'Rename it¶
          Name TempFile As Path & FileNoExtension & "-" & Format$( _¶
              i + 1, "000") & "." & Extension¶
        End If¶
      Next i¶
      'Finally, save the workbook !¶
      Book.SaveCopyAs Path & FileNoExtension & "-001." & Extension¶
      'Mark it as read only¶
      SetAttr PathName:=Path & FileNoExtension & "-001." & _¶
          Extension, Attributes:=vbReadOnly¶
    End If¶
    Exit Sub¶
  err_h:¶
    MsgBox "Error " & Err.Number & ", " & Err.Description, _¶
        vbCritical¶
  End Sub¶
```

Exl

```
' * * * * *¶
Function GetExtension(FileName As String) As String¶
  'Variable declaration¶
  Dim i As Long¶
  For i = Len(FileName) To 1 Step -1¶
    If Mid$(FileName, i, 1) = "." Then¶
      GetExtension = Mid$(FileName, i + 1)¶
      Exit Function¶
    End If¶
  Next i¶
End Function¶
' * * * * *¶
Function FileExists(sFullName As String) As Boolean¶
  FileExists = Len(Dir(PathName:=sFullName)) > 0¶
End Function¶
```

View the Appendix to learn how to store this procedure in a ThisWorkbook module.

```
Option Explicit¶
' * * * * *¶
Private Sub Workbook_BeforeSave(ByVal SaveAsUI As Boolean, _¶
  Cancel As Boolean)¶
    If SaveAsUI Then¶
      'Only save backup if the workbook is being saved from Excel¶
      SaveBackup Me¶
    End If¶
End Sub¶
```

The first part of the code goes in a standard module in the workbook or template of interest. The rest goes in the ThisWorkbook module of the same workbook.

Tip: Change the Path to the folder where the backups are to be stored and the History constant to the number of older versions to keep in the path.

Importing Your Contacts from Outlook

Use this procedure to import a list of all Microsoft Outlook contacts that meet specified criteria.

Exl

Scenario: Extracting information from the contacts in Outlook is useful, even if it is just to have a backup of the information. It is also possible to extract contacts that meet certain criteria.

Example file: E034.xls

	A	B	C	D	E
1	**Full Name**	**Last name**	**First name**	**Email**	**Business phone**
2	Bill Gates	Gates	Bill	bgates@microsoft.com	(555) 555-5555
3	Some Body	Body	Some	somebody@somedomain.com	
4	Some One	One	Some	someone@somedomain.com	
5	Any Body	Body	Any	anyboday@somedomain.com	
6					

Figure 35 – Extracted Access Contacts

View the Appendix to learn how to store this procedure in a Standard module.

```
Option Explicit¶
' * * * * *¶
Sub ImportContacts()¶
  'Variable declaration¶
'Outlook application¶
  Dim oApp As Object¶
'Outlook namespace¶
  Dim oNameSpace As Object¶
'Outlook MAPI folder¶
  Dim oFolder As Object¶
'Outlook Contact Item¶
  Dim oContact As Object¶
  Dim OutlookRunning As Boolean¶
  Dim WS As Worksheet¶
  'Turn off screen updating¶
  Application.ScreenUpdating = False¶
  'Create the Outlook references¶
  'Continue when error occurs¶
  On Error Resume Next¶
  Set oApp = GetObject(, "Outlook.Application")¶
  On Error GoTo 0¶
```

```
If oApp Is Nothing Then¶
  Set oApp = CreateObject("Outlook.Application")¶
  OutlookRunning = False¶
Else¶
  OutlookRunning = True¶
End If¶
Set oNameSpace = oApp.GetNamespace("MAPI")¶
Set oFolder = oNameSpace.GetDefaultFolder(10) 'olFolderContacts = 10¶
'Create a new sheet for this¶
Set WS = Workbooks.Add(xlWorksheet).Worksheets(1)¶
'Headers¶
With WS.Range("A1").Resize(1, 5)¶
  .Value = Array("Full Name", "Last name", "First name", _¶
      "Email", "Business phone")¶
  .Font.Bold = True¶
End With¶
'Loop through the available contacts¶
For Each oContact In oFolder.Items¶
  'Is it a Contact or a Distribution List¶
  If oContact.class = 40 Then      'olContact = 40¶
    'Next available row¶
    With WS.Cells(WS.Rows.Count, 1).End(xlUp).Offset(1)¶
      .Value = oContact.FullName¶
      .Offset(, 1).Value = oContact.LastName¶
      .Offset(, 2).Value = oContact.FirstName¶
      .Offset(, 3).Value = oContact.Email1Address¶
      .Offset(, 4).Value = oContact.BusinessTelephoneNumber¶
      'Other available properties¶
      '.Offset(, 5).Value = oContact.Birthday¶
      '.Offset(, 6).Value = oContact.BusinessAddress¶
      '.Offset(, 7).Value = oContact.BusinessAddressCity¶
      '.Offset(, 8).Value = oContact.CompanyName¶
      '.Offset(, 9).Value = oContact.Email1DisplayName¶
      '.Offset(, 10).Value = oContact.Gender¶
      '.Offset(, 11).Value = oContact.HomeAddress¶
      '.Offset(, 12).Value = oContact.HomeAddressCity¶
      '.Offset(, 13).Value = oContact.JobTitle¶
      '.Offset(, 14).Value = oContact.MailingAddress¶
      '.Offset(, 15).Value = oContact.MailingAddressCity¶
      '.Offset(, 16).Value = oContact.NickName¶
    End With¶
  End If¶
Next oContact¶
'Resize columns¶
WS.Cells.EntireColumn.AutoFit¶
'Check to see if Outlook needs to be closed¶
If Not OutlookRunning Then¶
  oApp.Quit¶
End If¶
```

Exl

```
    'Restore screen updating¶
    Application.ScreenUpdating = True¶
    'Destroy the variables and release memory¶
    Set oContact = Nothing¶
    Set oFolder = Nothing¶
    Set oNameSpace = Nothing¶
    Set oApp = Nothing¶
End Sub¶
```

Exl

Tip: The properties that are imported from Outlook can be changed. This code displays a few others that can be used. Remember to change the array size from "5" to the appropriate number and add additional column headers in the lines:

```
    With WS.Range("A1").Resize(1, 5)¶
        .Value = Array("Full Name", "Last name", "First name", _¶
"Email", "Business phone")¶
```

Tip: Also remember to uncomment (remove the apostrophe at left) the properties that are to be added:

```
'.Offset(, 5).Value = oContact.Birthday¶
'.Offset(, 6).Value = oContact.BusinessAddress¶
'.Offset(, 7).Value = oContact.BusinessAddressCity¶
'.Offset(, 8).Value = oContact.CompanyName¶
'.Offset(, 9).Value = oContact.Email1DisplayName¶
'.Offset(, 10).Value = oContact.Gender¶
'.Offset(, 11).Value = oContact.HomeAddress¶
'.Offset(, 12).Value = oContact.HomeAddressCity¶
'.Offset(, 13).Value = oContact.JobTitle¶
'.Offset(, 14).Value = oContact.MailingAddress¶
'.Offset(, 15).Value = oContact.MailingAddressCity¶
'.Offset(, 16).Value = oContact.NickName¶
```

E-mailing from Excel with Outlook

Use this procedure to e-mail a worksheet or a workbook using Microsoft Outlook as the e-mail application.

Example file:
E035.xls

> **Scenario:** Sending reports directly from Excel is very handy, especially with users who tend to forget to transmit them to the persons who are supposed to receive these files. Automating the task makes it much easier, and greatly increases the chances that the process will be done without error.

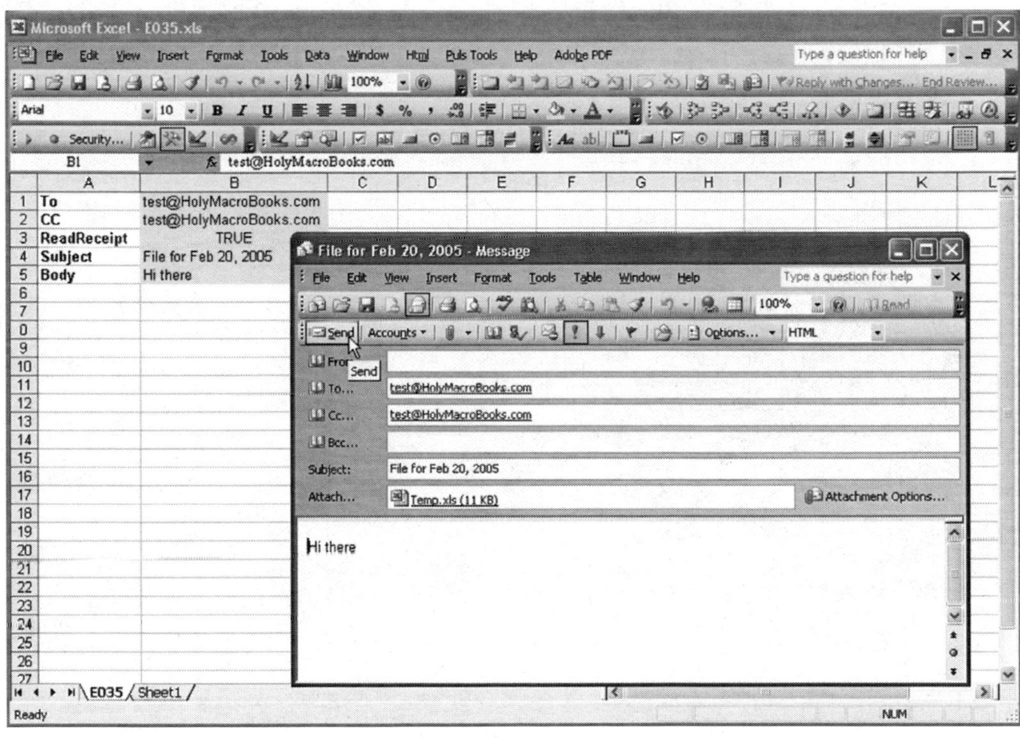

Figure 36 – E-mailing with Excel

Exl

View the Appendix to learn how to store this procedure in a Standard module.

```
Option Explicit¶
' * * * * * *¶
Sub EmailWithOutlook()¶
  'Variable declaration¶
'Outlook application¶
  Dim oApp As Object¶
'Outlook MailItem¶
  Dim oMail As Object¶
  Dim WB As Workbook¶
  Dim WS As Worksheet¶
  Dim FileName As String¶
  Dim SendSheetOnly As Boolean¶
  'Turn off screen updating¶
  Application.ScreenUpdating = False¶
  'Ask the user what to send¶
  Select Case MsgBox( _¶
      Prompt:="Do you want to send the active sheet only ?", _¶
      Buttons:=vbYesNoCancel)¶
  Case vbYes¶
    'Yes, make a copy of the active sheet.¶
    SendSheetOnly = True¶
    ActiveSheet.Copy¶
    Set WB = ActiveWorkbook¶
    'Save without formulas ?¶
    Cells.Copy¶
    Cells.PasteSpecial Paste:=xlPasteValues¶
    'Clear the clipboard¶
    Application.CutCopyMode = False¶
    FileName = "Temp.xls"¶
    'Continue when error occurs¶
    On Error Resume Next¶
    Kill "C:\" & FileName¶
    On Error GoTo 0¶
    WB.SaveAs FileName:="C:\" & FileName¶
  Case vbNo¶
    If Len(ActiveWorkbook.Path) = 0 Then¶
      'File hasn't been saved before¶
      MsgBox "Can't send an unsaved workbook", vbCritical¶
      GoTo exiting¶
    End If¶
    SendSheetOnly = False¶
    Set WB = ActiveWorkbook¶
  Case vbCancel¶
    'olDiscard = 1¶
    oMail.Close SaveMode:=1¶
    GoTo exiting¶
  End Select¶
```

```
  Set oApp = CreateObject("Outlook.Application")¶
  Set oMail = oApp.CreateItem(0)      'olMailItem = 0¶
  With oMail¶
    'Hard code To property¶
    .To = "test@HolyMacroBooks.com"¶
    'User input To property¶
    .To = Range("B1").Value¶
    'Hard code CC property¶
    .CC = "test@HolyMacroBooks.com"¶
    'User input CC property¶
    .CC = Range("B2").Value¶
    'Hard code Read Receipt Requested property¶
    .ReadReceiptRequested = True¶
    'User input Read Receipt Requested property¶
    .ReadReceiptRequested = Range("B3").Value¶
    'Hard code Subject property¶
    .Subject = "File for " & Format$(Date, "mmm dd, yyy")¶
    'User input Subject property¶
    .Subject = Range("B4").Value¶
    'Hard code Body property¶
    .Body = "Hi there"¶
    'User input Body property¶
    .Body = Range("B5").Value¶
    'Hard code Sensitivity property¶
    .Sensitivity = 3                'olConfidential = 3¶
    'Set attachment¶
    .Attachments.Add WB.FullName¶
    'Hard code importance¶
    ''olImportanceHigh = 2¶
    .Importance = 2¶
    'Send directly (remove apostrophe on line below to activate)¶
    '.Send¶
    'Display it¶
    .Display¶
  End With¶
  If SendSheetOnly Then¶
    WB.ChangeFileAccess Mode:=xlReadOnly¶
    Kill WB.FullName¶
    WB.Close SaveChanges:=False¶
  End If¶
exiting:¶
  'Restore screen updating¶
  Application.ScreenUpdating = True¶
  'destroy variables and restore memory¶
  Set oMail = Nothing¶
  Set oApp = Nothing¶
End Sub¶
```

Printing a UserForm

This procedure demonstrates how to print a UserForm with more flexibility than using the PrintForm method.

Exl

Example file:
E036.xls

Scenario: Printing a UserForm is a good way to store information; for example, you might want to print a UserForm that contains the information of a new customer for a hard-copy file. Unfortunately, there is not much flexibility in printing UserForms in Excel. Control over the paper orientation, margins, or any of the other settings that can normally be changed require code when printing UserForms.

This procedure uses Microsoft Word to print the UserForm.

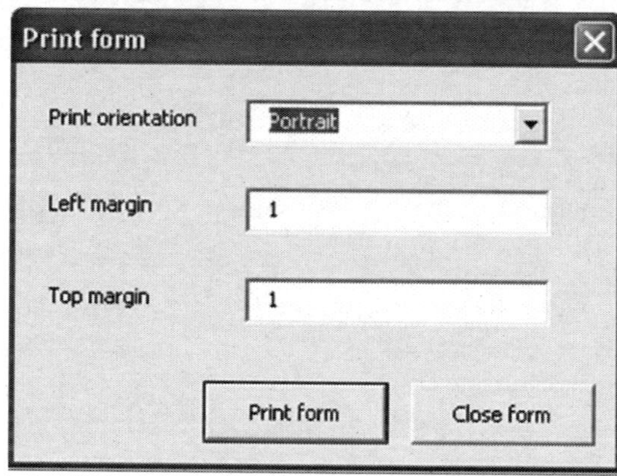

Figure 37 – Printing a UserForm

View the Appendix to learn how to store this procedure in a Standard module.

```
Option Explicit¶
' * * * * * *¶
Private Declare Sub keybd_event Lib "user32" (ByVal bVk As Byte, _¶
    ByVal bScan As Byte, ByVal dwFlags As Long, _¶
    ByVal dwExtraInfo As Long)¶
Private Const VK_SNAPSHOT = &H2C¶
```

```
' * * * * *¶
Sub Sample()¶
  fmPrint.Show¶
End Sub¶
' * * * * *¶
Sub PrintForm()¶
  'Variable declaration¶
  Dim wdApp As Object     'Word.Application¶
  Dim wdDoc As Object     'Word.Document¶
  'Simulate pressing Alt + Print Screen.¶
  'because of this, the UserForm *must* be visible¶
  'at the time the code is run¶
  'Press Print Screen¶
  keybd_event VK_SNAPSHOT, 1, 0, 0¶
  'Give the computer time to process the screen¶
  '(may need to be changed)¶
  Application.Wait Now + TimeSerial(0, 0, 1)¶
  'Turn off screen updating¶
  Application.ScreenUpdating = False¶
  'Create a word process¶
  Set wdApp = CreateObject("Word.Application")¶
  'Create a new document¶
  Set wdDoc = wdApp.Documents.Add()¶
  With wdDoc¶
    'Change the print settings¶
    With .PageSetup¶
      'Change this code to modify the print setup¶
      .Orientation = IIf(fmPrint.cbOrientation.Value = "Portrait", _¶
          0, 1)    'wdOrientPortrait = 0¶
                   'wdOrientLandscape = 1¶
      .LeftMargin = wdApp.InchesToPoints(Val(fmPrint.txLeft.Value))¶
      .TopMargin = wdApp.InchesToPoints(Val(fmPrint.txTop.Value))¶
    End With¶
    'Paste the image¶
    .Range.Paste¶
    'Print the document¶
    .PrintOut¶
    'Give Word time to send the document to the printer¶
    Do While wdApp.BackgroundPrintingStatus > 0¶
      DoEvents¶
    Loop¶
    'Close it without saving changes¶
    .Close SaveChanges:=False¶
  End With¶
  'Quit Word¶
  wdApp.Quit SaveChanges:=False¶
  'Kill the variables and free memory¶
  Set wdDoc = Nothing¶
  Set wdApp = Nothing¶
  'Done !¶
```

```
  MsgBox "Done !", vbInformation¶
  'Restore screen updating¶
  Application.ScreenUpdating = True¶
End Sub¶
```

The following code should be placed in a UserForm named 'fmPrint'. The example file has the form with the code already in it. To create from scratch, use Insert | UserForm from the menu bar and design the form with the controls that should be on it. This form has three labels, two text boxes, two command buttons, and a combo box arranged as indicated in the code:

View the Appendix to learn how to store this procedure in a UserForm.

```
Option Explicit¶
' * * * * *¶
Private Sub BCancel_Click()¶
  Unload Me¶
End Sub¶
' * * * * *¶
Private Sub BPrint_Click()¶
  PrintForm¶
End Sub¶
' * * * * *¶
Private Sub UserForm_Initialize()¶
  'Set the orientation options¶
  cbOrientation.List = Array("Portrait", "Landscape")¶
  'Choose 'Portrait'¶
  cbOrientation.ListIndex = 0¶
  'Default margins¶
  txLeft.Value = 1¶
  txTop.Value = 1¶
End Sub¶
```

The program needs all the code from the first section, except for the macro 'Sample'. The UserForm is only used in the sample to demonstrate how to use the code.

In the section 'Change this code to modify the print setup', modifying different things like margins, paper orientation, and paper size—in other words, the same settings that you modify to print a Microsoft Word document—can be set as desired.

Importing and Formatting a Text File

This procedure illustrates how to automate the process of importing, cleaning up, and formatting text files, and then to place the results in one unique workbook.

Note: This particular procedure is one of our more difficult Excel procedures. If you are not at all familiar with VBA, we suggest that you try some others first and get comfortable with the code before you attempt to customize this procedure for your own file. Otherwise, if you must use this procedure, you may want to get acquainted with the sample file.

Scenario: Importing a text file is another common task for which Excel is used. Almost all applications can create a text file that can be imported into another application so that application can use the information to some other purpose. In almost every case, there is a need to clean, delete, add, or format the information so that it can be used correctly at a later time.

Example file:
E037.xls

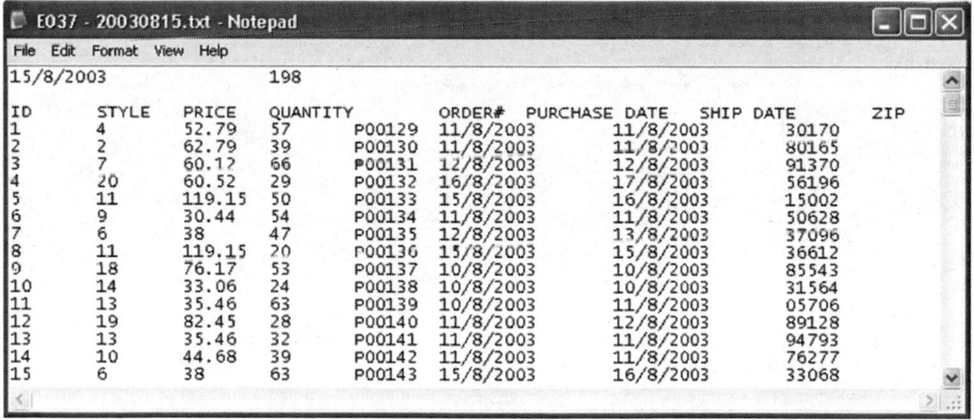

E037 - 20030815.txt - Notepad

File Edit Format View Help

15/8/2003 198

ID	STYLE	PRICE	QUANTITY	ORDER#	PURCHASE DATE	SHIP DATE	ZIP
1	4	52.79	57	P00129	11/8/2003	11/8/2003	30170
2	2	62.79	39	P00130	11/8/2003	11/8/2003	80165
3	7	60.12	66	P00131	12/8/2003	12/8/2003	91370
4	20	60.52	29	P00132	16/8/2003	17/8/2003	56196
5	11	119.15	50	P00133	15/8/2003	16/8/2003	15002
6	9	30.44	54	P00134	11/8/2003	11/8/2003	50628
7	6	38	47	P00135	12/8/2003	13/8/2003	37096
8	11	119.15	20	P00136	15/8/2003	15/8/2003	36612
9	18	76.17	53	P00137	10/8/2003	10/8/2003	85543
10	14	33.06	24	P00138	10/8/2003	10/8/2003	31564
11	13	35.46	63	P00139	10/8/2003	11/8/2003	05706
12	19	82.45	28	P00140	11/8/2003	12/8/2003	89128
13	13	35.46	32	P00141	11/8/2003	11/8/2003	94793
14	10	44.68	39	P00142	11/8/2003	11/8/2003	76277
15	6	38	63	P00143	15/8/2003	16/8/2003	33068

Figure 38 – Text File in Notepad

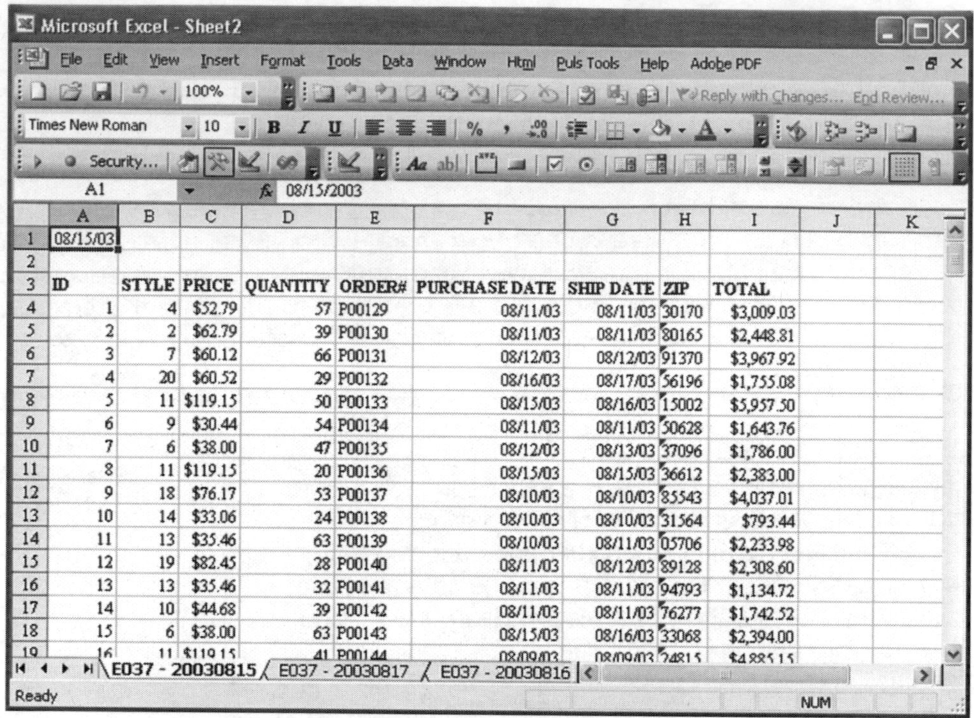

	A	B	C	D	E	F	G	H	I
1	08/15/03								
2									
3	ID	STYLE	PRICE	QUANTITY	ORDER#	PURCHASE DATE	SHIP DATE	ZIP	TOTAL
4	1	4	$52.79	57	P00129	08/11/03	08/11/03	30170	$3,009.03
5	2	2	$62.79	39	P00130	08/11/03	08/11/03	80165	$2,448.81
6	3	7	$60.12	66	P00131	08/12/03	08/12/03	91370	$3,967.92
7	4	20	$60.52	29	P00132	08/16/03	08/17/03	56196	$1,755.08
8	5	11	$119.15	50	P00133	08/15/03	08/16/03	15002	$5,957.50
9	6	9	$30.44	54	P00134	08/11/03	08/11/03	50628	$1,643.76
10	7	6	$38.00	47	P00135	08/12/03	08/13/03	37096	$1,786.00
11	8	11	$119.15	20	P00136	08/15/03	08/15/03	36612	$2,383.00
12	9	18	$76.17	53	P00137	08/10/03	08/10/03	85543	$4,037.01
13	10	14	$33.06	24	P00138	08/10/03	08/10/03	31564	$793.44
14	11	13	$35.46	63	P00139	08/10/03	08/11/03	05706	$2,233.98
15	12	19	$82.45	28	P00140	08/11/03	08/12/03	89128	$2,308.60
16	13	13	$35.46	32	P00141	08/11/03	08/11/03	94793	$1,134.72
17	14	10	$44.68	39	P00142	08/11/03	08/11/03	76277	$1,742.52
18	15	6	$38.00	63	P00143	08/15/03	08/16/03	33068	$2,394.00

Figure 39 – Text File in Excel

View the Appendix to learn how to store this procedure in a Standard module.

```
Option Explicit¶
' * * * * *¶
Sub ImportTextFile()¶
  'Variable declaration¶
  Dim File As Variant¶
  Dim i As Long¶
  Dim Book As Workbook¶
  'Ask for text files to open¶
  File = Application.GetOpenFilename( _¶
      FileFilter:="Text files (*.txt),*.txt", _¶
      Title:="Select the files to import", MultiSelect:=True)¶
  'Did the user cancel?¶
  If TypeName(File) = "Boolean" Then Exit Sub¶
  'Turn off screen updating¶
  Application.ScreenUpdating = False¶
```

```
  'Create a new workbook to store the imported files¶
  Set Book = Workbooks.Add(xlWorksheet)¶
  For i = LBound(File) To UBound(File)¶
    ProcessFile WhichFile:=CStr(File(i)), WhichBook:=Book¶
  Next i¶
  'Delete the first sheet (unused one)¶
  Application.DisplayAlerts = False¶
  Book.Sheets(1).Delete¶
  Application.DisplayAlerts = True¶
  'Restore screen updating¶
  Application.ScreenUpdating = True¶
End Sub¶
' * * * * *¶
Sub ProcessFile(ByVal WhichFile As String, _¶
    ByRef WhichBook As Workbook)¶
  'Variable definition¶
  Dim WS As Worksheet¶
  Dim ColumnInformation As Variant¶
  'Define the column types in the text file¶
  'All columns will be imported as general,¶
  'excepting columns 6, 7 and 8 which are dates¶
  '(in dd/mm/yy format) and zip codes¶
  ColumnInformation = Array(Array(1, 1), _¶
                            Array(2, 1), _¶
                            Array(3, 1), _¶
                            Array(4, 1), _¶
                            Array(5, 1), _¶
                            Array(6, 4), _¶
                            Array(7, 4), _¶
                            Array(8, 2))¶
  'xlGeneralFormat = 1¶
  'xlTextFormat = 2¶
  'xlDMYFormat = 4¶
  'To skip a column, use xlSkipColumn = 9¶
  'Open the text file using the TextImportWizard¶
  Workbooks.OpenText Filename:=WhichFile, Origin:=xlWindows, _¶
      StartRow:=1, DataType:=xlDelimited, _¶
      TextQualifier:=xlTextQualifierDoubleQuote, _¶
      ConsecutiveDelimiter:=True, Tab:=True, _¶
      FieldInfo:=ColumnInformation¶
  'Do some formatting to the book. This sample files have¶
  'the headers repeat every 50 records, make sure that¶
  'they are imported only once¶
  Do While Application.CountIf(Range("A4:A" & Rows.Count), _¶
      "ID") > 0¶
    Cells(Application.Match("ID", Range("A4:A" & Rows.Count), _¶
        0) + 3, 1).EntireRow.Delete Shift:=xlShiftUp¶
  Loop¶
```

```
    'Set the headers in Bold¶
    Range("3:3").Font.Bold = True¶
    'Add a "TOTAL" column in I¶
    'Use the value in B1 that contains the number of records¶
    Range("I3").Value = "TOTAL"¶
    Range("I4").Resize(Range("B1").Value).FormulaR1C1 = "=RC3*RC4"¶
    'And a Sum of all orders¶
    Range("I4").Offset(Range( _¶
        "B1").Value).FormulaR1C1 = "=SUM(R4C:R[-1]C)"¶
    'Remove cell "B1", which contains the total number of records¶
    Range("B1").ClearContents¶
    'Make sure that A1 is a date¶
    If Not Application.IsNumber(Range("A1")) Then¶
      Range("A1").Value = DateValue(Range("A1").Text)¶
    End If¶
    'Make sure that the zip codes are formatted correctly¶
    Range("H:H").NumberFormat = "00000"¶
    'Format the Total and Amount as currency¶
    Range("C:C, I:I").NumberFormat = "$#,##0.00"¶
    'Autofit all columns¶
    Cells.EntireColumn.AutoFit¶
    'Copy this worksheet to the WhichBook book (and close this file)¶
    With ActiveSheet¶
      .Copy After:=WhichBook.Sheets(WhichBook.Sheets.Count)¶
      .Parent.Close SaveChanges:=False¶
    End With¶
End Sub¶
```

Note: The 'ProcessFile' procedure takes a specific type of text file that was created just for this book. This code needs to be modified to adapt to the type of text files being imported. The easiest way to do that is to begin with a new workbook and then record a macro. While the recorder is running, open the text file, clean it, and apply the formatting that is needed. Compare your macro code with the code used in the procedure. Edit the procedure so that it uses some of the code that was recorded.

Extracting Numbers from a Text String

Using this procedure, you can extract only the numbers (digits from 0 to 9) from a range that contains text strings.

Scenario: When importing or pasting data from a different source, some information that contains the desired numbers can also include other characters, such as letters. In these cases, where the Text-Import wizard cannot help, having a way to extract only the numbers comes in very handy.

Example file:
E038.xls

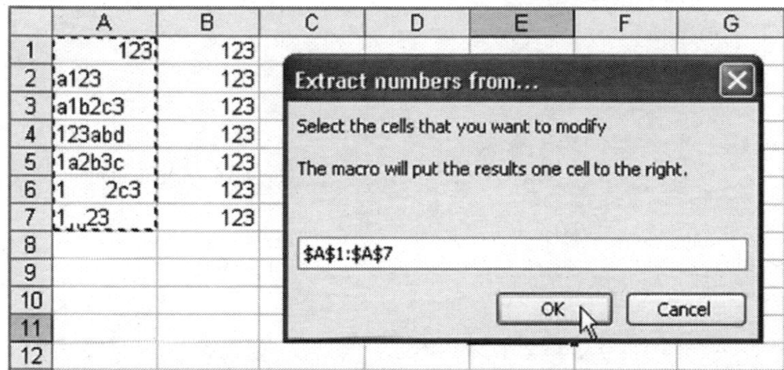

Figure 40 – Selecting Cells from Which to Extract Numbers

View the Appendix to learn how to store this procedure in a Standard module.

```
Option Explicit¶
' * * * * *¶
Sub ExtractNumbers()¶
  'Variable declaration¶
  Dim Rng As Range¶
  Dim Cll As Range¶
  Dim Ans As Variant¶
  'Select the cells to modify¶
  'Continue when error occurs¶
  On Error Resume Next¶
```

```
    Set Rng = Application.InputBox( _¶
        Prompt:="Select the cells that you want to modify" & vbCrLf & _¶
        vbCrLf & _¶
        "The macro will put the results one cell to the right.", _¶
        Title:="Extract numbers from...", Type:=8)¶
    On Error GoTo 0¶
    'Did the user cancel?¶
    If Rng Is Nothing Then¶
      Exit Sub¶
    End If¶
    'Turn off screen updating¶
    Application.ScreenUpdating = False¶
    For Each Cll In Rng.Cells¶
      'Try first using regular expressions¶
      Ans = WithRegExp(Cll.Value)¶
      'Did an error occur?¶
      If IsError(Ans) Then¶
        Ans = WithoutRegExp(Cll.Value)¶
      End If¶
      'Put it in the cell¶
      Cll.Offset(, 1).Value = Ans¶
      'Make sure that trailing zeros were not cleared¶
      If Cll.Offset(, 1).Text <> CStr(Ans) Then¶
        Cll.Offset(, 1).Value = "'" & CStr(Ans)¶
      End If¶
    Next Cll¶
    'Restore screen updating¶
    Application.ScreenUpdating = True¶
End Sub¶
' * * * * *¶
Function WithRegExp(ByVal Text As String) As Variant¶
    'Variable declaration¶
    Dim RegExp As Object¶
    Dim Pattern As String¶
    'Continue when error occurs¶
    On Error Resume Next¶
    Set RegExp = CreateObject("vbscript.regexp")¶
    If RegExp Is Nothing Then¶
      WithRegExp = CVErr(xlErrValue)¶
      Exit Function¶
    End If¶
    Pattern = "[^\d]+"¶
    'Set the properties of the Regular Expression¶
    RegExp.Global = True¶
    RegExp.Pattern = Pattern¶
    'Replace the matching characters¶
    WithRegExp = RegExp.Replace(Text, "")¶
    Set RegExp = Nothing¶
End Function¶
```

```
' * * * * *¶
Function WithoutRegExp(ByVal Text As String) As String¶
  'Variable declaration¶
  Dim i As Long¶
  For i = 1 To Len(Text)¶
    If Mid$(Text, i, 1) Like "#" Then¶
      WithoutRegExp = WithoutRegExp & Mid$(Text, i, 1)¶
    End If¶
  Next i¶
End Function¶
```


Finding and Deleting Erroneously Named Ranges

This procedure shows how to quickly find and delete all the names that contain reference errors (#REF!).

Scenario: When working with named ranges, it is likely that eventually one or more of those names will contain an error. For example, when deleting a row or column that points to a named range, that named range formula changes to =#REF!. This macro displays a list of all these named ranges, and provides an option to delete them.

Example file:
E039.xls

View the Appendix to learn how to store this procedure in a Standard module.

```
Option Explicit¶
' * * * * *¶
Sub DeleteBadNames()¶
  'Variable declaration¶
  Dim Nm As Name¶
  Dim Book As Workbook¶
  Dim ActBook As Workbook¶
  Dim DisplayList As Boolean¶
  'Turn off screen updating¶
  Application.ScreenUpdating = False¶
  Set ActBook = ActiveWorkbook¶
  Select Case MsgBox( _¶
      Prompt:="To display the bad names, click 'Yes'." & vbCrLf & _¶
      "To remove the bad names, click 'No'." & vbCrLf & _¶
      "To exit, press 'Cancel'.", _¶
      Buttons:=vbQuestion + vbYesNoCancel)¶
```

Exl

```
    Case vbYes¶
      DisplayList = True¶
      'Create a new workbook with one sheet¶
      Set Book = Workbooks.Add(xlWorksheet)¶
      With Book.Worksheets(1).Range("A1:B1")¶
        .Value = Array("Name", "RefersTo")¶
        .Font.Bold = True¶
      End With¶
    Case vbNo¶
      DisplayList = False¶
    Case vbCancel¶
      GoTo exiting¶
    End Select¶
    For Each Nm In ActBook.Names¶
      'Does the name include a #REF error ?¶
      If InStr(1, Nm.RefersTo, "#REF!") + InStr(1, Nm.RefersTo, _¶
          "#¡REF!") > 0 Then¶
        If DisplayList Then¶
          'Add it to the list¶
          With Book.Worksheets(1)¶
            With .Cells(.Rows.Count, 1).End(xlUp).Offset(1)¶
              .Value = Nm.Name¶
              .Offset(, 1).Value = "'" & Nm.RefersTo¶
            End With¶
          End With¶
        Else¶
          Application.DisplayAlerts = False¶
          Nm.Delete¶
          Application.DisplayAlerts = True¶
        End If¶
      End If¶
    Next Nm¶
exiting:¶
    'Restore screen updating¶
    Application.ScreenUpdating = True¶
End Sub¶
```

Logging Actions When a Cell Changes

This procedure demonstrates how to store specific information, such as the workbook name, worksheet, range, user, or date, whenever a cell changes in a workbook.

Scenario: Using the Track changes feature can help tremendously, but because it has to share the workbook as well, you may encounter limitations that Excel can't handle (such as protecting or unprotecting a sheet, changing data validation settings, etc.). When used to simply track who made which changes and where they made them, this macro will create a text file (which can be saved on a network server), with useful information such as the worksheet name, the cell(s) that changed, who did the changes and when the changes happened.

Example file:
E040.xls

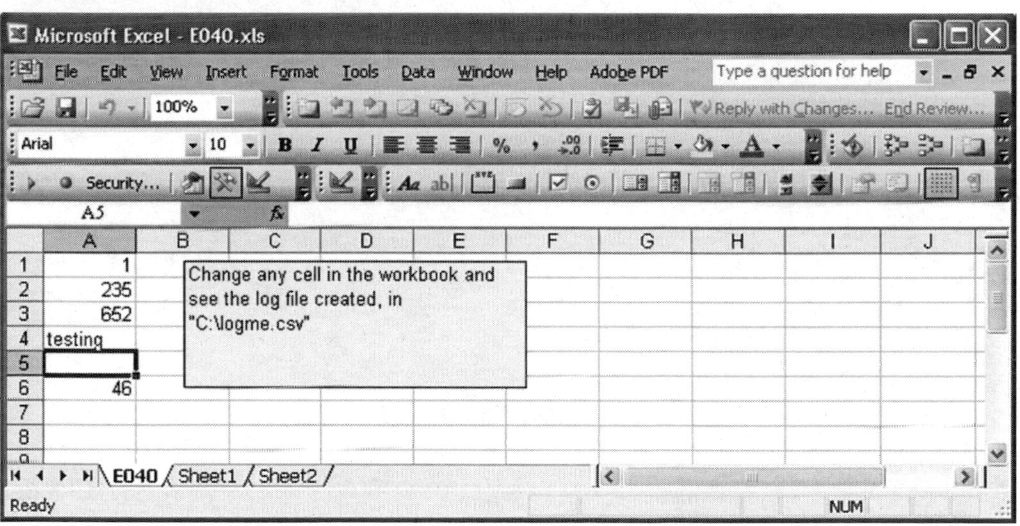

Figure 41 – Log Actions (Before Logging)

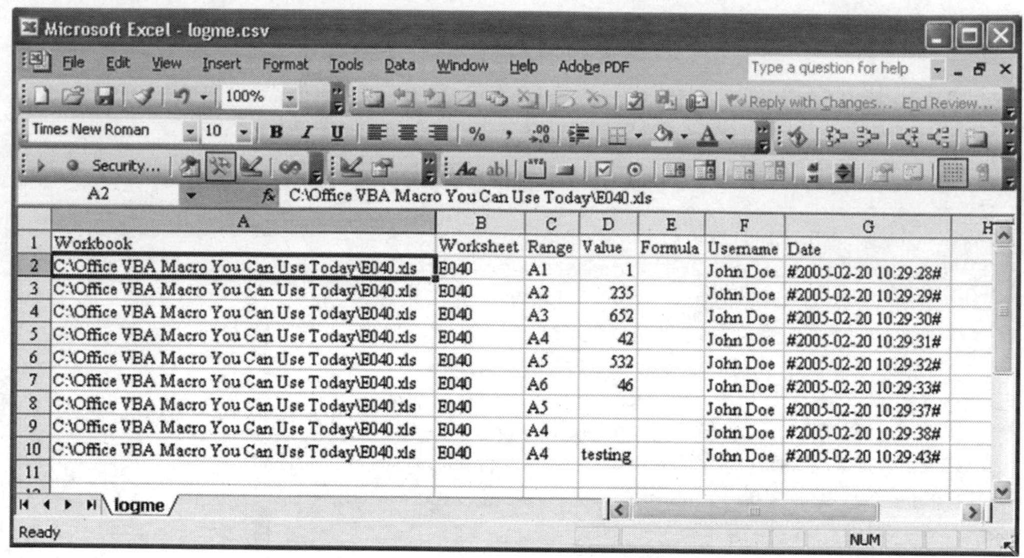

	A	B	C	D	E	F	G
1	Workbook	Worksheet	Range	Value	Formula	Username	Date
2	C:\Office VBA Macro You Can Use Today\E040.xls	E040	A1	1		John Doe	#2005-02-20 10:29:28#
3	C:\Office VBA Macro You Can Use Today\E040.xls	E040	A2	235		John Doe	#2005-02-20 10:29:29#
4	C:\Office VBA Macro You Can Use Today\E040.xls	E040	A3	652		John Doe	#2005-02-20 10:29:30#
5	C:\Office VBA Macro You Can Use Today\E040.xls	E040	A4	42		John Doe	#2005-02-20 10:29:31#
6	C:\Office VBA Macro You Can Use Today\E040.xls	E040	A5	532		John Doe	#2005-02-20 10:29:32#
7	C:\Office VBA Macro You Can Use Today\E040.xls	E040	A6	46		John Doe	#2005-02-20 10:29:33#
8	C:\Office VBA Macro You Can Use Today\E040.xls	E040	A5			John Doe	#2005-02-20 10:29:37#
9	C:\Office VBA Macro You Can Use Today\E040.xls	E040	A4			John Doe	#2005-02-20 10:29:38#
10	C:\Office VBA Macro You Can Use Today\E040.xls	E040	A4	testing		John Doe	#2005-02-20 10:29:43#

Figure 42 – Log Actions (After Logging)

View the Appendix to learn how to store this procedure in a Standard module.

```
Option Explicit¶
' * * * * *¶
Private Declare Function GetUserName Lib "advapi32.dll" Alias _¶
    "GetUserNameA" (ByVal lpBuffer As String, nSize As Long) As Long¶
' * * * * *¶
Sub LogInfo(ByVal Target As Range)¶
  'Variable declaration¶
  Dim FilePath As String¶
  Dim File As Long¶
  Dim Length As Long¶
  Dim Workbook As String¶
  Dim Worksheet As String¶
  Dim Address As String¶
  Dim Value As Variant¶
  Dim Username As String¶
  Dim TimeStamp As Date¶
  Dim Formula As String¶
  Dim Cell As Range¶
  'The log file will contain:¶
  'Workbook full name, Worksheet, Range address,¶
  'New Value, Formula, Username and a time stamp¶
  FilePath = "\\Server\apps\logme.csv"¶
  FilePath = "C:\logme.csv"¶
```

```
  'Open the file¶
  File = FreeFile¶
  Open FilePath For Append As #File¶
  Length = LOF(File)¶
  If Length = 0 Then¶
    'Put some headers¶
    Write #File, "Workbook", "Worksheet", "Range", "Value", _¶
        "Formula", "Username", "Date"¶
  End If¶
  'Loop through the cells¶
  For Each Cell In Target.Cells¶
    With Cell¶
      Workbook = .Worksheet.Parent.FullName¶
      Worksheet = .Worksheet.Name¶
      Address = .Address(RowAbsolute:=False, _¶
          ColumnAbsolute:=False)¶
      Value = .Value¶
      If .HasFormula Then¶
        Formula = .Formula¶
      Else¶
        Formula = ""¶
      End If¶
      Username = GetWinUserName()¶
      TimeStamp = Now()¶
    End With¶
    'Write the information¶
    Write #File, Workbook, Worksheet, Address, Value, Formula, _¶
        Username, TimeStamp¶
  Next Cell¶
  Close #File¶
End Sub¶
' * * * * *¶
Function GetWinUserName()¶
  'Variable declaration¶
  Dim strUserName As String¶
  strUserName = String(255, Chr$(0))¶
  GetUserName strUserName, 255¶
  strUserName = Left$(strUserName, InStr(strUserName, _¶
      Chr$(0)) - 1)¶
  GetWinUserName = strUserName¶
End Function¶
```

View the Appendix to learn how to store this procedure in a ThisWorkbook module.

```
Option Explicit¶
' * * * * *¶
Private Sub Workbook_SheetChange(ByVal Sh As Object, _¶
  ByVal Target As Range)¶
    If TypeName(Sh) = "Worksheet" Then¶
```

```
        LogInfo Target¶
    End If¶
End Sub¶
```

Synchronizing Page Fields of Pivot Tables

Exl

Use this procedure to overcome the limitation of Pivot Tables that do not stay synchronized whenever one of the Page fields is changed.

Example file:
E042.xls

Scenario: When you use a workbook that contains multiple tables based on the same database, displaying the information in a different way can become a real hassle. There is no way in Excel to "lock" the Page fields of pivot tables to display the same item, making it possible to easily compare the information between separate pivot tables.

This sample shows how to lock all the pivot tables in a worksheet or workbook, such that changing a page field in one affects the rest of the pivot tables as well.

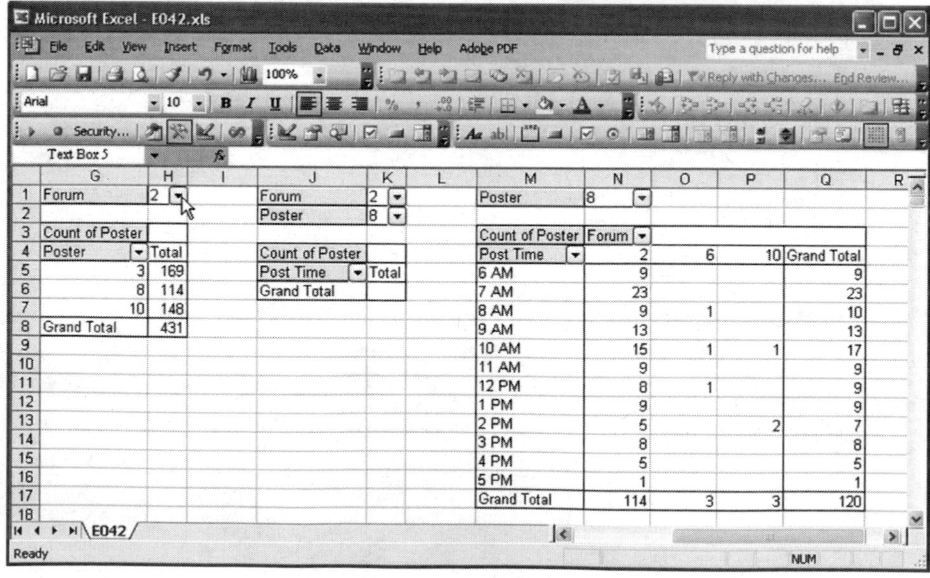

Figure 43 – Synchronizing Pivot Table Page Fields

View the Appendix to learn how to store this procedure in a Standard module.

```
Option Explicit¶
' * * * * *¶
Sub SynchPivotTables(BasePivot As PivotTable)¶
  'Variable declaration¶
  Dim Pivot As PivotTable¶
  Dim Sheet As Worksheet¶
  Dim BasePage As PivotField¶
  Dim Page As PivotField¶
  Dim Itm As PivotItem¶
  'Synchorize the Pivot Tables in the Active Sheet¶
  'Set Sheet = ActiveSheet¶
  'or, loop through all the Pivot tables in the active workbook¶
  For Each Sheet In ActiveWorkbook.Worksheets¶
    'Loop through the Pivots in the worksheet¶
    For Each Pivot In Sheet.PivotTables¶
      'Try to synch if is not the base pivot table¶
      If Not Pivot Is BasePivot Then¶
        'Loop through the page fields of the Base Pivot¶
        For Each BasePage In BasePivot.PageFields¶
          'Clear the old page value¶
          Set Page = Nothing¶
          'Check if its in the pages of the Pivot¶
          'Continue if error occurs¶
          On Error Resume Next¶
          Set Page = Pivot.PageFields(BasePage.Name)¶
          On Error GoTo 0¶
          'Is it there?¶
          If Not Page Is Nothing Then¶
            'Try to assign the current page¶
            On Error Resume Next¶
            Page.CurrentPage.Caption = _¶
                BasePage.CurrentPage.Caption¶
            'Succeed?¶
            If Page.CurrentPage <> BasePage.CurrentPage Then¶
              'Try, using the PivotItems collection¶
              For Each Itm In Page.PivotItems¶
                If Itm.Caption = BasePage.CurrentPage Then¶
                  Page.CurrentPage = Itm.Caption¶
                End If¶
              Next Itm¶
            End If¶
            On Error GoTo 0¶
          End If¶
        Next BasePage¶
      End If¶
    Next Pivot¶
  Next Sheet¶
End Sub¶
```

View the Appendix to learn how to store this procedure in a ThisWorkbook module.

```
Option Explicit¶
' * * * * *¶
Private Sub Workbook_SheetChange(ByVal Sh As Object, _¶
  ByVal Target As Range)¶
    If TypeName(Sh) = "Worksheet" Then¶
        On Error GoTo exiting:¶
        With Target.PivotTable¶
            Application.EnableEvents = False¶
            SynchPivotTables Target.PivotTable¶
            Application.EnableEvents = True¶
        End With¶
    End If¶
exiting:¶
End Sub¶
```

The first part of the code goes in a Standard module in the workbook or template of interest. The rest goes in the ThisWorkbook module of the same workbook.

Tip: This macro does not work in Excel 97 or Excel 2000, because changing a page field does not fire a Change event in those versions of Excel.

Word Procedures

By Cindy Meister

Applying Your Favorite Bullet/Number Format

This procedure demonstrates how to record a macro to quickly apply a favorite number format and to assign the macro to a toolbar button.

Scenario: To change the default numbering or bullets applied when clicking the numbering or bullets buttons on the Formatting toolbar requires a macro. Word offers no direct way to do this.

Example file:
There is no sample macro for this solution, because it is one based on individual preferences.

Don't be afraid to create this macro yourself! It is very easy to do. Once you determine the desired settings, you simply record the steps using the macro recorder. This is one of the few macros that IS easier and better to record than to write from scratch.

Follow these steps:

1. First, decide exactly how the numbering (or list, to use Word jargon) should look. Practice setting the options in Format | Bullets and Numbering | [type of list wanted] | Customize until the steps are familiar.
2. Start the macro recorder using Tools | Macro | Record new macro or by double-clicking the REC button in the Word window status bar.

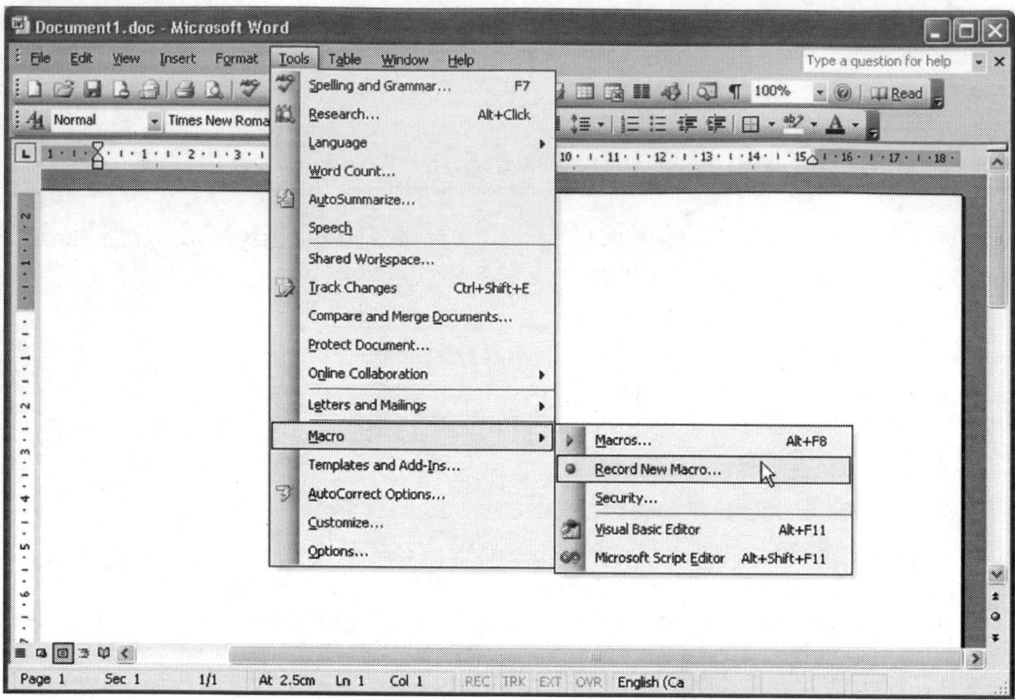

Figure 44 – Recording a Macro in Word

3. In the dialog box that appears, give the macro a descriptive name.

Tip: Macro names cannot contain spaces or punctuation and cannot begin with a number.

---

4. Type a detailed description about what the macro does. Select an appropriate place to save the macro so that it will be available all the time. Normal.dot or another global template is a good place. If it is needed only in a particular document, choose that document from the Store macro in list. For a set of documents created from a particular template, choose that template from the list.

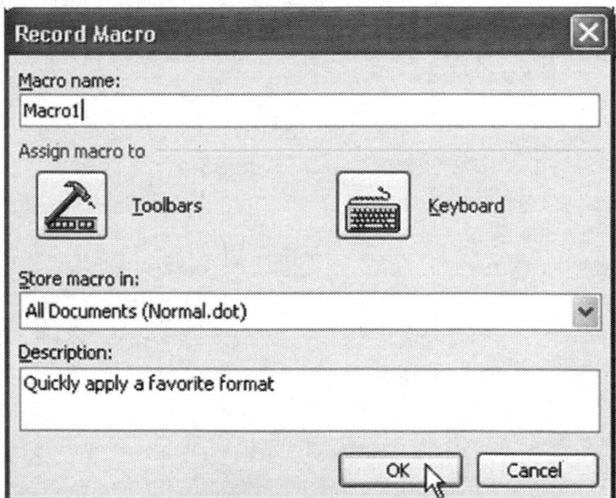

Figure 45 – Naming and Storing a Macro in Word

5. Once you click OK in the Customize dialog box, the macro recording begins. Go to Format | Bullets and Numbering and follow the steps required to create the preferred numbering format.
6. When you have finished making the settings and dismissed the Bullets and Numbering dialog box, stop the macro recorder by clicking the Stop button on the Stop recording toolbar, by double-clicking the REC button on the status bar, or by using the Tools | Macro | Stop Recording command.
7. Test the macro by selecting some paragraphs, then clicking on the new button.

Tip: If you make a mistake, simply start over. The macro recorder will overwrite the first macro if you give it the same name.

In order to view the macro, open the New Macros module in the project where the macro was created.

View the Appendix to learn how to open the VBE and locate the NewMacros module.

The macro recorder generates code for formatting all nine outline numbering levels, even if changes are only made to the settings for a few of the top levels.

Finding and Replacing in Multiple Documents

This procedure demonstrates how to use common Office dialogs and how to loop Find through all parts of a document.

Scenario: The macro recorder is useful, but when the result is played back, the behavior does not always correspond to what happens in the user interface. One excellent example of this is recording Edit | Find or Edit | Replace. In the user interface, Find and Replace processes the entire document, including headers, footers, footnotes and drawing objects. It is rather a nasty surprise to find out that the recorded macro only works in the current "document story"; that is, the main body OR the header, OR the footer, OR the drawing objects.

The macro recorder also cannot record looping through and processing all the files in a selected folder.

Example file:
W002_1.doc and
W002_2.doc

Wrd

This macro combines these two tasks. It loops through all Word files in the folder selected from the dialog box, opens each one in turn, searches for fields that link to outside files, and changes the file path. This approach can be adapted to find other things, such as the need to replace a company logo or to take a desired action.

View the Appendix to learn how to store this procedure in a Standard module.

```
Option explicit¶
'  * * * * *¶
'Finds a field code¶
Const FindText = "^d"¶
' * * * * *¶
Sub ChangeLinks()¶
    'Variable declaration¶
    Dim FilePath As String¶
    Dim linkPath As String¶
    Dim securitySetting As Long¶
    FilePath = GetFileFolder("Select folder to process")¶
    'User cancelled¶
    If Len(FilePath) = 0 Then Exit Sub¶
    linkPath = GetFileFolder("Select path to linked file")¶
    'User cancelled¶
    If Len(linkPath) = 0 Then Exit Sub¶
```

```
    'Debug.Print FilePath, LinkPath¶
    'Suppress screen flicker as much as possible¶
    Application.ScreenUpdating = False¶
    'Save the user's current macro security setting¶
    securitySetting = Application.AutomationSecurity¶
    'Suppress macro warnings¶
    Application.AutomationSecurity = msoAutomationSecurityLow¶
    'Suppress messages, as far as possible¶
    Application.DisplayAlerts = wdAlertsNone¶
    'Don't allow Automacros to run¶
    WordBasic.DisableAutoMacros¶
    ProcessFiles FilePath, linkPath¶
    'Restore original settings¶
    WordBasic.DisableAutoMacros 0¶
    Application.DisplayAlerts = wdAlertsAll¶
    Application.AutomationSecurity = securitySetting¶
End Sub¶
' * * * * *¶
Function GetFileFolder(DlgTitle As String) As String¶
    'Variable declaration¶
    Dim dlg As Office.FileDialog¶
    'Use the Office FileDialog box to get the path info¶
    Set dlg = Application.FileDialog(msoFileDialogFolderPicker)¶
    With dlg¶
        .AllowMultiSelect = False¶
        .ButtonName = "Select Folder"¶
        .InitialView = msoFileDialogViewList¶
        .Title = DlgTitle¶
        'User did not cancel¶
        If .Show = -1 Then¶
            GetFileFolder = .SelectedItems.Item(1)¶
        End If¶
    End With¶
End Function¶
' * * * * *¶
Sub ProcessFiles(FilePath As String, linkPath As String)¶
    'Variable declaration¶
    Dim doc As Word.Document¶
    ' !Remember to reference Microsoft Scripting Runtime!¶
    Dim fso As Scripting.FileSystemObject¶
    Dim f As Scripting.Folder, fil As Scripting.File¶
    Set fso = CreateObject("Scripting.FileSystemObject")¶
    'If the folder exists...¶
    If fso.FolderExists(FilePath) Then¶
        Set f = fso.GetFolder(FilePath)¶
        'Loop through each file in it¶
        For Each fil In f.Files¶
            'Check if it's a Word document¶
            If LCase(fil.Type) = "microsoft word document" Then¶
                'If yes, open it¶
                Set doc = Documents.Open(fil.Path)¶
```

Wrd

```
                ProcessDoc doc, linkPath¶
                'If changes were made, document was saved¶
                'before, so don't save again¶
                doc.Close SaveChanges:=wdDoNotSaveChanges¶
                Set doc = Nothing¶
            End If¶
        Next fil¶
    Else¶
        'folder not found. Unlikely, since was picked¶
        'from folder dialog.¶
    End If¶
    Set fso = Nothing¶
End Sub¶
' * * * * *¶
Sub ProcessDoc(ByRef doc As Word.Document, linkPath As String)¶
    'Variable declaration¶
    Dim rng As Word.Range¶
    'Loop through all parts of a document¶
    For Each rng In doc.StoryRanges¶
        'If appropriate field codes were found,¶
        'save the document¶
        If DoFind(rng, linkPath) Then doc.Save¶
        Do Until rng.NextStoryRange Is Nothing¶
            If DoFind(rng, linkPath) Then doc.Save¶
        Loop¶
    Next¶
End Sub¶
' * * * * *¶
Function DoFind(rng As Word.Range, linkPath As String) As Boolean¶
    'Variable declaration¶
    Dim bFound As Boolean¶
    Dim fieldCode As String¶
    Dim origRng As Word.Range¶
    'Determine where the original range first ended¶
    ' after a successful Find because the range being searched¶
    'changes to the found range¶
    Set origRng = rng.Duplicate¶
    Do¶
        'Make sure field codes are recognized¶
        'Else the macro won't find ^d¶
        rng.TextRetrievalMode.IncludeFieldCodes = True¶
        With rng.Find¶
            .ClearFormatting¶
            .Forward = True¶
            .MatchCase = False¶
            .MatchWholeWord = False¶
            .MatchWildcards = False¶
            .Text = FindText¶
            bFound = .Execute¶
            If bFound Then¶
                fieldCode = rng.Text¶
```

Wrd

```
                'Check whether it's a field that links¶
                'in an outside file¶
                If InStr(LCase(fieldCode), "includetext") <> 0 _¶
                  Or InStr(LCase(fieldCode), "includepicture") <> 0 _¶
                  Or InStr(LCase(fieldCode), "link") <> 0 Then¶
                  'If it is, replace the old path with the new¶
                  rng.Fields(1).Code.Text = NewFieldCode(fieldCode,
linkPath)¶
                  rng.Fields(1).Update¶
                  DoFind = True¶
                End If¶
            End If¶
        End With¶
        'Extend the search range again to¶
        'the end of the original range¶
        rng.Collapse wdCollapseEnd¶
        rng.End = origRng.End¶
    Loop While bFound¶
End Function¶
' * * * * *¶
Function NewFieldCode(ByRef fieldCode As String, linkPath As String) As
String¶
    'Variable declaration¶
    Dim startPos As Long, endPos As Long¶
    Dim newCode As String, docName As String¶
    'Find where the first space after the field name is¶
    startPos = InStr(3, fieldCode, " ")¶
    'If the file path contains spaces, it will¶
    'be enclosed in "quotes"¶
    'Get the position at the end of the path¶
    'either the closing quote, or the first space¶
    If Mid(fieldCode, startPos + 1, 1) = Chr$(34) Then¶
        endPos = InStr(startPos + 2, fieldCode, Chr$(34)) + 1¶
    Else¶
        endPos = InStr(startPos + 2, fieldCode, " ")¶
    End If¶
    'doc name is from the end of the path to¶
    'the first backslash¶
    docName = Mid(fieldCode, _¶
      InStrRev(fieldCode, "\", endPos) + 1, _¶
      endPos - InStrRev(fieldCode, "\", endPos) - 2)¶
    'Now put all the parts back together, with the¶
    'new link path¶
    newCode = Mid(fieldCode, 2, startPos - 1) & _¶
      Chr$(34) & linkPath & "\" & docName & Chr$(34) & _¶
      Mid(fieldCode, endPos, Len(fieldCode) - endPos)¶
    'Fieldcodes in Word need double backslashes¶
    newCode = DoubleBackslashes(newCode)¶
    NewFieldCode = newCode¶
End Function¶
```

Wrd

```
' * * * * *¶
Function DoubleBackslashes(s As String) As String¶
    'Variable declaration¶
    Dim newString As String, startPos As Long, endPos As Long¶
    startPos = 1¶
    'Locate each backslash and insert an additional one¶
    Do While InStr(startPos, s, "\") <> 0¶
        endPos = InStr(startPos, s, "\")¶
        newString = newString & Mid(s, startPos, endPos - startPos + 1) & "\"¶
        startPos = endPos + 1¶
    Loop¶
    newString = newString & Mid(s, startPos)¶
    DoubleBackslashes = newString¶
End Function¶
```


This tool is built modularly so that it can be adapted to various requirements fairly easily. For example, to do a regular Find and Replace, record a macro for the search to use, then substitute the recorded code for the code in the procedure DoFind.

This macro changes the path of linked objects that are formatted in-line with the text only (no text wrap formatting is applied). To combine this macro with text wrap, insert the linked object into a FRAME (from the Forms toolbar).

Highlighting a Selection

With this procedure, you can apply highlighting to selected text or highlight an entire word at the insertion point if there is no selection.

Scenario: Highlighting is a very useful functionality, but selecting text, moving to the toolbar button, then selecting the color quickly becomes a tedious task. Instead, it would be useful to simply hit a keyboard combination in order to apply highlighting; and, if no text is selected, to automatically apply it to the word in which the insertion point is currently blinking.

Example file:
W003

View the Appendix to learn how to store this procedure in a Standard module.

```
Option explicit¶
' * * * * *¶
Private Const highlightColor As Long = wdBrightGreen¶
'Alternate values: wdPink, wdYellow, wdTurquoise¶
'  wdGreen, wdBlue, wdRed, wdTeal, wdDarkRed, wdDarkYellow¶
'  wdDarkBlue, wdGray25, wdGray50, wdViolet, wdBlack¶
' * * * * *¶
Sub HighlightSelection()¶
    'Check if the selection is only an insertion point (IP)¶
    'If it is, extend the range to include the entire word¶
    'at the IP, or the one to which it is directly adjacent¶
    If Selection.Type = wdSelectionIP Then¶
        'Comment out the following line if retaining¶
        'a bracket only, and not highlighting an entire word¶
        'is desired if there is no selection¶
        Selection.Words(1).Select¶
    End If¶
    Selection.Range.HighlightColorIndex = highlightColor¶
End Sub¶
```


Tip: If you prefer a different highlight color, substitute one of the alternate values for wdBrightGreen, such as wdRed or wdViolet.

This macro should be assigned to a keyboard shortcut. The example file has the macro assigned to Alt+H.

Highlighting a Selection in Word 2002/XP

The basis of HighlightSelection may be of interest to Word 2002 users. Word 2002—in contrast to earlier and later versions—does not apply highlighting to commented text. The selected text is surrounded by very thin brackets, which are often hard to see. If no text is selected, there is simply a bar marking the place in the text, which makes it not only difficult to find, but also almost impossible to position the mouse pointer to display the comment in a tool tip. The following macro, InsertAnnotation, calls HighlightSelection to help create visible comments in Word 2002 documents.

View the Appendix to learn how to store this procedure in a Standard module.

```
Option explicit¶
' * * * * *¶
Sub InsertAnnotation()¶
    'Variable declaration¶
    Dim rng As Word.Range¶
    Dim cmt As Word.Comment¶
    'Optional: prompt to enter the comment text¶
    'Comment out the following 7 lines of code¶
    'if you do not want to be prompted¶
    Dim commentText As String¶
    Dim msgPrompt As String¶
    Dim msgTitle As String¶
    commentText = ""¶
    'Change the text in "quotes" to change the prompt¶
    msgPrompt = "Enter the comment text"¶
    'Change the text in "quotes" to change¶
    'the title at the top of the box¶
    msgTitle = "Comment text"¶
    commentText = InputBox(msgPrompt, msgTitle)¶
    If commentText = "" Then Exit Sub¶
    'Set the highlight¶
    HighlightSelection¶
    Set rng = Selection.Range¶
    'Create the comment¶
    Set cmt = ActiveDocument.Comments.Add(rng, commentText)¶
    'Optional: Display the Reviewing task pane¶
    'Comment out the following 6 code lines if¶
    'forcing display of the task pane is not desired.¶
    'If there's more than one task pane, check if the second one¶
    'is in Web View; if not, set the Revisions task pane¶
    If ActiveWindow.Panes.Count > 1 Then¶
        If ActiveDocument.ActiveWindow.Panes(2).View <> wdWebView _¶
        Then _¶
            ActiveWindow.View.SplitSpecial = wdPaneComments¶
    Else¶
            'if there's only one pane for the document¶
            'display the Revisions task pane¶
            ActiveWindow.View.SplitSpecial = wdPaneComments¶
    End If¶
End Sub¶
```

Removing All Highlighting

This procedure removes all highlighting in a document or part of a document.

Scenario: A technique used in working with Word documents is highlighting to make something visible while working in a document. This method is proposed in some of the macros in this book. At some point, you'll want to remove the highlighting that you applied.

Example file:
W004

Wrd

Tip: If you make a mistake and run the macro unintentionally, don't panic! Simply use Edit/Undo and the highlighting will be restored.

View the Appendix to learn how to store this procedure in a Standard module.

```
Option Explicit¶
' * * * * *¶
Sub RemoveHighlighting()¶
    If Selection.Type = wdSelectionIP Then¶
        ActiveDocument.Range.HighlightColorIndex _¶
        = wdNoHighlight¶
        ElseIf Selection.Type = wdSelectionNormal Then¶
        Selection.Range.HighlightColorIndex _¶
        = wdNoHighlight¶
    Else¶
        MsgBox "No text is selected."¶
    End If¶
End Sub¶
```

Inserting AutoText with No Formatting

This procedure lets you insert an AutoText entry as plain text.

Example file:
W005

Scenario: Prior to Word 97, there was a checkbox in the AutoText dialog box that let the user choose whether an AutoText entry should be inserted with its formatting or as "plain text", so that it would adapt to the formatting of the text at the insertion point. Although this functionality has since been lost to the user interface, it is still available through a macro.

This macro displays the built-in Insert | AutoText | AutoText dialog box so that the user can select from the entire range of AutoText entries. The dialog box does not execute, however. Instead, the macro takes care of inserting the AutoText, without any accompanying formatting.

View the Appendix to learn how to store this procedure in a Standard module.

```
Option explicit¶
' * * * * *¶
Sub InsertAutoTextNoFormatting()¶
    'Variable declaration¶
    Dim tmpl As Word.Template¶
    With Dialogs(wdDialogEditAutoText)¶
        .Display¶
        'Because "Display" is used, the macro¶
        'takes care of the actual insertion.¶
        'But only if the user chose the Insert button¶
        If .Insert = -1 Then¶
            'Loop through all loaded templates¶
            For Each tmpl In Application.Templates¶
                'Continue when error occurs¶
                On Error Resume Next¶
                tmpl.AutoTextEntries(.Name).Insert _¶
                Where:=Selection.Range, RichText:=False¶
                'If the AutoText name is not found in a¶
                'template, an error is generated.¶
                'Rather than displaying an error message,¶
                'the error code is checked. If it's 0, then¶
                'there was no error and the AutoText entry was¶
                'inserted successfully. The macro can end¶
```

```
                If Err.Number = 0 Then¶
                    Err.Clear¶
                    Exit For¶
                Else¶
                    Err.Clear¶
                End If¶
            Next¶
        End If¶
    End With¶
End Sub¶
```

Updating All Fields

Wrd

With this procedure, you can update all fields in all parts of a document at once.

Scenario: Depending on the location of fields in a document and which options are set, the data in a field may or may not be up-to-date. There is no way to tell Word, short of printing a document with "Update fields" activated in Tools | Options | Print, to update all the fields in the document.

This macro forces fields to update in every nook and cranny ("story") of a document, including drawing objects, headers and footers in every section, footnotes, endnotes, etc.

Example file:
W006

View the Appendix to learn how to store this procedure in a Standard module.

```
Option explicit¶
' * * * * *¶
Sub UpdateAllFields()¶
    'Variable declaration¶
    Dim story As Word.Range¶
    For Each story In ActiveDocument.StoryRanges¶
        story.Fields.Update¶
        Do Until story.NextStoryRange Is Nothing¶
            Set story = story.NextStoryRange¶
           story.Fields.Update¶
        Loop¶
    Next¶
End Sub¶
```

Setting Hyperlinks on Index Entries

This procedure processes the entries in an index range, creating hyperlinks to the first instance of the index term on the target page. It also showcases the use of a simple array in combination with a user-defined Type to keep track of multiple items.

Example file:
W007

Wrd

> **Scenario:** Since Word 97, it has been possible to click on an entry in a Table of Contents in order to jump to the text in the document that it references. An often-expressed wish of users is that the same process be possible with an index.
>
> This set of macros converts the index to plain text. It then works through each paragraph in the index range, checking whether the text at the right is a (page) number. If it is, the macro "walks" all the characters, from right to left, until it finds no more numbers. The text that remains is then searched on each of the pages listed for that entry, bookmarked, and a hyperlink is created for the bookmark.

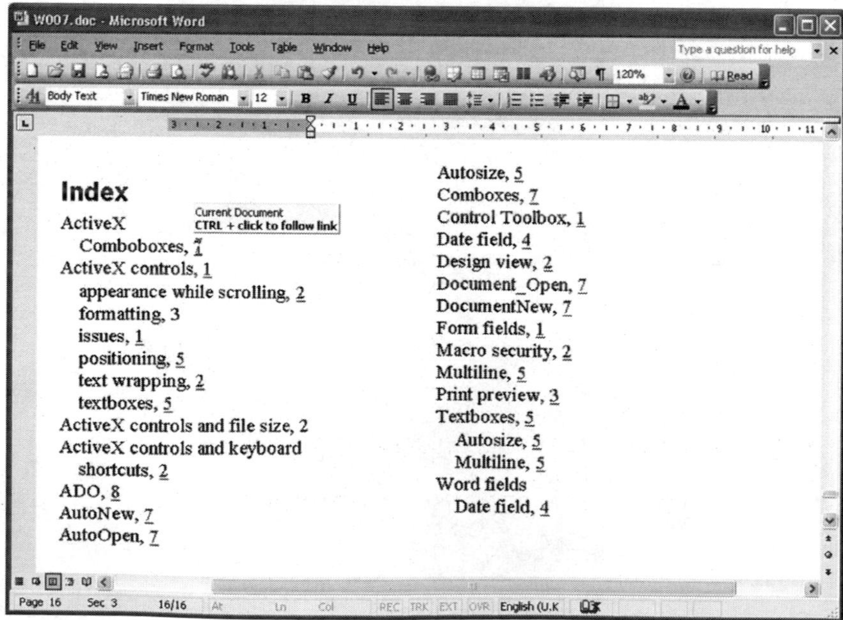

Figure 46 – Hyperlinked Index Entries

Tip: Click on any page number in the hyperlinked index to jump to the first instance of the index entry on the given page.

View the Appendix to learn how to store this procedure in a Standard module.

```
Option explicit¶
' * * * * *¶
Private EntryList() As IndexEntry¶
Private nrEntries As Long¶
Private Const bookmarkIdentifier = "_txt"¶
Private Type IndexEntry¶
    page As String¶
    posStart As Long¶
    posEnd As Long¶
End Type¶
' * * * * *¶
Sub HyperlinkIndex()¶
    'Variable declaration¶
    Dim doc As Word.Document¶
    Dim rngIndex As Word.Range¶
    Dim para As Word.Paragraph¶
    Dim rngEntry As Word.Range¶
    Dim entry As String¶
    Dim searchTerm As String¶
    Dim entryLength As Long¶
    Dim bookmarkName As String¶
    Dim linkCounter As Long¶
    'index term is used as basis for bookmark¶
    'hyperlink target¶
    'increment number for each bookmark target¶
    'in case of more than one entry with same name¶
    Application.ScreenUpdating = False¶
    nrEntries = 0¶
    Set doc = ActiveDocument¶
    Set rngIndex = GetIndexRange(doc)¶
    'Get the range with the index¶
    If rngIndex Is Nothing Then¶
        MsgBox "No index could be found in the active document.", _¶
          vbOKOnly + vbInformation, "Hyperlink index"¶
        Exit Sub¶
    End If¶
```

Wrd

```
    'Remove any bookmarks from previous runs¶
    DeleteAllIndexBookmarks doc, bookmarkIdentifier¶
    'turn it into plain text¶
    rngIndex.Fields.Unlink¶
    For Each para In rngIndex.Paragraphs¶
        'Process each paragraph in the index range¶
        Set rngEntry = para.Range¶
        'Pick up only the field result, not the code¶
        rngEntry.TextRetrievalMode.IncludeFieldCodes = False¶
        entry = rngEntry.Text¶
        entryLength = Len(entry) - 1 'cut off para mark¶
        If IsValidEntry(entry, entryLength) Then¶
            searchTerm = ExtractEntryInfo(rngEntry, _¶
              entry, entryLength)¶
            'Process each page number for the index entry¶
            bookmarkName = DeriveName(doc, searchTerm)¶
            For linkCounter = 0 To UBound(EntryList)¶
                CreateHyperlinkAndTarget doc, searchTerm, _¶
                  bookmarkName, linkCounter, rngIndex¶
            Next¶
        End If¶
        ReDim EntryList(0)¶
    Next para¶
End Sub¶
' * * * * *¶
'Find the Index, if it exists by looping through¶
'the fields and testing the type¶
'Returns "Nothing" if Index field is not present¶
Function GetIndexRange(doc As Word.Document) As Word.Range¶
    'Variable declaration¶
    Dim fld As Word.Field¶
    For Each fld In doc.Fields¶
        If fld.Type = wdFieldIndex Then¶
            Set GetIndexRange = fld.Result¶
            Exit For¶
        End If¶
    Next fld¶
End Function¶
' * * * * *¶
Sub DeleteAllIndexBookmarks(doc As Word.Document, _¶
  identifier As String)¶
    'Variable declaration¶
    Dim bkm As Word.Bookmark¶
    For Each bkm In doc.Bookmarks¶
        If Left(bkm.Name, Len(identifier)) = _¶
          identifier Then bkm.Delete¶
    Next¶
End Sub¶
```

Wrd

```
' * * * * *¶
Function IsValidEntry(entry As String, _¶
  entryLength As Long) As Boolean¶
    'Index entry must be at least 4 characters:¶
    'entry text, space or tab, page nr, para mark¶
    IsValidEntry = False¶
    If entryLength > 3 Then¶
        'Dont bother if no page number¶
        If IsNumeric(Mid(entry, entryLength, 1)) Then¶
            IsValidEntry = True¶
        End If¶
    End If¶
End Function¶
' * * * * *¶
Function ExtractEntryInfo(rngEntry As Word.Range, _¶
  entry As String, entryLength As Long) As String¶
    'Variable declaration¶
    Dim newEntry As IndexEntry¶
    Dim pageNumber As String¶
    Dim entryCounter As Long¶
    Do¶
        'Restart the list of pages for this entry¶
        ReDim Preserve EntryList(entryCounter)¶
        pageNumber = ""¶
        'end point for the hyperlink to be inserted¶
        newEntry.posEnd = rngEntry.End - _¶
          (Len(entry) - entryLength)¶
        'get all consecutive numerals (= page number)¶
        'at end of entry string¶
        Do While IsNumeric(Mid(entry, entryLength, 1))¶
            pageNumber = Mid(entry, entryLength, 1) & pageNumber¶
            entryLength = entryLength - 1¶
        Loop¶
        'Add the page number to the list for which¶
        'bookmark targets need to be created¶
        newEntry.page = pageNumber¶
        'start point for the hyperlink to be inserted¶
        newEntry.posStart = rngEntry.End - _¶
          (Len(entry) - entryLength)¶
        'Add this to the entry list that will be processed¶
        EntryList(entryCounter) = newEntry¶
        entryCounter = entryCounter + 1¶
        'skip any spaces between numbers¶
        Do While Mid(entry, entryLength, 1) = " "¶
            entryLength = entryLength - 1¶
        Loop¶
        'skip the , separating page numbers¶
        Do While Mid(entry, entryLength, 1) = ","¶
            entryLength = entryLength - 1¶
        Loop¶
```

```
        'skip any tab separator for right-aligned page numbers¶
        Do While Mid(entry, entryLength, 1) = vbTab¶
            entryLength = entryLength - 1¶
        Loop¶
        'skip any spaces up to the search entry¶
        Do While Mid(entry, entryLength, 1) = " "¶
            entryLength = entryLength - 1¶
        Loop¶
    Loop Until Not IsNumeric(Mid(entry, entryLength, 1))¶
    'When there are no more numbers left¶
    'the search term is what remains¶
    ExtractEntryInfo = Left(entry, entryLength)¶
End Function¶
' * * * * * *¶
Function DeriveName(doc As Word.Document, _¶
  searchTerm As String) As String¶
    'Variable declaration¶
    Dim counter As Long¶
    Dim bookmarkName As String¶
    'Continue when error occurs¶
    On Error Resume Next¶
    'Limit the base bookmark name to 24 characters¶
    'this allows up to four digits for the counter¶
    'plus four for the identifier¶
    For counter = 0 To 24¶
        'If the searchTerm is less than this limit, stop¶
        If counter = Len(searchTerm) Then Exit For¶
        'Loop through the characters in search term¶
        bookmarkName = bookmarkName & Mid(searchTerm, _¶
          counter + 1, 1)¶
        'Make sure the bookmark name doesn't contain any¶
        ' illegal characters by trying to use the name¶
        doc.Bookmarks.Add bookmarkName¶
        If Err.Number > 0 Then¶
            'If there's an error, drop the illegal character¶
            bookmarkName = Left(bookmarkName, _¶
              Len(bookmarkName) - 1)¶
        Else¶
            'delete the test bookmark¶
            doc.Bookmarks(bookmarkName).Delete¶
        End If¶
        Err.Clear¶
    Next counter¶
    On Error GoTo 0¶
    DeriveName = bookmarkIdentifier & bookmarkName¶
End Function¶
```

```
' * * * * *¶
Sub CreateHyperlinkAndTarget(doc As Word.Document, _¶
  searchTerm As String, bookmarkName As String, _¶
  linkCounter As Long, rngIndex As Word.Range)¶
    'Variable declaration¶
    Dim rngPage As Word.Range¶
    Dim rngAnchor As Word.Range¶
    'In order to assign a page to a range the¶
    'selection must be on that page. So be sure¶
    'the document being processed is the active one¶
    If Not doc Is ActiveDocument Then doc.Activate¶
    Selection.GoTo What:=wdGoToPage, _¶
      Count:=CLng(EntryList(linkCounter).page)¶
    Set rngPage = doc.Bookmarks("\Page").Range¶
    'Now search for the term on the given page¶
    'Be sure to also check the XE fields, even if¶
    'they are not displayed¶
    rngPage.TextRetrievalMode.IncludeHiddenText = True¶
    With rngPage.Find¶
        .ClearFormatting¶
        .Text = searchTerm¶
        .Forward = True¶
        If .Execute Then¶
            'If found, bookmark it¶
            bookmarkName = bookmarkName & CStr(nrEntries)¶
            doc.Bookmarks.Add Name:=bookmarkName, Range:=rngPage¶
            'get the range of the page number and¶
            Set rngAnchor = rngIndex.Duplicate¶
            rngAnchor.TextRetrievalMode.IncludeFieldCodes = False¶
            rngAnchor.SetRange _¶
              Start:=EntryList(linkCounter).posStart, _¶
              End:=EntryList(linkCounter).posEnd¶
            'Insert hyperlink to the bookmark in its place¶
            'With the page number as the display text¶
            doc.Hyperlinks.Add Anchor:=rngAnchor, _¶
              SubAddress:=bookmarkName, _¶
              TextToDisplay:=EntryList(linkCounter).page¶
            'For Word97, remove the TextToDisplay part¶
            nrEntries = nrEntries + 1¶
            End If¶
    End With¶
End Sub¶
```

Wrd

Tip: Be sure to update the index before running the macro, because the macro turns the index into static text. It does not matter whether or not the XE (index entry) fields are visible on screen.

If there is a subsequent need to update the index, delete the hyperlinked index, insert a new one, and then run the macro again.

This macro is designed to work with a generic index generated by the Insert | Reference | Index and Table of Contents | Index dialog box, of the Indent type. As it stands, it will not work with a Run-in type of index, although it could be modified for this type of index. The number of columns is not important, nor whether page numbers are right-aligned.

Displaying a Number in Millions as Text

Using this procedure, you can insert a complex set of nested fields to augment Word's * CardText and * DollarText formatting switches to display numbers in the millions as text. It also demonstrates how to check whether the selection is in a field.

Scenario: The Word object model provides no way to create a set of nested fields using VBA. But often a more or less complex set of Word fields is the only way to dynamically display or bring data into Word, thus saving the user lots of manual work.

In this example, to display a number in the millions as text, Word's internal * DollarText and * CardText switches only work up to 999,999.

Example file:
W008

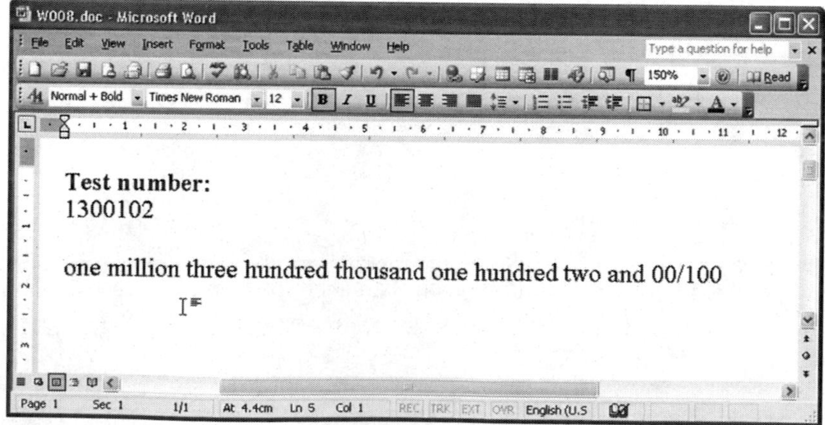

Figure 47 – Displaying Numbers as Text

View the Appendix to learn how to store this procedure in a Standard module.

```
Option explicit¶
' * * * * *¶
Sub CreateCardTextFieldMillions()¶
    'Variable declaration¶
    Dim fld As Word.Field, rng As Word.Range¶
    Dim szSepChar As String, szBkm As String¶
    Dim szQuotes As String¶
    szQuotes = Chr(34)¶
    szBkm = "bkm"¶
    szSepChar = System.PrivateProfileString( _¶
      "", "HKEY_CURRENT_USER\Control Panel\International", _¶
      "sList")¶
    'Insert the outermost level; QUOTE field¶
    Set fld = ActiveDocument.Fields.Add( _¶
      Range:=Selection.Range, Type:=wdFieldQuote, _¶
      Text:="bkm bkm bkm bkm", PreserveFormatting:=False)¶
    Set rng = fld.Code¶
    'Insert the second level, first SET field¶
    InsertFieldInFieldCode rng, szBkm, "Set n bkm"¶
    InsertFieldInFieldCode rng, szBkm, "NrToText"¶
    'Determine the millions part of the number¶
    InsertFieldInFieldCode rng, szBkm, "Set m bkm"¶
    InsertFieldInFieldCode rng, szBkm, "= int(bkm/1000000)"¶
    InsertFieldInFieldCode rng, szBkm, "n"¶
    'Determine the remainder¶
    InsertFieldInFieldCode rng, szBkm, "Set r bkm"¶
    InsertFieldInFieldCode rng, szBkm, "= MOD(bkm" & szSepChar _¶
      & "1000000)"¶
    InsertFieldInFieldCode rng, szBkm, "n"¶
    'Determine if NrToText number < or >= 1 million¶
    InsertFieldInFieldCode rng, szBkm, "If bkm < 1000000 " & _¶
      szQuotes & "bkm" & szQuotes & " " & szQuotes & "bkm" _¶
      & szQuotes & " \* lower \* CharFormat"¶
    InsertFieldInFieldCode rng, szBkm, "n"¶
    'If less, simply transform into dollartext¶
    InsertFieldInFieldCode rng, szBkm, "n \* dollartext"¶
    'Insert a container for concatenated result¶
    'if greater than or equal to¶
    InsertFieldInFieldCode rng, szBkm, _¶
      "Quote " & szQuotes & "bkm millionbkm" & szQuotes¶
    'If more than a million, insert the millions number as CardText¶
    InsertFieldInFieldCode rng, szBkm, "m \* cardtext"¶
    'If the remainder = 0...¶
    InsertFieldInFieldCode rng, szBkm, "If bkm < 1 " & szQuotes & _¶
      " and bkm/100" & szQuotes & " " & szQuotes & " bkm" & szQuotes¶
    InsertFieldInFieldCode rng, szBkm, "r"¶
```

```
    '...otherwise it has to precede the "/100" as a number¶
    InsertFieldInFieldCode rng, szBkm, "= bkm * 100 \# " & _¶
      szQuotes & "00" & szQuotes¶
    InsertFieldInFieldCode rng, szBkm, "r"¶
    'Format the rest as dollartext¶
    InsertFieldInFieldCode rng, szBkm, "r \* dollartext"¶
    fld.Update¶
End Sub¶
' * * * * *¶
Function InsertFieldInFieldCode( _¶
  ByRef rng As Word.Range, _¶
  ByRef szBkm As String, _¶
  ByRef szField As String, _¶
  Optional ByRef PF As Boolean = False) As Boolean¶
    InsertFieldInFieldCode = False¶
    With rng.Find¶
        .Text = szBkm¶
        .Execute¶
        If .Found Then¶
            ActiveDocument.Fields.Add _¶
              Range:=rng, Text:=szField, _¶
              PreserveFormatting:=PF¶
            InsertFieldInFieldCode = True¶
        End If¶
    End With¶
End Function¶
' * * * * *¶
Sub UpdateAllFields()¶
    'Variable declaration¶
    Dim sty As Word.Range¶
    Application.DisplayAlerts = wdAlertsNone¶
    For Each sty In ActiveDocument.StoryRanges¶
        sty.Fields.Update¶
    Next¶
    Application.DisplayAlerts = wdAlertsAll¶
End Sub¶
' * * * * *¶
Sub PasteFieldCodesAsText()¶
    'Variable declaration¶
    Dim rng As Word.Range¶
    Dim FieldString As String¶
    Dim NewString As String¶
    Dim i As Long¶
    Dim CurrChar As String¶
    Dim CurrSetting As Boolean¶
    Dim MyData As MSForms.DataObject¶
    'Make the preparations¶
    Set rng = Selection.Range¶
    NewString = ""¶
    Application.ScreenUpdating = False¶
```

```
    'Make sure to pick up the field codes¶
    rng.TextRetrievalMode.IncludeFieldCodes = True¶
    FieldString = rng.Text¶
    'Work through the characters in the selection, one-by-one¶
    'and build the result. If a field opening or closing brace¶
    'is encountered, put a brace-character in its place¶
    For i = 1 To Len(FieldString)¶
        CurrChar = Mid(FieldString, i, 1)¶
        Select Case CurrChar¶
            Case Chr(19)¶
                CurrChar = "{"¶
            Case Chr(21)¶
                CurrChar = "}"¶
            Case Else¶
        End Select¶
        NewString = NewString + CurrChar¶
    Next i¶
    'Put the result on the clipboard, so that¶
    'the user can paste it where ever needed¶
    Set MyData = New DataObject¶
    MyData.SetText NewString¶
    MyData.PutInClipboard¶
End Sub¶
```

The fields should be updated if the number is changed to reflect the change in the text. You can do this by running the Updating All Fields macro found on page 131.

Copying Nested Field Codes as Text

With this procedure, you can copy a set of nested field codes and paste the field codes as plain text, rather than the fields themselves.

> **Scenario:** It can be frustrating enough just to figure out certain field codes. Now, perhaps you want to share them with a coworker or to place one on a web page. You copy the field code and paste it, but only the result is pasted, even though you hit Alt+F9 to reveal the field codes!
>
> Using this macro, exchanging complex field solutions with colleagues, via e-mail or other methods, can be done without having to attach Word documents.

Example file:
W009

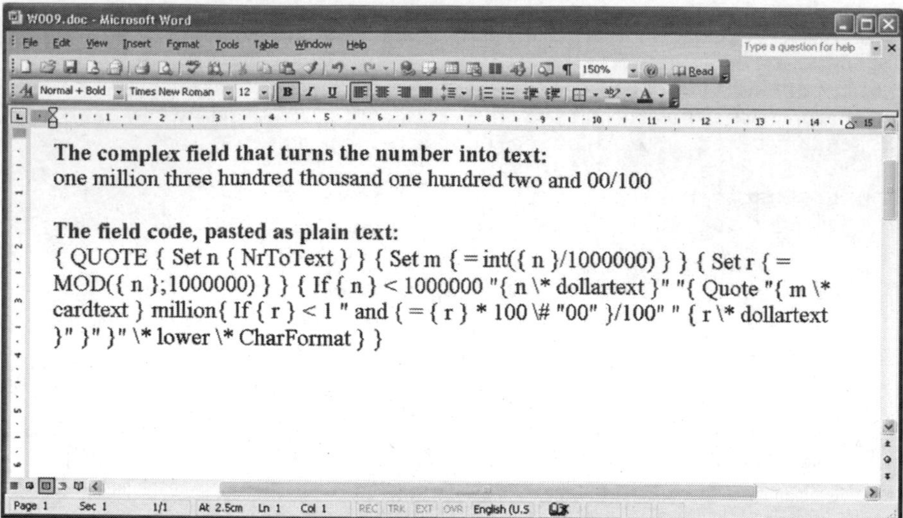

Figure 48 – Nested Field Codes Pasted as Text

View the Appendix to learn how to store this procedure in a Standard module.

```
Option explicit¶
' * * * * *¶
Function InsertFieldInFieldCode( _¶
  ByRef rng As Word.Range, _¶
  ByRef szBkm As String, _¶
  ByRef szField As String, _¶
  Optional ByRef PF As Boolean = False) As Boolean¶
    InsertFieldInFieldCode = False¶
    With rng.Find¶
        .Text = szBkm¶
        .Execute¶
        If .Found Then¶
            ActiveDocument.Fields.Add _¶
              Range:=rng, Text:=szField, _¶
              PreserveFormatting:=PF¶
            InsertFieldInFieldCode = True¶
        End If¶
    End With¶
End Function¶
' * * * * *¶
Sub PasteFieldCodesAsText()¶
    'Variable declaration¶
    Dim rng As Word.Range¶
    Dim FieldString As String¶
    Dim NewString As String¶
```

```
    Dim i As Long¶
    Dim CurrChar As String¶
    Dim CurrSetting As Boolean¶
    Dim MyData As MSForms.DataObject¶
    'Make the preparations¶
    Set rng = Selection.Range¶
    NewString = ""¶
    Application.ScreenUpdating = False¶
    'Make sure to pick up the field codes¶
    rng.TextRetrievalMode.IncludeFieldCodes = True¶
    FieldString = rng.Text¶
    'Work through the characters in the selection, one-by-one¶
    'and build the result. If a field opening or closing brace¶
    'is encountered, put a brace-character in its place¶
    For i = 1 To Len(FieldString)¶
        CurrChar = Mid(FieldString, i, 1)¶
        Select Case CurrChar¶
            Case Chr(19)¶
                CurrChar = "{"¶
            Case Chr(21)¶
                CurrChar = "}"¶
            Case Else¶
        End Select¶
        NewString = NewString + CurrChar¶
    Next i¶
    'Put the result on the clipboard, so that¶
    'the user can paste it wherever needed¶
    Set MyData = New DataObject¶
    MyData.SetText NewString¶
    MyData.PutInClipboard¶
End Sub¶
```

Select a field result (the entire result must be selected, not just an insertion point), run the macro, then position the cursor where the field code should be pasted.

Tip: This macro can also be used to paste into another application, such as an e-mail editor.

Note: Check that there is an active reference to the "Microsoft Forms 2.0 object library" in Tools | References in the Visual Basic Editor. If you forget to take this step, you'll receive an error: User-defined type not defined. In this case, stop the macro, add the reference, and try again.

Wrd

Converting AutoNumbered Text into Normal Text

This macro converts AutoNumbered text to plain text, including the numbers.

> **Scenario:** Perhaps you have been tasked with creating a readme file for your company's software product. Readme files are always created as TXT—plain text files, but your software manual was developed using many levels of AutonNumbering. When you copy and paste as unformatted text, or save as a TXT file, the numbering is lost.
>
> This macro illustrates a way to turn the numbering in the current selection into plain text so that the numbering is retained. You won't believe how simple it is!

Example file:
W010

Wrd

View the Appendix to learn how to store this procedure in a Standard module.

```
Option explicit¶
' * * * * *¶
Sub NumbersToPlainText()¶
    Selection.Range.ListFormat.ConvertNumbersToText¶
End Sub¶
```

Select the text you want to convert. Run the macro. Paste the text where desired.

Reverse Numbering

This macro numbers paragraphs in reverse order.

> **Scenario:** Usually, numbering things in ascending order is preferred, from 1 to 10, for example. But there are occasions when reverse order (a countdown) is desired, such as a "Top 10". This macro inserts numbering in reverse order at the beginning of each paragraph of the current selection.

Example file:
W011

Lines to number in reverse order:
7. Line one
6. Line two
5. Line three
4. Line four
3. Line five
2. Line six
1. Line seven

Figure 49 – Reverse Numbering

Wrd

View the Appendix to learn how to store this procedure in a Standard module.

```
Option explicit¶
' * * * * *¶
Sub ReverseNumbering()¶
'Numbers the selected paragraphs¶
'in reverse order¶
    'Variable declaration¶
    Dim rngSel As Word.Range¶
    Dim para As Word.Paragraph¶
    Dim nrLines As Long¶
    Dim separatorChars As String¶
    'What should stand between the number¶
    'and the paragraph text¶
    separatorChars = "." & vbTab¶
    Set rngSel = Selection.Range¶
    'Determines the starting number¶
    nrLines = rngSel.Paragraphs.Count¶
    For Each para In rngSel.Paragraphs¶
        'Insert the number info at the front¶
        'of each paragraph¶
        para.Range.InsertBefore CStr(nrLines) _¶
          & separatorChars¶
        'Get the next number¶
        nrLines = nrLines - 1¶
    Next¶
    'If using a tab, set the tabstop indent¶
    If InStr(separatorChars, vbTab) Then¶
        SetTabIndent rngSel, InchesToPoints(0.3)¶
        'If using the metric system, comment¶
        'out the above line and remove the comment¶
        'from the following line¶
        'SetTabIndent rngSel, CentimetersToPoint(0.6)¶
    End If¶
End Sub¶
```

```
' * * * * *¶
Sub SetTabIndent(rngSel As Word.Range, indnt As Single)¶
    rngSel.Paragraphs.TabStops.Add _¶
      Position:=rngSel.Information( _¶
        wdHorizontalPositionRelativeToTextBoundary) _¶
      + indnt¶
End Sub¶
```

Consider what to place as a separator between the number and the paragraph text. By default, the macro uses a point (period, dot) followed by a Tab. Substitute any character for the assignment to 'separatorChars'. For example, to use a parenthesis followed by a space:

```
separatorChars = ") "¶
```


Using a tab results in the macro setting a tab stop at .3 inches from the original left indent position of the text. This setting can be changed. For example, to have the text start at .5 inch from the left edge:

```
SetTabIndent rngSel, InchesToPoints(0.5) ¶
```

Select the paragraphs to be numbered in reverse order, and run the macro.

The result of this macro is static text. For more numbering solutions, visit http://homepage.swissonline.ch/cindymeister/.

Tables: Changing the Tab Direction

This macro changes the tab direction in tables so that you can tab down, then across, instead of left to right.

Scenario: In Word, the selection always moves with the flow of the text: across, then down. The same is true when Tab is pressed in a table: the selection moves across the row, then down to the next column. To change this to first move down the column, then across to the next column, as when reading text columns, a macro like the following is needed.

Example file:
W012

View the Appendix to learn how to store this procedure in a Standard module.

```
Option explicit¶
' * * * * *¶
Sub NextCell()¶
'Make sure the selection is in a table¶
    If Selection.Information(wdWithInTable) Then¶
        'Variable declaration¶
        Dim rcount As Long, ccount As Long¶
        Dim ri As Long, ci As Long¶
        Dim tbl As Word.Table¶
        Set tbl = Selection.Tables(1)¶
        'Where is selection?:¶
        'In which row is the selection?¶
        ri = Selection.Rows(1).Index¶
        'And in which column?¶
        ci = Selection.Columns(1).Index¶
        'How many rows are there?¶
        rcount = tbl.Rows.Count¶
        'And how many columns?¶
        ccount = tbl.Columns.Count¶
        'If selection is not in the last row¶
        If ri < rcount Then¶
            'Move down to the next cell¶
            tbl.Cell(ri + 1, ci).Select¶
        'If it is in the last table cell¶
        ElseIf ri = rcount And ci = ccount Then¶
            'Variable declaration¶
            Dim rng As Word.Range¶
            Set rng = tbl.Range¶
            'Move outside the table¶
            rng.Collapse wdCollapseEnd¶
            rng.Select¶
        'If the last row, but not the last column¶
        ElseIf ri = rcount Then¶
            'Move to the top of the next column¶
            tbl.Cell(1, ci + 1).Select¶
        Else¶
            'An unexpected situation has occurred¶
            MsgBox "There's a problem"¶
        End If¶
    End If¶
End Sub¶
```

The macro runs automatically.

Note: This macro MUST be named NextCell, which is the name of the Word internal command that is fired when Tab is pressed while your cursor is inside of a table. In Word, a macro named with the same name as an internal command will run in place of that command.

Tables: Suppressing New Rows When Tabbing

Use this procedure to suppress Word's default behavior, which creates a new row when Tab is pressed in the last cell of a table.

Scenario: In the previous macro, unlike the default behavior, no new row is created when Tab is pressed in the last cell. To do the same for normal table cell navigation behavior when pressing Tab, use this variation of the NextCell procedure.

Example file:
W013

View the Appendix to learn how to store this procedure in a Standard module.

```
Option explicit¶
' * * * * *¶
Sub NextCell()¶
    If Selection.Information(wdWithInTable) Then¶
        'Variable declaration¶
        Dim tbl As Word.Table, cel As Word.Cell¶
        Set tbl = Selection.Tables(1)¶
        Set cel = Selection.Cells(1)¶
        'If not in the last cell, move to the next¶
        If cel.RowIndex <> tbl.Rows.Count _¶
        Or cel.ColumnIndex <> tbl.Columns.Count Then¶
            WordBasic.NextCell¶
        Else¶
            'Move out of the table¶
            Dim rng As Word.Range¶
            Set rng = tbl.Range¶
            rng.Collapse wdCollapseEnd¶
            rng.Select¶
        End If¶
    End If¶
End Sub¶
```

The macro runs automatically.

Note: This macro MUST be named NextCell. NextCell is the name of the Word internal command that is fired when Tab is pressed while your cursor is inside of a table. In Word, a macro named with the same name as an internal command will run in place of that command.

Tables: Formatting Numbers in a Selection

This procedure applies a numeric "picture" to numbers in selected table cells.

Wrd

Example file:
W014

Scenario: Microsoft has always said that users who want spreadsheet functionality should use Excel. What Microsoft seems to have forgotten is that an Excel object in Word cannot break across pages.

One bit of spreadsheet functionality often desired in Word is the ability to format numbers without having to expressly type in the format. This macro applies a specified number format to every number that stands alone in a selected table cell. If it is the result of a field calculation, the number format is added to the field code.

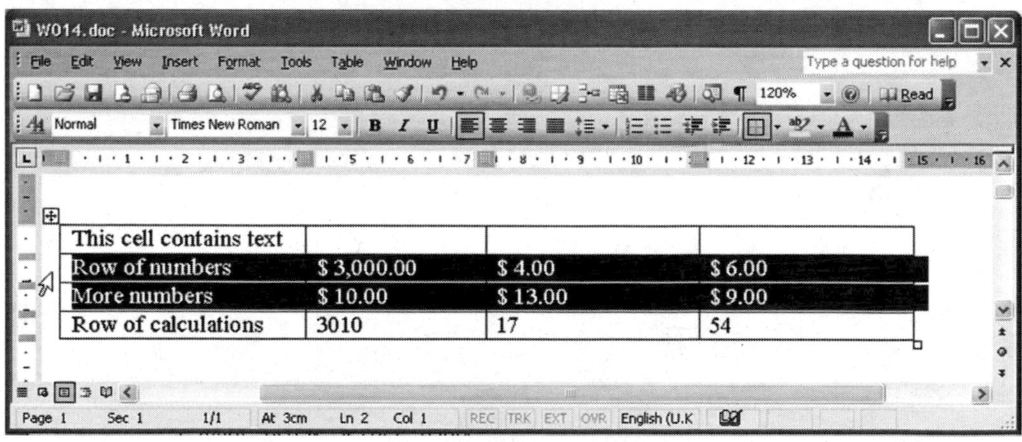

Figure 50 – Formatted Numbers

View the Appendix to learn how to store this procedure in a Standard module.

```
Option explicit¶
' * * * * *¶
Const NumberFormat As String = "$ #,0.00"¶
' * * * * *¶
Sub FormatNumbersInTableSelection()¶
    'Variable declarations¶
    Dim tbl As Word.Table¶
    Dim cel As Word.Cell¶
    Dim rng As Word.Range¶
    Dim fld As Word.Field¶
    Dim sCellContent As String¶
    Dim sFieldCode As String¶
    'Make sure the selection is in a table¶
    If Selection.Information(wdWithInTable) = True Then¶
        'Loop through the cells in the selection¶
        For Each cel In Selection.Cells¶
            Set rng = cel.Range¶
            sCellContent = TrimCellText(rng.Text)¶
            'Only proceed if a numerical value; ignore text¶
            If IsNumeric(sCellContent) Then¶
                If rng.Fields.Count = 0 Then¶
                    rng.Text = Format(sCellContent, _¶
                    NumberFormat)¶
                Else¶
                    Set fld = rng.Fields(1)¶
                    sFieldCode = fld.Code.Text¶
                    'If the number is generated by a field¶
                    'check that it doesn't already contain¶
                    'a number format¶
                    If InStr(sFieldCode, "\#") = 0 Then¶
                      fld.Code.Text = sFieldCode & "\# " & _¶
                       Chr$(34) & NumberFormat & Chr$(34) & " "¶
                      fld.Update¶
                    End If¶
                End If¶
            End If¶
        Next cel¶
    End If¶
End Sub¶
' * * * * *¶
Function TrimCellText(s As String) As String¶
    'Remove end-of-cell markers¶
    TrimCellText = Left(s, Len(s) - 2)¶
End Function¶
```

Set the number format you want to use for the Const NumberFormat value.

Note: The number format specified must correspond to the settings specified for the Windows Regional settings. For example, if a comma is set as the decimal separator in Windows, a comma must be used in the table number format.

Tip: To learn more about acceptable values for number formatting, search "number picture field switch" in Word's Help, as well as looking at the information on the Format function in the VBA Help.

Tables: Copying Formulas

This procedure copies formulas, while adjusting the row references.

Example file:
W015

Scenario: Microsoft encourages its customers to use Excel for anything that requires calculation, and to use Word for text-oriented tasks. There are times when inserting an Excel sheet into a Word document is not a workable solution.

Using Word for simple calculations in small tables presents no great problems. However, if the same formula needs to be used across many rows that references cells in those rows, the task becomes frustrating. Unlike Excel, Word uses absolute cell references that do not adapt automatically when a formula is copied to a different row, which means virtually every formula must be manually created.

This tool enables a formula to be copied to as many rows as desired.

This tool picks up the formula in the currently selected cell, displays a dialog box to confirm that this is the formula to be copied, and selects the parts of it that should be changed. Select the cells to which the formula should be pasted and click "Copy Formula". The Formula is copied to these cells with the appropriate corresponding row references.

In the illustrated example, all instances of (A2 * C2) in the original formula (top of dialog box) will be changed to (A3 * C3), (A4 * C4) and so on.

Wrd

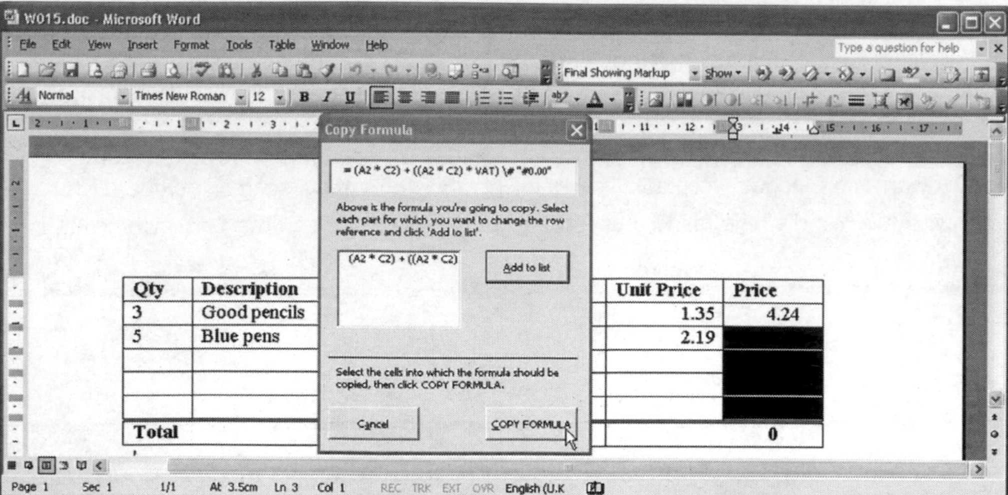

Figure 51 – Copying Formulas in Tables

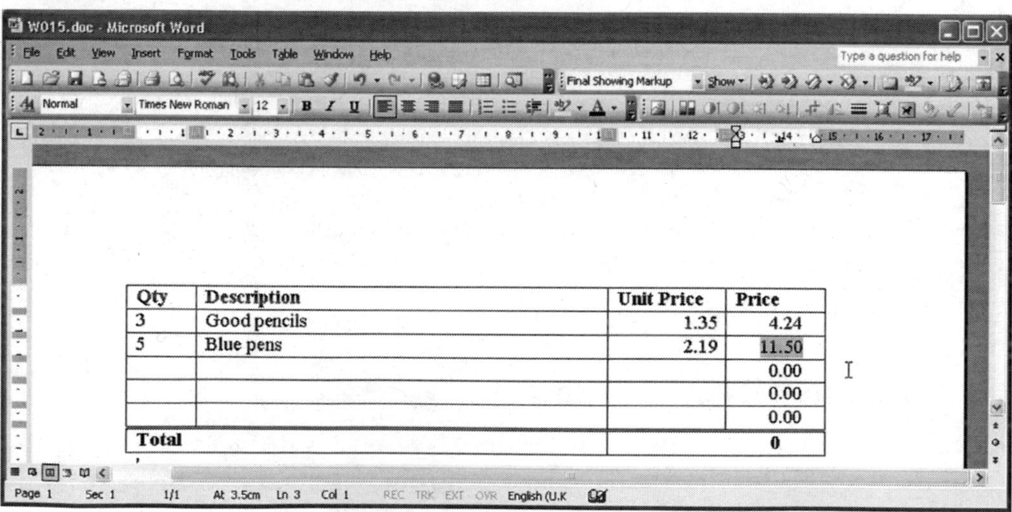

Figure 52 – Copied Formulas

View the Appendix to learn how to store this procedure in a Standard module (in a template).

```
Option explicit¶
' * * * * * *¶
Private frm As frmCopyFormula¶
Private startRow As Long¶
' * * * * * *¶
Sub StartCopyFormula()¶
    Dim sel As Word.Selection¶
    'Show the form¶
    'It may already be loaded, so check¶
    'and re-show if it is¶
    If UserForms.Count > 0 Then¶
        'Variable declaration¶
        Dim f As UserForm¶
        For Each f In UserForms¶
            If f.Caption = "Copy Formula" Then¶
                Exit For¶
            End If¶
        Next¶
    Else¶
        'If it's not, start a new one¶
        'and fill the field code¶
        Set sel = Selection¶
        'Make sure the selection is in a table cell¶
        'and that the cell contains a formula¶
        If SelectionIsValid(sel) Then¶
            startRow = sel.Rows(1).Index¶
                Set frm = New frmCopyFormula¶
                    frm.txtFieldCode.Text = _¶
                  sel.Cells(1).Range.Fields(1).Code¶
        Else¶
            MsgBox "The selection is invalid. " & _¶
              "Make sure the selection is in a cell " & _¶
              "with a formula.", vbCritical + vbOKOnly¶
        End If¶
    End If¶
    frm.Show¶
End Sub¶
' * * * * * *¶
Sub CopyFormula()¶
    'Variable declaration¶
    Dim sel As Word.Selection¶
    Dim cel As Word.Cell¶
    Dim partFormula As String¶
    Dim newFormula As String¶
    Dim updatedFormula As String¶
    Dim i As Long¶
    Dim posStart As Long, posEnd As Long¶
    'Get the new selection: target cells¶
    Set sel = Selection¶
    'Make sure it's valid: in a table¶
    If sel.Information(wdWithInTable) Then¶
```

```
        'Don't include the original cell¶
        'in the target¶
        Do While sel.Rows(1).Index = startRow¶
            MsgBox "The selection is still in the same row. " & _¶
              "The formula cannot be copied. " & _¶
              "Please try again.", vbCritical + vbOKOnly¶
            'Reshow the form¶
            StartCopyFormula¶
            Exit Sub¶
        Loop¶
        'Go through each cell in the contiguous¶
        'selection¶
        For Each cel In Selection.Cells¶
            newFormula = frm.txtFieldCode¶
            'Process each formula part the user¶
            'selected to be changed relative to the row¶
            For i = 0 To frm.lstFormulas.ListCount - 1¶
                partFormula = frm.lstFormulas.List(i)¶
                'get start position of the formula part¶
                posStart = InStr(newFormula, partFormula)¶
                'if it was found¶
                If posStart > 0 Then¶
                    'determine the end position¶
                    posEnd = posStart + Len(partFormula) - 1¶
                    'replace the row index in the formula¶
                    updatedFormula = UpdateFormula(partFormula, _¶
                      cel.Row.Index)¶
                    'replace the partial formula¶
                    newFormula = Replace(newFormula, _¶
                      partFormula, updatedFormula)¶
                End If¶
            Next¶
            'insert the field code in the cell¶
            'Variable declaration¶
            Dim rngCel As Word.Range¶
            Set rngCel = cel.Range¶
            rngCel.Collapse wdCollapseStart¶
            ActiveDocument.Fields.Add Range:=rngCel,
Type:=wdFieldEmpty, _¶
                Text:=newFormula, PreserveFormatting:=False¶
        Next¶
    Else¶
        MsgBox "The selection must be within a table", _¶
          vbCritical vbOKOnly¶
        StartCopyFormula¶
        Exit Sub¶
    End If¶
    Unload frm¶
End Sub¶
```

Wrd

```
' * * * * *¶
Function UpdateFormula(ByVal newFormula As String, _¶
  rw As Long) As String¶
    'Variable declaration¶
    Dim rowChange As Long¶
    Dim i As Long¶
    Dim nrToChange As String¶
    Dim posStart As Long¶
    'Difference between original and new row index¶
    rowChange = rw - startRow¶
    'Check each character in the formula¶
    For i = 1 To Len(newFormula)¶
        posStart = i¶
        'whether it's numeric¶
        'accumulate the numerals to get¶
        'complete number¶
        Do While IsNumeric(Mid(newFormula, i, 1))¶
            nrToChange = nrToChange & (Mid(newFormula, i, 1))¶
            i = i + 1¶
        Loop¶
        'If there's a number¶
        If Len(nrToChange) > 0 Then¶
            'increment that number and replace the original¶
            newFormula = Mid(newFormula, 1, posStart - 1) _¶
              & CStr(CLng(nrToChange) + rowChange) _¶
              & Mid(newFormula, i)¶
        End If¶
        nrToChange = ""¶
    Next¶
    UpdateFormula = newFormula¶
End Function¶
' * * * * *¶
Function SelectionIsValid(sel As Word.Selection) As Boolean¶
    SelectionIsValid = False¶
    If sel.Information(wdWithInTable) Then¶
        If Selection.Cells(1).Range.Fields.Count >= 1 Then¶
            If Selection.Cells(1).Range.Fields(1).Type _¶
              = wdFieldExpression Then¶
                SelectionIsValid = True¶
            End If¶
        End If¶
    End If¶
End Function¶
```

Wrd

View the Appendix to learn how to store this procedure in a UserForm.

```
Option explicit¶
' * * * * *¶
Private Sub btnAddToList_Click()¶
    If Me.txtFieldCode.SelLength > 1 Then¶
        lstFormulas.AddItem Me.txtFieldCode.SelText¶
    End If¶
End Sub¶
' * * * * *¶
Private Sub btnCancel_Click()¶
    Me.Hide¶
    DoUnload¶
End Sub¶
' * * * * *¶
Private Sub btnCopy_Click()¶
    Me.Hide¶
    CopyFormula¶
End Sub¶
```


Follow these steps:

1. Copy the first section of code to a module in a template or in Normal.dot. The second section of code goes in a UserForm. Transfer the UserForm, frmCopyFormula, to the same project either by using the Organizer or by dragging the UserForm in the Visual Basic Editor (VBE) to the template's project.

2. In the text box at the top of the dialog box, select the part of the formula that should be modified. Click the "Add to list" button. Note that text can be selected in the text box, but cannot be edited.

   The tool checks for the presence of the entire formula that is added to the list; for example, (A2 * A3). Only those parts of the formula that exactly match will be changed. Any other parts of the formula containing these cell references will not be changed unless they are also added to the list.

3. Repeat the above step for every separate part of the formula that should be modified. Click on the document. Select the cells to which the formula should be copied. Click the button "COPY FORMULA".

Using Calendar Wizard

Using this procedure, you can generate a calendar page for the specified month and year.

Scenario: Creating a calendar in Word is relatively easy technically: just set it up in a table. Of course, the task involves a lot of repetitive work, numbering the cells, and applying borders and shading. In other words, the perfect task for a macro.

One issue when using a Word table as an electronic calendar is that the entire cell is selected when tabbing through the days. It is all too easy to delete the date number or inadvertently incorporate it into the text entry.

Another aspect that sometimes needs to be considered is entering data from a databank or other application or extracting information from the Word calendar in order to use it elsewhere.

Example file:
W016

Wrd

This tool addresses all of the above problems. The calendar page is generated automatically based on the month and year typed into the InputBox. A new line character follows each number, and a form field is inserted on this line. The document is then protected, with the result that text can be typed only in the form fields; there is no danger of deleting the number or of typing text "around" it.

Tip: Each form field is bookmarked, so a macro or an outside application can open the document and extract the information. It is also possible to activate the Save data only for forms option in Tools | Options | Save to create a tab-delimited text file of the form's content.

Wrd

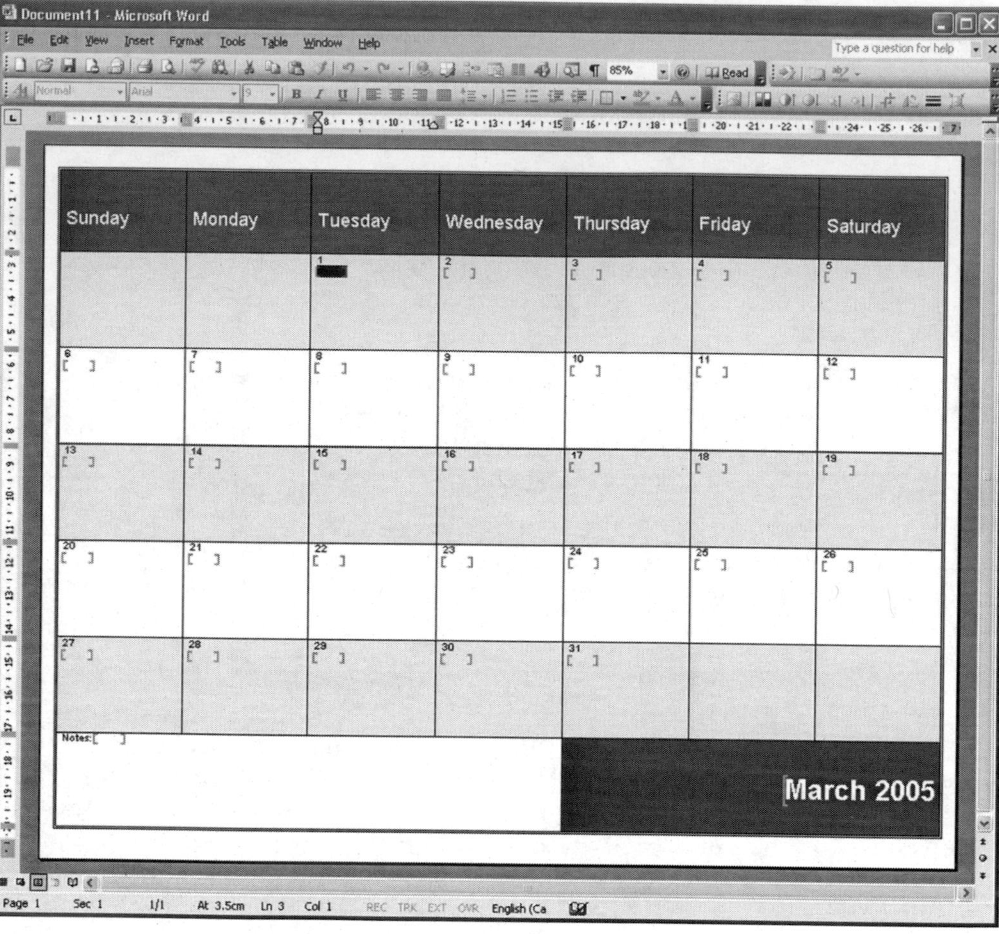

Figure 53 – Calendar Wizard

View the Appendix to learn how to store this procedure in a Standard module.

```
Option explicit¶
' * * * * *¶
Sub CreateCalendar()¶
    'Variable declaration¶
    Dim doc As Word.Document¶
    Dim tbl As Word.Table¶
    Dim rng As Word.Range¶
    Dim startDate As String¶
    Dim dat As Date¶
    Dim In1_4 As Single¶
```

```
    'Number of points in a quarter inch¶
    In1_4 = InchesToPoints(0.25)¶
    'Reduce screen flicker¶
    Application.ScreenUpdating = False¶
    'Loop until the user has entered a valid date¶
    Do¶
        startDate = InputBox( _¶
           "Enter the desired date in the form 'Month Year'." _¶
           & vbCr & "Example: January 2005")¶
        'The user clicked Cancel or didn't enter anything¶
        If startDate = "" Then Exit Sub¶
    Loop While Not IsDate(startDate)¶
    dat = CVDate(startDate)¶
    'Create new document; make page settings¶
    Set doc = Documents.Add¶
    With doc.PageSetup¶
        .PaperSize = wdPaperLetter¶
        .Orientation = wdOrientLandscape¶
        .RightMargin = In1_4¶
        .LeftMargin = In1_4¶
        .TopMargin = In1_4¶
        .BottomMargin = In1_4¶
    End With¶
    Set tbl = InsertCalendarTable(doc)¶
    FillCalendar tbl, dat¶
    FormatCalendar tbl¶
    SetViewOptions doc¶
End Sub¶
' * * * * *¶
Function InsertCalendarTable(doc As Word.Document) _¶
   As Word.Table¶
   'Variable declaration¶
   Dim tbl As Word.Table¶
   Dim cel As Word.Cell¶
   Dim nrRows As Long¶
   Dim nrCols As Long¶
   Dim counter As Long¶
   'Row 1: weekdays; rows 2-6 each week in the month¶
   'Row 7: space for notes and month label¶
   nrRows = 7¶
   nrCols = 7¶
    'For Word 2000 and later¶
    Set tbl = doc.Tables.Add(Range:=doc.Range, _¶
      NumRows:=nrRows, NumColumns:=nrCols, _¶
      DefaultTableBehavior:=wdWord8TableBehavior)¶
    'For Word 97¶
    'Set tbl = doc.Tables.Add(Range:=doc.Range, NumRows:=nrRows, _¶
      NumColumns:=nrCols)¶
```

Wrd

```
    'All rows same height, to fill page¶
    tbl.Rows.HeightRule = wdRowHeightExactly¶
    With doc.PageSetup¶
        tbl.Rows.Height = _¶
          ((.PageHeight - .TopMargin - .BottomMargin) _¶
          / nrRows)¶
    End With¶
    'Enter days of the week in top row¶
    For Each cel In tbl.Rows(1).Cells¶
        counter = counter + 1¶
        cel.Range.text = Format(weekDay(counter), "dddd")¶
    Next cel¶
    Set InsertCalendarTable = tbl¶
End Function¶
' * * * * *¶
Sub FillCalendar(tbl As Word.Table, dat As Date)¶
    'Variable declaration¶
    Dim startWeekDay As Long¶
    Dim nrDays As Long¶
    Dim monthName As String¶
    Dim nrRows As Long¶
    Dim nrCols As Long¶
    Dim cel As Word.Cell¶
    Dim ffld As Word.FormField¶
    Dim counter As Long¶
    nrRows = tbl.Rows.Count¶
    nrCols = tbl.Columns.Count¶
    startWeekDay = weekDay(dat)¶
    'Calculate the number of days in the specified month¶
    nrDays = DateDiff("d", dat, DateAdd("m", 1, dat))¶
    monthName = Format(dat, "MMMM") & " " & _¶
      Format(dat, "yyyy")¶
    'Start in the cell corresponding to first¶
    'weekday of the specified month¶
    tbl.Rows(2).Cells(startWeekDay).Select¶
    'Number the days of the month and¶
    'insert a formfield for text entry¶
    For counter = 1 To nrDays¶
        With Selection¶
            .Collapse wdCollapseStart¶
            .Font.Bold = True¶
            .TypeText counter¶
            .Font.Bold = False¶
            'New line¶
            .TypeText Chr$(11)¶
            Set ffld = .FormFields.Add( _¶
              Range:=.Range, Type:=wdFieldFormTextInput)¶
            ffld.name = Format(DateAdd("d", (counter - 1), _¶
            dat), "MMM_DD_YYYY")¶
            .Cells(1).Range.Next(wdCell, 1).Select¶
        End With¶
```

```
    Next¶
    'Enter month name bottom right¶
    'Merge cells for "Notes", bottom left unless¶
    'Month (except February) starts on Fri or Sat¶
    'then the Notes space is top left¶
    If (startWeekDay = 6 Or startWeekDay = 7) _¶
      And (nrDays >= 30) Then¶
        Set cel = tbl.Cell(2, 1)¶
        MergeAndLabelCell cel, "Notes", "Notes: ", 2, 5¶
        InsertFormFieldAtEndOfCell cel, "Notes"¶
        Set cel = tbl.Cell(nrRows, 5)¶
        MergeAndLabelCell cel, "Month", monthName, _¶
          nrRows, nrCols¶
    Else¶
        Set cel = tbl.Cell(nrRows, 1)¶
        MergeAndLabelCell cel, "Notes", "Notes: ", nrRows, 4¶
        InsertFormFieldAtEndOfCell cel, "Notes"¶
        Set cel = tbl.Cell(nrRows, 2)¶
        MergeAndLabelCell cel, "Month", monthName, _¶
          nrRows, cel.Range.Rows(1).Cells.Count¶
    End If¶
End Sub¶
' * * * * *¶
Sub MergeAndLabelCell(ByVal cel As Word.Cell, _¶
  Label As String, text As String, _¶
  lastCellRow As Long, lastCellCol As Long)¶
    cel.Merge mergeto:= _¶
      cel.Range.Tables(1).Cell(lastCellRow, lastCellCol)¶
    cel.Range.Bookmarks.Add name:=Label, Range:=cel.Range¶
    cel.Range.text = text¶
End Sub¶
' * * * * *¶
Sub InsertFormFieldAtEndOfCell(cel As Word.Cell, _¶
  name As String)¶
    'Variable declaration¶
    Dim rng As Word.Range¶
    Dim ffld As Word.FormField¶
    Set rng = cel.Range¶
    rng.Collapse wdCollapseEnd¶
    rng.MoveEnd wdCharacter, -1¶
    Set ffld = rng.FormFields.Add(Range:=rng, _¶
      Type:=wdFieldFormTextInput)¶
    ffld.name = name¶
End Sub¶
' * * * * *¶
Sub FormatCalendar(tbl As Word.Table)¶
    'Variable declaration¶
    Dim rng As Word.Range¶
    Dim counter As Long¶
    Dim lastRow As Word.Row¶
    Set rng = tbl.Range¶
```

Wrd

```
    Set lastRow = tbl.Rows(tbl.Rows.Count)¶
    'Set basic font and font size for table¶
    rng.Font.name = "Arial"¶
    rng.Font.Size = 9¶
    With tbl¶
        'Shade every second row light gray¶
        For counter = 2 To tbl.Rows.Count Step 2¶
            .Rows(counter).Shading.Texture = wdTextureNone¶
            .Rows(counter).Shading.BackgroundPatternColor _¶
              = wdColorGray10¶
        Next counter¶
        'Put double borders around the outside¶
        .Borders.OutsideLineStyle = wdLineStyleDouble¶
        'And single borders around the cells in the table¶
        .Borders.InsideLineStyle = wdLineStyleSingle¶
        'First row contains names of days of week¶
        With .Rows(1)¶
            'Shade dark gray with large, white text¶
            .Shading.BackgroundPatternColor = wdColorGray70¶
            .Range.Font.Size = 16¶
            .Range.Font.Color = wdColorWhite¶
            'Center text vertically¶
            'Since Word97 doesn't support vertical¶
            'cell alignment, calculate it¶
            .Range.ParagraphFormat.SpaceBefore = _¶
              (.Height - 16) / 2¶
            'First row smaller so everything fits on the page¶
            .Height = .Height - 10¶
        End With¶
        'Last cell contains name of month and year¶
        'Dark gray with very large, white, bold text¶
        With lastRow.Cells(lastRow.Cells.Count)¶
            .Range.Font.Size = 24¶
            .Range.Font.Bold = True¶
            .Range.Font.Color = wdColorWhite¶
            .Range.ParagraphFormat.Alignment = wdAlignParagraphRight¶
            .Range.ParagraphFormat.SpaceBefore = _¶
              (.Height - 24) / 2¶
            .Shading.BackgroundPatternColor = wdColorGray70¶
        End With¶
    End With¶
End Sub¶
' * * * * *¶
Sub SetViewOptions(doc As Word.Document)¶
    'Suppress second page by reducing¶
    'font size of last paragraph mark¶
    doc.Paragraphs.Last.Range.Font.Size = 1¶
    'Show whole page on screen¶
    doc.ActiveWindow.Panes(1).Zooms(3).PageFit _¶
      = wdPageFitFullPage¶
```

```
    'Go to top of doc¶
    Selection.HomeKey wdStory¶
    'Protect so form fields can be used¶
    doc.Protect Type:=wdAllowOnlyFormFields¶
    'Suppress field shading so that it doesn't print¶
    'And make sure bookmarks are displayed so that¶
    'user can see the fields¶
    doc.FormFields.Shaded = False¶
    doc.ActiveWindow.View.ShowBookmarks = True¶
End Sub¶
```

Formatting Your Calendar

Changing the Page Settings

Wrd

You can change the page formatting if you desire a different paper size or different margins.

Adjust the margin settings, paper size, etc., for the calendar sheet in the block of code beginning With doc.PageSetup in the procedure 'CreateCalendar'.

Note that margin settings must be in points. The value used by 'In1_4' (representing 1/4 inch) is generated using the 'InchesToPoints' function provided by Word's object model. To change this value, either type the values for the margins in directly or change the value assignment in the line In1_4 = InchesToPoints(0.25).

With the default settings, the first row is formatted dark gray and every second row light gray. The text is formatted white in the dark gray regions; black otherwise. This formatting is applied by the procedure 'FormatCalendar' and can be adjusted as follows:

Changing the Font

Change the font and font size for the entire calendar by assigning the desired values to these code lines:

```
rng.Font.name = "Arial"¶
rng.Font.Size = 9¶
```

The alternate row shading can be changed by substituting the value for Rows(counter).Shading.BackgroundPatternColor = wdColorGray10.

Changing the Borders

The style of the outside and inside borders can be changed in the code lines

```
.Borders.OutsideLineStyle = wdLineStyleDouble¶
.Borders.InsideLineStyle = wdLineStyleSingle¶
```

The attributes specific to the first row are found in the block under With .Rows(1).

To change the shading, font and font size here, as well, adjust the appropriate code lines as described above.

Wrd

Finally, to change how the cell at the bottom right is formatted under the block beginning With lastRow.Cells(lastRow.Cells.Count), the same instructions apply as above.

Note: For shading and borders, it is recommended that you delete the equal sign and everything to the right of it. Then type = again; Intellisense should display a list of supported shading values from which to select.

Inserting a Picture with Caption

With this procedure, you can insert a picture, format it with text wrapping, and add a caption.

Scenario: Inserting pictures into Word and adding a caption involves a number of individual steps. A much more efficient approach is a macro that prompts for choosing a picture from the folder of choice, inserts the picture, and then prompts for a caption.

In addition, if the text should wrap around the picture, it needs to be inserted into a frame. Why a frame? Because if the picture is formatted directly with text wrapping, the caption is placed in a text box.

Example file:
W017

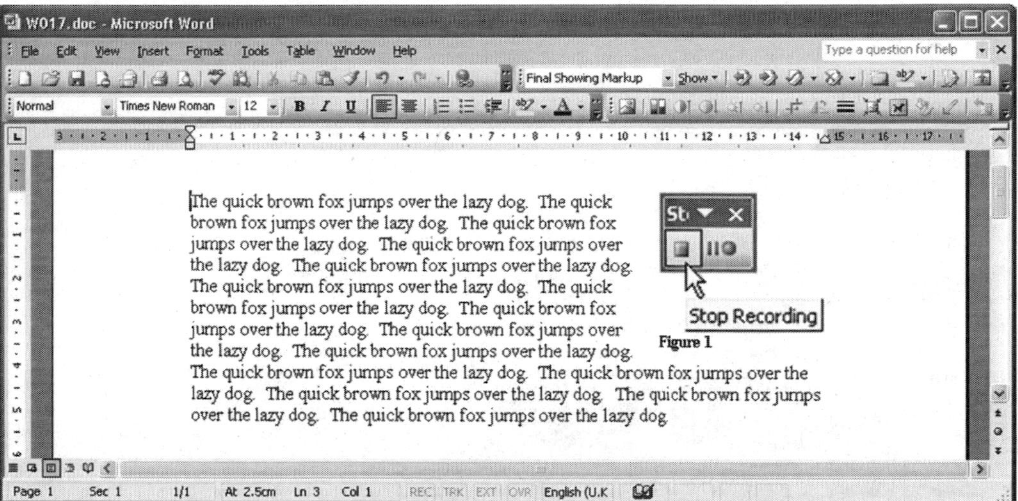

Figure 54 – Inserted Picture with Caption

Note: Word's cross-referencing feature or the Table of Contents generator does not pick up Captions in text boxes. What's more, if a picture is moved, its caption in a text box will not move with it. Placing both the picture and its caption in a frame solves these problems. The same objections apply to using a Canvas in Word 2002 or 2003.

View the Appendix to learn how to store this procedure in a Standard module.

```
Option explicit¶
' * * * * *¶
'Location where user selects graphic¶
Const StartFolder As String = "" '"C:\test\"¶
'Set how the picture is saved in the doc¶
Const LinkGraphic As Boolean = False¶
Const SaveInDoc As Boolean = True¶
'Set how frame and picture size¶
Const LimitPictureWidth As Long = _¶
  wdFrameExact 'wdFrameAuto¶
Const LimitPictureHeight As Long = _¶
  wdFrameAuto 'wdFrameExact¶
```

```
' * * * * *¶
Sub InsertPictureWithCaption()¶
    'Variable declaration¶
    Dim FileToInsert As String¶
    Dim rng As Word.Range¶
    Dim frm As Word.Frame¶
    FileToInsert = GetFileName¶
    'The user cancelled¶
    If Len(FileToInsert) = 0 Then Exit Sub¶
    Set rng = Selection.Range.Paragraphs(1).Range¶
    'When in a paragraph with text¶
    'move to the top, so that the frame¶
    'will be associated with this paragraph¶
    'and insert an empty paragraph¶
    If Len(rng.Paragraphs(1).Range.Text) <> 1 Then¶
        rng.Collapse wdCollapseStart¶
        rng.Text = vbCr¶
    End If¶
    'Put a frame around the paragraph¶
    Set frm = rng.Frames.Add(rng)¶
    'format the frame¶
    FormatFrame frm¶
    'Insert a picture into it¶
    rng.InlineShapes.AddPicture _¶
      FileName:=FileToInsert, _¶
      LinkToFile:=LinkGraphic, _¶
      SaveWithDocument:=SaveInDoc, _¶
      Range:=rng¶
    If frm Is Nothing Then¶
        AddaCaptionInaFrame rng¶
    Else¶
        AddaCaptionInaFrame frm.Range¶
    End If¶
        'Moves insertion point out of frame¶
        Selection.MoveRight Unit:=wdCharacter, Count:=1¶
End Sub¶
' * * * * *¶
Function GetFileName() As String¶
    'Variable declaration¶
    Dim dlg As Word.Dialog¶
    Set dlg = Dialogs(wdDialogInsertPicture)¶
    With dlg¶
        .Display¶
    End With¶
    GetFileName = dlg.Name¶
End Function¶
```

Wrd

```
' * * * * *¶
Function FormatFrame(ByRef frm As Word.Frame)¶
    'Set the borders¶
    frm.Borders.Enable = False¶
    If frm.Borders.Enable = True Then¶
        With frm.Borders¶
            .OutsideColorIndex = wdBlack¶
            .OutsideLineStyle = wdLineStyleSingle¶
            .OutsideLineWidth = wdLineWidth050pt¶
        End With¶
    End If¶
    'Determine how the frame sizes¶
    'The frame can size a picture proportionally¶
    'if an exact height OR width is set,¶
    'and let the other dimension size automatically¶
    'Use if the frame should be a certain height¶
    frm.HeightRule = LimitPictureHeight¶
    If LimitPictureHeight <> wdFrameAuto Then¶
        frm.HeightRule = LimitPictureHeight¶
        frm.Height = InchesToPoints(3)¶
    End If¶
    'Use if the frame should be a certain width¶
    frm.WidthRule = LimitPictureWidth¶
    If LimitPictureWidth <> wdFrameAuto Then¶
        frm.WidthRule = wdFrameAtLeast¶
        frm.Width = InchesToPoints(1.5)¶
    End If¶
    frm.RelativeHorizontalPosition = _¶
      wdRelativeHorizontalPositionColumn¶
    frm.HorizontalPosition = wdFrameRight¶
    'Corresponds to "Move with text"¶
    frm.RelativeVerticalPosition = _¶
      wdRelativeVerticalPositionParagraph¶
    frm.VerticalPosition = 0¶
    frm.LockAnchor = False¶
    frm.TextWrap = True¶
End Function¶
' * * * * *¶
Sub AddaCaptionInaFrame(rng As Word.Range)¶
    'Move to the end of the frame¶
    rng.Collapse wdCollapseEnd¶
    'Add a new line¶
    rng.InsertAfter vbCr¶
    'Select just that line¶
    If rng.Frames.Count = 1 Then¶
        'with frame¶
        rng.Collapse wdCollapseEnd¶
    Else¶
        'without frame¶
        rng.Collapse wdCollapseStart¶
    End If¶
```

Wrd

```
    rng.Select¶
    'Let the user add a caption¶
    Dialogs(wdDialogInsertCaption).Show¶
End Sub¶
```

Making Changes

You can change a number of items in this procedure.

Linking in a Picture

Wrd

Use the following to specify how the graphic is inserted and saved in the document:

```
Const LinkGraphic¶
Const SaveInDoc¶
```

In order to link to the file, set the first of these to True. In this case, the latter may be True or False (False will result in a smaller file size.) If Const LinkGraphic is set to False, then SaveInDoc must be set to True.

Inserting a Picture Without a Frame

To use the macro to simply insert pictures from the folder of choice, with default preferred settings, comment out the lines.

```
Set frm = rng.Frames.Add(rng)¶
FormatFrame frm.¶
```

Leaving off the Caption

To leave off the caption, comment out these lines by placing an apostrophe in front of each.

```
If frm Is Nothing Then¶
AddaCaptionInaFrame rng¶
Else¶
AddaCaptionInaFrame frm.Range¶
End If¶
```

Controlling the Picture Size

Inserting a picture into a frame, one side of which is set to an exact size, causes the picture to resize itself proportionally to fit. The other dimension should be set to "AutoFit".

Set the Const LimitPictureWidth and Const LimitPictureHeight values to the combination of wdFrameAuto and wdFrameExact that is preferred.

Setting Exact Height and Width

Set the height and/or width in inches for the frame in the 'FormatFrame' procedure by changing the numbers in parentheses in these lines:

```
frm.Height = InchesToPoints(3)¶
frm.Width = InchesToPoints(3)¶
```


Adding Borders

Put a border around the frame by setting frm.Borders.Enable to True.

Once this is done, the values under With frm.Borders takes effect. In order to change the color, line style, or line width, delete from the equals sign (=) to the end of the line. Then, type the equals sign again and Intellisense should show a list of values to choose from.

Positioning the Frame

The values for the following correspond to settings in the dialog box Format Frame. Here, again, deleting the equal sign and the text following it, then typing the equal sign again will present a list of valid values.

```
RelativeHorizontalPosition
HorizontalPosition
RelativeVerticalPosition
VerticalPosition
```

Frames can be formatted relative to the page, both vertically and horizontally, or relative to the text to which they are anchored (equivalent to activating "Move with text").

Wrapping Text Around the Frame

This is controlled by setting frm.TextWrap to True or False.

Changing the Path for Graphics Files

Change the path for the Const StartFolder to the folder where the graphics to be used are located. This won't disallow navigating to any other path; the Insert Picture dialog box simply uses this path as a starting point. To use the default file location set for a particular installation of Word, just remove the text between the quotes (but leave the quote pairs).

Tips: This code is constructed modularly to make it easy to customize the way the macro works, so that it can best suit various needs.

When using this macro with a caption, only set the width. Setting the height cuts off the caption.

Associating a Picture with a Page

Using a graphic's name, this procedure moves that graphic to the page where it should always reside.

Example file:
W018

Scenario: Word for Windows was originally conceived in the late 1980s purely as a word processing program. As users' expectations increased, Microsoft added numerous layout capabilities to it. One piece of functionality it is still missing, however, is the ability to "lock" a graphical object to a particular page.

Graphical objects formatted with text wrap are always anchored to a paragraph. They always appear on the same page as that paragraph. So even if an object has been positioned relative to the page (Move with text is turned off), as edits are made to the text, the object may move to another page.

Although this is "expected behavior" in Word, it can be extremely irritating. Repositioning the graphics is time consuming and somewhat error prone.

This tool can quickly reposition all graphics formatted with text wrap that are positioned relative to a page. It also includes a form for assigning names.

View the Appendix to learn how to store this procedure in a Standard module.

```
Option explicit¶
' * * * * *¶
Sub ShowGraphicName()¶
    frmNameGraphic.Show¶
End Sub¶
' * * * * *¶
Sub MoveGraphicToPage()¶
    'Variable declaration¶
    Dim shp As Word.Shape¶
    Dim PageNr As Long¶
    Dim iPos As Long¶
    For Each shp In ActiveDocument.Shapes¶
        'Don't process canvas content¶
        'Only valid in Word 2002, 2003¶
        If Not shp.Child Then¶
          With shp¶
            Select Case .RelativeVerticalPosition¶
                 'Positioned relative to the page¶
                Case wdRelativeVerticalPositionPage, _¶
                  wdRelativeVerticalPositionMargin¶
                    'Extract the page number;¶
                    'it's the 5th character in the name¶
                    iPos = 4¶
                   PageNr = ExtractNumber(shp.Name, iPos)¶
                    'Compare the current page number with¶
                    'the specified one¶
                    If shp.Anchor.Information(wdActiveEndPageNumber) _¶
                        <> Val(PageNr) Then¶
                            'Move the graphic to the correct page¶
                            'using the Clipboard¶
                            MoveGraphicViaClipboard shp, PageNr¶
                    End If¶
                Case wdRelativeVerticalPositionLine, _¶
                     wdRelativeVerticalPositionParagraph¶
                     'It's formatted to move with the text and¶
                     'is therefore not linked with a specific page¶
                Case Else¶
                'unknown Enum constant¶
            End Select¶
        End With¶
      End If¶
    Next shp¶
End Sub¶
' * * * * *¶
'Extract a number from a string,¶
'Starting at the offset position plus1¶
'until there are no more numerals¶
Function ExtractNumber(ByVal sString As String, _¶
```

```
  ByVal Offset As Long) As Long¶
    'iNr is declared as type "Variant" because¶
    'it can contain numbers as well as strings¶
    'Variable declaration¶
    Dim iNr As Variant¶
    Do¶
        Offset = Offset + 1¶
        iNr = iNr & Mid(sString, Offset, 1)¶
    Loop While IsNumeric(iNr)¶
    ExtractNumber = Left(iNr, Len(iNr) - 1)¶
End Function¶
' * * * * *¶
Sub MoveGraphicViaClipboard(shp As Word.Shape, _¶
  PageNr As Long)¶
    'Variable declaration¶
    Dim rngPage As Word.Range¶
    Dim rngPageStart As Word.Range¶
    Dim vw As Word.View¶
    Dim lViewType As Long¶
    Dim bWholePage As Boolean¶
    'Graphics can only be moved in the¶
    'Print Layout view. Save the user's¶
    'current view and restore it when done¶
    Set vw = shp.Parent.ActiveWindow.View¶
    lViewType = vw.Type¶
    vw.Type = wdPrintView¶
    'Turn off hidden text as that will¶
    'falsify page numbers¶
    vw.ShowHiddenText = False¶
    If Val(Application.Version) >= 10 Then¶
        'Graphics will be positioned incorrectly¶
        'if the target range is not in view¶
        'In Word 2002 and 2003 be sure to¶
        'display the top and bottom margins!¶
        bWholePage = vw.DisplayPageBoundaries¶
        vw.DisplayPageBoundaries = True¶
    End If¶
    'Put the graphic on the clipboard¶
    shp.Select¶
    Selection.Cut¶
    'Go to the required page¶
    Selection.GoTo What:=wdGoToPage, _¶
      Which:=wdGoToAbsolute, _¶
      Count:=PageNr¶
    Set rngPage = ActiveDocument.Bookmarks("\Page").Range¶
    'If the target page is the last page of the document¶
    'make sure to include the last paragraph mark¶
    If rngPage.Information(wdActiveEndPageNumber) = _¶
      rngPage.Information(wdNumberOfPagesInDocument) Then _¶
      rngPage.MoveEnd wdParagraph, 1¶
    Set rngPageStart = rngPage.Duplicate¶
```

```
    'Get the range for first para's starting point¶
    rngPageStart.End = rngPage.Paragraphs(1).Range.Start¶
    'If the beginning of the first para¶
    'is on the preceding page, then the¶
    'graphic must be anchored to the second para¶
    'in order for it to appear on this page¶
    If Val(rngPageStart.Information(wdActiveEndPageNumber)) _¶
        < PageNr Then¶
        rngPage.Paragraphs(2).Range.Paste¶
    Else¶
        rngPage.Paragraphs(1).Range.Paste¶
    End If¶
    vw.Type = lViewType¶
    If Application.Version > 10 Then vw.DisplayPageBoundaries _¶
      = bWholePage¶
End Sub¶
```


View the Appendix to learn how to store this procedure in a UserForm.

```
Option explicit¶
' * * * * *¶
Private Sub cmdCancel_Click()¶
    Unload Me¶
End Sub¶
' * * * * *¶
Private Sub cmdOK_Click()¶
    ChangeGraphicName¶
    Unload Me¶
End Sub¶
' * * * * *¶
Private Sub UserForm_Activate()¶
    'Variable declaration¶
    Dim sShapeName As String¶
    sShapeName = GetGraphicName¶
    If Len(sShapeName) = 0 Then¶
        MsgBox "You haven't selected a graphic." & vbCr & vbCr & _¶
            "Please select a graphic and try again.", _¶
            vbOKOnly + vbCritical¶
        Unload Me¶
        Exit Sub¶
    Else¶
```

```
        Select Case Selection.ShapeRange(1).RelativeVerticalPosition¶
             'Positioned relative to the page¶
            Case wdRelativeVerticalPositionPage,
wdRelativeVerticalPositionMargin¶
                If Left(sShapeName, 4) <> "Page" Then¶
                    sShapeName = "Page" & _¶
                        Selection.Information(wdActiveEndPageNumber) _¶
                        & "_" & sShapeName¶
                End If¶
            Case wdRelativeVerticalPositionLine, _¶
                 wdRelativeVerticalPositionParagraph¶
                 'It's formatted to move with the text and¶
                 'is therefore not linked with a specific page¶
            Case Else¶
            'unknown Enum constant¶
        End Select¶
        txtGrafikName.Text = sShapeName¶
    End If¶
End Sub¶
' * * * * *¶
Sub ChangeGraphicName()¶
    Selection.ShapeRange(1).Name = txtGrafikName.Text¶
End Sub¶
Function GetGraphicName() As String¶
    If Selection.ShapeRange.Count > 0 Then¶
        GetGraphicName = Selection.ShapeRange(1).Name¶
    Else¶
        GetGraphicName = vbNullString¶
    End If¶
End Function¶
```

Wrd

Copy the standard module to a document, to a template, or to Normal.dot. Transfer the user form 'frmNameGraphic' to the same project, either by using the Organizer or by dragging it in the Visual Basic Editor (VBE) to the template's project.

To prepare a graphic so that the tool will recognize it:

1. First, format it with text wrapping (in the Layout tab of the Format dialog box).
2. Then, position it relative to the page (click Advanced in the Layout tab of the Format dialog box, choose the Picture Position tab, and deactivate Move with the text).

Run the macro 'ShowGraphicName' and make sure the word "Page" plus the page number on which the graphic should appear are at the beginning of the graphic's name. Example: Page3 Picture of me

When you have finished editing the text, run the 'MoveGraphicToPage' macro to reposition the graphics.

Forms: Suppressing New Paragraphs in Form Fields

This procedure disables the Enter key when the user is typing in form fields. It also demonstrates assigning a macro to a keyboard shortcut.

Example file: W019

Wrd

Scenario: As a word processing program, Word is primarily concerned with text flow. The Textinput type of form field reflects this—by default, as much text as desired can be typed into the form. The form field wraps like any other text and displays its content on multiple lines.

While this is appropriate for some applications, forms that mimic paper forms need to restrict the amount of space a form field can occupy. Word provides no direct functionality to accomplish the task; most often, the form fields are placed in table cells with an exact height and width setting. In some cases, it may be desirable to prevent the Enter key from creating a new paragraph in the form field, or the Shift+Enter key combination from generating a new line. However, if the form contains unprotected sections where the user can type and edit freely, these key combinations should be allowed to work normally in these regions.

This set of macros dynamically changes the two keyboard assignments, depending on where the selection in the document is located.

View the Appendix to learn how to store this procedure in a Standard module.

```
Option explicit¶
' * * * * *¶
Sub ActivateKeyAssignmentsInCurrentFile()¶
     ' Changes the key assignments for the document¶
     ' or template which is active when the macro is run!¶
     ' To return the file to default Word behavior¶
     ' run the macro DeactivateEnterAndNewLineKeyAssignments¶
    CustomizationContext = ActiveDocument¶
   ' Assign the DisableEnterKeyInFormFields macro¶
   ' to the Enter key for this document¶
   KeyBindings.Add KeyCode:=wdKeyReturn, _¶
     KeyCategory:=wdKeyCategoryMacro,
Command:="DisableEnterKeyInFormFields"¶
   ' Assign the DisableNewLineInFormFields macro¶
   ' to the Shift+Enter key combintation in this document¶
   KeyBindings.Add KeyCode:=BuildKeyCode(wdKeyShift, wdKeyReturn), _¶
     KeyCategory:=wdKeyCategoryMacro,
Command:="DisableNewLineInFormFields"¶
End Sub¶
' * * * * *¶
Sub DisableEnterKeyInFormFields()¶
     ' Check whether the document is protected for forms¶
     ' and whether the protection is active in the current section.¶
     ' If insertion point is not in a protected section¶
     ' or a form field, allow new paragraphs to be inserted¶
   If ActiveDocument.ProtectionType = wdAllowOnlyFormFields And _¶
     Selection.Sections(1).ProtectedForForms Then¶
     Exit Sub¶
   End If¶
   Selection.TypeText Chr$(13)¶
End Sub¶
' * * * * *¶
Sub DisableNewLineInFormFields()¶
   If ActiveDocument.ProtectionType = wdAllowOnlyFormFields And _¶
     Selection.Sections(1).ProtectedForForms Then¶
     Exit Sub¶
   End If¶
   Selection.TypeText Chr$(11)¶
End Sub¶
' * * * * *¶
Sub DeactivateEnterAndNewLineKeyAssignments()¶
    CustomizationContext = ActiveDocument¶
    FindKey(BuildKeyCode(wdKeyReturn)).Clear¶
    FindKey(BuildKeyCode(wdKeyShift, wdKeyReturn)).Clear¶
End Sub¶
```

Follow these steps:

1. Copy 'DisableEnterKeyInFormFields' and 'DisableNewLineInFormFields' to the document or template in which the Enter and Shift+Enter keys should be disabled when the focus is in a form field.
2. Copy 'ActivateKeyAssignmentsInCurrentFile' and 'DeactivateEnterAndNewLineKeyAssignments' to the Normal.dot or any other global template add-in.
3. View the document or template into which 'DisableEnterKeyInFormFields' and 'DisableNewLineInFormFields' were copied.
4. Run 'ActivateKeyAssignmentsInCurrentFile' to map the Enter and Shift+Enter keys to the macros 'DisableEnterKeyInFormFields' and 'DisableNewLineInFormFields' in the active document or template.
5. In order to deactivate these assignments, view the document or template and run 'DeactivateEnterAndNewLineKeyAssignments'.

This tool consists of two sets of macros. The first pair, 'DisableEnterKeyInFormFields' and 'DisableNewLineInFormFields', controls the Enter and Shift+Enter key behaviors in the target document or template. The second pair, 'ActivateKeyAssignmentsInCurrentFile' and 'DeactivateEnterAndNewLineKeyAssignments' makes and removes the key assignments to the Enter and Shift+Enter key combinations in the target document.

After the key assignments have been made, 'ActivateKeyAssignmentsInCurrentFile' is no longer needed; 'DeactivateEnterAndNewLineKeyAssignments' is only required if a mistake is made and it is necessary to restore the Enter and Shift+Enter key combinations to the default state.

Note: A key combination assignment in a template carries over to all documents created from that template, as long as the template is available to the document.

Forms: Formatting Text Input in Form Fields

This procedure lets you apply bold, italic, and color formatting to the text entered in form fields and also demonstrates error handling.

Note: This tool currently provides for bold, italic, and underline formatting. The adventurous coder can expand it to include other types of formatting, by following the same pattern.

Scenario: Word's forms functionality is designed to allow text input only; no formatting is supported and formatting can only be applied in unprotected sections. Sometimes, this is exactly what is wanted. However, in some forms, allowing the user to apply simple formatting, such as bold or italics, is the desired functionality.

Example file:
W020

View the Appendix to learn how to store this procedure in a Standard module.

```
Option explicit¶
' * * * * *¶
'If the form has more than one table¶
'set this value to the number of the¶
'table to process with this code¶
Const TableIndex As Long = 1¶
'Name of the AutoText entry that contains¶
'the row that should be inserted¶
Const AutoTextName As String = "NewRow"¶
'Enter the number of rows that should remain¶
'below the row being inserted For example,¶
'this sample table has one row,¶
'the Totals row, that should stay at the end¶
'This and the password constant are shared¶
'with the DeleteCurrentRow macro¶
Public Const EndRowsIndex As Long = 1¶
'The password to unprotect (leave as is if¶
'not assigning a password to the form¶
Public Const password = ""¶
```

```
' * * * * *¶
Sub InsertNewTableRow()¶
    'Variable declaration¶
    Dim doc As Word.Document¶
    Dim tmpl As Word.Template¶
    Dim tbl As Word.Table¶
    Dim lastRow As Long¶
    Dim ffldName As String¶
    Dim rng As Word.Range¶
    Dim ffld As Word.FormField¶
    Dim nrFields As Long¶
    Dim increment As Long¶
    Dim aFieldNames() As String¶
    Dim counter As Long¶
    Set doc = ActiveDocument¶
    Set tmpl = doc.AttachedTemplate¶
    Set tbl = doc.Tables(TableIndex)¶
    'Calculate the row index after which the¶
    'new row should be inserted¶
    lastRow = tbl.Rows.Count - EndRowsIndex¶
    Set rng = tbl.Rows(lastRow).Range¶
    'Calculate the increment number for the new row¶
    'by picking up the text to the right of¶
    'the underscore just preceding it in the first form field¶
    ffldName = rng.FormFields(1).Name¶
    increment = CLng(Right(ffldName, _¶
      (Len(ffldName) - InStr(ffldName, "_")))) + 1¶
    'Collapse range so that newly inserted row¶
    'follows immediately after the rng-row¶
    rng.Collapse wdCollapseEnd¶
    If doc.ProtectionType <> wdNoProtection Then¶
        doc.Unprotect password:=password¶
    End If¶
    Set rng = tmpl.AutoTextEntries(AutoTextName).Insert( _¶
      Where:=rng, RichText:=True)¶
    'rng.Select¶
    'Store the list of original field names¶
    'in an array so checking against the array¶
    'for the field names used in any calculations¶
    'can be done.¶
    nrFields = rng.FormFields.Count¶
    ReDim aFieldNames(nrFields)¶
    For counter = 1 To nrFields¶
        aFieldNames(counter - 1) = rng.FormFields(counter).Name¶
    Next counter¶
```

Wrd

```
    'Add the increment to the field names, and to¶
    'the field names in any calculation¶
    'Run through from back to front because¶
    'executing the dialog box to force update¶
    'of the .Default property recreates the form field¶
    For counter = nrFields To 1 Step -1¶
        Set ffld = rng.FormFields(counter)¶
        ffld.Name = ffld.Name & "_" & CStr(increment)¶
        If ffld.TextInput.Valid Then¶
            If ffld.TextInput.Type = wdCalculationText Then¶
                ChangeCalculationCode ffld, increment, aFieldNames()¶
                DoEvents¶
            End If¶
        End If¶
    Next counter¶
    doc.Protect Type:=wdAllowOnlyFormFields, noreset:=True,
password:=password¶
    rng.FormFields(1).Select¶
End Sub¶
' * * * * *¶
Sub ChangeCalculationCode(ffld As Word.FormField, _¶
  nr As Long, aFieldNames() As String)¶
    'Variable declaration¶
    Dim calculationCode As String¶
    Dim counter As Long¶
    Dim ffldName As String¶
    calculationCode = ffld.TextInput.Default¶
    'cycle through the base field names that have been¶
    'incremented. If found, add the underscore¶
    'increment value to the field name in the calculation¶
    For counter = 0 To UBound(aFieldNames) - 1¶
        If InStr(calculationCode, aFieldNames(counter)) <> 0 Then¶
            ffldName = aFieldNames(counter)¶
            calculationCode = Left(calculationCode, _¶
              (InStr(calculationCode, ffldName) + Len(ffldName) - 1)) _¶
              & "_" & CStr(nr) & Mid(calculationCode, _¶
              (InStr(calculationCode, ffldName) + Len(ffldName)))¶
        End If¶
    Next¶
    ffld.TextInput.Default = calculationCode¶
    'Select it so that executing the dialog box¶
    'updates the changed calculation formula¶
    ffld.Select¶
    Application.Dialogs(wdDialogFormFieldOptions).Execute¶
    Selection.Range.FormFields(1).TextInput.Clear¶
End Sub¶
```

Wrd

```
Option explicit¶
' * * * * *¶
'First row containing form fields¶
'that should not be deleted¶
Const StartRowIndex As Long = 2¶
' * * * * *¶
Sub DeleteCurrentRow()¶
    'Variable declaration¶
    Dim doc As Word.Document¶
    Dim rng As Word.Range¶
    Dim totalRows As Long¶
    Set rng = Selection.Range¶
    If rng.Information(wdWithInTable) Then¶
        'Make sure user can't accidentally delete¶
        'any rows at the end, such as a totals row¶
        'nor the last remaining "data row" in table¶
        totalRows = rng.Tables(1).Rows.Count¶
        If rng.Rows(1).Index <= totalRows - EndRowsIndex _¶
          And totalRows > StartRowIndex + EndRowsIndex Then¶
            Set doc = rng.Parent¶
            If doc.ProtectionType <> wdNoProtection Then¶
                doc.Unprotect password:=password¶
            End If¶
            rng.Rows(1).Delete¶
            doc.Protect Type:=wdAllowOnlyFormFields, _¶
              noreset:=True, password:=password¶
        End If¶
    End If¶
End Sub¶
```

Follow these steps:

1. Copy the macros into a module in a forms document or in a template from which protected forms are generated. Create a new toolbar and be sure to save it in the same document or template as the macros.
2. Using Tools | Customize | Commands, with the category "Macros" selected, drag each of the format-specific macro names ('FormatBold', 'FormatItalic', and 'FormatUnderline') to the toolbar to create a button for each macro.
3. If the form is protected with a password, and the password is not specified, the form cannot be unprotected so that the macro can apply the formatting. If the form has no password, then the value for the constant should be a zero-length string (""), as in the code procedure example above.

If there is a password on the form, then enter that password at the top of the macro module, such as:

```
Const password as String = "password")¶
```

Changing Other Types of Formatting

As mentioned, this tool can be expanded to include other types of formatting, such as Small Caps or a particular color. For each new addition, follow these steps:

1. Create a format-specific macro following the pattern for the three macros presented above, where a representative term for the desired formatting is substituted, such as for "Underline" in the code ApplyFormat rng, "Underline".
2. Then, in the procedure 'ApplyFormat' create a new "Case" block that references the term, such as Case "Underline".
3. Finally, apply the required formatting to the range (rng) as in rng.Underline = wdUnderlineSingle. For example, in order to apply the color red to the range, the line of code would be rng.Font.Color = wdColorRed.

If you are unsure of the code you need in order to apply a particular format, use the macro recorder to record your steps while applying the formatting. The macro recorder provides, for example, Selection.Font.Bold. Copy the code to the Case block, then change Selection to rng.

Note: This tool does not work satisfactorily with form fields placed in table cells. Word does not allow the user to properly select text when a form field is in a table, so formatting could be applied only to the entire cell, or to the contents from the selection point to the beginning or end of the cell.

Forms: Inserting a New Table Row

Use this procedure to expand the number of rows provided in a table in a protected form.

Example file:
W021

> **Scenario:** Forms are often used to create offers, invoices, and other types of repetitive data entry that are best organized in a table. Knowing in advance how many rows the table should have in any particular form document is not typical.
>
> What's more, such forms may need to perform calculations with the data entered into the form fields. Such calculations are usually performed with the help of the bookmark names assigned to the form fields. Since bookmark names must be unique in a document, this means that each row's form field name has to be incremented, and the formulas adjusted to use these names.

As an example, look at the sample table on the following page. When the document is created, the table consists of three rows: the header row, a single, empty data row, and the totals row. The right-most column calculates Qty * Unit price for each row; the last cell in the table totals this column. The Qty and Unit price fields in each row are named with incrementing numbers: Qty_1, Qty_2, etc. and each Amount field must reference exactly the field names in its row: Qty_1*Price_1, Qty_2*Price_2, etc.

The macro takes care not only of inserting the new rows, but also renames the fields and updates any calculation formulas.

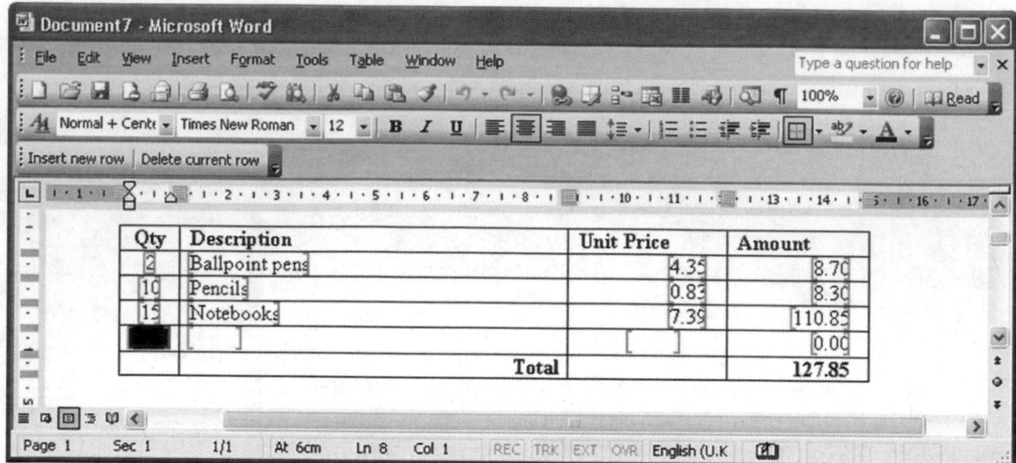

Figure 55 – Auto-inserting Table Rows

View the Appendix to learn how to store this procedure in a Standard module.

```
Option explicit¶
' * * * * *¶
'If the form has more than one table¶
'set this value to the number of the¶
'table to process with this code¶
Const TableIndex As Long = 1¶
'Name of the AutoText entry that contains¶
'the row that should be inserted¶
Const AutoTextName As String = "NewRow"¶
'Enter the number of rows that should remain¶
'below the row being inserted.¶
'For example, this sample table has one row,¶
'the Totals row, that should stay at the end¶
'This and the password constant are shared¶
'with the DeleteCurrentRow macro¶
Public Const EndRowsIndex As Long = 1¶
'The password to unprotect (leave as is if you're¶
'not assigning a password to the form¶
Public Const password = ""¶
' * * * * *¶
Sub InsertNewTableRow()¶
    'Variable declaration¶
    Dim doc As Word.Document¶
    Dim tmpl As Word.Template¶
    Dim tbl As Word.Table¶
    Dim lastRow As Long¶
    Dim ffldName As String¶
```

```
Dim rng As Word.Range¶
Dim ffld As Word.FormField¶
Dim nrFields As Long¶
Dim increment As Long¶
Dim aFieldNames() As String¶
Dim counter As Long¶
Set doc = ActiveDocument¶
Set tmpl = doc.AttachedTemplate¶
Set tbl = doc.Tables(TableIndex)¶
'Calculate the row index after which the¶
'new row should be inserted¶
lastRow = tbl.Rows.Count - EndRowsIndex¶
Set rng = tbl.Rows(lastRow).Range¶
'Calculate the increment number for the new row¶
'by picking up the text to the right of¶
'the underscore just preceding it in the first form field¶
ffldName = rng.FormFields(1).Name¶
increment = CLng(Right(ffldName, _¶
  (Len(ffldName) - InStr(ffldName, "_")))) + 1¶
'Collapse range so that newly inserted row¶
'follows immediately after the rng-row¶
rng.Collapse wdCollapseEnd¶
If doc.ProtectionType <> wdNoProtection Then¶
    doc.Unprotect password:=password¶
End If¶
Set rng = tmpl.AutoTextEntries(AutoTextName).Insert( _¶
  Where:=rng, RichText:=True)¶
'rng.Select¶
'Store the list of original field names¶
'in an array so that we can check against it¶
'for the field names used in any calculations¶
nrFields = rng.FormFields.Count¶
ReDim aFieldNames(nrFields)¶
For counter = 1 To nrFields¶
    aFieldNames(counter - 1) = rng.FormFields(counter).Name¶
Next counter¶
'Add the increment to the field names, and to¶
'the field names in any calculation¶
'Have run through from back to front because¶
'executing the dialog box to force update¶
'of the .Default property recreates the form field¶
For counter = nrFields To 1 Step -1¶
    Set ffld = rng.FormFields(counter)¶
    ffld.Name = ffld.Name & "_" & CStr(increment)¶
    If ffld.TextInput.Valid Then¶
        If ffld.TextInput.Type = wdCalculationText Then¶
            ChangeCalculationCode ffld, increment, aFieldNames()¶
            DoEvents¶
        End If¶
    End If¶
```

Wrd

```
    Next counter¶
    doc.Protect Type:=wdAllowOnlyFormFields, noreset:=True,
password:=password¶
    rng.FormFields(1).Select¶
End Sub¶
' * * * * *¶
Sub ChangeCalculationCode(ffld As Word.FormField, _¶
  nr As Long, aFieldNames() As String)¶
    'Variable declaration¶
    Dim calculationCode As String¶
    Dim counter As Long¶
    Dim ffldName As String¶
    calculationCode = ffld.TextInput.Default¶
    'cycle through the base field names that have been¶
    'incremented. If found, add the underscore¶
    'increment value to the field name in the calculation¶
    For counter = 0 To UBound(aFieldNames) - 1¶
        If InStr(calculationCode, aFieldNames(counter)) <> 0 Then¶
            ffldName = aFieldNames(counter)¶
            calculationCode = Left(calculationCode, _¶
              (InStr(calculationCode, ffldName) + Len(ffldName) - 1)) _¶
              & "_" & CStr(nr) & Mid(calculationCode, _¶
              (InStr(calculationCode, ffldName) + Len(ffldName)))¶
        End If¶
    Next¶
    ffld.TextInput.Default = calculationCode¶
    'Select it so that executing the dialog box¶
    'updates the changed calculation formula¶
    ffld.Select¶
    Application.Dialogs(wdDialogFormFieldOptions).Execute¶
    Selection.Range.FormFields(1).TextInput.Clear¶
End Sub¶
```

The following code is included for completeness. The next example details how it is used.

```
Option explicit¶
' * * * * *¶
'First row containing form fields¶
'that should not be deleted¶
Const StartRowIndex As Long = 2¶
' * * * * *¶
Sub DeleteCurrentRow()¶
    'varaible declaration¶
    Dim doc As Word.Document¶
    Dim rng As Word.Range¶
    Dim totalRows As Long¶
    Set rng = Selection.Range¶
    If rng.Information(wdWithInTable) Then¶
```

```
        'Make sure user can't accidentally delete¶
        'any rows at the end, such as a totals row¶
        'nor the last remaining "data row" in table¶
        totalRows = rng.Tables(1).Rows.Count¶
        If rng.Rows(1).Index <= totalRows - EndRowsIndex _¶
          And totalRows > StartRowIndex + EndRowsIndex Then¶
            Set doc = rng.Parent¶
            If doc.ProtectionType <> wdNoProtection Then¶
                doc.Unprotect password:=password¶
            End If¶
            rng.Rows(1).Delete¶
            doc.Protect Type:=wdAllowOnlyFormFields, _¶
              noreset:=True, password:=password¶
        End If¶
    End If¶
End Sub¶
```


Follow these steps:

1. In Word's VBE, once you have copied the InsertNewTableRow macro code into a module, change the Const values at the top to fit how the table is constructed, as follows:

   - **TableIndex** If the form contains more than one table, enter the number of the table on which the code should execute (1 for the first table, 2 for the second, and so on).
   - **AutoTextName** The name of the AutoText entry containing the basic data row.
   - **EndRowsIndex** If the table has rows beneath the data rows (a totals row, such as in the example), enter the number of such rows. All new rows will be inserted immediately before these end rows.
   - **Password** If the form is protected with a password, supply it here. In order to insert the AutoText entry, the macro needs to unprotect the form. The password is then used when protecting the form again.

2. Create a toolbar button for this macro, and be sure to save the change in this template (Tools | Customize | Commands, the Macros category).
3. Finish setting up the form and then protect it.
4. Set up the form and the basic table—a header row, if needed, and at least one "data row" containing form fields that will be repeated.

Double-click each form field in the data row to open the form field options dialog box. Enter a unique name for each form field in the row. Activate Calculate on Exit if the form contains any fields that should be updated dynamically. Set any other options for the field.

5. When defining the formula for a calculation type of form field, be sure to use the form field names that have been defined. Once the data row is set up and adequate testing has been conducted, select the entire row (click in the left margin). Go to Insert | AutoText | AutoText and enter a name for the entry being created. Be very careful to select the template from the Look in list so that the AutoText entry moves with the template (and isn't stored in Normal.dot). Click Add.

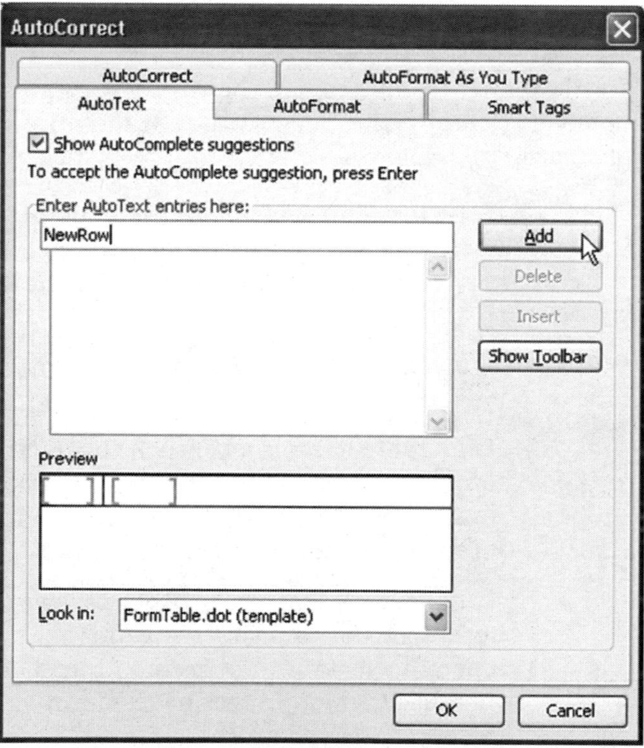

Figure 56 – Inserting an Autotext Entry

The macro runs from a toolbar that displays when a document is created using the template.

6. Now go back into each form field Options in the data row and append an underscore plus the number one (_1) to each form field name. This ensures that the names are different from those in the AutoText entry. For each calculation that references such form fields, update the names the calculation references to reflect the names that have been changed to include the underscore and number.

Note: This technique only works with a template, because only templates can store AutoText entries—documents cannot.

Forms: Deleting a Table Row

Delete the current row (the row at the insertion point) from a table in a protected form.

Scenario: A table set up in a form with multiple rows for data entry or set up using the 'InsertNewTableRow' macro (see preceding process) may at some point need to have superfluous rows removed.

The following macro removes the row in which the selection currently stands, unless it is the last data row in the table or is a designated header or footer row.

Example file: W022

View the Appendix to learn how to store this procedure in a Standard module.

```
Option explicit¶
' * * * * *¶
'First row containing form fields¶
'that should not be deleted¶
Const StartRowIndex As Long = 2¶
' * * * * *¶
Sub DeleteCurrentRow()¶
    'varaible declaration¶
    Dim doc As Word.Document¶
    Dim rng As Word.Range¶
    Dim totalRows As Long¶
    Set rng = Selection.Range¶
    If rng.Information(wdWithInTable) Then¶
```

```
        'Make sure user can't accidentally delete¶
        'any rows at the end, such as a totals row¶
        'nor the last remaining "data row" in table¶
        totalRows = rng.Tables(1).Rows.Count¶
        If rng.Rows(1).Index <= totalRows - EndRowsIndex _¶
          And totalRows > StartRowIndex + EndRowsIndex Then¶
            Set doc = rng.Parent¶
            If doc.ProtectionType <> wdNoProtection Then¶
                doc.Unprotect password:=password¶
            End If¶
            rng.Rows(1).Delete¶
            doc.Protect Type:=wdAllowOnlyFormFields, _¶
              noreset:=True, password:=password¶
        End If¶
    End If¶
End Sub¶
```


The following code is included for completeness. The next example details how it is used.

```
Option explicit¶
' * * * * *¶
'If the form has more than one table¶
'set this value to the number of the¶
'table to process with this code¶
Const TableIndex As Long = 1¶
'Name of the AutoText entry that contains¶
'the row that should be inserted¶
Const AutoTextName As String = "NewRow"¶
'Enter the number of rows that should remain¶
'below the row being inserted.¶
'For example, this sample table has one row,¶
'the Totals row, that should stay at the end¶
'This and the password constant are shared¶
'with the DeleteCurrentRow macro.¶
Public Const EndRowsIndex As Long = 1¶
'The password to unprotect (leave as is if you're¶
'not assigning a password to the form¶
Public Const password = ""¶
' * * * * *¶
Sub InsertNewTableRow()¶
    'Variable declaration¶
    Dim doc As Word.Document¶
    Dim tmpl As Word.Template¶
    Dim tbl As Word.Table¶
    Dim lastRow As Long¶
    Dim ffldName As String¶
    Dim rng As Word.Range¶
    Dim ffld As Word.FormField¶
    Dim nrFields As Long¶
    Dim increment As Long¶
```

```
    Dim aFieldNames() As String¶
    Dim counter As Long¶
    Set doc = ActiveDocument¶
    Set tmpl = doc.AttachedTemplate¶
    Set tbl = doc.Tables(TableIndex)¶
    'Calculate the row index after which the¶
    'new row should be inserted¶
    lastRow = tbl.Rows.Count - EndRowsIndex¶
    Set rng = tbl.Rows(lastRow).Range¶
    'Calculate the increment number for the new row¶
    'by picking up the text to the right of¶
    'the underscore just preceding it in the first form field¶
    ffldName = rng.FormFields(1).Name¶
    increment = CLng(Right(ffldName, _¶
      (Len(ffldName) - InStr(ffldName, "_")))) + 1¶
    'Collapse range so that newly inserted row¶
    'follows immediately after the rng-row¶
    rng.Collapse wdCollapseEnd¶
    If doc.ProtectionType <> wdNoProtection Then¶
        doc.Unprotect password:=password¶
    End If¶
    Set rng = tmpl.AutoTextEntries(AutoTextName).Insert( _¶
      Where:=rng, RichText:=True)¶
    'rng.Select¶
    'Store the list of original field names¶
    'in an array so that we can check against it¶
    'for the field names used in any calculations¶
    nrFields = rng.FormFields.Count¶
    ReDim aFieldNames(nrFields)¶
    For counter = 1 To nrFields¶
        aFieldNames(counter - 1) = rng.FormFields(counter).Name¶
    Next counter¶
    'Add the increment to the field names, and to¶
    'the field names in any calculation¶
    'Have run through from back to front because¶
    'executing the dialog box to force update¶
    'of the .Default property recreates the form field¶
    For counter = nrFields To 1 Step -1¶
        Set ffld = rng.FormFields(counter)¶
        ffld.Name = ffld.Name & "_" & CStr(increment)¶
        If ffld.TextInput.Valid Then¶
            If ffld.TextInput.Type = wdCalculationText Then¶
                ChangeCalculationCode ffld, increment, aFieldNames()¶
                DoEvents¶
            End If¶
        End If¶
    Next counter¶
    doc.Protect Type:=wdAllowOnlyFormFields, noreset:=True,
password:=password¶
    rng.FormFields(1).Select¶
End Sub¶
```

Wrd

```
' * * * * *¶
Sub ChangeCalculationCode(ffld As Word.FormField, _¶
  nr As Long, aFieldNames() As String)¶
    'Variable declaration¶
    Dim calculationCode As String¶
    Dim counter As Long¶
    Dim ffldName As String¶
    calculationCode = ffld.TextInput.Default¶
    'cycle through the base field names that have been¶
    'incremented. If found, add the underscore¶
    'increment value to the field name in the calculation¶
    For counter = 0 To UBound(aFieldNames) - 1¶
        If InStr(calculationCode, aFieldNames(counter)) <> 0 Then¶
            ffldName = aFieldNames(counter)¶
            calculationCode = Left(calculationCode, _¶
            (InStr(calculationCode, ffldName) + Len(ffldName) - 1)) _¶
              & "_" & CStr(nr) & Mid(calculationCode, _¶
              (InStr(calculationCode, ffldName) + Len(ffldName)))¶
        End If¶
    Next¶
    ffld.TextInput.Default = calculationCode¶
    'Select it so that executing the dialog box¶
    'updates the changed calculation formula¶
    ffld.Select¶
    Application.Dialogs(wdDialogFormFieldOptions).Execute¶
    Selection.Range.FormFields(1).TextInput.Clear¶
End Sub¶
```

Set the constant values, as follows:

- **StartRowIndex** The number of rows at the top of the table to "protect" from deletion by the macro.
- **EndRowsIndex** The number of rows at the end of the table to protect from deletion.
- **Password** If the form is protected with a password, supply it here. The macro must temporarily unprotect the form in order to delete the row. If no password has been assigned, use a zero-length string ("").

The macro runs from a toolbar that displays when a document is created using the template.

Forms: Placing a Picture in a Protected Form

Use this procedure to insert a picture into a protected section of a form.

Scenario: In a form, the Drawing tools and the entire graphics layer of the document is locked out. Pictures can be inserted into unprotected sections without difficulty; but only those positioned in-line with text can be manipulated after being inserted.

Inserting a picture in a protected section of the document is only possible with the help of a macro such as this one. The Insert Picture dialog box is displayed, the user chooses the graphic to insert, and the macro positions it, in-line with the text, at a bookmarked location.

Example file:
W023

Wrd

Tip: To get the text to flow around the graphic, use the Insert Frame tool on the Forms toolbar to draw a box. Insert the bookmark in the frame. Setting the height or the width of the frame to an exact setting resizes the picture relative to its original size to the limiting dimension.

View the Appendix to learn how to store this procedure in a Standard module.

```
Option explicit¶
' * * * * *¶
'Password to unprotect/protect form¶
Const password As String = ""¶
'Position where picture should be inserted¶
Const BookmarkTarget As String = "PicTarget"¶
Sub InsertPictureIntoForm()¶
    'variable declaration¶
    Dim doc As Word.Document¶
    Dim picPath As String¶
    Dim dlg As Word.Dialog¶
    Dim rng As Word.Range¶
    Dim ils As Word.InlineShape¶
    Set doc = ActiveDocument¶
    If doc.ProtectionType <> wdNoProtection Then¶
        doc.Unprotect password:=password¶
    End If¶
```

```
    'Display the Insert picture dialog box¶
    'But don't let it execute¶
    Set dlg = Dialogs(wdDialogInsertPicture)¶
    'If cancel was not clicked¶
    If dlg.Display <> 0 Then¶
        'Make sure the target exists¶
        If doc.Bookmarks.Exists(BookmarkTarget) Then¶
            Set rng = doc.Bookmarks(BookmarkTarget).Range¶
            'Delete any pictures currently in the bookmark¶
            If rng.InlineShapes.Count > 0 Then¶
                rng.InlineShapes(1).Delete¶
            End If¶
            'Insert the picture into the bookmark¶
            Set ils = doc.InlineShapes.AddPicture( _¶
                FileName:=dlg.Name, LinkToFile:=False, _¶
                SaveWithDocument:=True, Range:=rng)¶
            'Recreate the bookmark around the picture¶
            doc.Bookmarks.Add Name:=BookmarkTarget, _¶
                Range:=ils.Range¶
        Else¶
            'MsgBox "Target for picture not found"¶
        End If¶
    End If¶
    doc.Protect Type:=wdAllowOnlyFormFields, _¶
        NoReset:=True, password:=password¶
End Sub¶
```

Set the constant values:

- **Password** — If the form is protected with a password, supply it here. The macro must temporarily unprotect the form in order to delete the row. If no password has been assigned, use a zero-length string ("").
- **bookmarkTarget** — The name of the bookmark marking the target position for the picture being inserted.

The macro runs from a toolbar that displays when a document is created using the template.

Set up the form. Insert a bookmark at each location where the user should be able to insert a picture.

Mail Merge: Using a Relative Path for Data Source

This procedure lets you dynamically link to a data source in the same path as the main merge document.

Scenario: Word was originally designed to use absolute paths to all linked files. Over the last few versions, support for relative paths has been improved for some types of links, but the path to a mail merge data source is still stored in Word's binary file format as an absolute path. There is no way to change mail merge to store a relative path to the data source file.

This makes it difficult to distribute mail merge functionality; every user who does not work on the same machine is forced to relink manually to the data source.

Example file:
W025

The following set of macros takes on the burden of this task, linking to the data source file located in the same folder as the main merge document. The user is only prompted to search for the data source manually if it cannot be found.

View the Appendix to learn how to store this procedure in a Standard module.

```
Option explicit¶
' * * * * *¶
Const FileName As String = "MailMergeData.doc"¶
' * * * * *¶
Sub LinkToSourceFile()¶
    'Variable declaration¶
    Dim Path As String¶
    'Suppress the messages that display¶
    'if Word can't find a data source¶
    'Only works in Word 2002 and later¶
    'See AutoClose macro for Word 97 / 2000¶
    Application.DisplayAlerts = wdAlertsNone¶
    'Construct the full path to the data file¶
    Path = ActiveDocument.Path & "\" & FileName¶
    'If the data file can be found, link to it¶
    If Dir(Path) <> "" Then¶
        ActiveDocument.MailMerge.OpenDataSource _¶
            Name:=Path¶
    Else¶
```

```
        'Otherwise, display the dialog box¶
        'so that the user can select the data file¶
        Dialogs(wdDialogMailMergeOpenDataSource).Show¶
    End If¶
    'Turn the warnings back on¶
    Application.DisplayAlerts = wdAlertsAll¶
End Sub¶
' * * * * *¶
Sub AutoClose()¶
    'Unlink the data soruce for versions earlier¶
    'than 2002 so that no prompt about being unable¶
    'to find the data source appears when opening¶
    If Application.Version < 10 Then¶
        ActiveDocument.MailMerge.MainDocumentType _¶
          = wdNotAMergeDocument¶
    End If¶
    'Save this change. Note that any other changes¶
    'will also be saved! If choosing whether¶
    'or not to save changes is desired,¶
    'comment the next line out¶
    ActiveDocument.Save¶
End Sub¶
' * * * * *¶
Sub AutoOpen()¶
    LinkToSourceFile¶
End Sub¶
```

Wrd

Follow these steps:

1. Add a module to the mail merge main document or to the template from which the merge documents will be created. These are the files that will be dynamically linked to the data source.
2. Copy the LinkToDataSource and AutoOpen procedures into a standard module.
3. Change the file name for the CONST value to the file name of the data source. Alter the 'OpenDataSource' method in the 'LinkToDataSource' procedure so that it can link to the data source (see more below).

The macro runs automatically when the document is opened.

If you are using a Word document as the data source, there won't be a need to change anything in the 'OpenDataSource' method. For all other types of data sources, record a macro while you link to the data source. Copy the 'OpenDataSource' lines from the code generated by the macro recorder and use it to replace the 'OpenDataSource' lines in the sample code. Then substitute the Path variable everywhere a full file path exists in the recorded code.

Note: The macro recorder often (but not always) creates an 'OpenDataSource' method that works when it is run in a macro. The problems are largely restricted to Word 2002 and Word 2003 OLE DB connections (the default). Also keep in mind that 'OpenDataSource' does not necessarily work the same across all versions of Word, unless the data source is a Word document.

For all of the above situations, when not using Word documents or text files as the data source, ODBC connections are the most reliable. In order to force Word to create an ODBC connection:

- In Word 97 and Word 2000, activate the Select Method checkbox in the Open Data Source dialog box.
- In Word 2002 and Word 2003 Confirm Conversions on Open must be activated in Tools | Options | General before using the Open Data Source dialog box.
- In all cases, select ODBC in the list that follows. If the desired data table does not appear in the next dialog box, click Options and activate all the checkboxes in the next screen.

Here is an 'OpenDataSource' method recorded in Word 2003. Note how the file path is used in two places. In both instances, the file path needs to be replaced with the variable Path. If the macro should run under Word 97 or Word 2000, delete the last argument SubType:= wdMergeSubTypeOther, because this argument is not recognized by these versions.

```
ActiveDocument.MailMerge.OpenDataSource _¶
Name:="C:\Documents and Settings\User\My Documents\SalesData.xls", _¶
ConfirmConversions:=False, _¶
ReadOnly:=False, _¶
LinkToSource:=True, _¶
AddToRecentFiles:=False, _¶
PasswordDocument:="", _¶
PasswordTemplate:="", _¶
WritePasswordDocument:="", _¶
WritePasswordTemplate:="", _¶
Revert:=False, _¶
Format:=wdOpenFormatAuto, _¶
Connection:= _¶
"DSN=Excel Files;DBQ=C:\Documents and Settings\User\My
Documents\SalesData.xls;DriverId=790;MaxBufferSize=2048;PageTimeout=5;". _¶
SQLStatement:="SELECT * FROM `Sheet1$`", _¶
SQLStatement1:="", SubType:=wdMergeSubTypeOther¶
```

Below is the edited version. Notice that all the information about passwords can be deleted; they are irrelevant when opening a mail merge data source.

```
ActiveDocument.MailMerge.OpenDataSource _¶
Name:=Path, _¶
ConfirmConversions:=False, _¶
ReadOnly:=False, _¶
LinkToSource:=True, _¶
AddToRecentFiles:=False, _¶
Revert:=False, _¶
Format:=wdOpenFormatAuto, _¶
Connection:= _¶
"DSN=Excel Files;DBQ=Path;DriverId=790;MaxBufferSize=2048;PageTimeout=5;".
_¶
SQLStatement:="SELECT * FROM `Sheet1$`", _¶
SQLStatement1:="", SubType:=wdMergeSubTypeOther¶
```


Mail Merge: Displaying the Mail Merge Interface

You can display the mail merge toolbar or wizard task pane automatically when creating or opening a mail merge document using this procedure.

Example file:
W026

Scenario: For versions of Word up to and including Word 2000, the mail merge toolbar was automatically displayed when opening a document linked to a data source. Since Word 2002, this is no longer the case, which means there is no longer any indication to the user that the document is a mail merge document.

To display the desired interface, go through Tools | Letters and Mailings. This simple little macro takes care of all that for you.

View the Appendix to learn how to store this procedure in a Standard module.

```
Option explicit¶
' * * * * *¶
Sub DisplayMergeUserInterface()¶
    'If there is a data source attached¶
    'to the document being opened¶
    If ActiveDocument.MailMerge.MainDocumentType <> wdNotAMergeDocument
```

```
Then¶
        'Remove the apostrophe from the line¶
        'that you wish to have execute¶
        '''Display the Mail Merge Wizard task pane¶
        'Application.TaskPanes(wdTaskPanemailMerge).Visible = True¶
        '''Display the mail merge toolbar¶
        'Application.CommandBars("Mail merge").Visible = True¶
    End If¶
End Sub¶
' * * * * *¶
Sub AutoClose()¶
    Application.TaskPanes(wdTaskPanemailMerge).Visible = False¶
    Application.CommandBars("Mail merge").Visible = False¶
End Sub¶
' * * * * *¶
Sub AutoOpen()¶
    DisplayMergeUserInterface¶
End Sub¶
```


Copy the procedure 'DisplayMergeUserInterface' to a module in the Normal.dot template to make the functionality always available. Alternatively, you can copy it to a module in a main merge document to restrict it to that particular document.

For already existing AutoOpen or Document_Open procedures, simply enter the macro name in the procedure so that it is called. If no AutoOpen or Document_Open procedure exists, then copy the sample AutoOpen procedure into the same module with "InsertMergeField'. Do the same for the AutoClose macro.

Remove the comment (apostrophe) from before the code line for the mail merge interface to be displayed (toolbar and/or task pane).

This macro runs automatically when the file is open.

Tip: It is possible to combine linking the data source dynamically and displaying a user interface. In this case, the AutoOpen macro could look like this:

```
Sub AutoOpen()¶
  LinkToSourceFile¶
  DisplayMergeUserInterface¶
End Sub¶
```

Mail Merge: Creating a User-Friendly List of Fields

This procedure lets you display the list of merge fields in a dialog box while working in the document at the same time.

Example file:
W027

Scenario: No version of Word has an interface that allows the viewing of a list of merge fields, allows insertion, and at the same time allows working in the main merge document. One workaround is to have a drop-down list on the toolbar from which you can choose merge fields to insert. An alternative is to display a dialog box that has to be closed in order to work in the document (Word 2002 and Word 2003).

Wrd

This latter solution takes advantage of the non-modal capability of UserForms introduced in Word 2000 to make the interface with mail merge more efficient. You can edit the main merge document while at the same time displaying a UserForm such as that shown below. Double-click an entry, or select it and then click the Insert Field button in the form to insert the merge field into the document.

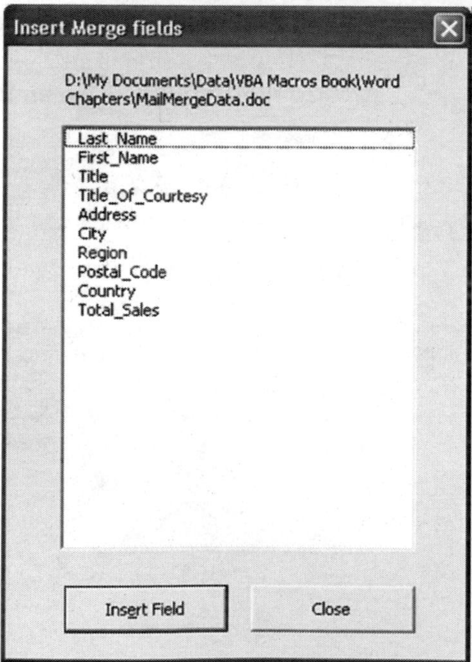

Figure 57 – User-Friendly Merge Field List

Note: The following code should be placed in the UserForm module of the UserForm that will use it.

```
Option explicit¶
' * * * * *¶
'Executes first when a UserForm is shown the first time¶
Private Sub UserForm_Initialize()¶
    'Generate the list of field names¶
    'Variable declaration¶
    Dim fld As Word.MailMergeDataField¶
    With ActiveDocument.MailMerge¶
        'Continue only if a merge document with linked data source¶
        If .MainDocumentType = wdNotAMergeDocument Then Exit Sub¶
        'Display the full path and name of the data source file ¶
        'above the list¶
        lblDatasource.Caption = .DataSource.Name¶
        'Loop through all the merge fields¶
        'in the data source, adding the name to the list¶
        For Each fld In .DataSource.DataFields¶
            Me.lstMergeFields.AddItem fld.Name¶
        Next fld¶
    End With¶
End Sub¶
' * * * * *¶
Private Sub UserForm_Activate()¶
'Only hide the form, without unloading it,¶
'so that time is not spent¶
'recreating the list each time it's shown¶
'Must catch whether the data source¶
'has been removed in the meantime.¶
'If so, and the form is shown again, close the form¶
    If ActiveDocument.MailMerge.MainDocumentType = wdNotAMergeDocument
Then¶
        Unload Me¶
        Exit Sub¶
    End If¶
End Sub¶
' * * * * *¶
Private Sub cmdClose_Click()¶
    'Close the UserForm without losing the list¶
    Unload Me¶
End Sub¶
' * * * * *¶
'Field can be inserted by clicking the button¶
Private Sub cmdInsertField_Click()¶
    'Insert the selected entry¶
    ActiveDocument.Fields.Add Range:=Selection.Range, _¶
        Type:=wdFieldMergeField, Text:=lstMergeFields.Text¶
End Sub¶
```

Wrd

```
' * * * * *¶
'As well as be double-clicking an entry in the list¶
Private Sub lstMergeFields_DblClick(ByVal Cancel As
MSForms.ReturnBoolean)¶
    'Insert the selected entry¶
    ActiveDocument.Fields.Add Range:=Selection.Range, _¶
        Type:=wdFieldMergeField, Text:=lstMergeFields.Text¶
End Sub¶
```

View the Appendix to learn how to store this procedure in a Standard module.

Wrd

```
Option explicit¶
'Display the UserForm¶
' * * * * *¶
Sub InsertMergeFields()¶
    'Variable declaration¶
    Dim frmMergeFields As frmListFields¶
    Set frmMergeFields = New frmListFields¶
    frmMergeFields.Show¶
    Set frmMergeFields = Nothing¶
End Sub¶
```

It will be easiest to use this macro from a toolbar button or menu command. In order to assign it to the mail merge toolbar:

1. Display the Commands tab in the Tools | Customize dialog box.
2. Select the Macros category.
3. Locate the InsertMergeField entry and drag it to the Mail Merge (or any other) toolbar.

Every time the button is clicked, the list of merge fields is displayed.

To create the form shown in the graphic, the controls and their attributes should be as follows:

- **Control Type:** Control properties
- **UserForm Name:** frmListFields
- **Label Name:** lblDataSource
- **List Box Name:** lstMergeFieldsMultiSelect:
0 — frmMultiSelectSingle

- **Button Name:** cmdInsertFieldDefault: True
- **Button Name:** cmdCloseCancel: True

Mail Merge: Making Placecards Using WordArt

Use this procedure to put the text result from a mail merge into a WordArt object, and rotate every other one to create placecards.

Example file:
W028

Wrd

> **Scenario:** Most recent versions of Word can rotate a graphic object at any rotation angle. Text, however, can only be rotated by 90 or 270 degrees; there is no way to make text "stand on its head" except as part of a picture (NOT a drawing object) or by using WordArt.
>
> This makes using mail merge for creating things like placecards something of a challenge. It is, of course, possible to rotate the page, then rotate the merge text by 90 and 270 degrees, or to put the paper into the printer upside-down to make a second printing pass. WordArt offers many ways to make the cards more lively, original, and attractive.
>
> This macro tool takes the mail merge result, places it into a WordArt object, then rotates every other one, as shown in the Associating a Picture with a Page procedure earlier in this chapter on page 181.

View the Appendix to learn how to store this procedure in a Standard module.

```
Option explicit¶
' * * * * *¶
Const AutoTextName = "WordArt"¶
' * * * * *¶
Sub MergePlacecards()¶
    'Variable declaration¶
    Dim docMain As Word.Document¶
    Dim docResult As Word.Document¶
    Dim tmpl As Word.Template¶
    Dim tbl As Word.Table¶
    Dim cel As Word.Cell¶
```

```
    Dim rng As Word.Range¶
    Dim PlacecardText As String¶
    Dim WordArt As Word.Shape¶
    Dim IsSecond As Boolean¶
    IsSecond = True¶
    Set docMain = ActiveDocument¶
    Set tmpl = docMain.AttachedTemplate¶
    'The merge should be a catalog/directory type¶
    If docMain.MailMerge.MainDocumentType <> wdCatalog Then Exit Sub¶
    With docMain.MailMerge¶
        .Destination = wdSendToNewDocument¶
        .Execute¶
    End With¶
    Set docResult = ActiveDocument¶
    docResult.AttachedTemplate = tmpl¶
    Set tbl = docResult.Tables(1)¶
    For Each cel In tbl.Range.Cells¶
        'Check whether there is text¶
        If Len(cel.Range.Text) > 2 Then¶
            Set rng = cel.Range¶
            'Get the text for the placecard¶
            PlacecardText = TrimCellText(rng.Text)¶
            'Then delete it before inserting the WordArt¶
            rng.Delete¶
            'A shape can't be inserted into the full cell range,¶
            'it must be collapsed so that it is only the inside¶
            'of the cell¶
            rng.Collapse wdCollapseStart¶
            'Insert the WordArt, stored as an AutoText¶
            tmpl.AutoTextEntries(AutoTextName).Insert Where:=rng,
RichText:=True¶
            Set WordArt = rng.Cells(1).Range.ShapeRange(1)¶
            'Put in the placecard text¶
            WordArt.TextEffect.Text = PlacecardText¶
            'Rotate every second one¶
            If IsSecond Then¶
                WordArt.Rotation = 180¶
            End If¶
            'Put it into the table cell so that it centers properly¶
            If CInt(Val(Application.Version)) = 11 Then¶
                WordArt.ConvertToInlineShape¶
            ElseIf CInt(Val(Application.Version)) < 10 And
CInt(Val(Application.Version)) > 8 Then¶
                WordArt.RelativeHorizontalPosition =
wdRelativeHorizontalPositionColumn¶
                WordArt.Left = ((cel.Width + cel.RightPadding +
cel.LeftPadding) - WordArt.Width) / 2¶
                WordArt.RelativeVerticalPosition =
wdRelativeVerticalPositionMargin¶
                WordArt.Top = (cel.Row.Height - WordArt.Height) / 2¶
```

```
            End If¶
            IsSecond = Not IsSecond¶
        End If¶
    Next cel¶
    MsgBox "Finished!", vbOKOnly + vbInformation¶
End Sub¶
' * * * * *¶
Function TrimCellText(s As String) As String¶
    'Remove end-of-cell markers¶
    TrimCellText = Left(s, Len(s) - 2)¶
End Function¶
```

Follow these steps:

1. Substitute the name of the AutoText entry for the value of Const AutoTextName.
2. Set up the main merge document as a catalog-type merge. Save the file as a template.
3. Create the basic WordArt with some sample text. Select it. Save it as an AutoText entry in this template. (Use Insert | AutoText | AutoText to create the entry and be sure to select this template from the list at the bottom of the dialog box.) Delete it.
4. Set up a table to match the place card paper stock. Insert the merge fields that will be converted to WordArt into the table cells.

Mail Merge: Creating a One-to-Many List

This procedure lets you create lists of multiple, related items for each data record in the mail merge result. It demonstrates how to link to Access, gather data, insert it into Word and format it as a table.

Scenario: Word's mail merge feature provides no way to generate lists of items belonging to a single entry. For example, a table of grades won't get Word to generate a list of grades for each pupil without resorting to a very complex set of nested field codes. Alternatively, mail merge can be bypassed entirely and the creation of the individual letters can be programmed in VBA.

Example file:
W029

Tip: Other methods are described at http://homepage.swissonline.ch/cindymeister and work in all versions of Word.

The following example is a relational database in Access designed to track pupils' grades. The Pupils table is the mail merge data source. The first two columns of the Semester Grades query provide the content of the table list in the letter to each pupil's parents.

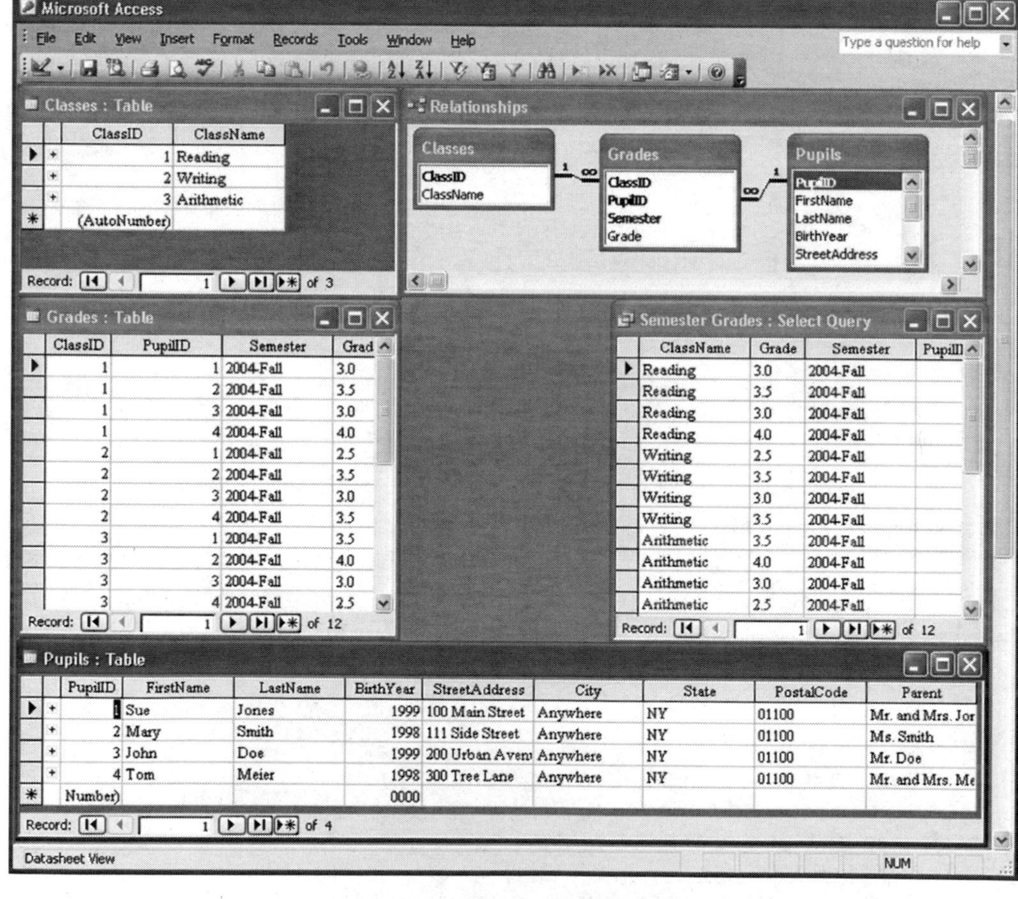

Figure 58 – Access Relationships

In Word 2002 many new features were added to mail merge, but this capability was not one of them. However, new events for mail merge were added and these offer an alternate path that makes it comparatively easy for a user to set up the main merge document, while VBA code behind the scenes does the actual list building.

With this tool, it is possible to specify a table of data containing lists of information related to the individual merge records. The record-specific data is extracted as each record is processed and inserted into the merge result for that record.

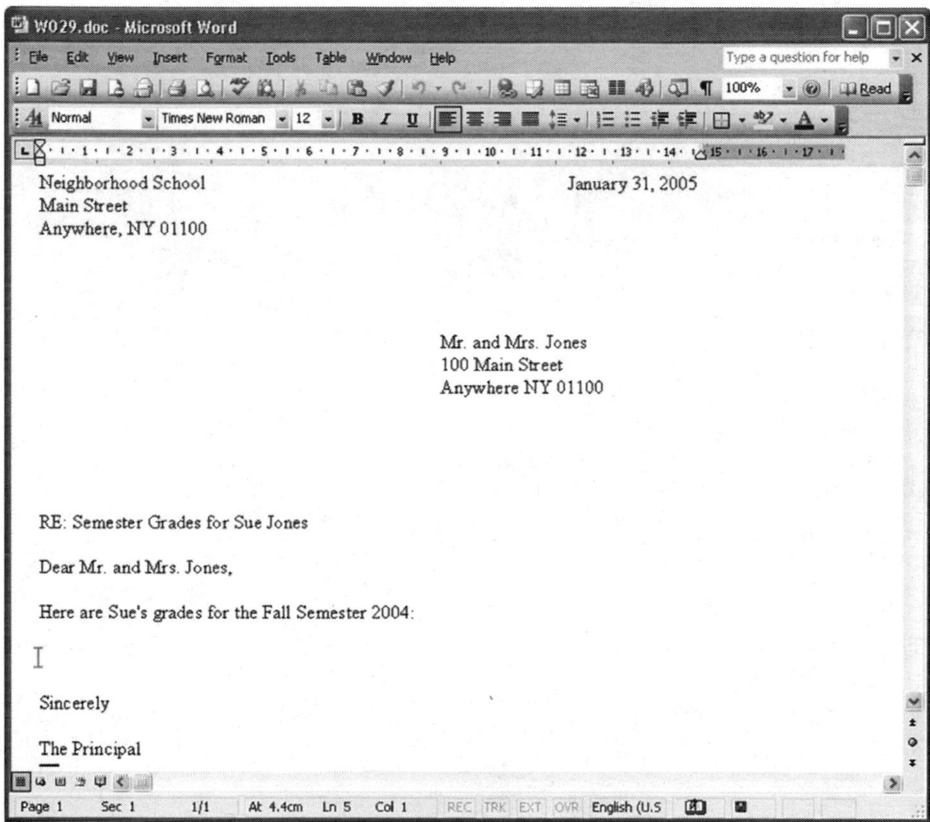

Figure 59 – Document Layout

The list of class grades in this mail merge result was generated by querying the database for all the grades belonging to the current merge record (pupil), as it was merged.

View the Appendix to learn how to store this procedure in a Standard module.

Wrd

```
Option explicit¶
' * * * * *¶
Public MergeEvents As New clsMergeEvents¶
Public BookmarkName As String¶
Public BeforeMergeExecuted As Boolean¶
Public CancelMerge As Boolean¶
Public recordIndex As Long¶
Private DatabasePath As String¶
Private FieldNames() As Variant¶
Private TableName As String¶
Private sepChar As String¶
' * * * * *¶
Sub DoOneToManyMerge()¶
    'Preset the global variables¶
    BeforeMergeExecuted = False¶
    CancelMerge = False¶
    recordIndex = 1¶
    'Set the user-specific variables¶
    Setup¶
    'The events in the class module¶
    'clsMergeEvents will be enabled¶
    ActivateEvents¶
    Application.ScreenUpdating = False¶
    'As each record is merged¶
    'the MailMergeBeforeMerge¶
    'event will be called¶
    ActiveDocument.MailMerge.Execute¶
    'Turn the events off so that they¶
    'only execute for this document¶
    DeactivateEvents¶
End Sub¶
' * * * * *¶
Sub Setup()¶
    'Bookmark target to insert the list¶
    BookmarkName = "GradeTable"¶
    'Full path to database containing the list¶
    DatabasePath = "C:\test\School.mdb"¶
    'The table or query with the list information¶
    TableName = "Semester Grades"¶
    'List the desired fields to show in¶
    'the table in the order they should appear¶
    'List the ID field name first (it links the data¶
    'for the list with the mail merge record)¶
    FieldNames() = Array("PupilID", "ClassName", "Grade")¶
    'Character to separate the fields' data¶
    'that's not present in the field data¶
    sepChar = "¦"¶
End Sub¶
```

```
' * * * * *¶
Sub GetData(ByRef rs As ADODB.Recordset)¶
    'Variable declaration¶
    Dim conn As ADODB.Connection¶
    Dim SQL As String¶
    SQL = "Select " & GetFieldNames(FieldNames()) & _¶
      " FROM [" & TableName & "] "¶
    Set conn = New ADODB.Connection¶
    conn.Open "Provider=Microsoft.Jet.OLEDB.4.0;" & _¶
           "Data Source=" & DatabasePath & ";" & _¶
           "User Id=admin;Password="¶
    rs.Open SQL, conn, adOpenStatic, adLockBatchOptimistic¶
    'Use a disconnected recordset¶
    rs.ActiveConnection = Nothing¶
    conn.Close¶
    Set conn = Nothing¶
End Sub¶
' * * * * *¶
Function GetFieldNames(lst() As Variant) As String¶
    'Variable declaration¶
    Dim i As Long, s As String¶
    For i = 0 To UBound(lst())¶
        s = s & "[" & lst(i) & "], "¶
    Next¶
    'Cut off the last comma-space¶
    s = Left(s, Len(s) - 2)¶
    GetFieldNames = s¶
End Function¶
' * * * * *¶
Function InsertList(bkm As Word.Bookmark, _¶
  rs As ADODB.Recordset, idfield, id As Long) _¶
  As String¶
    'Variable declaration¶
    Dim list As String¶
    'Get only the records for the current pupil¶
    FilterRecords rs, idfield, id¶
    'Stop if there aren't any records¶
    If rs.RecordCount <= 0 Then Exit Sub¶
    'Put the data into delimited string¶
    'that can be converted to a table¶
    list = GetDataList(rs)¶
    'Remove the record filter¶
    rs.Filter = ""¶
    CreateTable list, bkm, rs.Fields.Count - 1¶
End Function¶
' * * * * *¶
Sub FilterRecords(ByRef rs As ADODB.Recordset, _¶
    ByVal idfield As String, ByVal id As Long)¶
    'Variable declaration¶
    Dim filterString As String¶
```

```
    'string field values have to be in¶
    'single quotes; numeric not¶
    Select Case rs.Fields(idfield).Type¶
        Case adVarChar, adVarWChar 'String¶
            filterString = "(" & rs.Fields(idfield) _¶
              & " = '" & id & "')"¶
        Case adDate¶
            filterString = ""¶
        Case Else 'numeric¶
            filterString = "(" & idfield & " = " _¶
              & id & ")"¶
    End Select¶
    rs.MoveFirst¶
    rs.Filter = filterString¶
End Sub¶
' * * * * *¶
Function GetDataList(rs As ADODB.Recordset) As String¶
    'Variable declaration¶
    Dim nrCols As Long¶
    Dim counter As Long¶
    Dim list As String¶
    nrCols = rs.Fields.Count - 1¶
    'Get the table headers from the field names¶
    'Skip the first field (ID)¶
    For counter = 1 To nrCols¶
        list = list & rs.Fields(counter).Name & sepChar¶
    Next¶
    'Cut off the last field separator character¶
    'And append the record separator¶
    list = Left(list, Len(list) - 1) & vbCr¶
    'Now get the field data for each record¶
    Do While Not rs.EOF¶
        For counter = 1 To nrCols¶
            list = list & rs.Fields(counter).Value & sepChar¶
        Next¶
        list = Left(list, Len(list) - 1) & vbCr¶
        rs.MoveNext¶
    Loop¶
    GetDataList = list¶
End Function¶
' * * * * *¶
Sub CreateTable(list As String, bkm As Word.Bookmark, nrCols As Long)¶
    'Variable declaration¶
    Dim tbl As Word.Table¶
    Dim rng As Word.Range¶
    Set rng = bkm.Range¶
    'Delete any old, existing table¶
    If rng.Tables.Count > 0 Then¶
        rng.Tables(1).Delete¶
    End If¶
```

```
    'Insert the data string¶
    rng.Text = list¶
    'Convert it to a table¶
    Set tbl = rng.ConvertToTable(Separator:=sepChar,
NumColumns:=nrCols)¶
    'Restore the bookmark around the table¶
    rng.Parent.Bookmarks.Add Range:=tbl.Range, Name:=BookmarkName¶
    FormatTable tbl¶
End Sub¶
' * * * * *¶
Sub FormatTable(tbl As Word.Table)¶
    'Variable declaration¶
    Dim cel As Word.Cell¶
    Dim s As String¶
    'Bold the header row¶
    With tbl.Rows(1).Range.Font¶
        .Bold = True¶
        .Underline = wdUnderlineSingle¶
    End With¶
    'Center the last column¶
    tbl.Columns(tbl.Columns.Count).Select¶
    For Each cel In Selection.Cells¶
        cel.Range.Paragraphs.Alignment = wdAlignParagraphCenter¶
    Next cel¶
    tbl.Columns.AutoFit¶
    tbl.Borders.Enable = False¶
End Sub¶
' * * * * *¶
Sub ActivateEvents()¶
    Set MergeEvents.WdApp = Word.Application¶
End Sub¶
' * * * * *¶
Sub DeactivateEvents()¶
    Set MergeEvents = Nothing¶
End Sub¶
```

View the Appendix to learn how to store this procedure in a Class module.

```
Option explicit
' * * * * *¶
Public WithEvents WdApp As Word.Application¶
Const sMergeMessage As String = "The merge process can take some time."
& _¶
  vbCr & vbCr & "Word may pause and seem to hang while the charts
update." _¶
  & vbCr & vbCr & "Please do NOT try to work " & _¶
  "in Word until the 'finish' message has been displayed!"¶
Private rs As ADODB.Recordset¶
```

Wrd

```
Private Sub WdApp_MailMergeAfterMerge(ByVal Doc As Document, _¶
  ByVal DocResult As Document)¶
    'Release the data¶
    rs.Close¶
    Set rs = Nothing¶
    'Delete the last table and restore the bookmark¶
    If Doc.Bookmarks.Exists(BookmarkName) Then¶
        'Variable declaration¶
        Dim rng As Word.Range¶
        Set rng = Doc.Bookmarks(BookmarkName).Range¶
        If rng.Tables.Count > 0 Then¶
            rng.Tables(1).Delete¶
        End If¶
        Doc.Bookmarks.Add Range:=rng, Name:=BookmarkName¶
    End If¶
    MsgBox "Merge process has finished!"¶
    'Display the merge result document¶
    If Not DocResult Is Nothing Then¶
        DocResult.ActiveWindow.View.TableGridlines = False¶
        DocResult.Activate¶
    End If¶
End Sub¶
' * * * * *¶
Private Sub WdApp_MailMergeBeforeRecordMerge( _¶
 ByVal Doc As Document, Cancel As Boolean)¶
    'Variable declaration¶
    Dim bkm As Word.Bookmark¶
    'If something is wrong, don't continue¶
    'processing each record¶
    If CancelMerge = True Then¶
        Debug.Print "Cancelled. Record: " & CStr(recordIndex)¶
        Cancel = True¶
        Exit Sub¶
    End If¶
    'The file containing the data for the merge¶
    'should only be opened once. Therefore,¶
    'track when the merge has started¶
    If BeforeMergeExecuted = False Then¶
        BeforeMergeExecuted = True¶
        MsgBox sMergeMessage, vbCritical + vbOKOnly¶
        Set rs = New ADODB.Recordset¶
        rs.CursorLocation = adUseClient¶
        'Retrieve the entire recordset¶
        'then get the individual records for each pupil¶
        GetData rs¶
    End If¶
    If rs.RecordCount <= 0 Then¶
        MsgBox "There is no data to process."¶
        CancelMerge = True¶
        Cancel = True¶
        Exit Sub¶
```

```
    End If¶
    'If there is no target, then¶
    'don't try to insert the table¶
    If Doc.Bookmarks.Exists(BookmarkName) Then¶
        'Variable declaration¶
        Dim idfield As String¶
        Set bkm = Doc.Bookmarks(BookmarkName)¶
        idfield = rs.Fields(0).Name¶
        'Create and format table¶
        InsertList bkm, rs, idfield, _¶
          Doc.MailMerge.DataSource.DataFields(idfield).Value¶
        DoEvents¶
        Cancel = False¶
    Else¶
        MsgBox "The bookmark " & BookmarkName & "is missing."¶
        Cancel = True¶
        Exit Sub¶
    End If¶
End Sub¶
```


Follow these steps:

1. Locate the 'Setup' procedure in the standard module. Change the information pertinent to the operating system and mail merge that needs to be specified as follows:

   - **BookmarkName** Name of the bookmark where the list should be inserted
   - **DatabasePath** Full path to the database holding the list

     (This does not have to be the same database or application containing the data for the mail merge.)
   - **TableName** Name of the table or query with the list data
   - **FieldNames():** Array of the field names with the list data

     a. Type each field name in between a pair of "quotes".

     b. Separate each field name from the next using a comma.

     c. The very first field name must be the field that links the mail merge records with the data list information. Most often, this is an

ID number, but it can be any value unique to each merge record.

d. If this field's value needs to be displayed in the list result, this field name must be specified twice because the same value would repeat for each list entry, which is usually not desired.

- **sepChar:** Delimiting character

  (The list of data is read from the table into a delimited string of text.)

  a. Delimited means that each field's and each record's value are separated from the others by a particular character. Word can convert a delimited text string into a table.

  b. The record separator must always be a paragraph mark; the field separator can be any character. Choose one that is not present in the data.

2. Prepare the mail merge main document normally. Place a bookmark where the list should be inserted. In the sample macro it is named GradeTable, but you can use any name you wish. Just be sure to change it in the macro, as described further down.
3. Go into Tools | References in the VBE and activate the checkbox next to one of the Microsoft ActiveX Data Object libraries (ADO). Any version will do; the sample file references version 2.0.
4. ADO connections are application-specific. If an Excel table is used instead of an Access database, a different connection ('conn' in the procedure 'GetData') is needed.

   Find the code for an Excel connection on page 371 in the Filling a Word Combo Box with Data from Excel procedure in the Combined Procedures Section. For other database types, see the information on ADO OLE DB connections at http://www.able-consulting.com/tech.htm. If the data is in a Word table, see the code for generating an MS Graph chart in the 'Mail Merge: Merging with a Chart' process, which follows.

Mail Merge: Merging with a Chart

This procedure allows you to create a chart for each mail merge record, based on a sample chart in the main mail merge document, and demonstrates automating MS Graph using mail merge events.

Scenario: Just as Word's mail merge doesn't support merging one-to-many item lists, it also provides no way to create a chart for each record.

Example file:
MailMergeData,
MailMergePieChartLetter,
MailMergePieChartData,
MailMergeColChartLetter, and
MailMergeColChartData

Wrd

There are four basic ways to accomplish this; all of these methods require a macro if there are a substantial number of records to be merged.

1. Create a chart for each record in Excel. Add a column to the data table and enter the name of the appropriate chart for each record. Use this merge field in LINK field in the mail merge document.
2. Use a database field in the main merge document to create a data table for each merge record
   See http://www.knowhow.com/Guides/DatabaseInfo/DatabaseInfo.htm for details.
   Select the table and link it to an MS Graph. Preview the merge data, one record at a time, and print each individually. Executing the merge would remove the bookmark that links the table to the chart, resulting in the same chart for all records.
3. Create the chart for each record chart in the mail merge result document, after the mail merge has executed.
4. Create the charts on-the-fly, as the mail merge executes.

This macro applies the fourth method. Since it relies on the mail merge events introduced in Word 2002, it only works with that version or later versions. The other three methods work with all versions of Word.

View the Appendix to learn how to store this procedure in a Standard module.

```
Option explicit¶
' * * * * *¶
Public x As New clsMergeEvents¶
Public BeforeMergeExecuted As Boolean¶
Public CancelMerge As Boolean¶
Public recordIndex As Long¶
Const ChartDataDoc As String = "MailMergePieChartData.doc"¶
' * * * * *¶
Sub MergeWithChart()¶
    'Preset the global variables¶
    BeforeMergeExecuted = False¶
    CancelMerge = False¶
    recordIndex = 1¶
    'The events in the class module¶
    'clsMergeEvents will be enabled¶
    ActivateEvents¶
    'As each record is merged¶
    'the MailMergeBeforeMerge¶
    'event will be called¶
    ActiveDocument.MailMerge.Execute¶
    'Turn the events off so that they¶
    'only execute for this document¶
    DeactivateEvents¶
End Sub¶
' * * * * *¶
Sub ActivateEvents()¶
    Set x.WdApp = Word.Application¶
End Sub¶
' * * * * *¶
Sub DeactivateEvents()¶
    Set x.WdApp = Nothing¶
End Sub¶
' * * * * *¶
Function OpenChartDataFile(LocalPath As String) _¶
 As Word.Document¶
    'Variable declarations¶
    Dim FilePath As String¶
    'Combine the path where the main merge doc¶
    'is stored plus the specified name of the¶
    'document containing the data for the chart¶
    FilePath = LocalPath & "\" & ChartDataDoc¶
    'Make sure the data file exists¶
    'before trying to open it¶
    If Dir(FilePath) <> "" Then¶
    Set OpenChartDataFile = Documents.Open( _¶
        FileName:=FilePath, _¶
        ReadOnly:=True, _¶
        AddToRecentFiles:=False, _¶
        Visible:=False)¶
    End If¶
End Function¶
```

Wrd

```
' * * * * *¶
Sub EditChart(rng As Word.Range, _¶
  DataDoc As Word.Document)¶
    'Variable declaration¶
    Dim of As Word.OLEFormat¶
    Dim oChart As Graph.Chart¶
    Dim oDataSheet As Graph.DataSheet¶
    Dim tbl As Word.Table¶
    Dim chartType As Long¶
    Set tbl = DataDoc.Tables(1)¶
    'Activate the MS Graph object in the¶
    'main merge document¶
    Set of = rng.InlineShapes(1).OLEFormat¶
    of.DoVerb wdOLEVerbInPlaceActivate¶
    'Pick up the chart for automation¶
    Set oChart = of.Object¶
    'Is chart a pie chart or not?¶
    chartType = oChart.chartType¶
    'Data sheet required¶
    Set oDataSheet = oChart.Application.DataSheet¶
    oChart.DisplayBlanksAs = xlNotPlotted¶
    FillDataSheet oDataSheet, tbl, chartType¶
    'Finish with the chart¶
    oChart.Application.Update¶
    oChart.Application.Quit¶
    DoEvents¶
    Set oChart = Nothing¶
End Sub¶
' * * * * *¶
Sub FillDataSheet(ByRef ds As Graph.DataSheet, _¶
  tbl As Word.Table, chartType As Long)¶
    'Variable declaration¶
    Dim nrDataCols As Long¶
    recordIndex = recordIndex + 1¶
    nrDataCols = tbl.Columns.Count¶
    'Delete all entries in the datasheet¶
    ds.Cells.ClearContents¶
    If chartType = xlPie Then¶
        ProcessPieChart ds, tbl, nrDataCols¶
    Else¶
        ProcessOtherChart ds, tbl, nrDataCols¶
    End If¶
    DoEvents¶
End Sub¶
```

```
' * * * * *¶
Sub ProcessPieChart(ByRef ds As Graph.DataSheet, _¶
  tbl As Word.Table, ByVal nrDataCols As Long)¶
    'Variable declaration¶
    Dim rwData As Word.Row¶
    Dim datavalue As Double¶
    Dim rwLabels As Word.Row¶
    Dim colcounter As Long, i As Long¶
    colcounter = 1¶
    'Data series in rows!¶
    ds.Application.PlotBy = xlRows¶
    'First column contains record ID¶
    'Following columns contain data¶
    'One row per record¶
    'First row contains Legend labels¶
    Set rwLabels = tbl.Rows(1)¶
    Set rwData = tbl.Rows(recordIndex)¶
    'Loop through the data columns¶
    For i = 2 To nrDataCols¶
        With ds¶
            datavalue = CDbl(Val( _¶
              TrimCellText(rwData.Cells(i).Range.Text)))¶
            'Don't carry over 0 values¶
            'If 0 values should be used¶
            'comment out If and End If lines¶
            If datavalue > 0 Then¶
                colcounter = colcounter + 1¶
                'carry over the column header¶
                .Cells(1, colcounter).Value _¶
                  = TrimCellText(rwLabels.Cells(i).Range.Text)¶
                'and the data to the data sheet¶
                .Cells(2, colcounter).Value _¶
                  = datavalue¶
              End If¶
        End With¶
    Next i¶
End Sub¶
' * * * * *¶
Sub ProcessOtherChart(ByRef ds As Graph.DataSheet, _¶
  tbl As Word.Table, ByVal nrDataCols As Long)¶
    'Variable declaration¶
    Dim rwData As Word.Row¶
    Dim rwLabels As Word.Row¶
    Dim rowCounter As Long¶
    Dim totalRows As Long¶
    Dim ID As String¶
    Dim datavalue As Double¶
    Dim colcounter As Long, i As Long¶
    colcounter = 1¶
    rowCounter = 1¶
    totalRows = tbl.Rows.Count¶
```

Wrd

```
    'Data series in columns!¶
    ds.Application.PlotBy = xlColumns¶
    'First column contains record ID¶
    'Second column contains legend labels¶
    'Following columns contain data¶
    'First row contains x-axis labels¶
    Set rwLabels = tbl.Rows(1)¶
    Set rwData = tbl.Rows(recordIndex)¶
    'There can be multiple rows / merge record¶
    'therefore loop through table rows until¶
    'ID (value in col 1) changes¶
    Do¶
        colcounter = 1¶
        rowCounter = rowCounter + 1¶
        ID = TrimCellText(rwData.Cells(1).Range.Text)¶
        'carry over row header to datasheet¶
        ds.Cells(rowCounter, 1).Value = _¶
          TrimCellText(rwData.Cells(2).Range.Text)¶
        'loop through the columns¶
        For i = 3 To nrDataCols¶
            colcounter = colcounter + 1¶
            With ds¶
                'carry over column header only on first pass¶
                If rowCounter = 2 Then¶
                    .Cells(1, colcounter).Value _¶
                      = TrimCellText(rwLabels.Cells(i).Range.Text)¶
                End If¶
                'and the data to the data sheet¶
                .Cells(rowCounter, colcounter).Value _¶
                  = TrimCellText(rwData.Cells(i).Range.Text)¶
            End With¶
        Next i¶
        recordIndex = recordIndex + 1¶
        'Stop if the end has been reached¶
        If totalRows < recordIndex Then Exit Do¶
        'Otherwise, move to the next row¶
        'Then perform the ID check before looping back¶
        Set rwData = tbl.Rows(recordIndex)¶
    Loop While ID = TrimCellText(rwData.Cells(1).Range.Text)¶
    'Reset in order to start with correct row for next record¶
    recordIndex = recordIndex - 1¶
End Sub¶
' * * * * *¶
Function TrimCellText(s As String) As String¶
    'Remove end-of-cell markers¶
    TrimCellText = Left(s, Len(s) - 2)¶
End Function¶
```

View the Appendix to learn how to store this procedure in a Class module.

```
Option explicit¶
' * * * * * *¶
Public WithEvents WdApp As Word.Application¶
Private DataDoc As Word.Document¶
Const BookmarkName As String = "PieChart"¶
Const sMergeMessage As String = "The merge process can take some time."
& _¶
  vbCr & vbCr & "Word may pause and seem to hang while the charts
update." _¶
  & vbCr & vbCr & "Please do NOT try to work " & _¶
  "in Word until the 'finish' message has been displayed!"¶
Private Sub WdApp_MailMergeAfterMerge(ByVal Doc As Document, _¶
  ByVal DocResult As Document)¶
    DataDoc.Close SaveChanges:=wdDoNotSaveChanges¶
    Set DataDoc = Nothing¶
    MsgBox "Merge process has finished!"¶
    'Display the merge result document¶
    If Not DocResult Is Nothing Then¶
     DocResult.Activate¶
    End If¶
End Sub¶
' * * * * *¶
Private Sub WdApp_MailMergeBeforeRecordMerge( _¶
 ByVal Doc As Document, Cancel As Boolean)¶
    'Variable declaration¶
    Dim rngChart As Word.Range¶
'    Dim rngControl As Word.Range¶
'    Dim EmployeeName As String¶
    Debug.Print Doc.Characters.Count, Asc(Doc.Characters.Last)¶
    'If something is wrong, don't continue¶
    'processing each record¶
    If CancelMerge = True Then¶
        Debug.Print "Cancelled. Record: " & CStr(recordIndex)¶
        Cancel = True¶
        Exit Sub¶
    End If¶
    'The file containing the data for the merge¶
    'should only be opened once. Therefore,¶
    'track when the merge has started¶
    If BeforeMergeExecuted = False Then¶
        BeforeMergeExecuted = True¶
        MsgBox sMergeMessage, vbCritical + vbOKOnly¶
        Set DataDoc = OpenChartDataFile(Doc.Path)¶
    End If¶
    If DataDoc Is Nothing Then¶
        MsgBox "The data document could not be opened."¶
        CancelMerge = True¶
        Cancel = True¶
        Exit Sub¶
    End If¶
    'If there is no target for the chart, then¶
```

Wrd

```
    'don't try to insert it¶
    If Doc.Bookmarks.Exists(BookmarkName) Then¶
        Set rngChart = Doc.Bookmarks(BookmarkName).Range¶
        EditChart rngChart, DataDoc¶
        DoEvents¶
        Cancel = False¶
    Else¶
        MsgBox "The bookmark " & BookmarkName & "is missing."¶
        Cancel = True¶
        Exit Sub¶
    End If¶
    'Make sure the changes to the chart¶
    'are carried over to the merge result¶
    rngChart.Fields.Update¶
End Sub¶
```

Wrd

Prepare the chart data: The data should be in a Word table, in a Word document, saved in the same folder as the main merge document.

If the data is in a table in another application, such as Access or Excel, simply copy and paste it into a Word document. Take care that the records are sorted in the same order as for the mail merge, and that there is at least one row of data for each record.

The following data table was copied from an Access query and pasted into a Word document. Then the first row (containing the query name) was deleted.

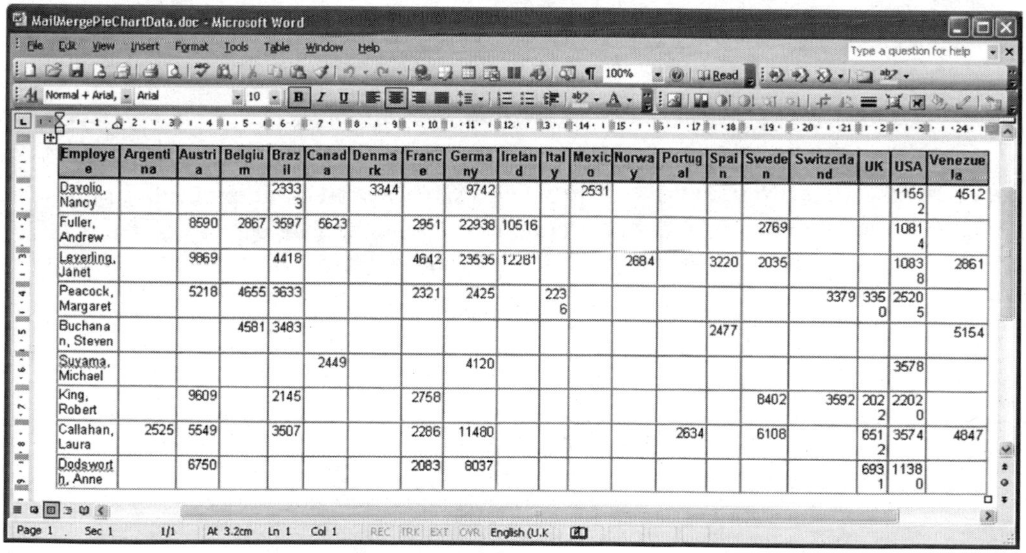

Employee	Argentina	Austria	Belgium	Brazil	Canada	Denmark	France	Germany	Ireland	Italy	Mexico	Norway	Portugal	Spain	Sweden	Switzerland	UK	USA	Venezuela
Davolio, Nancy				23333		3344		9742			2531							11552	4512
Fuller, Andrew		8590	2867	3597	5623		2951	22938	10516						2769			10814	
Leverling, Janet		9869		4418			4642	23535	12281			2684		3220	2036			10838	2861
Peacock, Margaret		5218	4655	3633			2321	2425		2236						3379	3350	25205	
Buchanan, Steven			4581	3483										2477					5154
Suyama, Michael					2449			4120										3578	
King, Robert		9609		2145			2758								8402	3592	2022	22020	
Callahan, Laura	2525	5549		3507			2286	11480					2634		6108		6512	3574	4847
Dodsworth, Anne		6750					2083	8037									6931	11380	

Figure 60 – Mail Merge with Charts

The first column contains the ID information relating to the merge record. The second and following columns provide the data for a pie chart, such as shown in Figure 61.

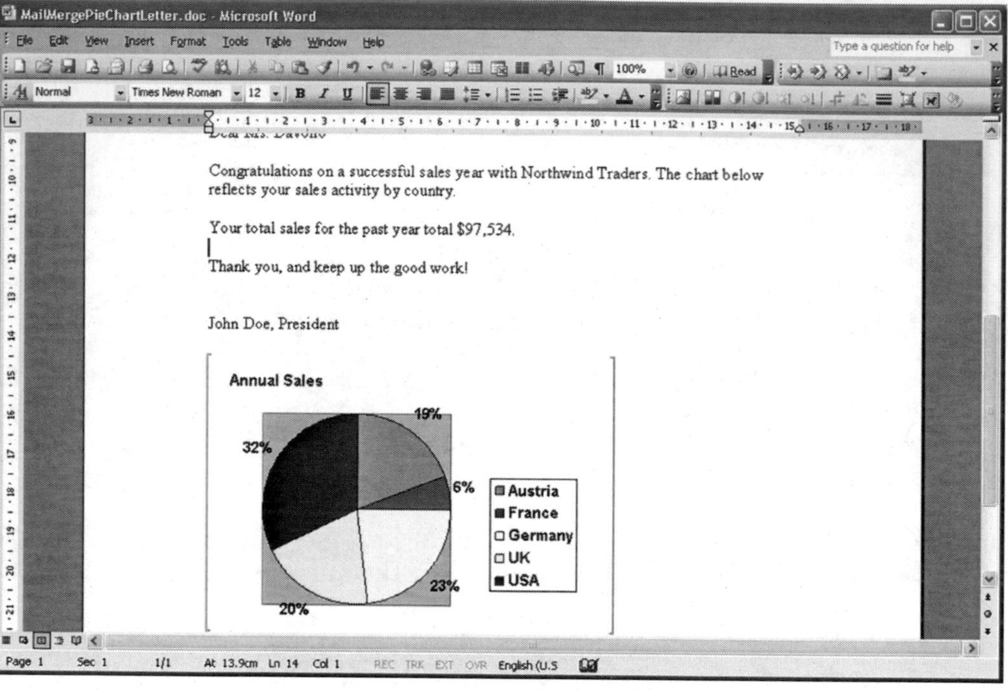

Figure 61 – Letter with Chart Merged

The code can also produce other kinds of charts as well. The example below shows the source data for a column chart. In this case, the second column corresponds to the x-axis labels of the column chart, and the remaining columns contain the data.

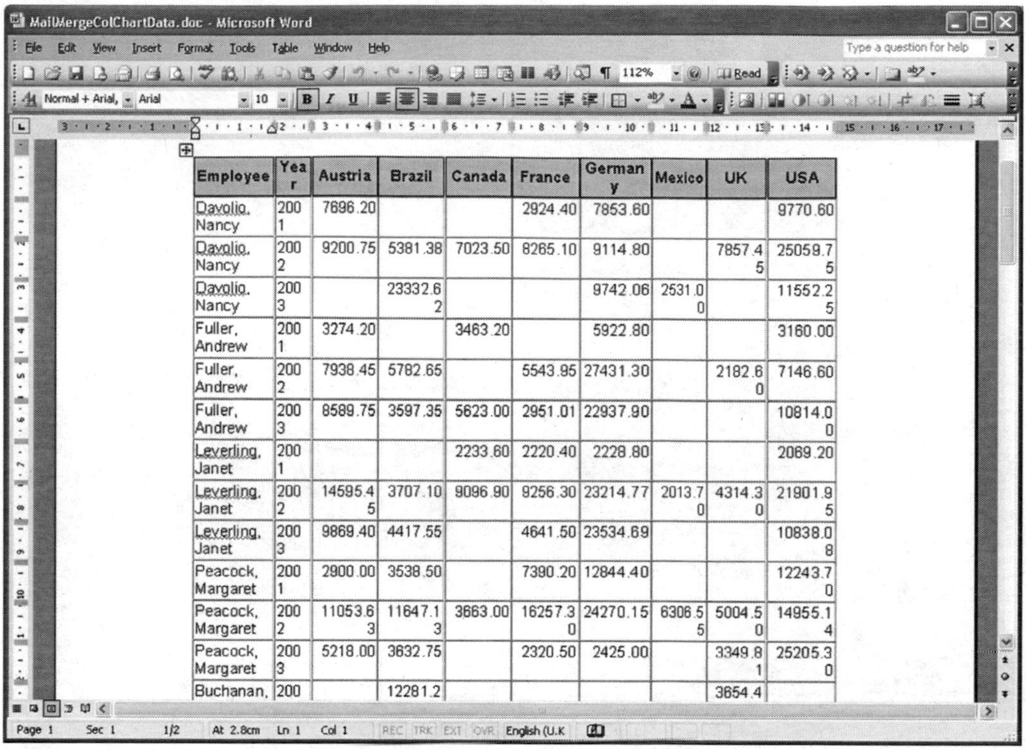

Employee	Year	Austria	Brazil	Canada	France	Germany	Mexico	UK	USA
Davolio, Nancy	2001	7696.20			2924.40	7853.60			9770.60
Davolio, Nancy	2002	9200.75	5381.38	7023.50	8265.10	9114.80		7857.45	25059.75
Davolio, Nancy	2003		23332.62			9742.06	2531.00		11552.25
Fuller, Andrew	2001	3274.20		3463.20		5922.80			3160.00
Fuller, Andrew	2002	7938.45	5782.65		5543.95	27431.30		2182.60	7146.60
Fuller, Andrew	2003	8589.75	3597.35	5623.00	2951.01	22937.90			10814.00
Leverling, Janet	2001			2233.60	2220.40	2228.80			2069.20
Leverling, Janet	2002	14595.45	3707.10	9096.90	9256.30	23214.77	2013.70	4314.30	21901.95
Leverling, Janet	2003	9869.40	4417.55		4641.50	23534.69			10838.08
Peacock, Margaret	2001	2900.00	3538.50		7390.20	12844.40			12243.70
Peacock, Margaret	2002	11053.63	11647.13	3663.00	16257.30	24270.15	6306.55	5004.50	14955.14
Peacock, Margaret	2003	5218.00	3632.75		2320.50	2425.00		3349.81	25205.30
Buchanan,	200		12281.2					3654.4	

Figure 62 – Letter with Column Chart Merged

Figure 63 shows the resulting letter with a column chart embedded.

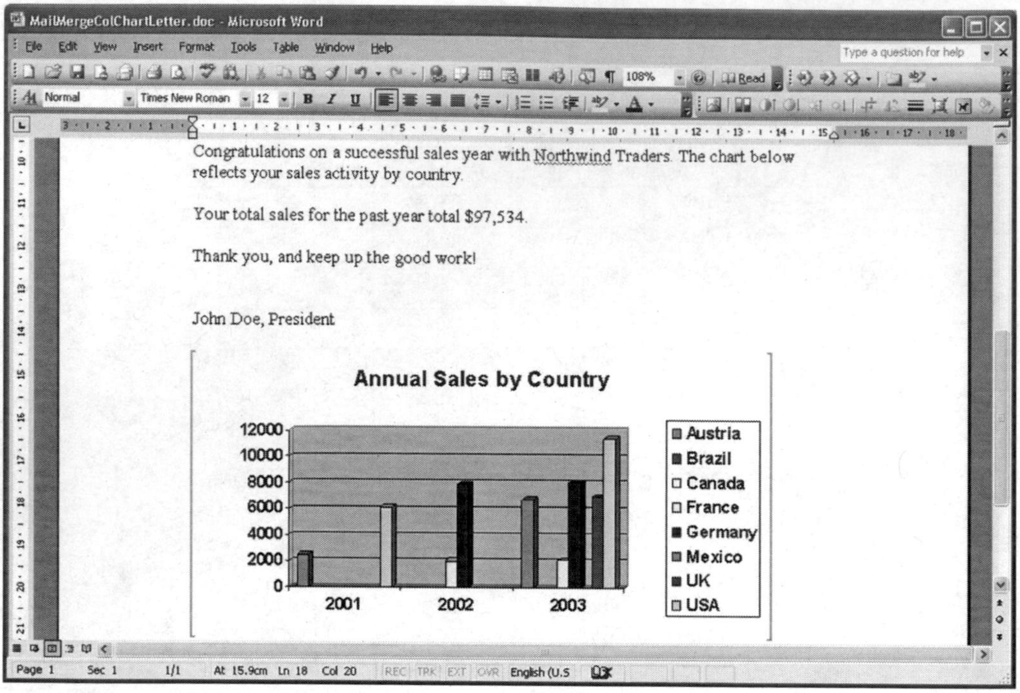

Figure 63 – Chart with Legend

In both cases, the first row contains the legend text for the chart.

Tip: Because it simply fills the datasheet of an MS Graph object that is inserted and formatted, the macro solution can be used with any kind of chart.

Follow these steps:

1. Save the data document and substitute its name for the code line Const ChartDataDoc.

2. Set up the main merge document as a form letter in the normal fashion. Use Insert | Object to insert a Microsoft Graph Chart. Choose the type of chart you want and format it as desired. The macro changes only the data in the data sheet. Select the chart, then over Insert | Bookmark, insert a bookmark named PieChart.

Tips: The chart and bookmark can be in a table cell or a frame in order to have text flow around the chart.

If a different bookmark name is used, just remember to change the information for the code line Const BookmarkName.

3. Go into Tools | References in the Visual Basic Editor (VBE) and activate the checkbox next to Microsoft Office Graph 10.0 Object Library (Office 2002) or Microsoft Office Graph 11.0 Object Library (Office 2003).
4. There are sample files for both pie and column chart merges. Both use MailMergeData.doc for the data source; link the sample mail merge letter files to them before running the 'MergeToChart' code.

Note: Pay attention to the message that is displayed at the start! The updating of the MS Graph charts in the document can take a number of seconds, and Word may appear to hang. It hasn't. Be patient and wait until the finishing message has been displayed.

Transferring a Selection to a New Document

This procedure demonstrates how to access page setup properties, headers, footers, and page numbers.

Scenario: One request for help seen quite often, especially for persons moving to Word from WordPerfect, is how to save a selection to a new file. While copying the selection and pasting it into a new document is one solution, there are two major issues involved: additional steps that are required, and lost formatting due to differences in margins, styles, headers, and footers in the new document as opposed to the original document.

With this macro, a selection can be quickly transferred into a new document, retaining all the original formatting.

Example file:
W031

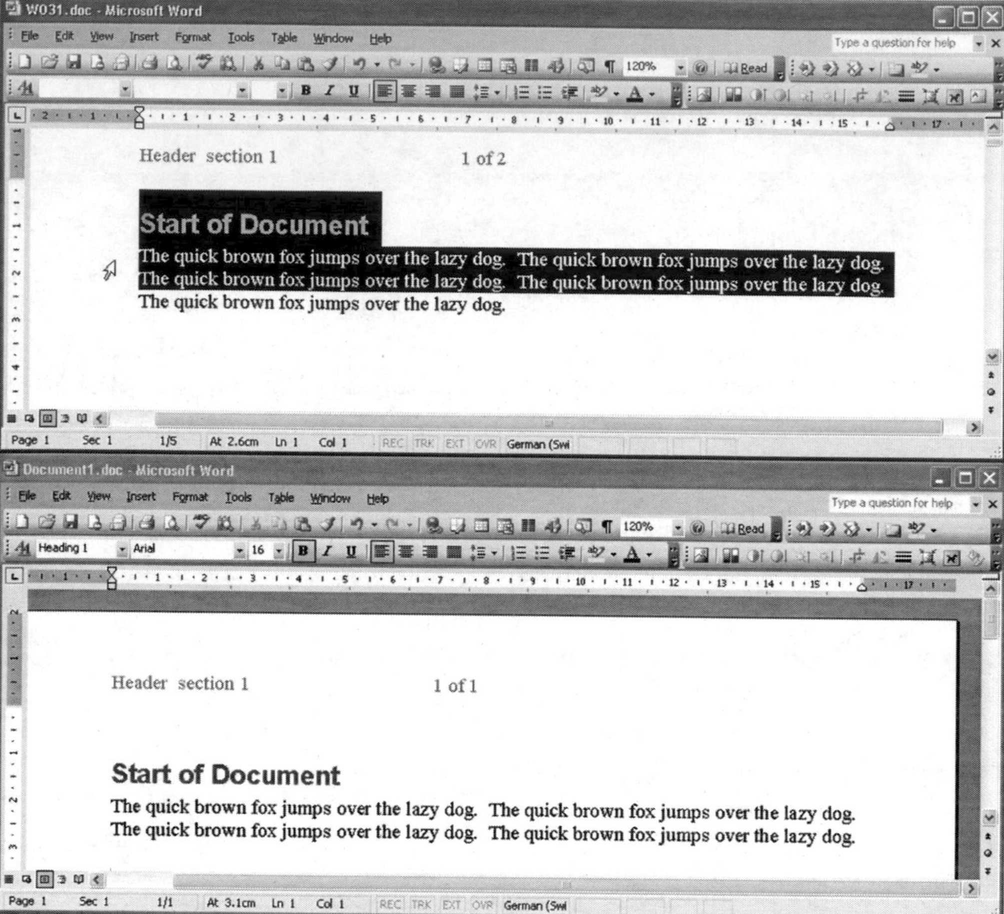

Figure 64 – Transferring a Selection to a New Document

View the Appendix to learn how to store this procedure in a Standard module.

```
Option explicit¶
' * * * * *¶
Sub SaveSelectionAsNewFile()¶
    'Variable declaration¶
    Dim rngSel As Word.Range¶
    Dim origSetup As Word.PageSetup¶
    Dim docNew As Word.Document¶
```

```
'Assign the selection to its variable¶
Set rngSel = Selection.Range¶
Set origSetup = rngSel.Sections(1).PageSetup¶
'Create a new document from the current document¶
'So that styles, etc. are all present¶
Set docNew = Documents.Add(ActiveDocument.FullName)¶
'Delete everything¶
docNew.Range.Delete¶
'Put the selection into the new document¶
docNew.Range.FormattedText = rngSel.FormattedText¶
'Set the page properties to correspond¶
'to the settings for the section in which¶
'the selection was made¶
With docNew.Sections(1).PageSetup¶
    .BottomMargin = origSetup.BottomMargin¶
    .TopMargin = origSetup.TopMargin¶
    .LeftMargin = origSetup.LeftMargin¶
    .RightMargin = origSetup.RightMargin¶
    .Gutter = origSetup.Gutter¶
    'Comment out the next two lines for Wor97¶
    'and Word 2000¶
    .GutterPos = origSetup.GutterPos¶
    .GutterStyle = origSetup.GutterStyle¶
    .DifferentFirstPageHeaderFooter = _¶
      origSetup.DifferentFirstPageHeaderFooter¶
    .OddAndEvenPagesHeaderFooter = _¶
      origSetup.OddAndEvenPagesHeaderFooter¶
    .FooterDistance = origSetup.FooterDistance¶
    .HeaderDistance = origSetup.HeaderDistance¶
    .MirrorMargins = origSetup.MirrorMargins¶
    .Orientation = origSetup.Orientation¶
    .PaperSize = origSetup.PaperSize¶
    .PageHeight = origSetup.PageHeight¶
    .PageWidth = origSetup.PageWidth¶
    With .TextColumns¶
        .SetCount numcolumns:=origSetup.TextColumns.Count¶
        .EvenlySpaced = origSetup.TextColumns.EvenlySpaced¶
        .LineBetween = origSetup.TextColumns.LineBetween¶
        If .Count > 1 And .EvenlySpaced Then¶
                'Variable declaration¶
                Dim i As Long¶
            .Spacing = origSetup.TextColumns.Spacing¶
            If .Spacing = False Then¶
                For i = 1 To .Count¶
                    .Item(i).SpaceAfter = _¶
                      origSetup.TextColumns(i).SpaceAfter¶
                    .Item(i).Width = _¶
                      origSetup.TextColumns(i).Width¶
                Next¶
            End If¶
```

Wrd

```
            ElseIf .Count > 1 And Not .EvenlySpaced Then¶
                For i = 1 To .Count¶
                 .Width = origSetup.TextColumns(i).Width¶
                Next¶
            End If¶
        End With¶
    End With¶
    'Define headers, footers and page numbers¶
    Dim pgNr As Long¶
    'Get the starting page number¶
    rngSel.Collapse wdCollapseStart¶
    pgNr = rngSel.Information(wdActiveEndAdjustedPageNumber)¶
    'Disables different first page if selection is not on a first page¶
    'Comment out the following first, and fourth through seventh¶
    ' lines to see first page headers/footers¶
    ' in result document if present in original even if¶
    ' selection is not originally on a first page¶
    If pgNr = 1 Then¶
        ProcessHeadersFooters wdHeaderFooterFirstPage, _¶
          rngSel.Sections(1), docNew.Sections(1)¶
    Else¶
        docNew.Sections(1).PageSetup. _¶
          DifferentFirstPageHeaderFooter = False¶
    End If¶
    'To NOT retain the original page number,¶
    'comment out the next four lines¶
    With docNew.Sections(1).Headers(wdHeaderFooterPrimary)¶
        .PageNumbers.RestartNumberingAtSection = True¶
        .PageNumbers.StartingNumber = pgNr¶
    End With¶
    ProcessHeadersFooters wdHeaderFooterPrimary, _¶
      rngSel.Sections(1), docNew.Sections(1)¶
    ProcessHeadersFooters wdHeaderFooterEvenPages, _¶
      rngSel.Sections(1), docNew.Sections(1)¶
    'Display the FileSaveAs dialog box¶
    Dialogs(wdDialogFileSaveAs).Show¶
End Sub¶
' * * * * *¶
'Carry over formatted text for the selected section¶
'from original document and update the fields¶
Sub ProcessHeadersFooters(typ As Long, _¶
  sec1 As Word.Section, sec2 As Word.Section)¶
    sec2.Headers(typ).Range.FormattedText = _¶
      sec1.Headers(typ).Range.FormattedText¶
    sec2.Headers(typ).Range.Fields.Update¶
    sec2.Footers(typ).Range.FormattedText = _¶
      sec1.Footers(typ).Range.FormattedText¶
    sec2.Footers(typ).Range.Fields.Update¶
End Sub¶
```

It was difficult to decide exactly what to include in this tool because there are varying requirements as to what kinds of setup formatting should be retained or discarded. Comment out any of the property assignments under With docNew.Sections(1).PageSetup that should not transfer to the new document.

If the original document has page numbers, consider whether it is better to retain the original page number or to let the new document begin counting at 1. To do the latter, comment out these four lines in the procedure:

```
With docNew.Sections(1).Headers _ (wdHeaderFooterPrimary)¶
.PageNumbers.RestartNumberingAtSection = True¶
.PageNumbers.StartingNumber = pgNr¶
End With¶
```


If DifferentFirstPage is activated for headers and footers, decide whether the new document should reflect this or if it should begin with the header and footer used on the page on which the selection begins. To not suppress DifferentFirstPage when the original selection does not begin on a first page, comment out these lines, EXCEPT for the second and third lines.

```
If pgNr = 1 Then¶
ProcessHeadersFooters wdHeaderFooterFirstPage, _¶
rngSel.Sections(1), docNew.Sections(1)¶
Else¶
docNew.Sections(1).PageSetup. _¶
DifferentFirstPageHeaderFooter = False¶
End If¶
```

Select some text, and then run the macro.

Splitting a Document into Multiple Files

This procedure shows you chow to split a document into separate files according to heading styles applied to the text. It also shows you how to work with Subdocuments.

Example file: W032

Scenario: Sometimes, it is necessary to split up a document into separate files; for instance, to allow a number of persons to edit different chapters at the same time. Another case would be to create a website from the document.

The easiest way in Word to pull a document apart or to bring separate documents together is with the Master/Subdocument feature, available in the Outline view. Over the last decade, this feature has caused lots of problems primarily because people have tried to use it in ways the developers never intended. For the basic task of splitting or combining documents, however, it's quite reliable.

Tip: Key points for staying out of trouble when using Master documents:

1. Make back-up copies of the sub-documents frequently.
2. Never, ever edit subdocuments when they are open in a Master document. Consider the Master document as a throw-away container for pulling individual documents together for printing or viewing purposes.

This macro tool splits a document into sub-documents based on heading styles. You can specify the heading levels to which the document should be split.

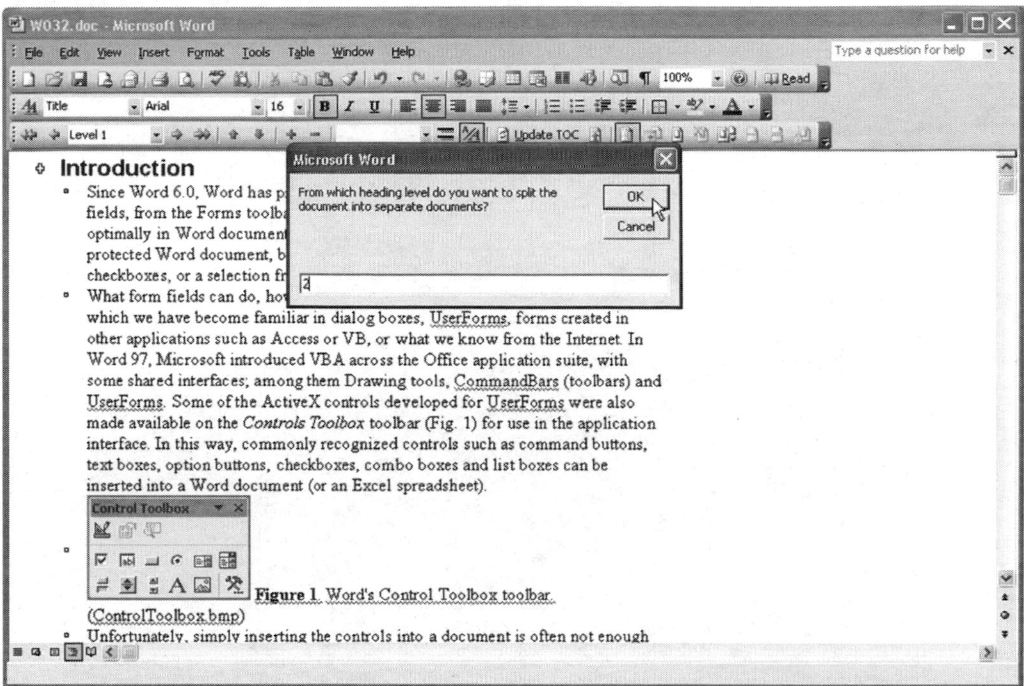

Figure 65 – Defining the Heading Level for Splitting a Document

---

Tip: The tool is language independent; for example, it doesn't matter whether the style in the active document is named "Heading 1" or "Überschrift 1".

View the Appendix to learn how to store this procedure in a Standard module.

```
Option explicit¶
' * * * * *¶
Sub SplitDocIntoFiles()¶
    'Variable declaration¶
    Dim doc As Word.Document¶
    Set doc = ActiveDocument¶
    'Recommended to save to a new name¶
    'as original document will not¶
    'be recoverable¶
    Dialogs(wdDialogFileSaveAs).Show¶
    SplitByLevel doc¶
```

```
    'Saving automatically saves subdocs¶
    'to names using text of first paragraph¶
    doc.Save¶
    '''Save merge result to¶
    '''separate files¶
    ' Convert all sections to Subdocs¶
    ' (for mail merge result, for example)¶
    'AllSectionsToSubDoc(doc)¶
    ' Save each Subdoc as a separate file¶
    'SaveAllSubDocsFromMerge¶
End Sub¶
' * * * * *¶
Sub SplitByLevel(doc As Word.Document)¶
    'Variable declaration¶
    Dim outlineLevel As String¶
    Dim i As Long¶
    Dim rngSearch As Word.Range¶
    Dim styleName¶
    Dim bFound As Boolean¶
    outlineLevel = InputBox( _¶
      "From which heading level do you want to " & _¶
        "split the document into separate documents?")¶
    'Invalid entry: outline levels from 1 to 9¶
    If outlineLevel = "" Then¶
        Exit Sub¶
    ElseIf CLng(outlineLevel) < 1 _¶
      Or CLng(outlineLevel) > 9 Then¶
        Exit Sub¶
    End If¶
    'Must be in MasterView to work with¶
    'Subdocs as separate files¶
    With doc.ActiveWindow.View¶
        .Type = wdMasterView¶
        'And all text must be showing¶
        .ShowHeading 9¶
        .ShowAllHeadings¶
    End With¶
    For i = 1 To CLng(outlineLevel)¶
        Set rngSearch = doc.Range¶
        styleName = GetStyleName(doc, i)¶
        Do¶
            With rngSearch.Find¶
                .ClearFormatting¶
                .Forward = True¶
                .Format = True¶
                .MatchCase = False¶
                .MatchWholeWord = False¶
                .MatchWildcards = False¶
                .Style = styleName¶
                .Text = ""¶
                .Wrap = wdFindStop¶
```

```
                bFound = .Execute¶
            End With¶
            If bFound Then¶
                rngSearch.Select¶
                Set rngSearch = doc.Bookmarks( _¶
                  "\HeadingLevel").Range¶
                'Sub docs can't go across¶
                'section / subdoc boundaries¶
                Do While Asc(rngSearch.Characters( _¶
                  Len(rngSearch.Text))) = 12¶
                    rngSearch.MoveEnd wdCharacter, -1¶
                Loop¶
                doc.Subdocuments.AddFromRange _¶
                  rngSearch¶
            End If¶
            rngSearch.Collapse wdCollapseEnd¶
            rngSearch.MoveStart wdCharacter, 1¶
            rngSearch.End = doc.Range.End¶
            rngSearch.Select¶
        Loop While bFound¶
    Next¶
End Sub¶
' * * * * *¶
Function GetStyleName(doc As Word.Document, _¶
  outlineLevel As Long) As String¶
    'Variable declaration¶
    Dim styleName As String¶
    Select Case outlineLevel¶
        Case 1¶
            styleName = doc.Styles(wdStyleHeading1).NameLocal¶
        Case 2¶
            styleName = doc.Styles(wdStyleHeading2).NameLocal¶
        Case 3¶
            styleName = doc.Styles(wdStyleHeading3).NameLocal¶
        Case 4¶
            styleName = doc.Styles(wdStyleHeading4).NameLocal¶
        Case 5¶
            styleName = doc.Styles(wdStyleHeading5).NameLocal¶
        Case 6¶
            styleName = doc.Styles(wdStyleHeading6).NameLocal¶
        Case 7¶
            styleName = doc.Styles(wdStyleHeading7).NameLocal¶
        Case 8¶
            styleName = doc.Styles(wdStyleHeading8).NameLocal¶
        Case 9¶
            styleName = doc.Styles(wdStyleHeading9).NameLocal¶
    End Select¶
    GetStyleName = styleName¶
End Function¶
```

```
' * * * * *¶
Function AllSectionsToSubDoc(ByRef doc As Word.Document) As Boolean¶
    'Variable declaration¶
    Dim secCounter As Long¶
    Dim NrSecs As Long¶
    NrSecs = doc.Sections.Count¶
    If NrSecs <= 1 Then¶
        AllSectionsToSubDoc = False¶
        Exit Function¶
    End If¶
    'Start from the end because creating¶
    'Subdocs inserts additional sections¶
    For secCounter = NrSecs - 1 To 1 Step -1¶
        doc.Subdocuments.AddFromRange _¶
          doc.Sections(secCounter).Range¶
    Next secCounter¶
    AllSectionsToSubDoc = True¶
End Function¶
' * * * * *¶
Sub SaveAllSubDocsFromMerge(ByRef doc As Word.Document)¶
    'Variable declaration¶
    Dim subdoc As Word.Subdocument¶
    Dim newdoc As Word.Document¶
    Dim docCounter As Long¶
    docCounter = 1¶
    For Each subdoc In doc.Subdocuments¶
        Set newdoc = subdoc.Open¶
        'Remove NextPage section breaks¶
        'originating from mailmerge¶
        RemoveAllSectionBreaks newdoc¶
        With newdoc¶
            .SaveAs FileName:="MergeResult" & CStr(docCounter)¶
            .Close¶
        End With¶
        docCounter = docCounter + 1¶
    Next subdoc¶
End Sub¶
' * * * * *¶
Sub RemoveAllSectionBreaks(doc As Word.Document)¶
    With doc.Range.Find¶
    .ClearFormatting¶
    .Text = "^b"¶
        With .Replacement¶
        .ClearFormatting¶
        .Text = ""¶
        End With¶
    .Execute Replace:=wdReplaceAll¶
    End With¶
End Sub¶
```

Wrd

Follow these steps:

1. When prompted to save the document under a different name, you can do so or not. Doing so is recommended, because there is NO WAY to go back to the original file once the macro has finished.
2. In the next dialog box, enter the heading level down to which the document should split. Enter 2, for example, and the tool saves all the text between heading level 1 and heading level 2 to new documents. Note that in this example, the documents created from heading level 1 will have sub-document links to the heading level 2 documents. These can be deleted along with their section breaks.
3. If the goal is to create a set of web pages from the original document, copy the hyperlinks to a position outside the sub-document "block" before deleting the sub-document sections.
4. When the macro has finished, each of the subdocuments will have been saved as a separate file in the same folder as the master document from which they were created. The heading level text from which they were generated serves as the file name. The master document file can now safely be deleted.
5. Make sure that each paragraph is formatted where the document should be split with a heading style. If these paragraphs should not appear different than other paragraphs, change the definition of the Heading style.

Creating a Folder Tree Menu

This procedure displays the contents of a folder and its sub-folders as a drop-down menu and demonstrates how to create drop-down menus (pop-ups).

Example file:
MenuTree

Scenario: Microsoft provides the My Documents folder for storing the files. If you regularly work with more than 20 files or so, it's not expedient to have them all listed together in the same place. Generally, files get organized in sets of folders, according to a criterion—by project, for example—so that they can be found more easily.

Wrd

The drawback to being organized this way is that it takes longer to navigate through the folder paths when you need to open a file. Displaying the contents of a set of folders in drop-down menus helps to quickly find and choose the file that is needed: the menus open up automatically when the mouse hovers over them—no clicking required except for selecting the file to work with.

Selecting a file will open it in Word or insert it in the current document, as appropriate for the file type.

The following macro drills down through a folder structure to up to three levels and presents a list of all Word, Excel, PowerPoint, plain text, HTML, RTF, and graphics files in each folder. When an entry is selected, the Word, text, HTML or RTF file will be opened; Excel, PowerPoint, and graphics files will be embedded in the current document as objects.

In addition, for Word 2002 or Word 2003, an icon designating the file type next to the filename can be displayed.

View the Appendix to learn how to store this procedure in a Standard module.

```
Option explicit¶
' * * * * *¶
Const BaseFolderPath As String = "C:\Test\"¶
Const ToolbarTarget As String = "Menu Bar"¶
Const ButtonName As String = "My Files"¶
```

```
' * * * * *¶
Sub CreateFolderTreeMenu()¶
    'Variable declaration¶
    Dim aLevOneEntries() As String¶
    Dim cb As Office.CommandBar¶
    Dim ctlPopupMain As Office.CommandBarPopup¶
    Dim i As Long¶
    'Get the list of files and folders from the¶
    'base folder specified in the Const BaseFolderPath¶
    aLevOneEntries() = GetMenuEntries(BaseFolderPath)¶
    'Make sure the changes will be stored in¶
    'the Normal.dot template¶
    CustomizationContext = NormalTemplate¶
    'Specify in which toolbar the new menu¶
    'will be created¶
    Set cb = CommandBars(ToolbarTarget)¶
    'Check to see if the button already exists¶
    'and remove it if it does¶
    If buttonExists(cb, ButtonName) = True Then¶
        cb.Controls(ButtonName).Delete¶
    End If¶
    'Create the top-level drop-down¶
    'at the end of the toolbar¶
    Set ctlPopupMain = CreateNewPopup(cb, ButtonName, 0)¶
    'Create entries for first-level files¶
    For i = LBound(aLevOneEntries, 2) To UBound(aLevOneEntries, 2)¶
        'Ignore any empty entries¶
        If Len(aLevOneEntries(0, i)) <> 0 Then¶
            CreateMenuButton ctlPopupMain.CommandBar, aLevOneEntries(0,
i), BaseFolderPath¶
        End If¶
    Next i¶
    'Create entries for first-level sub-folders¶
    'Loop through folders in reverse order since¶
    'each successive folder entry is inserted¶
    'at the top of the list. Keeps them alphabetical¶
    For i = UBound(aLevOneEntries, 2) To LBound(aLevOneEntries, 2) Step
-1¶
        If Len(aLevOneEntries(1, i)) <> 0 Then¶
            'Variable declaration¶
            Dim newPopup As Office.CommandBarPopup¶
            'Create the popup entry¶
            'position it at the top of the list (1)¶
            Set newPopup = CreateNewPopup(ctlPopupMain.CommandBar,
aLevOneEntries(1, i), 1)¶
            'Process the lists for the second level popup¶
            'Variable declaration¶
            Dim aLevTwoEntries() As String¶
            Dim LevTwoPath As String¶
            Dim j As Long¶
            LevTwoPath = BaseFolderPath & aLevOneEntries(1, i) & "\"¶
```

Wrd

```
            aLevTwoEntries() = GetMenuEntries(LevTwoPath)¶
            'Create buttons for the second level files¶
            For j = LBound(aLevTwoEntries, 2) To UBound(aLevTwoEntries,
2)¶
                If Len(aLevTwoEntries(0, j)) <> 0 Then¶
                    CreateMenuButton newPopup.CommandBar,
aLevTwoEntries(0, j), LevTwoPath¶
                End If¶
            Next j¶
            'Now do any sub-folders at the second level¶
            For j = LBound(aLevTwoEntries, 2) To UBound(aLevTwoEntries,
2)¶
                If Len(aLevTwoEntries(1, j)) <> 0 Then¶
                    'Variable declaration¶
                    Dim newPopup2 As Office.CommandBarPopup¶
                    Set newPopup2 = CreateNewPopup(newPopup.CommandBar,
aLevTwoEntries(1, i), 1)¶
                    'Get the thirdlevel entries¶
                    'Variable declaration¶
                    Dim aLevThreeEntries() As String¶
                    Dim k As Long¶
                    aLevThreeEntries() = GetMenuEntries(LevTwoPath &
aLevTwoEntries(1, i) & "\")¶
                    'Only show files, for this level¶
                    For k = LBound(aLevThreeEntries, 2) To
UBound(aLevThreeEntries, 2)¶
                        If Len(aLevThreeEntries(0, k)) <> 0 Then¶
                            CreateMenuButton newPopup2.CommandBar,
aLevThreeEntries(0, k), LevTwoPath & aLevTwoEntries(1, j) & "\"¶
                        End If¶
                    Next k¶
                End If¶
            Next j¶
        End If¶
    Next i¶
End Sub¶
'Remove the entire menu, with all sub-entries¶
'by removing the top-level popup¶
Sub DeleteTree()¶
    'Variable declaration¶
    Dim cb As Office.CommandBar¶
    CustomizationContext = NormalTemplate¶
    Set cb = CommandBars(ToolbarTarget)¶
    If buttonExists(cb, ButtonName) = True Then¶
        cb.Controls(ButtonName).Delete¶
    End If¶
End Sub¶
```

Wrd

```
' * * * * *¶
'Get all files and folders in the specified path¶
'and return them in an array¶
Function GetMenuEntries(path As String) As Variant¶
    'Variable declaration¶
    Dim folderContent As String¶
    Dim filePath As String¶
    Dim aEntries() As String¶
    Dim iFileEntry As Long¶
    Dim iDirEntry As Long¶
    'Store the type (file or directory) and¶
    'name in an array, to pass back¶
    'The array has two dimensions¶
    'All entries with 0 in the first dimension¶
    'are file names; all entries with 1¶
    'in the first dimension are folders¶
    ReDim aEntries(1, 0)¶
    'Start processing the folder tree in the base path...¶
    folderContent = Dir(path, vbDirectory + vbNormal)¶
    'Looping through each entry in the folder¶
    'until no more are found¶
    Do While folderContent <> ""¶
        filePath = path & folderContent¶
        'Determine which kind of entry is being dealt with¶
        Select Case GetAttr(filePath)¶
            Case vbArchive, vbNormal¶
                'Only increment the second array dimension¶
                'as necessary¶
                If iFileEntry >= iDirEntry Then¶
                    ReDim Preserve aEntries(1, iFileEntry)¶
                End If¶
                'add file to the appropriate array dimension¶
                aEntries(0, iFileEntry) = folderContent¶
                'increment the counter for this type¶
                iFileEntry = iFileEntry + 1¶
            Case vbDirectory¶
                'Don't pick up the folder itself,¶
                'nor its "parent"¶
                If folderContent <> "." And folderContent <> ".." Then¶
                    'Only increment the second array dimension¶
                    'as necessary¶
                    If iDirEntry >= iFileEntry Then¶
                        ReDim Preserve aEntries(1, iDirEntry)¶
                    End If¶
                    aEntries(1, iDirEntry) = folderContent¶
                    iDirEntry = iDirEntry + 1¶
                End If¶
            Case Else¶
        End Select¶
```

Wrd

```
            'Go to the next entry¶
            folderContent = Dir¶
        Loop¶
        GetMenuEntries = aEntries()¶
End Function¶
' * * * * *¶
Function CreateNewPopup( _¶
    cb As CommandBar, _¶
    s As String, _¶
    Pos As Long) As Office.CommandBarPopup¶
        'Variable declaration¶
        Dim ctl As Office.CommandBarPopup¶
        'If 0 is passed in, then the entry should appear¶
        'at the end of the list¶
        If Pos = 0 Then¶
            Set ctl = cb.Controls.Add(Type:=msoControlPopup)¶
        Else¶
        'Otherwise, place it at the top¶
           Set ctl = cb.Controls.Add(Type:=msoControlPopup, Before:=Pos)¶
        End If¶
        With ctl¶
            'The folder name is the caption¶
            .Caption = s¶
            .Enabled = True¶
            .Visible = True¶
        End With¶
        Set CreateNewPopup = ctl¶
End Function¶
' * * * * *¶
Function CreateMenuButton( _¶
    cb As CommandBar, _¶
    filename As String, _¶
    path As String)¶
        'Variable declaration¶
        Dim ctl As Office.CommandBarButton¶
        Dim filetype As String¶
        'Determine what kind of file by the extension¶
        filetype = GetFileType(path & filename)¶
        'Don't include unwanted file types¶
        'to deal with¶
        If filetype = "unknown" Then Exit Function¶
        'Create the new button¶
        Set ctl = cb.Controls.Add(Type:=msoControlButton)¶
        With ctl¶
            .Caption = filename¶
            .Enabled = True¶
            .Visible = True¶
            'The macro to run when the button is clicked¶
            'in this case, all buttons run the same macro¶
            .OnAction = "ProcessFile"¶
```

Wrd

```
        'Store the path in the Tag property¶
        'so that OnAction macro can access it¶
        .Tag = path¶
        'Only Word 2002/2003 support adding a¶
        'picture from a file¶
        If Application.Version >= 10 Then¶
            AddButtonPicture ctl, filetype¶
        End If¶
    End With¶
End Function¶
' * * * * *¶
Function GetFileType(s As String) As String¶
   'Variable declaration¶
    Dim ext As String¶
    Dim loc As Long¶
    'The file extension follows the last .¶
    'in the filename. Determine¶
    'at which position this is¶
    loc = InStr(s, ".")¶
    'Loop until no more . are found¶
    'What's left in the ext string is the file extension¶
    Do¶
        ext = Mid(s, loc + 1)¶
        loc = InStr(ext, ".")¶
        s = ext¶
    Loop Until loc = 0¶
    'Set the file type, based on the extension¶
    Select Case ext¶
        Case "doc", "dot", "htm", "html", _¶
          "rtf", "txt", "csv"¶
            GetFileType = "Word"¶
        Case "xls"¶
            GetFileType = "Excel"¶
        Case "ppt"¶
            GetFileType = "Powerpoint"¶
        Case "bmp", "gif", "jpg", "tif"¶
            GetFileType = "Graphic"¶
        Case Else¶
            GetFileType = "unknown"¶
    End Select¶
End Function¶
' * * * * *¶
Function buttonExists( _¶
  cb As Office.CommandBar, _¶
  s As String) As Boolean¶
    Dim c As Office.CommandBarControl¶
    buttonExists = False¶
```

```
    'Determine whether the button already¶
    'exists in the specifed toolbar,¶
    'based on its caption¶
    For Each c In cb.Controls¶
        If c.Caption = s Then¶
            buttonExists = True¶
            Exit For¶
        End If¶
    Next c¶
End Function¶
' * * * * *¶
'Common macro executed by all buttons¶
'for valid file types¶
Sub ProcessFile()¶
    Dim ctl As Office.CommandBarButton¶
    Dim filetype As String¶
    Dim filename As String¶
    'The ActionControl property gives us¶
    'the button that was clicked¶
    Set ctl = Application.CommandBars.ActionControl¶
    'Determine the file type, based on the extension¶
    filetype = GetFileType(ctl.Caption)¶
    filename = ctl.Tag & ctl.Caption¶
    'Depending on the file type, perform an action¶
    Select Case filetype¶
        Case "Word"¶
            'Word and text files are opened¶
            Documents.Open ctl.Tag & ctl.Caption¶
        Case "Excel"¶
            'Excel files are inserted as Excel¶
            'spreadsheet objects¶
            ActiveDocument.InlineShapes.AddOLEObject _¶
              ClassType:="Excel.Sheet.8", _¶
              filename:=filename, _¶
              Range:=Selection.Range¶
        Case "Powerpoint"¶
            'Powerpoint files are inserted as¶
            'presentation objects¶
            ActiveDocument.InlineShapes.AddOLEObject _¶
              ClassType:="PowerPoint.Show.8", _¶
              filename:=filename, _¶
              Range:=Selection.Range¶
        Case "Graphic"¶
            'Graphics are inserted as embedded pictures¶
            ActiveDocument.InlineShapes.AddPicture _¶
              filename:=filename, _¶
              Range:=Selection.Range¶
        Case "unknown"¶
        Case Else¶
    End Select¶
End Sub¶
```

Wrd

```
' * * * * *¶
Option explicit¶
'Place in a separate module if unsure¶
'whether code will be used in Word 2000¶
'Word 2000 does not support adding pictures¶
'from file! Code in a separate module only¶
'compiles if it is called¶
Const IconPath As String = "C:\OffMacroBook\SampleFiles\"¶
' * * * * *¶
Sub AddButtonPicture(ctl As Office.CommandBarButton, filetype As
String)¶
    'Variable declaration¶
    Dim pic As IPictureDisp¶
    Dim mask As IPictureDisp¶
    Dim IconFile As String¶
    'Add a picture to the button,¶
    'based on the type of file¶
    Select Case filetype¶
        Case "Word"¶
            IconFile = IconPath & "WordIcon.bmp"¶
        Case "Excel"¶
            IconFile = IconPath & "XLIcon.bmp"¶
        Case "Powerpoint"¶
            IconFile = IconPath & "PPTIcon.bmp"¶
        Case "Graphic"¶
            IconFile = IconPath & "GrphIcon.bmp"¶
        Case Else¶
    End Select¶
    'Make sure the specified graphics file exists¶
    If Dir(IconFile) <> "" Then¶
        Set pic = stdole.StdFunctions.LoadPicture(IconFile)¶
        Set mask = stdole.StdFunctions.LoadPicture(IconFile)¶
        ctl.Picture = pic¶
    End If¶
End Sub¶
```

Follow these steps:

1. Copy the procedures to a module in a template or document. The example file uses two modules. The code specific to Word 2002 and 2003 is contained in the second module. This routine is called only when the version number indicates it is needed. Since the code is contained in a separate module, it is not compiled until it is called.

2. Edit the file paths in the Const declarations to reflect what the macro should do:

   - **BaseFolderPath** The top-level folder, the contents of which should appear in the main menu drop-down

Wrd

- **ToolbarTarget** The toolbar to which the menu should be added
- **ButtonName** The caption for the new button

3. To add a file extension to a category of recognized file extensions (xml to be opened like a document, for example), edit the procedure 'GetFileType'.
4. Locate the Case code line for the category to which the extension should be appended.
5. Type a comma, a space, then the extension in "quotes", as in the example below, where xml is added after csv.


```
Select Case ext
Case "doc", "dot", "htm", "html", _
"rtf", "txt", "csv", "xml"
```

6. If running Word 2002/2003 and including icons next to the file names, copy the 'AddButtonPicture' procedure to the same module, or to another module. Add the Const declaration to the top of the same module and edit the path to the folder where the bitmaps are located. Copy the bitmap files from the CD to that folder.

   If running Word 2000 or previous versions, adding pictures cannot be done using the technique in 'AddButtonPicture'. In this case, leave it off completely or place it in a different module so that, if upgraded to a more recent Word version, it becomes available.

Note: In order for the macro to work reliably, make sure the display of file extensions is enabled on the computer. In Windows Explorer, go to Tools | Folder Options | View and deactivate the checkbox 'Hide extensions for known file types'.

7. In order to remove the set of menus entirely, run the procedure 'DeleteTree'.
8. To add additional sets of menus, simply change the information in the Const declarations at the top of the module.

Changing Custom Dictionaries On-the-Fly

With this procedure, you can change the active custom dictionary to which words are added during spell check.

Scenario: Back in the days of Word 6.0 and Word 95, when the spell check was run, you could select the custom dictionary to which a word was added in the spell check dialog box. With the advent of Word 97, this functionality disappeared from the user interface. Thus, when you "Add to dictionary", it is uncertain as to which custom dictionary a word will be added.

This problem is especially critical when working with multiple languages prior to Word 2002, as well as when using project-specific dictionaries for special terminology. The only interface provided by Word is under Tools | Options | Spelling and Grammar | Custom Dictionaries. How much more convenient it would be to not have to click through four menu levels to change the active custom dictionary!

Example file:
W034

Tip: Starting in version 2002, Word maintains a separate default custom dictionary for every language. See Tools | Options | Spelling and Grammar | Custom Dictionaries.

One workable solution is to have a list of custom dictionaries in a toolbar. Simply select the dictionary that you want as the active custom dictionary from the list. This macro tool works best in a global template that loads when Word is started. It makes sure the toolbar is displayed with an up-to-date list of available custom dictionaries.

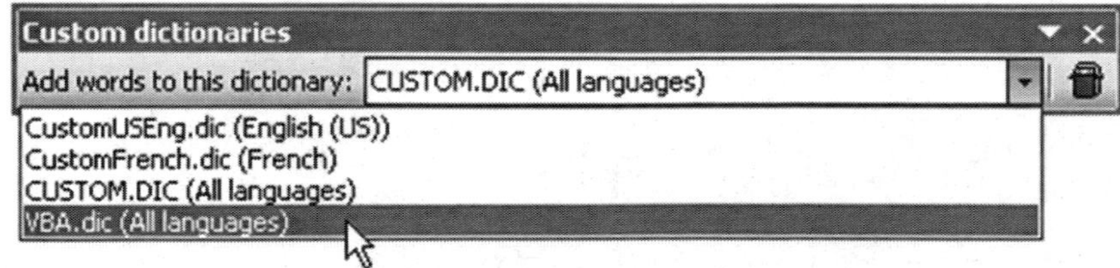

Figure 66 – Changing the Custom Dictionary

View the Appendix to learn how to store this procedure in a Standard module.

```
Option explicit¶
' * * * * *¶
Sub AutoExec()¶
    Dim errCounter As Long¶
    'Loop as long as it takes for Word to¶
    'load the toolbar when starting¶
    'Continue when error occurs¶
    On Error Resume Next¶
    Do¶
        errCounter = errCounter + 1¶
        Application.CommandBars("Custom dictionaries").Visible = True¶
    Loop While Err.Number <> 0 And errCounter < 50¶
    On Error GoTo 0¶
    FillDicList¶
    ThisDocument.Save¶
End Sub¶
' * * * * *¶
Sub FillDicList()¶
    'Variable declaration¶
    Dim theCtrl As Office.CommandBarComboBox¶
    Dim dic As Dictionary, dicCounter As Long¶
    Set theCtrl = CommandBars("Custom dictionaries").Controls(1)¶
    With theCtrl¶
        .Clear¶
        For Each dic In Application.CustomDictionaries¶
            dicCounter = dicCounter + 1¶
            theCtrl.AddItem dic.Name & " (" &
LanguageIDText(dic.LanguageID) & ")"¶
            If dic =
Application.CustomDictionaries.ActiveCustomDictionary Then _¶
                .ListIndex = dicCounter¶
        Next¶
    End With¶
    ThisDocument.Save¶
End Sub¶
' * * * * *¶
Sub ActivateDic()¶
    'Variable declaration¶
    Dim theCtrl As Office.CommandBarComboBox¶
    Dim szDic As String¶
    Set theCtrl = CommandBars.ActionControl¶
    szDic = theCtrl.Text¶
    szDic = Left(szDic, InStr(szDic, "(") - 2)¶
    Application.CustomDictionaries.ActiveCustomDictionary =
Application.CustomDictionaries(szDic)¶
    ThisDocument.Save¶
End Sub¶
```

```
' * * * * *¶
Function LanguageIDText(varLang As Variant) As String¶
    Select Case varLang¶
        Case 0¶
            LanguageIDText = "All languages"¶
        Case 2055¶
            LanguageIDText = "German (Swiss)"¶
        Case 1031¶
            LanguageIDText = "German (Germany)"¶
        Case 3079¶
            LanguageIDText = "German (Austrian)"¶
        Case 5127¶
            LanguageIDText = "German (Liechtenstein)"¶
        Case 4103¶
            LanguageIDText = "German (Luxemburg)"¶
        Case 2057¶
            LanguageIDText = "English (UK)"¶
        Case 1033¶
            LanguageIDText = "English (US)"¶
        Case 3081¶
            LanguageIDText = "English (AU)"¶
        Case 4105¶
            LanguageIDText = "English (CA)"¶
        Case 5129¶
            LangaugeIDText = "English (NZ)"¶
        Case 10249¶
            LanguageIDText = "English (Belize)"¶
        Case 9225¶
            LanguageIDText = "English (Caribbean)"¶
        Case 14345¶
            LanguageIDText = "English (Indonesian)"¶
        Case 6153¶
            LanguageIDText = "English (Ireland)"¶
        Case 8201¶
            LanguageIDText = "English (Jamaica)"¶
        Case 13321¶
            LanguageIDText = "English (Philippines)"¶
        Case 7177¶
            LanguageIDText = "English (SA)"¶
        Case 11273¶
            LanguageIDText = "English (TrinidadTobago)"¶
        Case 12297¶
            LanguageIDText = "English (Zimbabwe)"¶
        Case 1036¶
            LanguageIDText = "French"¶
        Case 3084¶
            LanguageIDText = "French (CA)"¶
        Case Else¶
            LanguageIDText = CStr(varLang)¶
    End Select¶
End Function¶
```

Follow these steps:

1. Copy the code to a template. Use the Organizer to copy the "Custom dictionaries" toolbar from the sample document to the template.
2. Without the sample document, use the code at the end of this section to generate the toolbar. Copy it into the same template and run it once.
3. The macro works best when run from a template in the Startup folder. Save the template to the Word Startup folder. The next time Word is started, it will be loaded in the background as a global template and the 'AutoExec' macro will run, displaying the toolbar.

Tip: To find the location of the Word Startup folder, look in Tools | Options | File locations.

Tip: The 'CreateCustomDicToolbar' macro code can be run from the Visual Basic Editor to create the toolbar initially.

View the Appendix to learn how to store this procedure in a Standard module.

```
Sub CreateCustomDicToolbar()¶
    'Variable declaration¶
    Dim cb As Office.CommandBar¶
    Dim cbo As Office.CommandBarComboBox¶
    Dim btn As Office.CommandBarButton¶
    Application.CustomizationContext = ThisDocument¶
    Set cb = Application.CommandBars.Add(Name:="Custom dictionaries 2")¶
    With cb¶
        Set cbo = .Controls.Add(Type:=msoControlComboBox)¶
        With cbo¶
            .Caption = "Add words to this dictionary"¶
            .OnAction = "ActivateDic"¶
            .Style = msoComboLabel¶
            .Width = 400¶
        End With¶
        Set btn = .Controls.Add(Type:=msoControlButton)¶
        With btn¶
            .Caption = "Update list"¶
            .OnAction = "FillDicList"¶
            .Style = msoButtonIcon¶
        End With¶
    End With¶
    cb.Visible = True¶
End Sub¶
```

4. Run the macro once to create the toolbar and toolbar controls. The toolbar button on the right won't have an icon. To give it the face of choice:
   a. Right-click the button.
   b. Customize.
   c. Right-click it again.
   d. Change button face.
   e. Choose the preferred icon.

Formatting Spelling Errors for Printing

You can format a document so that spelling errors are visible in the print document using this procedure.

Example file:
W035

Scenario: Since Word 95, spelling and grammar errors have been displayed on-screen by wavy red and green lines under the text. Starting with Word 2002, the colors of the wavy lines can be changed. There has, however, never been anyway to print out a document with these errors indicated.

With this macro, the text marked as being spelled incorrectly is formatted so that it is visible when printed out, as illustrated in Figure 67. There is also a choice to have the macro write a list of the spelling errors found to a new document, with the page number and context in which the error occurs.

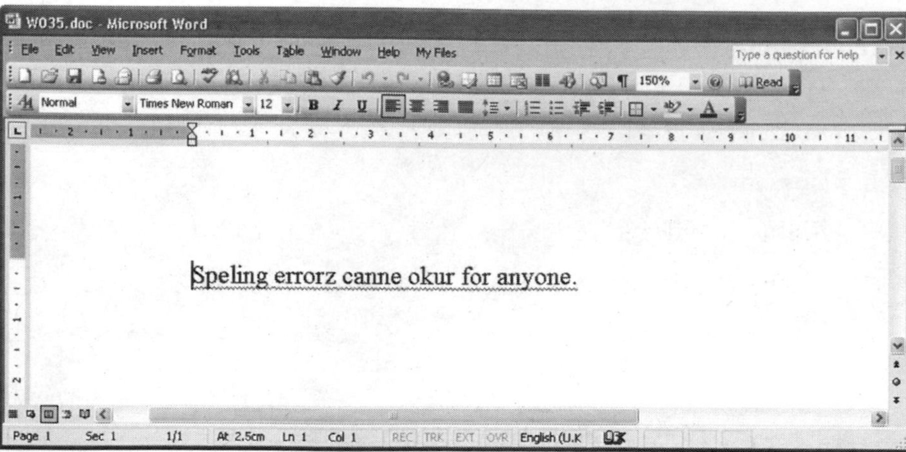

Figure 67 – Formatted Spelling Errors

You can choose to change the font, to underline, and/or to highlight the errors. In this example, the errors are underlined with bold dots.

The macro saves the original document under a new name because it physically applies direct formatting to these text ranges. You can specify the type of formatting desired for the macro to apply.

View the Appendix to learn how to store this procedure in a Standard module.

```
Option explicit¶
' * * * * *¶
Const NewNameExtension As String = "_SpellingErrors"¶
Const FormatAsColor As Boolean = False¶
Const FormatAsUnderline As Boolean = True¶
Const FormatAsHighlight As Boolean = False¶
Const WriteToTable As Boolean = True¶
Const sepChar As String = "¦"¶
' * * * * *¶
Sub MarkSpellingErrorsForPrintout()¶
    'Variable declaration¶
    Dim doc As Word.Document¶
    Dim docNewName As String¶
    Dim rng As Word.Range¶
    Dim pageCounter As Long¶
    Dim spErr As Range¶
    Dim TableData As String¶
    Set doc = ActiveDocument¶
    'Save any changes the user has made¶
```

```
doc.Save¶
'Save the document to be processed¶
'under a different name, but in the same path¶
'so that the original file is not changed.¶
docNewName = GetNewName(doc, NewNameExtension)¶
doc.SaveAs FileName:=doc.Path & docNewName, _¶
  AddToRecentFiles:=False¶
'Be sure to start on the first page¶
Selection.HomeKey wdStory¶
Set rng = ActiveDocument.Range¶
'Don't continue if there aren't any¶
'spelling errors¶
If doc.SpellingErrors.Count > 0 Then¶
    'If there are lots of errors¶
    'in a document, spellcheck doesn't¶
    'process well. Break it down, therefore,¶
    'and go page by page¶
    For pageCounter = 1 To _¶
      doc.Range.Information(wdNumberOfPagesInDocument)¶
        'In order to place an entire page in a range¶
        'use the built in \Page bookmark¶
        Set rng = Selection.Bookmarks("\Page").Range¶
        For Each spErr In rng.SpellingErrors¶
            With spErr¶
                'Use the old Word97 command ColorIndex¶
                'for the font color so that the macro¶
                'runs in all versions¶
                If FormatAsColor = True Then _¶
                    .Font.ColorIndex = wdDarkRed¶
                If FormatAsUnderline = True Then _¶
                    .Font.Underline = wdUnderlineDotDash¶
                If FormatAsHighlight = True Then _¶
                    spErr.HighlightColorIndex = wdGray25¶
                If WriteToTable = True Then _¶
                    TableData = TableData & CStr(pageCounter) _¶
                      & sepChar & spErr.Text & sepChar _¶
                      & TrimEndParas(spErr.Sentences(1).Text) & vbCr¶
            End With¶
        Next spErr¶
        Selection.GoTo What:=wdGoToPage, Which:=wdGoToNext¶
    Next pageCounter¶
    If WriteToTable = True Then¶
        'Variable declaration¶
        Dim rngTable As Word.Range¶
        Dim tbl As Word.Table¶
        Dim docLogErrors As Word.Document¶
        Set docLogErrors = Documents.Add¶
        Set rngTable = docLogErrors.Range¶
        'Trim off the last paragraph mark¶
        TableData = Left(TableData, Len(TableData) - 1)¶
```

Wrd

```
            'Add column headings¶
            rngTable.Text = "Page" & sepChar & "Error" & _¶
              sepChar & "Context" & vbCr & TableData¶
            Set tbl = rngTable.ConvertToTable( _¶
              Separator:=sepChar, Numcolumns:=3)¶
            tbl.Rows(1).Range.Font.Bold = True¶
        End If¶
    End If¶
End Sub¶
' * * * * *¶
Function GetNewName(doc As Word.Document, _¶
  ext As String) As String¶
    'Variable declaration¶
    Dim s As String¶
    Dim loc As Long¶
    s = doc.Name¶
    'Cut off the file extension¶
    loc = InStr(s, ".doc")¶
    s = Left(s, loc - 1)¶
    GetNewName = s & ext¶
End Function¶
' * * * * *¶
Function TrimEndParas(s As String) As String¶
    Do While Asc(Right(s, 1)) = 13¶
        s = Left(s, Len(s) - 1)¶
    Loop¶
    TrimEndParas = s¶
End Function¶
```

Wrd

Follow these steps:

1. Set the Const values at the beginning for the preferred options to use, as follows:

   - **NewNameExtension** The macro saves the file under a new name so that the original file remains unchanged. It keeps the original name, but adds a suffix. Put what should be added to the original name in this constant.
   - **FormatAsColor** To have the macro change the text color where a spelling error is found, set this to True; otherwise, set it to False.
   - **FormatAsUnderline** To have the macro underline the text where a spelling error is found, set this to True; otherwise, set it to False.

- **FormatAsHighlight** — To have the macro highlight text where a spelling error is found, set this to True; otherwise, set it to False.
- **WriteToTable** — To get a separate list of the errors, the page on which they were found, and the context they are in, set this to True; otherwise, set it to False. The table is created in a new, separate document.
- **sepChar** — To have the errors listed in a separate file, specify the separator character the macro should use when collecting the data. This can be any character; choose one that doesn't appear anywhere in the text, such as a pipe: " | ".

2. Click the Save button in order to save the changes.
3. Make sure that Tools | Options | Spelling and Grammar has the 'Check Spelling as you type' box checked.
4. For any of the "FormatAs" options that are set to True, go down to the set of IF statements in the code that check these values and specify the details of the formatting. If Intellisense is turned on in the VBE, when code is deleted and an equals sign (=) is retyped, a list of valid options will appear. Select the one that is desired, then press Enter. You can change the color for the font or highlight or even change the type of underline by using this technique.

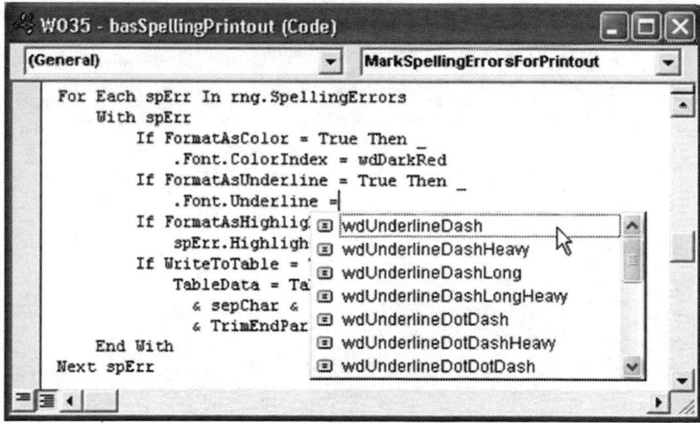

Figure 68 – Intellisense in the VBE

Entering Data Easily Using a Custom Dialog Box

Use this procedure to show a dialog box to get information and put it into bookmark targets in the document.

Example file:
W036

Scenario: Over 90% of the time, Word is not used for reports or writing books. Primarily, a person performs daily, repetitive tasks such as correspondence. While mail merge makes it easy to send large numbers of identical documents to many people, Word does not have a good facility for writing one-off letters, memos, or faxes.

Corporations and many power-users create templates for each type of correspondence worked with on a regular basis. Templates provide ready-made formatting in the form of styles and boilerplate text that correspond to company standards and corporate identity.

Even better is a template that gathers all the standard information in a single interface and takes the task of inserting it into the proper locations off the user's hands. A fairly simple, standard example is shown on the following page.

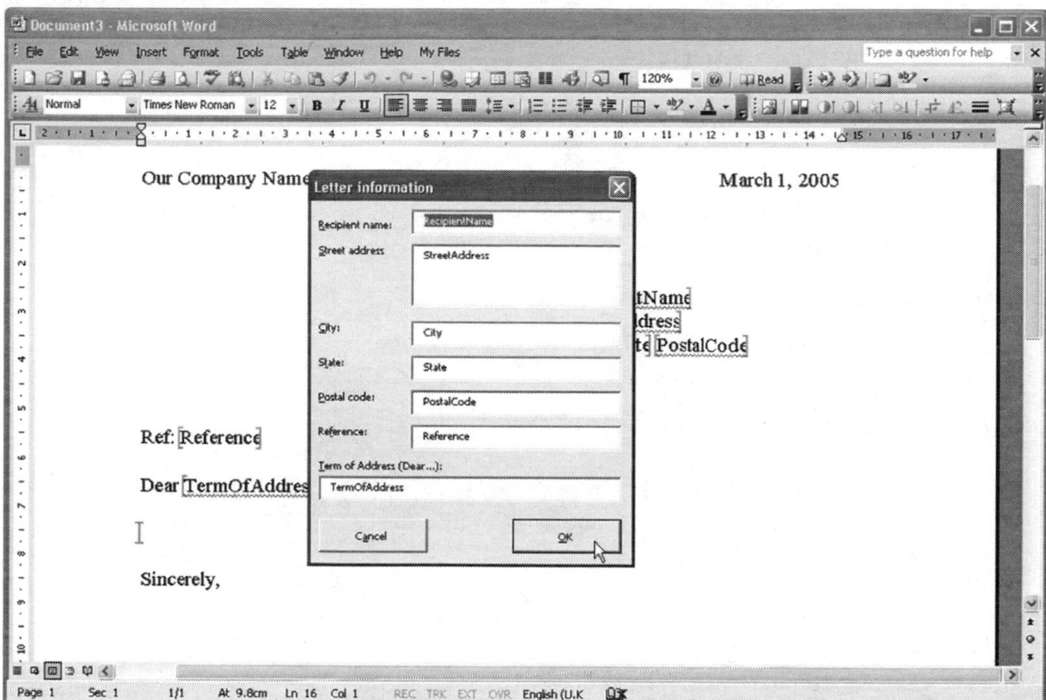

Figure 69 – Easy Data Entry Dialog Box

This macro tool can be adapted to all correspondence needs.

The form gathers user input and inserts it into appropriate areas of the document. After it finishes, the user can begin typing the body of the letter immediately. The tool is set up to be reusable in a document: the macro always picks up the bookmark contents that match the text box names, if the bookmarks are present in the document.

View the Appendix to learn how to store this procedure in a Standard module.

```
Option explicit¶
' * * * * *¶
Sub AutoNew()¶
    GetUserInput¶
End Sub¶
' * * * * *¶
Sub GetUserInput()¶
```

```
    'Variable declaration¶
    Dim frm As frmUserInput¶
    Dim doc As Word.Document¶
    Set doc = ActiveDocument¶
    If doc.Bookmarks.Count < 1 Then¶
        MsgBox "Invalide document. " & _¶
          "No bookmarks could be found.", _¶
          vbCritical + vbOKOnly¶
        Exit Sub¶
    End If¶
    Set frm = New frmUserInput¶
    GetDataFromDocument frm, doc¶
    frm.Show¶
    If frm.Tag = "OK" Then¶
        PutDataIntoDocument frm, doc¶
    End If¶
    Unload frm¶
    If doc.Bookmarks.Exists("txtStartBody") Then¶
        doc.Bookmarks("txtStartBody").Range.Select¶
    End If¶
End Sub¶
' * * * * *¶
Sub GetDataFromDocument(frm As UserForm, doc As Word.Document)¶
    'Variable declaration¶
    Dim ctl As MSForms.Control¶
    Dim firstControl As Boolean¶
    For Each ctl In frm.Controls¶
        If doc.Bookmarks.Exists(ctl.Name) Then¶
            ctl.Text = doc.Bookmarks(ctl.Name).Range.Text¶
            If Not firstControl Then¶
                ctl.SelStart = 0¶
                ctl.SelLength = Len(ctl.Text)¶
                firstControl = True¶
            End If¶
        End If¶
    Next¶
End Sub¶
' * * * * *¶
Sub PutDataIntoDocument(frm As UserForm, doc As Word.Document)¶
    'Variable declaration¶
    Dim ctl As MSForms.Control¶
    Dim rng As Word.Range¶
    For Each ctl In frm.Controls¶
        If doc.Bookmarks.Exists(ctl.Name) Then¶
            Set rng = doc.Bookmarks(ctl.Name).Range¶
            rng.Text = ctl.Text¶
            doc.Bookmarks.Add Name:=ctl.Name, Range:=rng¶
        End If¶
    Next¶
End Sub¶
```

Follow these steps:

1. Copy the macro code to the correspondence template's VBA project.
2. Transfer the UserForm frmUserInput to the same project using either the Organizer, or by dragging it in the Visual Basic Editor (VBE) to the template's project. The code for this UserForm module is below for reference.

View the Appendix to learn how to store this procedure in a UserForm.


```
Option explicit¶
' * * * * *¶
Private Sub btnCancel_Click()¶
     Me.Hide¶
    Me.Tag = "Cancel"¶
End Sub¶
' * * * * *¶
Private Sub btnOK_Click()¶
     Me.Hide¶
    Me.Tag = "OK"¶
End Sub¶
```

The code in the example file also includes the 'basCreateBookmark' module, which is utilized in the Creating a Bookmark from a Selection entry found on page 260. It is included below for reference.

```
Option explicit¶
' * * * * *¶
Const varName As String = "BookmarkCounter"¶
Const varDuplicateName As String _¶
= "DuplicateBookmarkCounter"¶
' * * * * *¶
Sub CreateBookmark()¶
'Variable declaration¶
Dim rng As Word.Range¶
Dim BookmarkName As String¶
Dim var As Word.Variable¶
'Check whether the document variable that stores¶
'a counter for bookmarks without content exists¶
If varExists(ActiveDocument, varName) = False Then¶
    'If not, create it and assign it the value 1¶
    ActiveDocument.Variables.Add _¶
    Name:=varName, Value:="1"¶
End If¶
Set var = ActiveDocument.Variables(varName)¶
Set rng = Selection.Range¶
If Selection.Type = wdSelectionIP Then¶
```

```
    'The user didn't select any text; a bookmark without¶
    'content will be inserted with¶
    'an incremented name txt#¶
    'Calculate that name¶
    BookmarkName = "txt" & var.Value¶
    var.Value = CStr(CLng(var.Value) + 1)¶
    'Alternately, a prompt can be displayed¶
    'to ask the user for the name¶
    'Uncomment the next two lines to use that method¶
    'BookmarkName = InputBox( _¶
    'No text is selected. Type in a bookmark name.")¶
Else¶
    'Get the bookmark name based on the selected text¶
    BookmarkName = ProcessBookmarkName(rng.Text)¶
End If¶
'Check if the bookmark name already exists;¶
'if it does it will be incremented with a counter¶
BookmarkName = "txt" & CheckIfDuplicateName( _¶
ActiveDocument, BookmarkName)¶
'Insert the bookmark¶
ActiveDocument.Bookmarks.Add _¶
Name:=BookmarkName, Range:=rng¶
End Sub¶
' * * * * *¶
Function ProcessBookmarkName(s As String) As String¶
'Variable declaration¶
Dim i As Long¶
'Maximum length of a bookmark name is 40 characters¶
'Because txt will be added to the beginning¶
'therefore cut off at 37¶
If Len(s) > 37 Then s = Left(s, 37)¶
    'Replace all spaces with underline characters¶
    s = Replace(s, " ", "_")¶
    'Remove any numbers at the beginning¶
    Do While IsNumeric(Left(s, 1)) = True¶
        s = Mid(s, 2)¶
        Debug.Print s¶
    Loop¶
    'Remove invalid characters¶
    '(following list is not comprehensive)¶
    For i = 1 To Len(s)¶
        Select Case Mid(s, i, 1)¶
            Case "§", "°", "+", "¦", "@", Chr$(34), "*", _¶
            "#", "%", "&", "", "/", "|", "(", "¢", ")", _¶
            "=", "?", "'", "´", "^", "`", "~", "[", "]", _¶
            "¨", "!", "{", "}", "$", "£", "<", ">", "<", _¶
            ".", ",", ":", ";", "-"¶
            s = Left(s, i - 1) & Mid(s, i + 1)¶
        Case Else¶
            'Otherwise, do nothing¶
        End Select¶
```

```
    Next i¶
ProcessBookmarkName = s¶
End Function¶
' * * * * *¶
Function CheckIfDuplicateName(doc As Word.Document, _¶
BookmarkName As String) As String¶
'Variable declaration¶
Dim var As Word.Variable¶
If varExists(doc, varDuplicateName) = False Then¶
    ActiveDocument.Variables.Add _¶
    Name:=varDuplicateName, Value:="1"¶
End If¶
Set var = ActiveDocument.Variables(varDuplicateName)¶
If doc.Bookmarks.Exists(BookmarkName) Then¶
    'Calculate incremented name¶
    BookmarkName = Left(BookmarkName, _¶
    Len(BookmarkName) - Len(var.Value)) & var.Value¶
    var.Value = CStr(CLng(var.Value) + 1)¶
End If¶
CheckIfDuplicateName = BookmarkName¶
End Function¶
' * * * * *¶
Function varExists(doc As Word.Document, _¶
s As String) As Boolean¶
'Variable declaration¶
Dim var As Word.Variable¶
varExists = False¶
'Loop through the list of document variables¶
'and check whether it already exists by¶
'comparing the name¶
For Each var In doc.Variables¶
    If var.Name = s Then¶
        varExists = True¶
        Exit For¶
    End If¶
Next var¶
End Function¶
```


3. Create bookmarks in the template where the data items in the form should be inserted (select the location, then Insert | Bookmark). The bookmark names should match the names of the text boxes in the UserForm. Some of the text boxes used in the example are txtRecipient, txtStreetAddress, and txtCity.

4. To see and change the text box names in the Visual Basic Editor (VBE), click on a text box and then look at the Name information in the Properties window (it is usually the first entry listed). Type the correct name in the box if changes need to be made.

Tip: See the following entry, Creating a Bookmark from a Selection, for a tool to quickly create bookmarks from text selections.

5. Insert a bookmark named txtStartBody in the location where the user should start typing once the macro has finished. Deciding not to use a bookmark simply means that the macro skips selecting that location if a bookmark isn't present.
6. Feel free to change the form to fit various requirements. Deleting and adding labels and text boxes won't detrimentally affect the macro tool. Just be careful not to delete the buttons.
7. This tool contains an 'AutoNew' procedure so that the form appears whenever the user creates a new document from the template. Comment out the procedure if this is unwanted.
8. To make it easy to edit the input at a later time, assign the procedure 'GetUserInput' to a toolbar button. The macro automatically picks up the bookmarked content when it displays the user form.

Creating a Bookmark from a Selection

This procedure creates a bookmark from the current selection in a document and bases the bookmark name on the selected text.

Scenario: Using a macro to place text into a Word document, whether the text originates from a UserForm, a database, or an InputBox, requires that a target be specified in the document. Most often, bookmarks serve as targets. Bookmarks are also used to mark information for cross-referencing and generating Tables of Content for specific parts of a document.

While creating bookmarks is simple enough—select a range of characters, then Insert | Bookmark, type in a name and click Insert—it is time-consuming to repeatedly go through the menu and display the dialog box.

Example file:
W038

The following macro bookmarks the current selection in the document, using the selected text as the bookmark name. If the selection is long, only the first 40 characters (maximum number of characters for a bookmark name) are used. Invalid characters will be removed, according to the following rules:

- Bookmark names may not begin with numbers. Any numbers at the beginning of a selection are cut off from the bookmark name.
- Punctuation, such as periods and commas, are not allowed and are removed.
- Spaces are replaced with underscores.

View the Appendix to learn how to store this procedure in a Standard module.


```
Option explicit¶
' * * * * *¶
Const varName As String = "BookmarkCounter"¶
Const varDuplicateName As String _¶
= "DuplicateBookmarkCounter"¶
' * * * * *¶
Sub CreateBookmark()¶
'Variable declaration¶
Dim rng As Word.Range¶
Dim BookmarkName As String¶
Dim var As Word.Variable¶
'Check whether the document variable that stores¶
'a counter for bookmarks without content exists¶
If varExists(ActiveDocument, varName) = False Then¶
    'If not, create it and assign it the value 1¶
    ActiveDocument.Variables.Add _¶
    Name:=varName, Value:="1"¶
End If¶
Set var = ActiveDocument.Variables(varName)¶
Set rng = Selection.Range¶
If Selection.Type = wdSelectionIP Then¶
    'The user didn't select any text; a bookmark without¶
    'content will be inserted with¶
    'an incremented name txt#¶
    'Calculate that name¶
    BookmarkName = "txt" & var.Value¶
    var.Value = CStr(CLng(var.Value) + 1)¶
    'Alternately, a prompt can be displayed¶
    'to ask the user for the name¶
    'Uncomment the next two lines to use that method¶
    'BookmarkName = InputBox( _¶
    'No text is selected. Type in a bookmark name.")¶
Else¶
    'Get the bookmark name based on the selected text¶
```

```
    BookmarkName = ProcessBookmarkName(rng.Text)¶
End If¶
'Check if the bookmark name already exists;¶
'if it does, it is incremented with a counter¶
BookmarkName = "txt" & CheckIfDuplicateName( _¶
ActiveDocument, BookmarkName)¶
'Insert the bookmark¶
ActiveDocument.Bookmarks.Add _¶
Name:=BookmarkName, Range:=rng¶
End Sub¶
' * * * * *¶
Function ProcessBookmarkName(s As String) As String¶
'Variable declaration¶
Dim i As Long¶
'Maximum length of a bookmark name is 40 characters¶
'Because txt will be added to the beginning¶
'therefore cut off at 37¶
If Len(s) > 37 Then s = Left(s, 37)¶
    'Replace all spaces with underline characters¶
    s = Replace(s, " ", "_")¶
    'Remove any numbers at the beginning¶
    Do While IsNumeric(Left(s, 1)) = True¶
        s = Mid(s, 2)¶
        Debug.Print s¶
    Loop¶
    'Remove invalid characters¶
    '(following list is not comprehensive)¶
    For i = 1 To Len(s)¶
        Select Case Mid(s, i, 1)¶
            Case "§", "°", "+", "¦", "@", Chr$(34), "*", _¶
            "#", "%", "&", "", "/", "|", "(", "¢", ")", _¶
            "=", "?", "´", "^", "`", "~", "[", "]", _¶
            "¨", "!", "{", "}", "$", "£", "<", ">", "<", _¶
            ".", ",", ":", ";", "-"¶
            s = Left(s, i - 1) & Mid(s, i + 1)¶
        Case Else¶
            'Otherwise, do nothing¶
        End Select¶
    Next i¶
ProcessBookmarkName = s¶
End Function¶
' * * * * *¶
Function CheckIfDuplicateName(doc As Word.Document, _¶
BookmarkName As String) As String¶
'Variable declaration¶
Dim var As Word.Variable¶
If varExists(doc, varDuplicateName) = False Then¶
    ActiveDocument.Variables.Add _¶
    Name:=varDuplicateName, Value:="1"¶
End If¶
Set var = ActiveDocument.Variables(varDuplicateName)¶
```

```
If doc.Bookmarks.Exists(BookmarkName) Then¶
    'Calculate incremented name¶
    BookmarkName = Left(BookmarkName, _¶
    Len(BookmarkName) - Len(var.Value)) & var.Value¶
    var.Value = CStr(CLng(var.Value) + 1)¶
End If¶
CheckIfDuplicateName = BookmarkName¶
End Function¶
' * * * * *¶
Function varExists(doc As Word.Document, _¶
s As String) As Boolean¶
'Variable declaration¶
Dim var As Word.Variable¶
varExists = False¶
'Loop through the list of document variables¶
'and check whether it already exists by¶
'comparing the name¶
For Each var In doc.Variables¶
    If var.Name = s Then¶
        varExists = True¶
        Exit For¶
    End If¶
Next var¶
End Function¶
```

Wrd

Follow these steps:

1. Copy the entire set of macros to a module in the document, in its template, in Normal.dot, or in any template that will be loaded as a global Add-in. Then assign it to a toolbar button and/or keyboard shortcut. See Running a Macro from a Toolbar Button on page 418 or Running a Macro Using Shortcut Keys on page 419 for help in assigning a macro to a toolbar button or a keyboard shortcut.
2. The incremental numbers for duplicate names and bookmarks without content are stored in document Variables. The names for the Variables are set as Const values at the beginning of the module. To use different names, change the values in quotation marks.
3. To type in a bookmark name when no text is selected to provide the bookmark name, remove the apostrophes from the lines of code below, and comment out the original code:

```
If Selection.Type = wdSelectionIP Then¶
    'The user didn't select any text; a bookmark without¶
    'content will be inserted with¶
    'an incremented name txt#¶
    'Calculate that name¶
    BookmarkName = "txt" & var.Value¶
    var.Value = CStr(CLng(var.Value) + 1)¶
    'Alternately, a prompt can be displayed¶
```

```
    'to ask the user for the name¶
    'Uncomment the next two lines to use that method¶
    'BookmarkName = InputBox( _¶
    'No text is selected. Type in a bookmark name.")¶
Else¶
```

Making Bookmarks Visible

With this procedure, you can highlight bookmarks in a document and place their names in comments to make them easier to manage.

Wrd

Scenario: When setting up a document with many bookmarks, it is often difficult to keep track of their locations and names. One way to obtain an overview is to highlight them, and put their names in comments.

Example file:
W039

Tip: In Word 2002 and 2003, comments can be displayed in the right margin, with connecting lines. In Word 97, Word 2000, and Word 2003, the bookmark name appears in tip flags when the mouse hovers over a comment.

View the Appendix to learn how to store this procedure in a Standard module.

```
Option explicit¶
' * * * * *¶
Sub HighLightBookmarks()¶
    'Variable declaration¶
    Dim bkm As Word.Bookmark¶
    Dim rng As Word.Range¶
    For Each bkm In ActiveDocument.Bookmarks¶
        Set rng = bkm.Range¶
        rng.HighlightColorIndex = wdYellow¶
        ActiveDocument.Comments.Add _¶
          Range:=rng, Text:=bkm.Name¶
        Set rng = Nothing¶
    Next bkm¶
End Sub¶
' * * * * *¶
Sub RemoveHighlighting()¶
    If Selection.Type = wdSelectionIP Then¶
        ActiveDocument.Range.HighlightColorIndex = wdNoHighlight¶
    ElseIf Selection.Type = wdSelectionNormal Then¶
```

```
        Selection.Range.HighlightColorIndex = wdNoHighlight¶
    Else¶
        MsgBox "No text is selected."¶
    End If¶
End Sub¶
```

To change the highlight color, delete the text = wdYellow; type the equals sign (=) again, and a list of values should appear. Select one of the values and press Enter.

Forcing the User to Enable Macros

These procedures provide methods to prevent users from successfully working with a document if macros are not enabled.

Wrd

Scenario: When distributing macros that manage templates or documents, it is important that the user have macros enabled; otherwise the macros won't work. For obvious reasons, it is not possible to create a macro that changes macro security settings; if it were, macro security would be useless. This section discusses a number of ways to prevent the user from working with a project unless macros are enabled. There are a couple of code examples to demonstrate how the techniques are applied.

Example file:
WordProtection.doc,
DocFromCode.doc,
WeeklyReport.xls

Generating the Document Using VBA

Certainly, the most effective way is to generate the entire document when it is opened or created from a template. The 'Document_Open' and 'AutoOpen' procedures fire when a document is opened. A 'Document_New' or 'AutoNew' procedure fires when a new document is created from a template.

In the document body, place a message telling the user how to enable macro security so that the document can be created. If macros can be run, a macro removes the message text and replaces it with the document, as shown by the following sample code.

Tip: To open one of the sample documents without the AutoOpen macros running, hold down the Shift key while it is opening. Holding the Shift key down when opening a file prevents macros from executing. If this step is forgotten (happens all the time), just close the document without saving the changes and try again.

The sample code demonstrates many of the basics: how to insert text, fields, links to outside files, and how to apply formatting.

View the Appendix to learn how to store this procedure in a Standard module.

```
Option explicit¶
' * * * * *¶
'Path to be used in the field code¶
'linking in the Excel file¶
'Field codes need double backslashes¶
Const ReportPath As String = "C:\\test\\WeeklyReport.xls"¶
' * * * * *¶
Sub GenerateDocument()¶
    'Variable declaration¶
    Dim doc As Word.Document¶
    Dim rng As Word.Range¶
    Dim fld As Word.Field¶
    Set doc = ActiveDocument¶
    Set rng = doc.Range¶
    rng.Text = "Weekly Report" & vbCr¶
    rng.Style = wdStyleTitle¶
    rng.Collapse wdCollapseEnd¶
    rng.Text = "Regional Sales (East coast)" & vbCr¶
    rng.Style = wdStyleHeading1¶
    rng.ParagraphFormat.PageBreakBefore = True¶
    rng.Collapse wdCollapseEnd¶
    rng.Style = wdStyleBodyText¶
    Set fld = doc.Fields.Add(Range:=rng, _¶
        Type:=wdFieldMacroButton, _¶
        Text:="no macro " & _¶
        "Click here and type East coast regional sales info", _¶
        PreserveFormatting:=False)¶
    rng.Start = fld.Result.End¶
    rng.InsertAfter vbCr & vbCr¶
    rng.Collapse wdCollapseEnd¶
    Set fld = doc.Fields.Add(Range:=rng, _¶
        Type:=wdFieldEmpty, _¶
        Text:="LINK Excel.Sheet.8 " & Chr$(34) _¶
            & ReportPath & Chr$(34) & " " & Chr$(34) _¶
            & "EastCoast!EastCoast" & Chr$(34) _¶
            & " \a \r", _¶
        PreserveFormatting:=False)¶
    fld.Result.Tables(1).Columns.AutoFit¶
    Set rng = fld.Result¶
    fld.Unlink¶
    rng.Collapse wdCollapseEnd¶
End Sub¶
```


Wrd

View the Appendix to learn how to store this procedure in the ThisDocument module.

```
Option explicit¶
' * * * * *¶
Private Sub Document_Open()¶
    GenerateDocument¶
End Sub¶
```

Using Forms Protection

Generating an entire document from scratch can be a challenge. Somewhat easier is the method of protecting the file as a Word form (don't confuse this with a UserForm) with a password by using Tools | Protect document. The 'Document_Open', 'Auto Open', 'Document_New', or 'AutoNew' procedure can be built to remove the protection and do any other preparatory work (such as removing a message to the user at the beginning of the document about activating macro security), as this sample code demonstrates.

View the Appendix to learn how to store this procedure in a Standard module.

```
Sub RemoveProtection()¶
    ActiveDocument.Unprotect "test"¶
    'Remove macro message¶
    ActiveDocument.Paragraphs(1).Range.Delete¶
End Sub¶
```

The only real problem with this approach is that it is not 100% secure. Anyone can, from a blank document, use Insert | File and choose the protected document to open it in an unprotected state, even if it has been password protected.

If the main concern is to restrict the user from accidentally working with the file without the macros, then form field protection is certainly an acceptable approach.

Macros in Files Opened by Code

A related problem is macro security for other documents your code might need to open. If the user has set macro security to "Medium", a prompt appears if any files opened by the code contain macros. This can be irritating to the user if the solution should run without interruption. Or, it may be that open files should not have any macros they contain execute.

A new property was introduced in Word 2002 that allows macro security to be adjusted while code is executing. Once it has finished, reset security to the user's original setting. Here are the three available settings:

- **msoAutomationSecurityByUI** — Uses the security setting specified in the Security dialog box
- **msoAutomationSecurityForceDisable** — Disables all macros in all files opened programmatically without showing any security alerts
- **msoAutomationSecurityLow** — Enables all macros
  This is the default value of the property.
  This technique is used in Finding and Replacing in Multiple Documents on page 122.

View the Appendix to learn how to store this procedure in a Standard module.

```
Option explicit¶
' * * * * *¶
Private Security As Long¶
Sub AutoOpen()¶
    RemoveProtection¶
    SetMacroSecurity¶
    'Open other documents¶
    Application.AutomationSecurity = Security¶
End Sub¶
' * * * * *¶
Sub RemoveProtection()¶
    ActiveDocument.Unprotect "test"¶
    'Remove macro message¶
    ActiveDocument.Paragraphs(1).Range.Delete¶
End Sub¶
' * * * * *¶
Sub SetMacroSecurity()¶
    Security = Application.AutomationSecurity¶
    Application.AutomationSecurity = msoAutomationSecurityForceDisable¶
End Sub¶
```

Outlook Procedures

By Suat Ozgur

Most of the Outlook procedures do not have sample files because Outlook does not store its procedures in files.

Creating Control Buttons

This procedure automatically creates control buttons with VBA code.

The following code shows how to create a custom control button in Outlook. In the example shown here, a custom button called "Create New Task" is created.

Figure 70 – Creating a Custom Control Button

View the Appendix to learn how to store this procedure in a Standard module.

```
Option Explicit¶
' * * * * *¶
Public Sub CreateOutlookCommandBarButton()¶
  'Remove the button if it is already existing¶
  Call RemoveOutlookCommandBarButton¶
  'Create new control button¶
  'Temporary:=True  : Available from now on¶
  'Temporary:=False : Available only this Outlook session¶
  With ActiveExplorer.CommandBars("Standard").Controls. _¶
                      Add(msoControlButton, Temporary:=True)¶
    'Caption to display on button¶
    .Caption = "Create New Task"¶
    'Procedure name to run when button is clicked¶
    .OnAction = "CreateTask"¶
    'Button Style - msoButtonCaption = 2¶
    .Style = 2¶
    'Show new button¶
    .Visible = True¶
  End With¶
End Sub¶
```

```
' * * * * *¶
Public Sub RemoveOutlookCommandBarButton()¶
  'Error handler if control is not existing¶
  'Continue if an error occurs¶
  On Error Resume Next¶
  'Remove custom control button¶
  ActiveExplorer.CommandBars("Standard") _¶
             .Controls("Create New Task").Delete False¶
End Sub¶
```

The following code shows how to create a custom control button in other Office applications.

View the Appendix to learn how to store this procedure in a Standard module.

Out

```
Option Explicit¶
' * * * * *¶
Public Sub CreateCommandBarButton()¶
  'Remove the button if it is already existing¶
  Call RemoveCommandBarButton¶
  'Create new control button¶
  'Temporary:=True  : Available from now on¶
  'Temporary:=False : Available only this session¶
  With Application.CommandBars("Standard").Controls. _¶
                    Add(msoControlButton, Temporary:=True)¶
    'Caption to display on button¶
    .Caption = "New Button"¶
    'Procedure name to run when button is clicked¶
    .OnAction = "MyMacro"¶
    'Button Style - msoButtonCaption = 2¶
    .Style = 2¶
    'Show new button¶
    .Visible = True¶
  End With¶
End Sub¶
' * * * * *¶
Public Sub RemoveCommandBarButton()¶
  'Error handler if control is not existing¶
  On Error Resume Next¶
  'Remove custom control button¶
  Application.CommandBars("Standard") _¶
             .Controls("New Button").Delete False¶
End Sub¶
```

Saving E-mail Attachments in a Specified Folder

This macro saves all e-mail attachments in the active Outlook folder into the specified folder. It automatically renames the saved files in the folder by producing auto-incremented version numbers.

Scenario: You sent out a questionnaire to 1,000 employees in the company in the form of a Word document. You received all the responses back as Word document attachments. The attachments all have the same name. You know that this book provides code to extract data from Word forms, but you can't figure out how to quickly get all the documents saved from the e-mails into a folder so you can use that macro. This entry solves your dilemma.

View the Appendix to learn how to store this procedure in a Standard module.

```
Option Explicit¶
' * * * * *¶
Public Sub SaveAttachments()¶
'Outlook Application Objects declaration¶
Dim objApp    As Outlook.Application¶
Dim objFolder As Outlook.MAPIFolder¶
Dim objItem   As Object¶
Dim itemAttc  As Outlook.Attachment¶
'FileSystemObject Objects declaration¶
Dim fso As Object   'FileSystemObject¶
Dim fld As Object   'Folder¶
Dim fil As Object   'File¶
Dim i   As Long     'Counter¶
'Array variable to store file name and extension¶
Dim strFileName() As String¶
  On Error GoTo ErrHandler¶
  'Create FileSystemObject object¶
  Set fso = CreateObject("Scripting.FileSystemObject")¶
```

```
  'Create target directory object that is used for saving¶
  'attachments¶
  Set fld = fso.GetFolder(SelectFolder)¶
  'Set objApp object¶
  Set objApp = Outlook.Application¶
  'Set source folder as the currently activated folder¶
  Set objFolder = objApp.ActiveExplorer.CurrentFolder¶
  'Confirmation¶
  If MsgBox("Do you want to extract all attached items " & _¶
          "in " & objFolder.Name & _¶
          " and save into " & fld.path & " directory?", _¶
          vbYesNo + vbQuestion, "Confirmation") = vbNo _¶
          Then GoTo ErrHandler¶
  'Explore all mail items in selected folder¶
  For Each objItem In objFolder.Items¶
    'If item is mail object then continue processing item¶
    If objItem.Class = olMail Then¶
      'Explore all attachments in email message¶
      For Each itemAttc In objItem.Attachments¶
        'Increase counter for attachment count¶
        i = i + 1¶
        'Retrieve file name and extension¶
        'Calls ExplodeFileName custom function¶
        strFileName = ExplodeFileName(itemAttc.FileName)¶
        'Create new file name if the same file is already¶
        'existing in folder¶
        'Simply adds _X at the end of the file¶
        'X is the incrementing number¶
        strFileName = CreateFileName(strFileName, fso, fld)¶
        'Finally save attachment as file by given path¶
        itemAttc.SaveAsFile fld.path & "\" & _¶
          strFileName(0) & strFileName(1)¶
      Next itemAttc¶
    End If¶
  Next objItem¶
  'Inform user about completion and saved number¶
  'of attachment¶
  MsgBox i & " attachments have been succesfully saved in " _¶
        & fld.path¶
ExitSub:¶
  'Release object variables and memory¶
  Set fso = Nothing¶
  Set objApp = Nothing¶
  Exit Sub¶
```

Out

```
ErrHandler:¶
  Select Case Err.Number¶
  Case 76     'Target directory doesn't exist¶
    MsgBox "Selected directory doesn't exist.", _¶
           vbOKOnly + vbExclamation, "Error"¶
  Case Is <> 0  'Another critical error¶
    MsgBox Err.Number & "-" & Err.Description, _¶
           vbOKOnly + vbExclamation, "Error"¶
  End Select¶
  Resume ExitSub¶
End Sub¶
' * * * * *¶
Private Function SelectFolder() As String¶
  SelectFolder = "C:\Temp"¶
  'Alternative method might be using a user selected module¶
End Function¶
' * * * * *¶
Private Function ExplodeFileName(strFileName As String)¶
'Variable declaration¶
Dim dotPos    As Integer¶
Dim strArr(1) As String¶
    'Find the last dot position to parse strFileName¶
    'InStrRev function is being used to start from the¶
    'end of string¶
    dotPos = InStrRev(strFileName, ".")¶
    If dotPos = 0 Then¶
        'There is no extension¶
        strArr(0) = strFileName¶
        strArr(1) = ""¶
    Else¶
        'Parse file name¶
        strArr(0) = Left(strFileName, dotPos - 1)¶
        'Parse file extension¶
        strArr(1) = Right(strFileName, Len(strFileName) _¶
                    - dotPos + 1)¶
    End If¶
    'Return an array¶
    'First item is the file name¶
    'Second item is the file extension¶
    ExplodeFileName = strArr¶
End Function¶
```

Out

```
' * * * * *¶
Private Function CreateFileName(strFileName() As String, _¶
                                fso As Object, fld As Object)¶
'Variable declaration¶
Dim strSuffix As String¶
Dim intSuffix As Integer¶
Dim strFinalFileName(1) As String¶
  'Increment intSuffix until file is not existing¶
  'FileExists method returns True if there is a file named¶
  'with parameter string¶
  Do Until Not fso.FileExists(fld.path & "\" & _¶
                 strFileName(0) & strSuffix & strFileName(1))¶
    intSuffix = intSuffix + 1¶
    'Create file name suffix¶
    strSuffix = "_" & CStr(intSuffix)¶
  Loop¶
  strFinalFileName(0) = strFileName(0) & strSuffix¶
  strFinalFileName(1) = strFileName(1)¶
  'Return an array¶
  'First item is the final file name¶
  'Second item is the file extension¶
  CreateFileName = strFinalFileName¶
End Function¶
```

Out

Note: The target folder in the SelectFolder function procedure should be set to the desired path.

Creating a Contacts Database

This macro creates an Access database file by using contacts information stored in the Outlook Contacts folder. If the database file already exists, then the user is prompted to update it or recreate (overwrite) it.

Scenario: Extracting information from the contacts in Outlook is useful, even if it is for as simple a reason as to have a backup of the information. The Excel section showed how to do this to an Excel spreadsheet. Another option is to save this information in an Access database.

View the Appendix to learn how to store this procedure in a Standard module.

```
Option Explicit¶
' * * * * *¶
'Set database file name and table name¶
Const strFileName   As String = "C:\MyContactsDatabase.mdb"¶
Const tblName       As String = "tblContacts"¶
' * * * * *¶
Public Sub CreateContactsDatabase()¶
'Outlook Application Objects declaration¶
Dim objApp      As Outlook.Application¶
Dim objNS       As Outlook.NameSpace¶
Dim objFolder   As Outlook.MAPIFolder¶
Dim objContact  As Object¶
'Database file properties¶
Dim blnFileExists   As Boolean¶
Dim objConn         As Object¶
Dim objSchema       As Object¶
Dim i As Integer  'Counter¶
  On Error GoTo ErrHandler¶
  'Verify if database file exists¶
  If Dir(strFileName, vbNormal) <> "" Then¶
    If MsgBox(strFileName & " is an existing file." & _¶
              vbCrLf & "Do you want to update database?", _¶
              vbYesNo + vbQuestion, _¶
              "Update Database") = vbYes Then¶
              'Use existing database to update¶
              blnFileExists = True¶
    Else¶
      'Delete existing database¶
      Kill strFileName¶
    End If¶
  End If¶
  If Not blnFileExists Then¶
    'Create database file¶
    Call CreateNewAccessDatabase(strFileName)¶
  End If¶
  'Create database connection object¶
  Set objConn = CreateObject("ADODB.Connection")¶
  objConn.Open "PROVIDER=Microsoft.Jet.OLEDB.4.0;" & _¶
               "DATA SOURCE=" & strFileName & ";"¶
  'Search for the table in database¶
  'in case it already exists¶
  'adSchemaTables = 20¶
  Set objSchema = objConn.OpenSchema(20)¶
  Do Until objSchema.EOF¶
    If objSchema.Fields("TABLE_NAME") = tblName Then¶
      'If table is found then skip CreateTable step¶
      objSchema.Close¶
      GoTo SaveContacts¶
    End If¶
```

Out

```
    objSchema.MoveNext¶
  Loop¶
  'Table does not exist in database file¶
  'Create new table¶
  Call CreateTable(objConn)¶
SaveContacts:¶
  'Set objApp object¶
  Set objApp = Outlook.Application¶
  'Set NameSpace object¶
  Set objNS = objApp.GetNamespace("MAPI")¶
  'Set source folder as default Contacts folder¶
  Set objFolder = objNS.GetDefaultFolder(olFolderContacts)¶
  'Save each contact as a new record in database table¶
  For Each objContact In objFolder.Items¶
      DoEvents¶
      If objContact.Class = olContact Then¶
          Call SaveData(objContact, objConn)¶
          i = i + 1¶
      End If¶
  Next objContact¶
  MsgBox i & " contact items have been saved in " & _¶
         strFileName¶
  'Launch Microsoft Access application¶
  Call OpenDatabaseInAccess¶
ErrHandler:¶
  If Err <> 0 Then¶
    'Critical error¶
    MsgBox Err.Number & "-" & Err.Description, _¶
           vbOKOnly + vbExclamation, _¶
           "Error"¶
  End If¶
  'Release object variables and free memory¶
  Set objApp = Nothing¶
End Sub¶
' * * * * *¶
Private Sub CreateNewAccessDatabase(strFileName As String)¶
'ADODB Catalog Object declaration¶
Dim objDB   As Object¶
'Database format¶
Dim intVer  As Integer¶
  'Create ADODB Catalog object¶
  'to create a new database file¶
  Set objDB = CreateObject("ADOX.Catalog")¶
  intVer = 5   'Access 2000 database file format¶
  'Create new database file¶
  objDB.Create "Provider=Microsoft.Jet.OLEDB.4.0;" & _¶
               "Jet OLEDB:Engine Type=" & intVer & _¶
               ";Data Source=" & strFileName¶
  'Release object variables and free memory¶
  Set objDB = Nothing¶
End Sub¶
```

```
' * * * * *¶
Private Sub CreateTable(objConn As Object)¶
'ADODB Command Object declaration¶
Dim objCmd  As Object¶
  'Create ADODB Command object to execute SQL command¶
  Set objCmd = CreateObject("ADODB.Command")¶
  'ADODB Command object needs to know the Connection¶
  'object that it is working with¶
  Set objCmd.ActiveConnection = objConn¶
  'Create table by using Outlook Contact fields names¶
  'Set SQL string to execute with ADODB Command object¶
  objCmd.CommandText = "CREATE TABLE " & tblName & _¶
                  "([EntryID] STRING(255) PRIMARY KEY," & _¶
                  "[FullName] STRING(255)," & _¶
                  "[Email1Address] STRING(255)," & _¶
                  "[Email2Address] STRING(255)," & _¶
                  "[Email3Address] STRING(255)," & _¶
                  "[WebPage] STRING(255)," & _¶
                  "[BusinessPhone] STRING(255)," & _¶
                  "[BusinessFax] STRING(255)," & _¶
                  "[HomePhone] STRING(255)," & _¶
                  "[MobilePhone] STRING(255)," & _¶
                  "[PagerNumber] STRING(255)," & _¶
                  "[Address] STRING(255)," & _¶
                  "[AddressCity] STRING(255)," & _¶
                  "[AddressCountry] STRING(255)," & _¶
                  "[AddressPostalCode] STRING(255)," & _¶
                  "[AddressPostOfficeBox] STRING(255)," & _¶
                  "[AddressState] STRING(255)," & _¶
                  "[AddressStreet] STRING(255)," & _¶
                  "[Categories] STRING(255))"¶
  'Execute ADODB Command object¶
  'Similar to running a query in Access¶
  'adCmdText = 1 to evaluate command text as SQL statement¶
  objCmd.Execute , , 1¶
  'Release object variables and free memory¶
  Set objCmd = Nothing¶
End Sub¶
' * * * * *¶
Private Sub SaveData(objContact As Object, objConn As Object)¶
'ADODB Recordset Object declaration¶
Dim objRs As Object¶
  'Create ADODB Recordset object¶
  Set objRs = CreateObject("ADODB.Recordset")¶
  'Open recordset by using SELECT statement of SQL¶
  'in requested connection¶
  objRs.Open "SELECT * " & _¶
             "FROM " & tblName & _¶
             " WHERE EntryID=" & Chr(34) & _¶
             objContact.EntryID & Chr(34), objConn, 2, 3¶
  With objRs¶
```

Out

```
      'Verify if contact already exists in the table¶
      If .EOF Then¶
        'New contact, start new record¶
        .AddNew¶
      End If¶
      'Set field values¶
      .Fields(0).Value = objContact.EntryID¶
      .Fields(1).Value = objContact.FullName¶
      .Fields(2).Value = objContact.Email1Address¶
      .Fields(3).Value = objContact.Email2Address¶
      .Fields(4).Value = objContact.Email3Address¶
      .Fields(5).Value = objContact.WebPage¶
      .Fields(6).Value = objContact.BusinessTelephoneNumber¶
      .Fields(7).Value = objContact.BusinessFaxNumber¶
      .Fields(8).Value = objContact.HomeTelephoneNumber¶
      .Fields(9).Value = objContact.MobileTelephoneNumber¶
      .Fields(10).Value = objContact.PagerNumber¶
      .Fields(11).Value = objContact.MailingAddress¶
      .Fields(12).Value = objContact.MailingAddressCity¶
      .Fields(13).Value = objContact.MailingAddressCountry¶
      .Fields(14).Value = objContact.MailingAddressPostalCode¶
      .Fields(15).Value = objContact.MailingAddressPostOfficeBox¶
      .Fields(16).Value = objContact.MailingAddressState¶
      .Fields(17).Value = objContact.MailingAddressStreet¶
      .Fields(18).Value = objContact.Categories¶
      'Update and close the recordset¶
      .Update¶
      .Close¶
    End With¶
    'Release object variables and free memory¶
    Set objRs = Nothing¶
End Sub¶
' * * * * *¶
Private Sub OpenDatabaseInAccess()¶
'Access Application Object declaration¶
Dim accApp As Object¶
    On Error GoTo ErrHandler¶
    'Create an Access Application¶
    Set accApp = CreateObject("Access.Application")¶
    'Open contacts database¶
    With accApp¶
      .Visible = True¶
      .OpenCurrentDatabase strFileName¶
      .DoCmd.OpenTable tblName¶
    End With¶
    MsgBox "Access database has been opened."¶
ErrHandler:¶
    If Err.Number = 429 Then¶
      'MS Access is not installed in this system¶
      MsgBox "You must have MS Access installed to " & _¶
             "open database in Access." & vbCrLf & _¶
```

Out

```
            "Database Path : " & strFileName, _¶
            vbOKOnly + vbExclamation, "Error"¶
  ElseIf Err Then¶
    'Another critical error¶
    MsgBox Err.Number & "-" & Err.Description, _¶
            vbOKOnly + vbExclamation, "Error"¶
  End If¶
End Sub¶
```

Set the strFileName and tblName variables to the desired values.

Sending a Web Page as the Body of an E-mail Message

This macro creates an e-mail message that includes a web page at a given URL.

Scenario: Even though a web page does not offer an "e-mail this page" type of link, an e-mail of the page can still be done using this code.

Alternatively, you could create an advertisement for your website in HTML that you want to e-mail to your favorite clients exactly as it appears. Use this procedure.

Out

View the Appendix to learn how to store this procedure in a Standard module.

```
Option Explicit¶
' * * * * *¶
'API Declaration¶
Private Declare Function GetTempPath Lib "kernel32" _¶
        Alias "GetTempPathA" (ByVal nSize As Long, _¶
        ByVal lpBuffer As String) As Long¶
Private Declare Function URLDownloadToFile Lib "urlmon" _¶
        Alias "URLDownloadToFileA" (ByVal pCaller As Long, _¶
        ByVal szURL As String, ByVal szFileName As String, _¶
        ByVal dwReserved As Long, ByVal lpfnCB As Long) _¶
        As Long¶
Private Declare Function InternetOpen Lib "wininet" _¶
        Alias "InternetOpenA" (ByVal sAgent As String, _¶
        ByVal lAccessType As Long, _¶
        ByVal sProxyName As String, _¶
        ByVal sProxyBypass As String, _¶
        ByVal lFlags As Long) As Long¶
```

```
Private Declare Function InternetCloseHandle _¶
        Lib "wininet" (ByVal hInet As Long) As Integer¶
' * * * * *¶
Sub SendWebPage()¶
'Outlook Mail Item Object declaration¶
Dim objMail  As MailItem¶
'String variable declaration¶
Dim strHTML As String 'HTML code variable¶
Dim URL     As String 'URL address varialbe¶
  'Request web page address¶
  URL = InputBox("Please enter URL address. " & _¶
        "(sample: www.mrexcel.com)", "Enter URL")¶
  'Exit if URL is null string¶
  If Trim(URL) = "" Then Exit Sub¶
  'Cannot send ftp address¶
  'Verify if given address is not an ftp one¶
  If InStr(LCase(URL), "ftp.") = 1 Or _¶
     InStr(LCase(URL), "ftp:") = 1 Then¶
     MsgBox "You cannot send ftp type url. Please verify " _¶
            & "the URL you entered.", _¶
            vbOKOnly + vbExclamation, _¶
            "The page cannot be displayed"¶
    Exit Sub¶
  End If¶
  'Modify given URL if "http://" prefix has not been given¶
  If Not LCase(Left(LCase(URL), 7)) = "http://" Then¶
    URL = "http://" & URL¶
  End If¶
  'Retrieve HTML code of given web page¶
  strHTML = GetHTMLCode(URL)¶
  'If returned HTML code is empty then exit application¶
  If Trim(strHTML) = "" Then¶
    MsgBox "The page cannot be displayed. Please check " & _¶
           "the URL you entered.", _¶
           vbOKOnly + vbExclamation, _¶
           "The page cannot be displayed"¶
    Exit Sub¶
  End If¶
  'Create mail item in Outlook application¶
  Set objMail = ThisOutlookSession.CreateItem(olMailItem)¶
  'Insert "<BASE>" tag to refer internal items in given¶
  'web page¶
  'Basically telling HTML code to refer to the real¶
  'web server for the objects and style sheets in web page¶
  If Not InStr(1, UCase(strHTML), "<HEAD>") = 0 Then¶
      strHTML = Left(strHTML, InStr(1, UCase(strHTML), _¶
                "</HEAD>") - 1) & "<BASE HREF = " & _¶
                URL & " TARGET=_self>" & _¶
                Right(strHTML, Len(strHTML) - _¶
                InStr(1, UCase(strHTML), "</HEAD>") + 1)¶
  End If¶
```

Out

```
  'Create mail item body by using HTML code that is created¶
  objMail.HTMLBody = strHTML¶
  'Show mail item as ready to post¶
  objMail.Display¶
  'Release objects and free memory¶
  Set objMail = Nothing¶
End Sub¶
' * * * * *¶
Private Function GetHTMLCode(ByVal strURL As String) _¶
                              As String¶
'Variable declaration¶
Dim tmpHTML As String¶
Dim strHTML As String¶
Dim strTemp As String¶
Dim i       As Integer¶
  'Retrieve current temporary system folder path¶
  strTemp = Space$(256)¶
  Call GetTempPath(Len(strTemp), strTemp)¶
  'Remove unwanted chars from the path variable¶
  i = InStr(strTemp, Chr$(0))¶
  If i Then¶
     strTemp = Left$(strTemp, i - 1)¶
  End If¶
  'Create temporary html file in local computer¶
  '(in previously retrieved temporary folder)¶
  'Use a unique name by current time¶
  tmpHTML = strTemp & "webpageemail" & _¶
            Format(Now, "mmddyyhhmm") & ".html"¶
  Call SaveTmpFile(strURL, tmpHTML)¶
  'Retrieve HTML code from saved file¶
  Open tmpHTML For Binary As #1¶
  strHTML = Space(LOF(1))¶
  Get #1, , strHTML¶
  Close #1¶
  'Delete temporary HTML file¶
  Kill tmpHTML¶
  'Return HTML code¶
  GetHTMLCode = strHTML¶
End Function¶
' * * * * *¶
Private Function SaveTmpFile(strURL As String, _¶
                            tmpHTML As String) As Boolean¶
'API function variables declaration¶
Dim lngret  As Long¶
Dim lngInet As Long¶
Dim hInet¶
  'Open web page and save its HTML code into the¶
  'given temporary HTML file¶
  If lngInet = 0 Then hInet = InternetOpen("", 1, _¶
                              vbNullString, vbNullString, 0)¶
```

Out

```
   'Download web page source code as HTML¶
   lngret = URLDownloadToFile(0, strURL, tmpHTML, 0, 0)¶
   'Close internet connection¶
   InternetCloseHandle lngInet¶
End Function¶
```

Notes: FTP web pages cannot be sent using this macro.

Recipients will not be able to read the web page if their e-mail is set to receive text-only e-mails.

Sending a Message Individually to Multiple Recipients

This macro sends the same e-mail message (that has been saved as a draft in Outlook) to more than one recipient.

Scenario: You need to send out the same e-mail message to a group of recipients, but your Internet Service Provider's spam filters prevent you from sending it to all of them at one time. This macro can help you to bypass spam filters that may have been put in place by your Internet Service Provider by sending an individual e-mail to each recipient over a period of time.

This application lets the user select a saved mail item in the Drafts folder to send to the addresses listed in an Excel worksheet; it is triggered from Excel, not Outlook itself.

Example file:
O005.xls

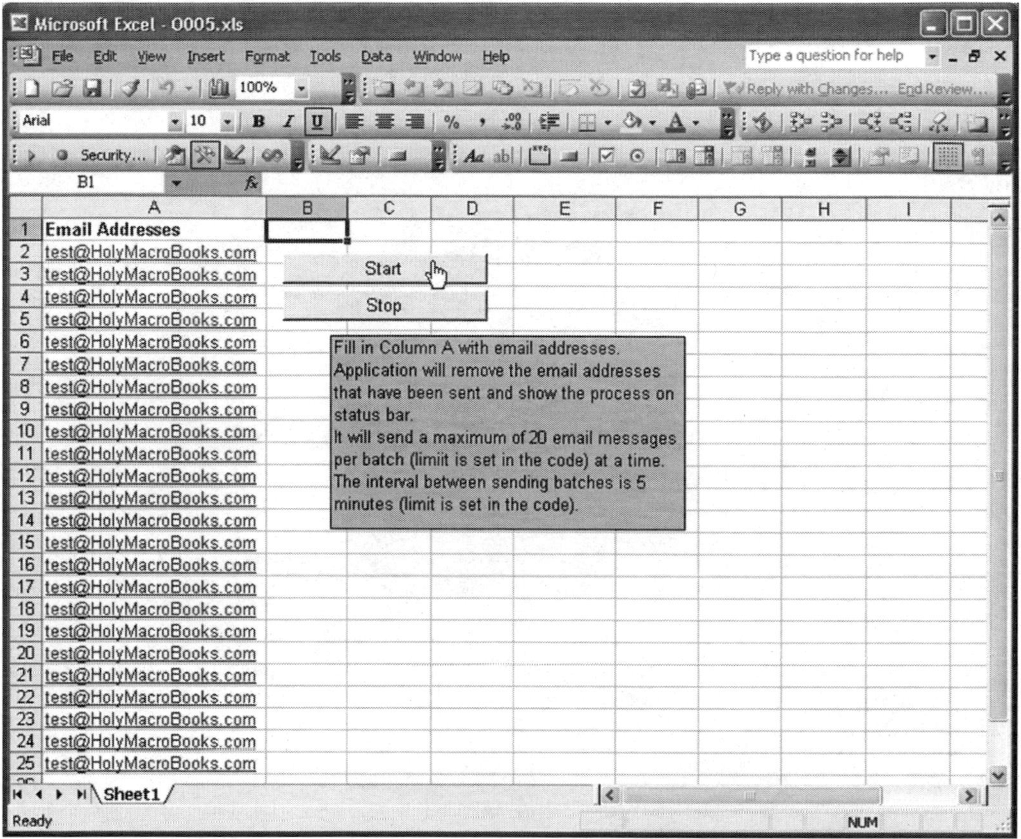

Figure 71 – Sending E-mail Messages to Multiple Recipients

View the Appendix to learn how to store this procedure in a Standard (Excel) module.

```
Option Explicit¶
' * * * * *¶
'Outlook Application Objects declaration¶
Dim objItem As Object 'Outlook.MailItem¶
'Applicaton Ontime variable declaration¶
Dim myRunTime As Double¶
'Send & Receive interval in second - set to desired interval¶
Const myInterval = 5 * 60¶
'How many emails to send in a single Send & Receive¶
'Set as needed¶
Const howMany = 20¶
'Excel Worksheet Object¶
```

Out

```
'Declaring this object variable in this section¶
'to make its lifetime along this application¶
'to recognize the active sheet that code¶
'started working with¶
Dim sht As Worksheet¶
' * * * * *¶
Sub SendEmail()¶
'Outlook Application Objects declaration¶
Dim objMail  As Object 'Outlook.MailItem¶
'Excel Application Objects declaration¶
Dim rng As Range¶
Dim cll As Range¶
  'Validate if this is the first attempt¶
  'to run this procedure¶
  'If first attempt then ask user to¶
  'select a mail item to send¶
  If objItem Is Nothing Then¶
    Call SetMailItem¶
  End If¶
  'Mail item cannot be set¶
  'Stop execution¶
  If objItem Is Nothing Then Exit Sub¶
  'Set worksheet object¶
  'Considering active sheet is being used¶
  'If it has been set during previous attempt to run¶
  'this module then skip it¶
  If sht Is Nothing Then¶
    Set sht = ActiveSheet¶
  End If¶
  'Set range that includes email addresses - Column A¶
  Set rng = sht.Range(sht.Cells(2, 1), _¶
                        sht.Cells(65536, 1).End(xlUp))¶
  If rng.Cells(1, 1).Row = 1 Then Exit Sub¶
  'Inform user about progress¶
  Application.StatusBar = "Remaining " & _¶
        (rng.Rows.Count - howMany) & " addresses : " & _¶
        Int(rng.Rows.Count / howMany * myInterval / 60) _¶
        & " minutes..."¶
  'If the selected range has a row count more than the number¶
  'of emails to be delivered then reselect the range by using¶
  'exact number of rows indicated by the howMany variable value¶
  If rng.Rows.Count > howMany Then¶
    Set rng = sht.Range(sht.Cells(2, 1), _¶
      sht.Cells(howMany + 1, 1))¶
  End If¶
  'Send every single user an email message¶
  For Each cll In rng.Rows¶
    If Trim(cll.Value) <> "" Then¶
      Set objMail = objItem.Copy¶
      objMail.To = cll.Cells(1, 1).Value¶
      objMail.Send¶
```

```
    End If¶
  Next cll¶
  'Clear email sent addresses¶
  rng.Delete xlUp¶
  'Reset email addresses range¶
  Set rng = sht.Range(sht.Cells(2, 1), _¶
    sht.Cells(65536, 1).End(xlUp))¶
  'If there is only one row selected then¶
  'there is no more email address to execute¶
  If rng.Cells(1, 1).Row = 1 Then¶
      'Stop Timer¶
      Call KillTimer(True)¶
      'Inform user about finalizing¶
      MsgBox "Done!"¶
      'Stop process¶
      Exit Sub¶
  End If¶
  'Set next time to send next range of email addresses¶
  'Using Send & Receive time that has been set in the¶
  'declaration section¶
  myRunTime = Now + TimeSerial(0, 0, myInterval)¶
  Application.OnTime myRunTime, "SendEmail", , True¶
End Sub¶
' * * * * *¶
Sub KillTimer(Optional auto As Boolean)¶
'Stop timer¶
  'continue when error occurs¶
  On Error Resume Next¶
  'Reset Status Bar message¶
  Application.StatusBar = False¶
  'Delete scheduled action on requested time¶
  Application.OnTime myRunTime, "SendEmail", , False¶
  'If user clicked on button to stop timer¶
  'then auto variable will be false¶
  'Confirm user about stopping timer¶
  If Not auto Then MsgBox "Timer stopped"¶
End Sub¶
' * * * * *¶
Private Sub SetMailItem()¶
'Outlook Application Objects declaration¶
Dim objApp  As Object 'Outlook.Application¶
Dim objFolder  As Object 'Outlook.MAPIFolder¶
Dim objNS   As Object 'Outlook.NameSpace¶
Dim retval¶
Dim i          As Integer¶
Dim strItems  As String¶
  'Continue running when error occurs¶
  On Error Resume Next¶
  'Get running instance of Outlook Application¶
  Set objApp = GetObject(, "Outlook.Application")¶
```

Out

```
    'Error occurs if Outlook Application is not running¶
    If Err Then¶
      'If error then launch Outlook Application¶
      Set objApp = CreateObject("Outlook.Application")¶
      Err.Clear¶
    End If¶
    'Create Name Space object to access folder object¶
    Set objNS = objApp.GetNamespace("MAPI")¶
    'Create folder object to look at the Drafts folder for¶
    'prepared email message¶
    'olFolderDrafts = 16¶
    Set objFolder = objNS.GetDefaultFolder(16)¶
    'Ask user to select a mail item from Drafts folder¶
    With objFolder.Items¶
      For i = 1 To .Count¶
        'Looking for mail items¶
        'olMail = 43¶
        If .Item(i).Class = 43 Then¶
          strItems = strItems & vbCrLf & i & "-" & .Item(i) _¶
                                                        .subject¶
        End If¶
      Next i¶
    End With¶
    retval = InputBox("Please select email message to send " & _¶
                      "receipents." & vbCrLf & strItems, _¶
                      "Select Email Message")¶
    'Validate if choice is a numeric value¶
    If Not IsNumeric(retval) Then¶
      GoTo ExitSub¶
    'Validate if choice is a valid item number¶
    ElseIf Not (retval > 0 And retval < i + 1) Then¶
      GoTo ExitSub¶
    End If¶
    'Set mail item object by user selection¶
    Set objItem = objFolder.Items.Item(CInt(retval))¶
ExitSub:¶
    'Validate if Outlook Application has been set by this code¶
    If Not objApp Is Nothing Then¶
      'Validate if Outlook Application has a visible explorer¶
      'If there is no visible explorer then¶
      'it means Outlook Application has been launched from¶
      'this code¶
      If objApp.ActiveExplorer Is Nothing Then¶
          objApp.Quit¶
      End If¶
      Set objApp = Nothing¶
    End If¶
End Sub¶
```

View the Appendix to learn how to store this procedure in the ThisWorkbook module.

```
Option Explicit¶
' * * * * *¶
Private Sub Workbook_BeforeClose(Cancel As Boolean)¶
    Call KillTimer(True)¶
End Sub¶
```

Follow these steps:

1. The first code section goes in a Standard module. The second code section goes in the ThisWorkbook module of the Excel workbook that contains the list of e-mail addresses.
2. Set the myInterval value as the Send & Receive time setting. Set the howMany value as the number of e-mails that the Outlook application can send within the Send & Receive time.
3. This macro runs from Microsoft Excel. The example file has assigned this macro to a button for easy use.

Sending Daily Attachments to Certain Recipients

This macro sends an e-mail to specific recipients with a local file attached by using a recurring task entry.

Scenario: A method similar to the one used in the Sending a Message Individually to Multiple Recipients section on page 285 can be used to send daily updated files from a local computer via e-mail. Suppose it is your responsibility to send an Excel file to all department heads each day at 3:00 p.m., but you often forget to do it until it's time to go home.

To send out updated files via e-mail on a daily basis, create a Recurring Task Item by using a custom category and reminder, and then enter a local file name into the task body. A custom category to tell the macro that the code should process a Task Item is necessary. The 'Daily Report Sender' category name is used in this sample code.

Create the Task Item as shown on the following page:

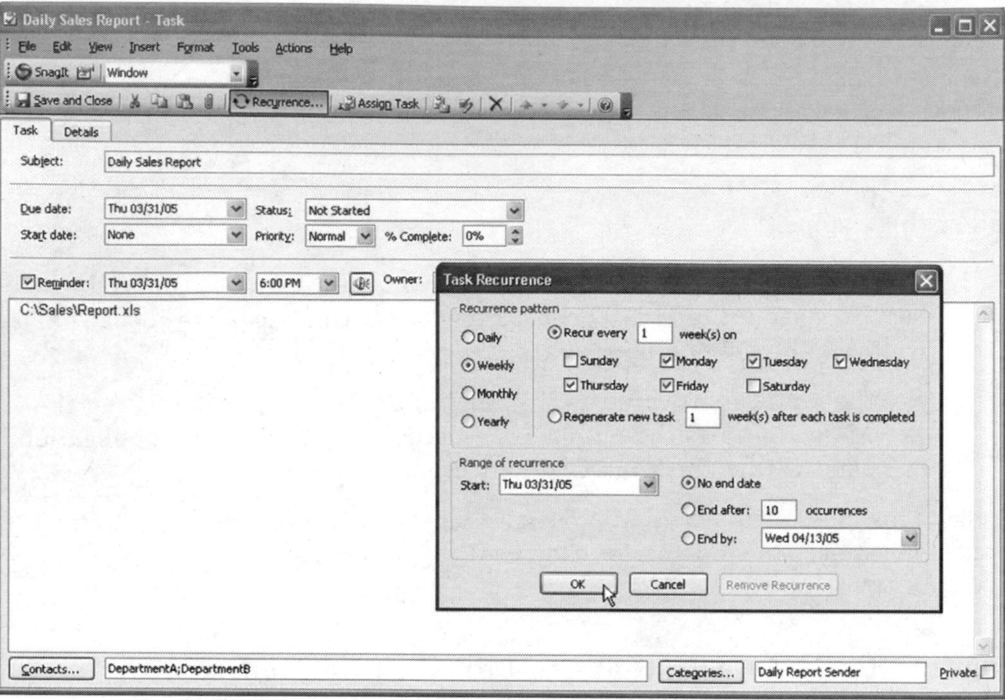

Figure 72 – Creating a Recurrent Task

The Sample Task Item has been set by using a reminder to recur everyday at 06:00 PM. Two sample contacts from the Address Book and sample file name in body section, C:\Sales\Report.xls, will be sent an e-mail automatically.

View the Appendix to learn how to store this procedure in the ThisOutlookSession module.

```
Option Explicit¶
' * * * * *¶
Private Sub Application_Reminder(ByVal Item As Object)¶
  'Occurs immediately before the reminder is displayed¶
  'And calls the macro that will do the job¶
  Call SendFiles(Item)¶
End Sub¶
```

```
' * * * * *¶
Private Sub SendFiles(objTask As TaskItem)¶
'Outlook objects declaration¶
Dim objMail     As Outlook.MailItem¶
Dim strCategoryName As String¶
Dim strFileName     As String¶
Dim strContact¶
Dim i As Integer  'Counter¶
  On Error GoTo ErrHandler¶
  'Custom category that was created to use for this¶
  'action¶
  strCategoryName = "Daily Report Sender"¶
  'If category name doesn't match then quit process¶
  'And let reminder run normally¶
  If Not objTask.Categories = strCategoryName Then Exit Sub¶
  'Verify if specified file exists¶
  'Quit process if it does not exist¶
  If Dir(objTask.Body) = "" Then Exit Sub¶
  'File name that is specified in task body section¶
  strFileName = Trim(objTask.Body)¶
  'Create mail object¶
  Set objMail = Outlook.CreateItem(olMailItem)¶
  With objMail¶
    'Use same subject with Task Item¶
    .Subject = objTask.Subject¶
    'Attach related file¶
    .Attachments.Add strFileName¶
    'Add recipients¶
    'Contact Names stores contact names with commas between¶
    'DepartmentA, DepartmentB, DepartmentC¶
    'So the names are split by using comma as delimiter¶
    strContact = Split(objTask.ContactNames, ",")¶
 'Checking if language settigns require using¶
' “;” as list separator¶
If Not IsArray(strContact) Then _¶
  strContact = Split(objTask.ContactNames, “;”)¶
End if ¶
  'Adding recipients to new email message¶
    For i = 0 To UBound(strContact)¶
      .Recipients.Add strContact(i)¶
    Next i¶
    'Send message immediately¶
    .Send¶
  End With¶
  With objTask¶
    'Close reminder popup¶
    .ReminderSet = False¶
    .Close olSave¶
  End With¶
ExitSub:¶
  Exit Sub¶
```

Out

```
ErrorHandler:¶
  'Critical error¶
  MsgBox Err.Number & "-" & Err.Description, _¶
        vbOKOnly + vbExclamation, "Error"¶
  GoTo ExitSub¶
End Sub¶
```

Change the file in the body of the task to whatever file is desired and set the time and the recurring period to appropriate values.

This macro is triggered by the recurring task.

Creating Reminders Automatically

This application shows how to create Task Items, such as eBay auctions, automatically.

Scenario: EBay auctions expire at a set time. In order to check an auction for the final bid, a reminder can be set in Outlook to inform the user that the auction is nearing the end. While eBay may send you an e-mail hours in advance, Outlook has the added advantage of being able to provide a sound notification when a reminder goes off.

View the Appendix to learn how to store this procedure in a Standard module.

```
Option Explicit¶
' * * * * *¶
'API Declaration¶
Private Declare Function GetTempPath Lib "kernel32" _¶
        Alias "GetTempPathA" (ByVal nSize As Long, _¶
        ByVal lpBuffer As String) As Long¶
Private Declare Function URLDownloadToFile Lib "urlmon" _¶
        Alias "URLDownloadToFileA" (ByVal pCaller As Long, _¶
        ByVal szURL As String, ByVal szFileName As String, _¶
        ByVal dwReserved As Long, ByVal lpfnCB As Long) _¶
        As Long¶
Private Declare Function InternetOpen Lib "wininet" _¶
        Alias "InternetOpenA" (ByVal sAgent As String, _¶
        ByVal lAccessType As Long, _¶
        ByVal sProxyName As String, _¶
        ByVal sProxyBypass As String, _¶
```

```
        ByVal lFlags As Long) As Long¶
Private Declare Function InternetCloseHandle _¶
        Lib "wininet" (ByVal hInet As Long) As Integer¶
Public Sub CreateAuctionReminder()¶
'Outlook Task object declaration¶
Dim objTask As Outlook.TaskItem¶
'variable declaration¶
Dim strHTML   As String  'HTML code variable¶
Dim URL       As String  'URL address variable¶
Dim aucNum    As String  'ebay Auction number¶
Dim strEnding As String  'Auction Ending Date¶
Dim strItem   As String  'Item name¶
Dim EndTime   As String  'Ending time of auction¶
Dim dt        As Variant 'Date¶
  'Request Auction ID¶
  aucNum = InputBox("Please enter Auction Number", _¶
                    "Auction Number")¶
  'Verify Auction ID and stop process if¶
  'something is wrong¶
  If IsNull(aucNum) Or Trim(aucNum) = "" Then Exit Sub¶
  If Not IsNumeric(aucNum) Then¶
    MsgBox "Invalid Auction Number.", _¶
              vbOKOnly + vbExclamation, "Error"¶
    Exit Sub¶
  End If¶
  On Error GoTo ErrHandler¶
  'Web Site URL for requested item listing¶
  URL = "http://cgi.ebay.com/ws/eBayISAPI.dll?" & _¶
          "ViewItem&item=" & aucNum¶
  'Retrieve HTML code of given web page¶
  strHTML = GetHTMLCode(URL)¶
  'If returned HTML code is empty then exit application¶
  If Trim(strHTML) = "" Then¶
    MsgBox "The page cannot be displayed. Please check " & _¶
            "the URL you entered.", _¶
            vbOKOnly + vbExclamation, _¶
            "The page cannot be displayed"¶
    Exit Sub¶
  End If¶
  'Retrieve title of web page¶
  strHTML = Mid(strHTML, _¶
          InStr(1, strHTML, "<title>", vbTextCompare), _¶
          InStr(1, strHTML, "</title>", vbTextCompare) _¶
          - InStr(1, strHTML, "<title>", vbTextCompare))¶
  'Find ending time from the title¶
  'Currently ebay web page returns this information in title¶
  'eBay item <aucNum> (Ends <ending time>) - Item Description¶
  'All that is required is to parse this string¶
  strHTML = Right(strHTML, _¶
             Len(strHTML) - InStr(strHTML, "Ends") - 4)¶
```

```
   'Retrieve ending time from the title¶
   strEnding = Left(strHTML, InStr(strHTML, ")") - 5)¶
   dt = strEnding¶
   strEnding = Replace(Left(dt, InStrRev(dt, " ") - 1), _¶
                  Chr(13) & Chr(10), "")¶
   'Verify if retrieved data is a valid date¶
   If Not IsDate(strEnding) Then Exit Sub¶
   'Format retrieved date in more readable format¶
   strEnding = Format(dt, "mm/dd/yyyy hh:mm AM/PM")¶
   'Retrieve item name¶
   strItem = Replace(Right(strHTML, Len(strHTML) _¶
                - InStr(strHTML, ")") - 1), _¶
                Chr(13) & Chr(10), "")¶
   'Create new task item for this item¶
   Set objTask = Application.CreateItem(olTaskItem)¶
   With objTask¶
     .StartDate = strEnding¶
     .DueDate = strEnding¶
     .Subject = aucNum & strItem¶
     .ReminderSet = True¶
     .ReminderOverrideDefault = True¶
     .ReminderPlaySound = True¶
     'Set reminder time for 5 minutes before¶
     'Auction ending¶
     .ReminderTime = Format(DateValue(dt) & " " & _¶
         TimeSerial(Hour(strEnding), Minute(strEnding) - 5, 0), _¶
         "mm/dd/yyyy HH:MM AM/PM")¶
     'Auction information¶
     .Body = "Reminder for " & strItem & vbCrLf & _¶
           "Auction Number : " & aucNum & vbCrLf & _¶
           "Ends : " & strEnding¶
     .Save¶
  End With¶
ExitSub:¶
  Exit Sub¶
ErrHandler:¶
  'Critical Error¶
  MsgBox "Cannot parse related html page.  " & _¶
        "May be wrong Auction Number", _¶
        vbOKOnly + vbExclamation, "Error"¶
  GoTo ExitSub¶
End Sub¶
' * * * * *¶
Private Function GetHTMLCode(ByVal strURL As String) _¶
                              As String¶
'Variable declaration¶
Dim tmpHTML As String¶
Dim strHTML As String¶
Dim strTemp As String¶
Dim i       As Integer¶
```

Out

```
   'Retrieve current temporary system folder path¶
   strTemp = Space$(256)¶
   Call GetTempPath(Len(strTemp), strTemp)¶
   'Remove unwanted chars from the path variable¶
   i = InStr(strTemp, Chr$(0))¶
   If i Then¶
      strTemp = Left$(strTemp, i - 1)¶
   End If¶
   'Create temporary html file in local computer¶
   '(in previously retrieved temporary folder)¶
   'Use a unique name by current time¶
   tmpHTML = strTemp & "webpageemail" & _¶
             Format(Now, "mmddyyhhmm") & ".html"¶
   Call SaveTmpFile(strURL, tmpHTML)¶
   'Retrieve HTML code from saved file¶
   Open tmpHTML For Binary As #1¶
   strHTML = Space(LOF(1))¶
   Get #1, , strHTML¶
   Close #1¶
   'Delete temporary HTML file¶
   Kill tmpHTML¶
   'Return HTML code¶
   GetHTMLCode = strHTML¶
End Function¶
' * * * * *¶
Private Function SaveTmpFile(strURL As String, _¶
                             tmpHTML As String) As Boolean¶
'API function variables declaration¶
Dim lngret  As Long¶
Dim lngInet As Long¶
Dim hInet¶
   'Open web page and save its HTML code into the¶
   'given temporary HTML file¶
   If lngInet = 0 Then hInet = InternetOpen("", 1, _¶
                              vbNullString, vbNullString, 0)¶
   'Download web page source code as HTML¶
   lngret = URLDownloadToFile(0, strURL, tmpHTML, 0, 0)¶
   'Close internet connection¶
   InternetCloseHandle lngInet¶
End Function¶
```

EBay auctions have been used as sample data. The user simply enters an auction number that is listed on eBay and the application returns the necessary information for the item and sets a reminder five minutes before the ending time of the selected auction.

Note: EBay often changes their web layout, which could make this macro worthless as it is written, making adjustments necessary.

Out

Creating Task Items Automatically in Outlook

This application creates Task Items for the records in a database. Adding or modifying a record in the database form will help manage related Task Items in Outlook by using database form events.

> **Scenario:** The sample database is an Order Entry database that has been created by using the Access Wizard.

Example file:
O012.mdb

The OLTaskItemID field has been added to the Orders table to store the Task Item EntryID to relate order records by Task Items.

- **OLTaskItemID field settings**
- **Parent Table: Orders**
- **Data Type: Text Field**
- **Field Size: 255**
- **Allow Zero Length: True**

The following code has been added to the default Orders form in the auto-generated database. There are three form event procedures (found on page 299) that are affected by this code:

- **Form_BeforeUpdate:** Creates task by adding/modifying a record
- **Form_Delete:** Stores deleted record's Task Item Entry ID
- **Form_AfterDelConfirm:** Deletes related Task Item object in Outlook

Additional code is contained in the 'Orders' Form. The Access Wizard generated this additional code. All Wizard-generated code and the associated Form are listed in the table that follows the Remarks for this macro.

```
'Option Compare statement specifies the string comparison method¶
'(Binary, Text, or Database) for a module. If a module doesn't¶
'include an Option Compare statement, the default text comparison¶
'method is Binary.¶
Option Compare Database¶
Option Explicit¶
' * * * * *¶
'Day before count for the reminder¶
Const RemindBefore  As Integer = 7¶
'Task Entry ID variable to store deleted record's OLTaskItemID¶
```

```
'Refer to Form_Delete event to see how it is being set¶
'Variable declaration¶
Dim DelTaskID       As String¶
' * * * * *¶
Private Sub AddOLTask()¶
'Outlook Application Objects declaration¶
Dim olApp       As Object 'Outlook.Application¶
Dim olNS        As Object 'Outlook.NameSpace¶
Dim olTask      As Object 'Outlook.TaskItem¶
Dim varShipDate As Date¶
  'Validate if current date field value and saved OLTaskItemID¶
  'for this record¶
  'If both value are invalid then cannot add/edit a Task Item¶
  If Not IsDate(Me.ShipDate) And IsNull(Me!OLTaskItemID) _¶
        Then Exit Sub¶
  'Continue if an error occurs¶
  On Error Resume Next¶
  Set olApp = GetObject(, "Outlook.Application")¶
  'Error occurs if Outlook Application is not running¶
  If Err Then¶
    'If error then launch Outlook Application¶
    Set olApp = CreateObject("Outlook.Application")¶
    Err.Clear¶
  End If¶
  'Create Name Space by using MAPI data source¶
  'for current Outlook session to manage objects¶
  Set olNS = olApp.GetNamespace("MAPI")¶
  'Validate OLTaskItemID field value for current record¶
  If IsNull(Me!OLTaskItemID) Then¶
    'There is not a saved Task Item for this record¶
    'Create new Task Item object¶
    ''olTaskItem = 3¶
    Set olTask = olApp.CreateItem(3)¶
  ElseIf Not Trim(Me!OLTaskItemID) = "" Then¶
    'There is a saved Task Item for this record¶
    'Get it to modify by using modified record¶
    Set olTask = olNS.GetItemFromID(Me!OLTaskItemID)¶
    'Make sure if Task Item is succesfully retrieved¶
    'Otherwise create new Task Iteim¶
    If olTask Is Nothing Then¶
      Set olTask = olApp.CreateItem(3)¶
    Else¶
      'Validate existing Task Item's current parent folder¶
      If olTask.Parent.Class = 2 Then¶
        'If Task Item was deleted then code will still find it¶
        'by using EntryID (OLTaskItemID)¶
        'Validate if it was deleted and move into Tasks folder¶
        'in case it was¶
        'Validation is being done by matching Deleted Items¶
        'and Task Item's parent folder names¶
        'olFolderDeletedItems = 3¶
```

Out

```
        If olTask.Parent.Name = olNS.GetDefaultFolder(3).Name _¶
            Then¶
          'olFolderTasks = 13¶
          olTask.Move _¶
            olNS.GetNamespace("MAPI").GetDefaultFolder(13)¶
        End If¶
      End If¶
    End If¶
  End If¶
  'Set error handler for general errors¶
  On Error GoTo ErrHandler¶
  'Make sure if Task Item has been set succesfully¶
  If Not olTask Is Nothing Then¶
    'Set Task Item properties by using current record data¶
    With olTask¶
      varShipDate = Me.ShipDate¶
      .Subject = "Shipping for " & Me.PurchaseOrderNumber.Value¶
      'Set Due Date for Task item specified days before¶
      'the event date¶
      .StartDate = varShipDate - RemindBefore¶
      .DueDate = varShipDate - RemindBefore¶
      'Set importance - High Importance¶
      'Available options¶
      ''olImportanceHigh  = 2¶
      ''olImportanceLow   = 0¶
      ''olImportanceNormal= 1¶
      .Importance = 2¶
      'Set reminder for the requested day¶
      'Time used by 13:00 as default¶
      .ReminderSet = True¶
      .ReminderTime = Format((varShipDate) & _¶
                      " 13:00", "mm/dd/yyyy hh:mm")¶
      'Play a sound ?¶
      .ReminderPlaySound = True¶
      'Retrieve record information for current record¶
      .Body = GetOrderInformation¶
      'Save Task Item¶
      .Save¶
      'Save recently saved Task Item's unique EntryID¶
      'to relate this Task Item and current record for¶
      'later modifications¶
      Me!OLTaskItemID = .EntryID¶
      'Close Task Item by saving it¶
      'Available options¶
      'olSave          = 0 'Required for silent automation¶
      'olPromptForSave = 2¶
      ' olDiscard      = 1 'Cannot be used for this code¶
      .Close 0¶
    End With¶
  End If¶
```

Out

```
ExitSub:¶
  'Validate if Outlook Application has been set by this code¶
  If Not olApp Is Nothing Then¶
    'Validate if Outlook Application has a visible explorer¶
    'If there is no visible explorer then¶
    'it means Outlook Application has been launched from¶
    'this code¶
    If olApp.ActiveExplorer Is Nothing Then¶
      'Quit Outlook Application¶
      olApp.Quit¶
    End If¶
    'Release objects¶
    Set olApp = Nothing¶
  End If¶
  Exit Sub¶
ErrHandler:¶
  'An error occured¶
  MsgBox Err.Number & "-" & Err.Description, _¶
        vbOKOnly + vbExclamation, "Error"¶
  Resume ExitSub¶
End Sub¶
' * * * * *¶
Private Function GetOrderInformation() As String¶
'This function Returns Record Information¶
'for the Task Item body as text¶
Dim strBody As String¶
Dim rcset As Recordset¶
  'Collect information from data fields for the current record¶
  With Me¶
    strBody = "PO#:" & vbTab & .PurchaseOrderNumber & vbCrLf & _¶
      "Employee:" & vbTab & .EmployeeID.Column(1) & vbCrLf & _¶
      "SalesTax %:" & vbTab & .SalesTaxRate & vbCrLf & _¶
      "Order Date:" & vbTab & .OrderDate & vbCrLf & _¶
      "Ship Date:" & vbTab & .ShipDate & vbCrLf & _¶
      "Ship by:" & vbTab & .ShippingMethodID.Column(1) & vbCrLf & _¶
      vbCrLf & _¶
      "Products" & vbTab & "Price" & vbTab & "Qty" & vbTab & _¶
      "Dis" & vbTab & "Total" & vbCrLf & _¶
      String(100, "-")¶
    'Products from subform recordset¶
    With .Order_Details_Subform.Form¶
      Set rcset = .Form.Recordset¶
      If Not rcset.EOF And Not rcset.BOF Then¶
        rcset.MoveFirst¶
      End If¶
      Do Until rcset.EOF¶
        strBody = strBody & vbCrLf & _¶
                  ![ProductID].Column(1) & vbTab & _¶
                  ![UnitPrice].Value & vbTab & _¶
                  ![Quantity].Value & vbTab & _¶
                  ![Discount].Value & vbTab & _¶
```

```
                 ![Line Total].Value & vbTab¶
          rcset.MoveNext¶
        Loop¶
      End With¶
      strBody = strBody & vbCrLf & _¶
      String(100, "-") & vbCrLf & _¶
      "SubTotal:" & vbTab & Format(.Order_Subtotal, "Currency") & vbCrLf & _¶
      "Freight Chr:" & vbTab & Format(.FreightCharge, "Currency") & vbCrLf & _¶
      "Sales Tax:" & vbTab & Format(.Sales_Tax, "Currency") & vbCrLf & _¶
      "Order Total:" & vbTab & Format(.Order_Total, "Currency") & vbCrLf & _¶
      "Payments:" & vbTab & Format(.Total_Payments, "Currency") & vbCrLf & _¶
      "Amount Due:" & vbTab & Format(.Amount_Due, "Currency")¶
    End With¶
    'Return complete data set¶
    GetOrderInformation = strBody¶
End Function¶
' * * * * *¶
Private Sub RemoveOLTask(DelTaskID As String)¶
'Deletes a Task Item¶
'Record deleting causes this action¶
'And remove related Task Item by identifying¶
'related OLTaskItemID for the record¶
'Outlook Application Objects declaration¶
Dim olApp  As Object¶
Dim olTask As Object¶
    'Continue when an error occurs¶
    On Error Resume Next¶
    'Validate if there is a valid Task Entry ID saved for deleting¶
    If Not IsNull(DelTaskID) Then¶
        Set olApp = GetObject(, "Outlook.Application")¶
        If Err Then¶
            Set olApp = CreateObject("Outlook.Application")¶
        End If¶
        On Error GoTo ErrHandler¶
        Set olTask =
olApp.GetNamespace("MAPI").GetItemFromID(DelTaskID)¶
        If Not olTask Is Nothing Then¶
            'Delete retrieved Task Item¶
            olTask.Delete¶
        End If¶
    End If¶
ExitSub:¶
    If Not olApp Is Nothing Then¶
        If olApp.ActiveExplorer Is Nothing Then¶
            olApp.Quit¶
        End If¶
        Set olApp = Nothing¶
    End If¶
    Exit Sub¶
```

```
ErrHandler:¶
    MsgBox Err.Number & "-" & Err.Description, _¶
           vbOKOnly + vbExclamation, "Error"¶
    Resume ExitSub¶
End Sub¶
' * * * * *¶
Private Sub Form_AfterDelConfirm(Status As Integer)¶
  'Status tells if record has been deleted or not¶
  If Status = acDeleteOK Then¶
    'If record is deleted then validate if there is a¶
    'saved EntryID to delete the related Task Item¶
    'in DelTaskID variable¶
    If Not Trim(DelTaskID) = "" Then¶
      'Start Task Item Removal procedure¶
      Call RemoveOLTask(DelTaskID)¶
    End If¶
  End If¶
End Sub¶
' * * * * *¶
Private Sub Form_BeforeUpdate(Cancel As Integer)¶
    'Before updating a record¶
    'Create or Edit a Task Item for this record¶
    Call AddOLTask¶
End Sub¶
' * * * * *¶
Private Sub Form_Delete(Cancel As Integer)¶
  'If record is being deleted¶
  'then this event procedure is the last chance to¶
  'save necessary OLTaskItemID value into a form variable¶
  'for using Task Item Removal procedure after deletion¶
  If IsNull(Me!OLTaskItemID.Value) Then¶
    'There is no OLTaskItemID has been saved for this record¶
    'Clean the DelTaskID value¶
    DelTaskID = ""¶
  Else¶
    'Save deleted record's OLTaskItemID value¶
    DelTaskID = Me!OLTaskItemID.Value¶
  End If¶
End Sub¶
```

The code for this macro goes into the module for the Orders form. In the Project window (top left) of the VBE, right-click on the name 'Form_Orders' and select the View Code option from the pop up menu. The example file already has the code in the form.

View the Appendix to learn how to Navigate the Visual Basic Editor.

Out

To use this with another database, make these changes:

- **OLTaskItemID field** — Should be added into the items table
- **PurchaseOrderNumber control name** — Should be changed by using the key field control name on the related form (AddOLTask module)
- **ShipDate control name** — Should be changed by using the date field control name on the related form (AddOLTask module)
- **GetOrderInformation function** — Should be changed by using corresponding field control names on form (GetOrderInformation module)
- **Modified code** — Should be copied & pasted into the related form declaration modules.

This macro runs automatically.

The forms in the example database contain code that was created by the Form Wizard.

Special: Outlook Security

Outlook Security provides protection against malicious scripts and asks the user for confirmation to allow scripts to run. This can cause an automated solution to be more trouble than it's worth.

One possible solution is to use a third-party COM object called Redemption. See http://www.dimastr.com/redemption/ for more information and a free installation package. To enable automated solutions to run properly, simply set the Mail Item object as the Safe Mail Item object using this COM object. Using this new object to execute actions and access its properties avoids the script confirmation problem.

In the following sections, we provide code entries modified to use the Redemption object.

Auto Replying to Selected E-mail Messages

With this procedure you can send a predefined message as a reply to selected e-mail messages.

Note: This procedure provides code using the Redemption object, which requires installation of the Redemption COM Object.

View the Appendix to learn how to store this procedure in a Standard module.

```
Option explicit¶
' * * * * *
Public Sub SendAutoReply()¶
'Outlook Application Objects declaration¶
Dim objExp  As Outlook.Explorer¶
Dim objMail As Outlook.MailItem¶
Dim objItem As Object¶
'Redemption SafeMail object declaration¶
Dim objSafeMail As Object¶
'Auto Reply message variable¶
Dim strReplyMessage As String¶
  'Set this variable as desired¶
  strReplyMessage = "Thank you! Your order will be " & _¶
    "processed immediately!"¶
  'Set active explorer object¶
  Set objExp = Application.ActiveExplorer¶
  'Loop in selected items in Active Explorer¶
  For Each objItem In objExp.Selection¶
    'If selected item is a mail item then execute¶
    'auto reply function¶
    If objItem.Class = olMail Then¶
      'Set mail item object as the selected item¶
      Set objMail = objItem¶
      'Create a reply mail object by using selected mail object¶
      Set objMail = objMail.Reply¶
      'Redemption Addition starts here¶
      'Create Redemption SafeMail object¶
      'Use this object to send message without¶
      'security warning¶
      Set objSafeMail = CreateObject("Redemption.SafeMailItem")¶
      Set objSafeMail.Item = objMail¶
      'Redemption Addition stops here¶
      'Add requested auto message to current message as reply¶
      With objSafeMail 'Using Redemption Safe Mail Item object¶
        .HTMLBody = strReplyMessage & vbCrLf & .HTMLBody¶
        'For Plain Text reply, use the following¶
```

Out

```
        'Body property setting instead HTMLBody¶
        'Please comment out the previous code line¶
        '.Body = strReplyMessage & vbCrLf & .Body¶
        'Send reply immediately¶
        .Send¶
      End With¶
    End If¶
  'Continue with next selected item in active explorer¶
  Next objItem¶
End Sub¶
```

To send the same reply to specific e-mail messages received, set the strReplyMessage variable that stores the predefined text message in the code. Set the .HTMLbody and .body properties to use either one or the other. Comment out the unwanted property by placing an apostrophe to the left of the property you do not want to run. The macro as written uses the .HTMLbody property.

Out

Select the mail items in the active folder then run the macro.

Remote Control with Outlook E-mail Message

This macro shows how to turn the Outlook Application into a Remote Control tool.

Scenario: Each day, you are required send an e-mail to a particular person. Today you forgot, and now you're over at a friend's house. To send this daily e-mail out from a remote location, you only need to send a special e-mail message to yourself. The code tracks the folder events, and when specific criteria are met, it then runs the code and attaches the requested file in the reply to the incoming e-mail message.

CAUTION! Using this code involves some risk. To make this code more secure, use a very specific subject line, and do not share it.

Note: This procedure provides code using the Redemption object, which requires installation of the Redemption COM Object.

View the Appendix to learn how to store this procedure in the ThisOutlookSession module.

```
Dim myFolderEventsClass As clsRemoteControl¶
Public Sub Application_Startup()¶
  'Create class object for handling receiving email items¶
  Set myFolderEventsClass = New clsRemoteControl¶
End Sub¶
```

The following code goes in a new class module. In the Properties window, change the name to clssRemoteControl by typing in the box to the right of Name. Copy and paste the following code into the 'clsRemoteControl' object class module in Outlook VBA.

View the Appendix to learn how to store this procedure in a Class module.

```
Option explicit¶
'* * * * *¶
Public WithEvents myOlItems As Outlook.Items¶
Private Sub Class_Initialize()¶
  Set myOlItems = Outlook.Session _¶
    .GetDefaultFolder(olFolderInbox).Items¶
End Sub¶
'* * * * *¶
Private Sub myOlItems_ItemAdd(ByVal Item As Object)¶
  'Verify if item is a MailItem¶
  If TypeName(Item) = "MailItem" Then¶
    'Run main module to send email¶
    Call AutoSendEmail(Item)¶
  End If¶
End Sub¶
'* * * * *¶
Private Sub AutoSendEmail(objMail As MailItem)¶
'Variable declaration¶
Dim strSubject    As String¶
Dim strFileName   As String¶
Dim strReplyMsg   As String¶
Dim fileNameStart As Long¶
Dim fileNameEnd   As Long¶
'Redemption SafeMail object declaration¶
Dim objSafeMail As Object¶
  'Set variables here¶
  strSubject = "Send me file."¶
  strReplyMsg = "Your file is attached."¶
  'Redemption Additional starts here¶
  'Create Redemption SafeMail object¶
```

Out

```
    'Use this object to send message without¶
    'security warning¶
    Set objSafeMail = CreateObject("Redemption.SafeMailItem")¶
    Set objSafeMail.Item = objMail¶
    'Redemption Additional stops here¶
    '1- Verify Subject¶
    If objSafeMail.Subject <> strSubject Then Exit Sub¶
    '2- Verify if file is existing¶
    ''  File name is supposed to be send in¶
    ''  body section of incoming email message¶
    strFileName = objSafeMail.Body¶
    'File name must be written in parenthesis¶
    'Parse required file name¶
    fileNameStart = InStr(strFileName, "(")¶
    fileNameEnd = InStr(strFileName, ")")¶
    'Verify if file name is a valid string¶
    If fileNameStart = 0 Or fileNameEnd = 0 Or _¶
      fileNameEnd < fileNameStart Then Exit Sub¶
    strFileName = Trim(Mid(strFileName, fileNameStart + 1, _¶
      fileNameEnd - fileNameStart - 1))¶
    'Verify if file is existing¶
    If Dir(strFileName) = "" Then Exit Sub¶
    'Create reply email¶
    'Set same object as the reply that would be send back¶
    Set objSafeMail = objMail.Reply¶
    With objSafeMail¶
      'Custom reply message¶
      .Body = strReplyMsg & vbCrLf & .Body¶
      'Insert Attachment¶
      .Attachments.Add strFileName¶
      'Send reply¶
      .Send¶
    End With¶
End Sub¶
```

Out

The sender's name, reply string and the subject line should be set as desired.

The macro runs automatically. Quit Outlook and re-launch to activate tracking incoming e-mail messages.

Tip: Additional checks can be added to increase security. For every additional check, an additional If-Then statement needs to be added.

PowerPoint Procedures

By Bill Dilworth

Inserting a Predefined Number of Slides

This procedure adds a specified number of slides to the active presentation.

Scenario: Adding new slides, all at once, is often necessary when building a presentation. Use this macro to insert many blank slides at once, a procedure that can be done manually—one at a time—by hitting Insert | New Slide.

Example file: P001.ppt

View the Appendix to learn how to store this procedure in a Standard module.

```
Option Explicit¶
' * * * * *¶
Sub BigInsert()¶
    'Variable declaration¶
    Dim intInsertCount As Integer¶
    Dim strInsertCount As String¶
    Dim i As Integer¶
    'The default number of slides to display¶
    strInsertCount = InputBox("How many slides?", _¶
        "Bulk Insert Macro", "3")¶
    If IsNumeric(strInsertCount) Then¶
        intInsertCount = Val(strInsertCount)¶
        Else¶
        'If the user removes the 3 or replaces with text¶
        'the macro tells the user there's a problem¶
        MsgBox "Input not understood.", vbOKOnly, "Error"¶
        '...and exit the macro¶
        Exit Sub¶
        End If¶
    'Check to make sure the number is valid¶
    If intInsertCount <= 1 Then¶
        'Number is too low¶
        MsgBox "Enter a number higher than 1", vbOKOnly, _¶
            "Number Too Low Error"¶
        Exit Sub¶
        End If¶
    If intInsertCount > 100 Then¶
```

Pwr

```
        'Number is big, better double check¶
        If MsgBox("Confirm -- add " & intInsertCount & _¶
            " slides.", vbYesNo, "Confirm large addition") _¶
            <> vbYes Then Exit Sub¶
        End If¶
    'Add the number of slides by looping¶
    For i = 1 To intInsertCount¶
        'Adds a new slide to the end of the presentation (count +1)¶
        'using the normal bulleted text layout¶
        ActivePresentation.Slides.Add _¶
            ActivePresentation.Slides.Count + 1, _¶
            ppLayoutText¶
        'Loop back if there are more to add.¶
        Next i¶
End Sub¶
```

Tip: The ppLayoutText portion of the line can be changed to any of the 29 values in the intellisense list that appears when typing the line.

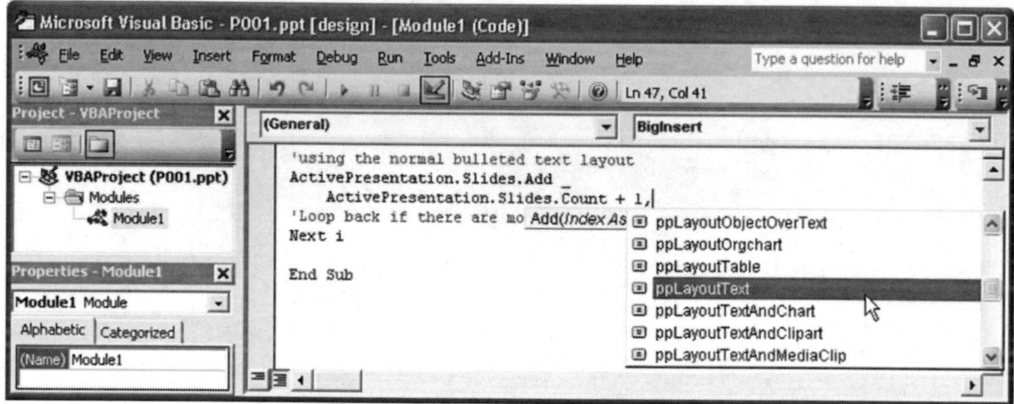

Figure 73 – Intellisense in the VBE

Manipulating AutoShapes

When building a presentation, it is often necessary to change the color of some of the shapes within a presentation. Because the basic presentation is used for several purposes, it is not desirable to have to redesign the slides each time the colors need to be changed. It is easy to automatically change the shape's color based on the shape that is selected when a macro is run.

Example file:
P002.ppt

Scenario: The goal of this macro is two-fold.

First, if a colored rectangle is selected, change all the rest of the rectangle auto-shapes in the presentation to the same color.

Second, if the selected object is not a square, then change all of the rectangular auto-shapes to blue. This demonstrates the use of shape selections and how to change a shape's properties.

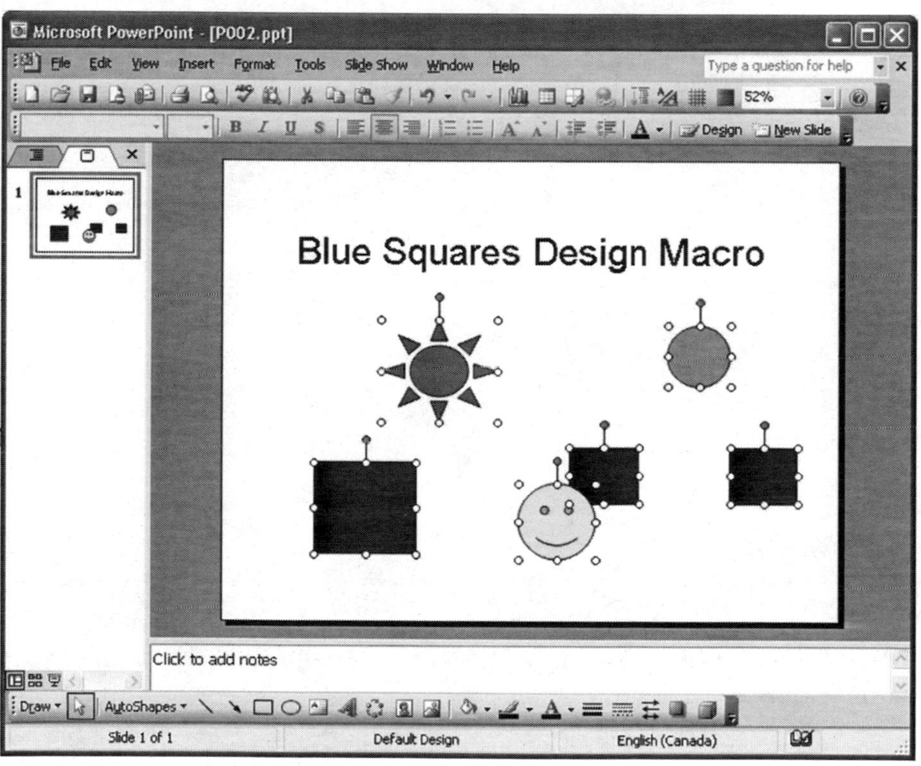

Figure 74 – Changing the Design of AutoShapes

View the Appendix to learn how to store this procedure in a Standard module.

```
Option Explicit¶
' * * * * *¶
Sub BlueSquares()¶
'Declare the counter variables used to cycle¶
'     thru the objects and slides¶
Dim varSlideNumber As Integer¶
Dim varShapeNumber As Integer¶
With ActivePresentation¶
  For varSlideNumber = 1 To .Slides.Count Step 1¶
  With .Slides(varSlideNumber)¶
    For varShapeNumber = 1 To .Shapes.Count Step 1¶
      With .Shapes(varShapeNumber)¶
        Select Case .AutoShapeType¶
         Case Is = msoShapeRectangle¶
           If ActiveWindow.Selection.ShapeRange(1).AutoShapeType = _¶
            msoShapeRectangle Then¶
             .Fill.ForeColor.RGB = _¶
                ActiveWindow.Selection.ShapeRange(1).Fill.ForeColor.RGB¶
                Else¶
                 .Fill.ForeColor.RGB = RGB(0, 0, 255)¶
            End If¶
              Case Else¶
              'Insert code for objects other than autoshapes here.¶
              'Close each of the selecting tools, loops and with
statements in turn.¶
               End Select¶
               End With¶
            Next varShapeNumber¶
        End With¶
    Next varSlideNumber¶
End With¶
End Sub¶
```

Grabbing All Text

This procedure exports all the text from every shape or text box in a PowerPoint presentation to a simple text file with the option to label which text came from which slide/shape.

> **Scenario:** The boss loved the presentation on the product and wants to send the wording only over to the Advertising department. The entire text from the presentation needs to be extracted. One way to do this is to cut and paste each text section into a text application from PowerPoint, but this is very slow and tedious. This macro exports all the text from a presentation into a single simple text file that can be imported to any other application.

Example file:
P003.ppt

Pwr

View the Appendix to learn how to store this procedure in a Standard module.

```
Option Explicit¶
' * * * * *¶
Sub AllTextOut()¶
'Variable declaration¶
Dim intSlide As Integer¶
Dim intShape As Integer¶
Dim strFileName As String¶
Dim strDummy As String¶
'Set the file name that the output text will be sent to.¶
strFileName = "c:\Textout.txt"¶
strDummy = MsgBox("Do you want to include labels?", _¶
    vbQuestion + vbYesNoCancel, "Label text")¶
If strDummy = vbCancel Then Exit Sub¶
'Open the output file specified earlier.¶
'If file already exists, running again will replace¶
'old contents with new contents.  Use different file¶
'name to keep old data.¶
Open strFileName For Output As #1¶
With ActivePresentation¶
    'Add filename label if required¶
    If strDummy = vbYes Then¶
        'Items printed to #1 are output to the text file¶
        Print #1, "strFileName " & .Name¶
        Print #1, "-----"¶
        Print #1, ""¶
        End If¶
    'Begin a loop to run thrugh each slide in the presentation¶
    For intSlide = 1 To .Slides.Count¶
        'Add label if required¶
        If strDummy = vbYes Then Print #1, "Slide: " & intSlide¶
        'Add to the assumed prefix¶
        With .Slides(intSlide)¶
            'Begin the loop to cycle through each shape on the slide¶
            For intShape = 1 To .Shapes.Count¶
                'Add to the assumed prefix¶
                With .Shapes(intShape)¶
                'Add label if required¶
                If strDummy = vbYes Then Print #1, "Shape: " & _¶
                    intShape & "   " & .Name¶
                'Check if there is a text frame to hold text¶
                If .HasTextFrame Then¶
                    'If there is, then output that text to the file¶
                    Print #1, .TextFrame.TextRange.Text¶
                    End If¶
                    'End the shapes assumption on the prefix¶
                    End With¶
```

Pwr

```
                'If labeling then a blank line is needed _¶
                    here in the text file¶
                If strDummy = vbYes Then Print #1, ""¶
                'Loop to the next shape or, if done, proceed¶
                Next intShape¶
            'End the slide assumption on the prefix¶
            End With¶
        'If labeling, a line is needed in the text file here¶
        If strDummy = vbYes Then Print #1, "========"¶
        'Loop to the next slide or, if done, proceed¶
        Next intSlide¶
    'End the presentation assumed prefix¶
    End With¶
'Close output text file¶
Close #1¶
End Sub¶
```

The output file is hard-coded into the macro.

Note: This is a PowerPoint design mode macro. Change the line strFileName = "c:\Textout.txt" to contain the desired file name.

Pwr

Moving Shapes and Graphics During Presentation

This procedure allows the user to move some shapes or pictures around the screen during a presentation by using Action Setting-triggered macros.

Scenario: During a presentation, the desire is to select one of several images being displayed and to move each of them individually; for example, to pick who will be on which team in the upcoming softball game. To illustrate this graphically, the desire is to move the picture of each of the players to their team's side of the slide.

Example file:
P004.ppt

View the Appendix to learn how to store this procedure in a Slide module.

```
Option Explicit¶
' * * * * *¶
'Variable declaration¶
```

```
'This string is dimmed outside of the subs _¶
    so that the variable will remain in force _¶
    between subs¶
Dim varShapeName As String¶
' * * * * *¶
Private Sub SpinButton1_SpinDown()¶
    'Identify which shape is to be modified.¶
        With ActivePresentation.Slides(1).Shapes(varShapeName)¶
        'Shift the object a little to the left by moving¶
        'its placement, but only if it will not run off¶
        'the screen.¶
        If .Left > 0 Then .Left = .Left - 5¶
        End With¶
End Sub¶
' * * * * *¶
Private Sub SpinButton1_SpinUp()¶
    With ActivePresentation.Slides(1).Shapes(varShapeName)¶
        'Shift the object a little to the left by moving¶
        'its placement, but only if it will not run off¶
        'the screen.¶
        If .Left < SlideShowWindows(1).Width - .Width Then .Left =
.Left + 5¶
        End With¶
End Sub¶
' * * * * *¶
Private Sub SpinButton2_SpinUp()¶
    With ActivePresentation.Slides(1).Shapes(varShapeName)¶
        'When this is activated, the object moves up¶
        'towards the top of the screen¶
        If .Top > 0 Then .Top = .Top - 5¶
        End With¶
End Sub¶
' * * * * *¶
Private Sub SpinButton2_SpinDown()¶
    With ActivePresentation.Slides(1).Shapes(varShapeName)¶
        'And down, but not off the bottom¶
        If .Top < SlideShowWindows(1).Height - .Height Then .Top = .Top
+ 5¶
        End With¶
End Sub¶
' * * * * *¶
Sub SpinCCW()¶
    With ActivePresentation.Slides(1).Shapes(varShapeName)¶
        'Because the rotation will reset if less than zero _¶
        'to its positive counter part, we do not have to _¶
        'stipulate conditions on the rotation.  In this _¶
        'case counter-clockwise¶
        .Rotation = .Rotation - 1¶
        End With¶
End Sub¶
```

```
' * * * * *¶
Sub SpinCW()¶
    With ActivePresentation.Slides(1).Shapes(varShapeName)¶
        'And clockwise¶
        .Rotation = .Rotation + 1¶
        End With¶
End Sub¶
' * * * * *¶
Sub NameIt(objShape As Shape)¶
    'When an object is clicked and has the action setting _¶
       'set to this Macro, that object's name will become the _¶
       'value of varShapeName.  In each of the other Macros, _¶
       'that object will be moved, at least until another _¶
       'object that triggers this Macro is clicked¶
    varShapeName = objShape.Name¶
End Sub¶
```

The slide to which the code relates must have three pictures or autoshapes on the top portion.

On the bottom half, add Two Spin Buttons from the Control Toolbox

Pwr

1. View the Control Toolbox by choosing click View | Toolbars | Control Toolbox from the PowerPoint application window. The buttons are automatically named SpinButton1 and SpinButton2.

2. Use the handles on the shapes to make the first one wider than it is tall. This should cause the arrows to point to the sides.

3. Make SpinButton2 taller than it is wide so the arrows point up and down.

4. Double-click on either of the spin controls to bring up the VBE window for the slide-based code. Replace any code found in the VBE window with the code provided above.

Note: The code must already be added to the presentation for the next steps to work.

Assign one of the three pictures the Action Setting of "NameIt" on mouse click.

1. To do this, right-click on the picture, then follow this sequence:

Action Setting... | Mouse Click | Run Macro | NameIt.

2. Click OK to get out of the dialog boxes. Repeat for the other pictures or shapes.

Add two Auto-shapes:

1. Curved Up Arrow
   Assign action setting "SpinCCW" on mouse click.
2. Curved Down Arrow
   Assign action setting "SpinCW" on mouse click.

Now, if a picture is clicked during a show, it will be selected as the object to be moved via the "NameIt" macro, and the macro will move that picture.

Notes: This macro is event driven. It runs when a shape is selected and a button is pressed.

This is a PowerPoint presentation mode macro. Presentation mode macros operate during slide shows; therefore, viewing the show is necessary to use this macro.

Making a Random Jump to Another Slide

This procedure allows the user to click on an assigned shape/picture object during a presentation and to jump to a random slide within a presentation, or, alternately, to a random slide from a pre-set list of slides.

Scenario: While building a presentation that needs to be viewed by 30,000 employees, the boss decides that each should get a slightly different show. Random (or semi-random) jumps within the presentation to make it a little different for each employee must be incorporated.

Example file:
P005.ppt

View the Appendix to learn how to store this procedure in a Standard module.

```
Option Explicit¶
' * * * * * *¶
Sub RandomJumpAny()¶
SlideShowWindows(1).View.GotoSlide _¶
    (Rnd * (ActivePresentation.Slides _¶
    .Count - 1)) + 1¶
End Sub¶
' * * * * * *¶
Sub RandomJumpList()¶
'Variable declaration¶
Dim intDestinationSlide(4) As Integer¶
'Load the array with the slide numbers of slides to jump¶
'to.  These can be changed as required.  If more than 5¶
'choices are required, the array needs to be resized.¶
'Dim intDestinationSlide(4) As Integer¶
'Replace the 4 with the desired number of slides (less one)¶
'Assign specific slide numbers to the array.¶
intDestinationSlide(0) = 4¶
intDestinationSlide(1) = 6¶
intDestinationSlide(2) = 7¶
intDestinationSlide(3) = 8¶
intDestinationSlide(4) = 10¶
'Jump to a random slide by picking one of the destinations¶
SlideShowWindows(1).View.GotoSlide _¶
    intDestinationSlide(Rnd * (UBound(intDestinationSlide)))¶
End Sub¶
```


The list of potential slides to jump to in the non-random routine can be changed as needed. Text in the AutoShape must be changed to reflect this as well.

Assign the shapes the Action Setting of one of the two macros: either RandomJumpAny or RandomJumpList.

Note: This is a PowerPoint presentation mode macro. Presentation mode macros operate during slide shows; therefore, viewing the show is necessary to use this macro.

Random Madness

This macro changes the color, shape, size, and rotation of objects at random during an active PowerPoint presentation.

Scenario: Create a visually active filler slide to use between slides in presentations.

Example file:
P006.ppt

View the Appendix to learn how to store this procedure in a Standard module.

```
Option Explicit¶
' * * * * *¶
Sub RandomMadness()¶
'Variable declaration¶
Dim intSld As Integer¶
Dim RandomShape As Integer¶
'Determine current slide¶
'Store the result in the variable IntSld¶
intSld = ActivePresentation.SlideShowWindow.View.CurrentShowPosition¶
Do While SlideShowWindows.Count > 0 And _¶
    ActivePresentation.SlideShowWindow.View.CurrentShowPosition = intSld¶
'Pick the shape number of a random shape on this slide¶
RandomShape = Int((Rnd *
(ActivePresentation.Slides(intSld).Shapes.Count)) + 1)¶
'Reseed the random number generator¶
Randomize¶
With ActivePresentation.Slides(intSld).Shapes(RandomShape)¶
    'Change the horizontal position of the shape¶
    'to fall in the range between -6 and +6¶
    .Left = .Left + Int(Rnd * 7) - 4¶
    'Change the vertical position in a similar fashion¶
    .Top = .Top + Int(Rnd * 7) - 4¶
    'Change the rotation by -3 to + 3¶
    .Rotation = .Rotation + Int(Rnd * 7) - 3¶
    'Reseed the random numer generator¶
    Randomize¶
    'Change the width¶
    .Width = .Width + ((Rnd * 5) - 2)¶
    'Change the Height¶
    .Height = .Height + ((Rnd * 5) - 2)¶
    'Change the color¶
    .Fill.ForeColor.RGB = RGB(Rnd * 256, Rnd * 256, Rnd * 256)¶
    End With¶
    'Catch up on events¶
    DoEvents¶
```

Pwr

```
'Do it again, as long as the 2 conditions are still true¶
Loop¶
End Sub¶
```

Create a number of auto-shapes, pictures, and text boxes on any slide. On at least one shape, use the Action Setting to fire the macro 'RandomMadness' on click.

When the show is running, click on the shape that has the action setting and all of the shapes on that slide will begin to move, re-color, and resize at random. Advancing the slide or exiting the slide show stops the macro.

Note: This is a PowerPoint presentation mode macro. Presentation mode macros operate during slide shows; therefore, viewing the show is necessary to use this macro.

Sending Word Outline to Notes Section of PowerPoint

Pwr

Use this procedure to enhance the abilities of the 'Send to PowerPoint' feature of MS Word. The Word feature does not support sending notes to PowerPoint, just Titles and Text to the slides based on outline levels. This macro converts level-six outline text in Word to Notes for each of the slides in a presentation.

Scenario: Using the Send to PowerPoint feature in Microsoft Word's File menu to create the slides for a weekly presentation works great, but does not include Notes to be added to the Notes section of the presentation. This macro provides for that capability.

Example file:
P007.ppt and
P007.doc

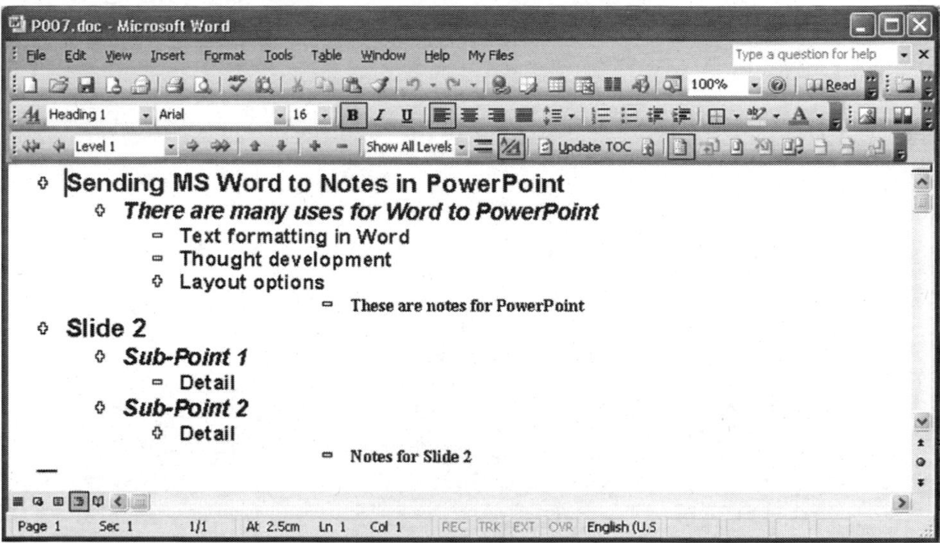

Figure 75 – Word's Outline View

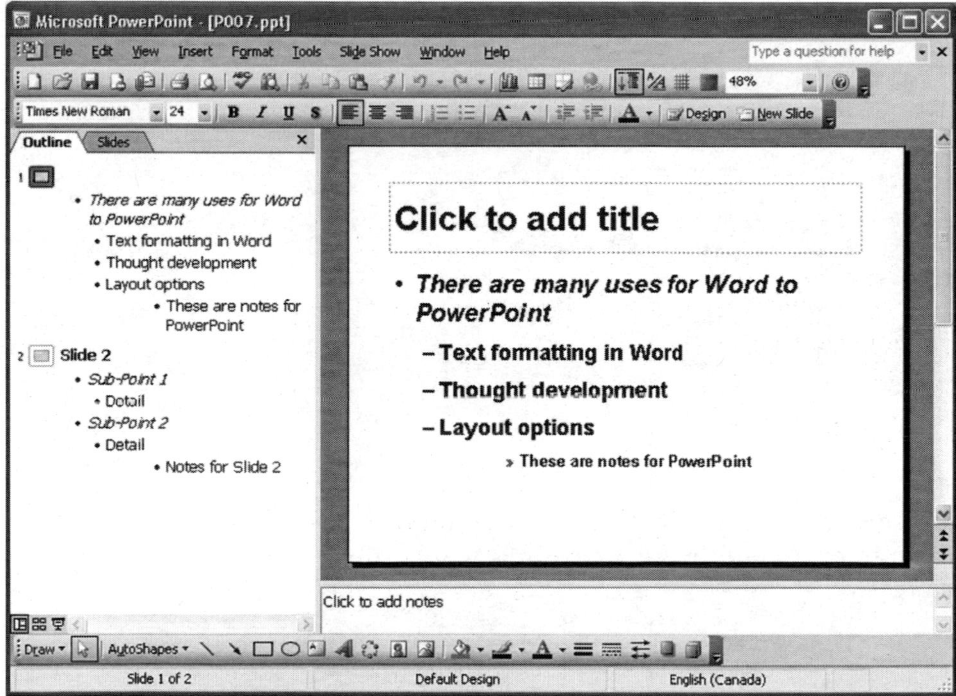

Figure 76 –PowerPoint's Outline View

Pwr

View the Appendix to learn how to store this procedure in a Standard module.

```
Option Explicit¶
' * * * * *¶
Sub OutlineLevel2Notes()¶
'Variable declaration¶
Dim varSlideNum As Integer¶
Dim varLineNum As Integer¶
With ActivePresentation¶
  For varSlideNum = 1 To .Slides.Count¶
    With .Slides(varSlideNum).Shapes.Placeholders(2)¶
      'Check if there is a text frame, if not, then there really _¶
        is not any point in looking at this slide any longer¶
      If .HasTextFrame Then¶
        With .TextFrame.TextRange¶
          'Now loop thru the lines of text _¶
            within the placeholder textbox,but go backwards.¶
          For varLineNum = .Lines.Count To 1 Step -1¶
            If .Lines(varLineNum).IndentLevel > 4 Then¶
              ActivePresentation.Slides(varSlideNum) _¶
                .NotesPage.Shapes(2) _¶
                .TextFrame.TextRange.Text = _¶
                .Lines(varLineNum).Text & vbCr & _¶
                ActivePresentation.Slides(varSlideNum) _¶
                .NotesPage.Shapes(2) _¶
                .TextFrame.TextRange.Text¶
              'removes text from frame¶
              .Lines(varLineNum).Text = ""¶
            End If¶
          'Proceed to the next slide.¶
          Next varLineNum¶
        End With¶
      'Done checking if there is a textframe¶
      End If¶
    End With¶
  'Proceed to the next slide.¶
  Next varSlideNum¶
End With¶
End Sub¶
```

The presentation created AFTER using the File | Send to | Microsoft PowerPoint command from the menu is where the Standard module should be inserted.

Tip: This is a PowerPoint design mode macro. That means it will not run while viewing a PowerPoint show.

Pwr

Note: Placeholders is a special designation given to shapes that are used to pre-format a slide to a custom layout. There are several types: pictures, clipart, text, and titles. They are used to locate the various fields on the master slide.

It is not possible to add additional placeholders to a layout. Additional shapes and text boxes can be added, just not as placeholders.

Wrapping Text to the Next Slide

This macro wraps text from one slide to a new one when it overflows the number of lines in a text box that has been specified. The new slide retains the formatting and appearance of the original slide.

Scenario: A long piece of text that needs to be added to the slide show is too long. Unfortunately, there is more text than there is room to show in one slide's text box. Copying the slide and manually deleting some text from each slide can be time consuming. Automate the process with this macro.

Example file: P008.ppt

View the Appendix to learn how to store this procedure in a Standard module.

```
Option Explicit¶
' * * * * *¶
Sub WrapOver()¶
'Variable declaration¶
Dim SldCnt As Integer¶
Dim SldNum As Integer¶
Dim WrapCnt As Integer¶
Dim OldCnt As Integer¶
'How many slides will be checked?¶
SldCnt = ActivePresentation.Slides.Count¶
'Set the recheck counter to the current number of slides¶
OldCnt = SldCnt¶
'Find out from the user how many lines are allowed in the _¶
    textbox placeholder¶
WrapCnt = InputBox("'Wrap' text in placeholder " & _¶
    "if they exceed how many lines?", "Wrap after" & _¶
    "input", "6") 'Default to 6 if user does not enter a number¶
```

```
'Keep it reasonable, between 2 and 15 lines in the textbox¶
If WrapCnt > 15 Or WrapCnt < 2 Then¶
    'If it isn't in this range then tell the user what they did wrong¶
    MsgBox "Please enter a number between 2 and 15" & _¶
    ", when you re-run this macro", vbCritical + _¶
    vbOKOnly, "Input range error"¶
    'Stop doing anything in this sub routine. They will have _¶
        to re-run it and enter a valid number¶
    Exit Sub¶
    End If¶
'Initialize the slide counter¶
SldNum = 0¶
With ActivePresentation¶
'This is a line label.  It can be referenced in a goto¶
'statement which is why it is used here.¶
NextSlide:¶
    'Increment the slide counter¶
    SldNum = SldNum + 1¶
    'If this slide is more than the total number of _¶
        slides then the macro is done and can goto the _¶
        ending routine that is used¶
    If SldNum > SldCnt Then GoTo EndRoutine¶
        'Check if the number of lines in the textbox _¶
            placeholder merits being wrapped to the next slide¶
        If .Slides(SldNum).Shapes.Placeholders(2) _¶
            .TextFrame.TextRange.Lines _¶
            .Count <= WrapCnt Then GoTo NextSlide¶
        'If it does need to be wrapped over to the next slide, _¶
            then start by making a duplicate slide¶
        .Slides(SldNum).Duplicate¶
        'Now add one to the total number of slides because _¶
            of the added slide¶
        SldCnt = SldCnt + 1¶
        'Get rid of all the lines on the original slide that _¶
            will be repeated on the wrap over slide¶
        .Slides(SldNum).Shapes.Placeholders(2) _¶
            .TextFrame.TextRange.Lines(WrapCnt + 1, _¶
            .Slides(SldNum).Shapes.Placeholders(2) _¶
            .TextFrame.TextRange.Lines.Count).Delete¶
        'On the second slide, get rid of all the lines _¶
            that were on the first slide¶
        .Slides(SldNum + 1).Shapes.Placeholders(2) _¶
            .TextFrame.TextRange.Lines(1, WrapCnt).Delete¶
    'Check the next slide¶
    GoTo NextSlide¶
EndRoutine:¶
    End With¶
```

Pwr

```
    'Tell the user what was done and how many slides were added¶
    MsgBox "Task complete.  " & SldCnt - OldCnt & _¶
        " slides were added.", vbOKOnly, WrapCnt & _¶
        " line max. macro"¶
End Sub¶
```

Note: This is a PowerPoint design mode macro. That means it runs while you create a presentation and not while you view it.

Saving the Show Point

With this macro, you can quickly resume a slide show where it left off. This could be very useful for presentations that span multiple sessions, such as semester classes or weekend seminars.

Scenario: When using a single presentation to teach a class that will span several weeks (because of how much or how little will be able to be covered in a given class period), the entire semester can be run from a single PowerPoint presentation. In order to resume the presentation where the class left off last time, you can use a reminder note that you might lose or, alternatively, you can use a macro to mark the spot.

Example file:
P009.ppt

Pwr

View the Appendix to learn how to store this procedure in a Standard module.

```
Option Explicit¶
' * * * * *¶
Sub SavePoint()¶
SaveSetting "PowerPointMacros", "SlideSavePoint",
ActivePresentation.Name,
Str(ActivePresentation.SlideShowWindow.View.CurrentShowPosition)¶
End Sub¶
' * * * * *¶
Sub GotoSavePoint()¶
ActivePresentation.SlideShowWindow.View.GotoSlide
Val(GetSetting("PowerPointMacros", "SlideSavePoint",
ActivePresentation.Name, "1")), msoTrue¶
End Sub¶
```

This macro is event driven. Clicking a shape fires the macro. This is achieved by setting the action setting of 'On mouse click' to 'Run Macro'. The macro to run depends on what the shape should do. Assign 'SavePoint' to shapes that will save the place in the presentation. Assign 'GotoSavePoint' to shapes that will send the user to the save point.

The shapes can be placed on the slides in a few different ways, as follows:

- The shapes can be drawn on slides where they may be used, and then manually assign the action setting.
- The shapes can be copied and pasted on as many slides as may be needed.
- The shapes can be placed on the Master slides to make them available throughout the presentation.

The SavePoint shape must be placed on the Master Slide and both the SavePoint and the GotoSavePoint shapes must be placed on the Title Master Slide.

Note: This is a PowerPoint presentation mode macro. Presentation mode macros operate during slide shows; therefore, viewing the show is necessary to use this macro.

Personalizing a Presentation

This macro allows personalization of a presentation.

Scenario: The boss wants a personalized computer-based quiz system designed for the company. There are 30,000 employees and typing each of the names on a custom presentation must be avoided.

Example file:
P010.ppt

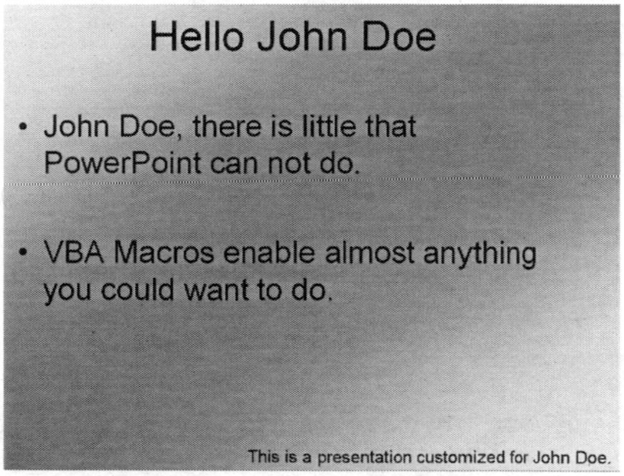

Figure 77 – Customized Presentation

View the Appendix to learn how to store this procedure in a Slide module.

```
Option Explicit¶
' * * * * *¶
Private Sub CommandButton1_Click()¶
'Variable declaration¶
Dim strReplace As String¶
'This is the string that the macro will look for _¶
    and replace with the name from the text box on slide 1¶
strReplace = "<<NAME>>"¶
'Check that there is something in the textbox¶
If TextBox1.Text = "" Then¶
        'If there isn't, then tell the user what to do¶
        MsgBox "Please enter your name in the box"¶
        'End the sub routine until they do it¶
        Exit Sub¶
    'If there is text in the textbox (Textbox1.Text = "" is not true) _¶
        then this code will execute¶
    Else¶
        'Tell the user what will happen¶
        MsgBox "The macro will now replace all instances of " & _¶
            strReplace & ", with " & TextBox1.Text¶
    'Close the If statement¶
    End If¶
'Variable declaration¶
Dim oPres As Presentation¶
Dim oSld As Slide¶
Dim oShp As Shape¶
```

```
'Use the current presentation as this object¶
Set oPres = ActivePresentation¶
For Each oSld In oPres.Slides¶
    For Each oShp In oSld.Shapes¶
      'Check if it has a text frame¶
      If oShp.HasTextFrame Then¶
      'If there is a text frame, then check if the replacement _¶
      string is there and replace it until there are no more _¶
      instances of it.¶
      'While...Wend loops allow the program to loop while the statement¶
      'is acurate, in this case, while there is a replacement string¶
      'in the text frame¶
      While InStr(1, oShp.TextFrame.TextRange.Text, strReplace)¶
      'Use the oShp object (in this case it is assigned to each shape _¶
      on each slide one after another) and replace the targeted
replacement _¶
      text with the text from the textbox on the first slide.¶
      oShp.TextFrame.TextRange.Replace strReplace, TextBox1.Text¶
               Wend¶
            'Close the If statement¶
            End If¶
        'Progress to the next shape on the slide¶
        Next oShp¶
    'Progress to the next slide¶
    Next oSld¶
'Reset variables and free memory¶
Set oPres = Nothing¶
Set oSld = Nothing¶
Set oShp = Nothing¶
'Clear the text box¶
Slide1.TextBox1.Text = ""¶
'Advance the presentation¶
SlideShowWindows(1).View.GotoSlide 2¶
End Sub¶
```

Pwr

Creating a New Presentation

Follow these steps:

On slide 1

1. Open the command toolbox (if it is not already open) by selecting View on the pull down menu and then selecting Toolbars. Select Command Toolbox from the list.
2. Insert an object from the command toolbox called a text box. This will automatically be named TextBox1.
   Place this text box object where it should appear on the slide. Please note that this text box is a command text box and so is

different from the normal text boxes that are used on a slide to display text.

3. Insert a command button from the control toolbox.
   This will be auto-labeled CommandButton1.
   Again, place and resize this control as desired.

On slide 2

4. Insert several lines of text in whatever shapes or placeholders will be used.
   Be sure to include the replacement string "<<NAME>>" (without the quotes) in a few places.

On slide 1

5. Double-click on the Command Button. This should open the Visual Basic Editor (VBE) with a slide-based module begun (including the first and last line of the code below). Type the code so that what is seen in the VBE code window matches the code above. Close the VBE window.

6. Select the Command Button and right-click. Select properties and the properties window will open. Under the line labeled 'Caption', change the value (in the box to the right of the word caption) to Go.

Pwr

Tip: Additional data (besides a name) could be collected and incorporated into the slide show presentation using different replacement fields and adding code lines that would replace them with the additional data.

Note: This macro runs automatically. This is a PowerPoint presentation-mode macro. Presentation-mode macros operate during slide shows; therefore, viewing the show is necessary to use this macro.

Access Procedures

By Nico Altink

Splitting Names

This procedure demonstrates how to separate the different parts of a name in a field using a supporting form.

> **Scenario:** Some files may contain names that incorporate unlike data, making it difficult to parse data appropriately. Such is the case with the titles in the data shown below. Extracting them properly requires VBA, where other text extractions may not. What to do when titles exist (perhaps even two titles!) is now presented.

Example file:
A005.mdb with frmSplitNames

To split strings of text based on a selected portion of the field, use the form 'frmSplitNames' with some code. The table looks like Figure 78:

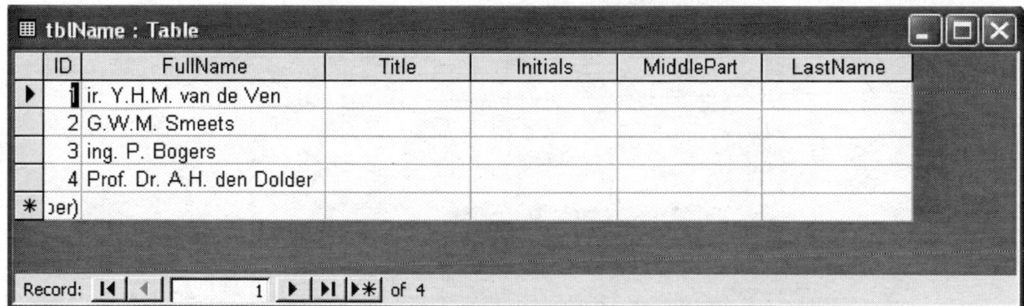

tblName : Table
ID
FullName
Title
Initials
MiddlePart
LastName
1 ir. Y.H.M. van de Ven
2 G.W.M. Smeets
3 ing. P. Bogers
4 Prof. Dr. A.H. den Dolder
Record: 1 of 4

Figure 78- Table Behind frmSplitNames

The desired format is to split the names as shown below:

Titles	Initials	MiddlePart	LastName
ir.	Y.H.M.	van de	Ven
	G.W.M.		Smeets

Titles	Initials	MiddlePart	LastName
ing.	P.		Bogers
Prof. Dr.	A.H.	den	Dolder

Splitting the field into Title, Initials, and LastName is done by identifying the selection, the portion in front of the selection, and the portion behind the selection. To get the MiddlePart, the same kind of split is done on the LastName field.

Follow these steps:

1. With Forms selected, press the New button on the database window to create a form from which to run this code. Leave the default choice of Design view. From the combo box at the bottom, select the table tblName as shown in Figure 79:

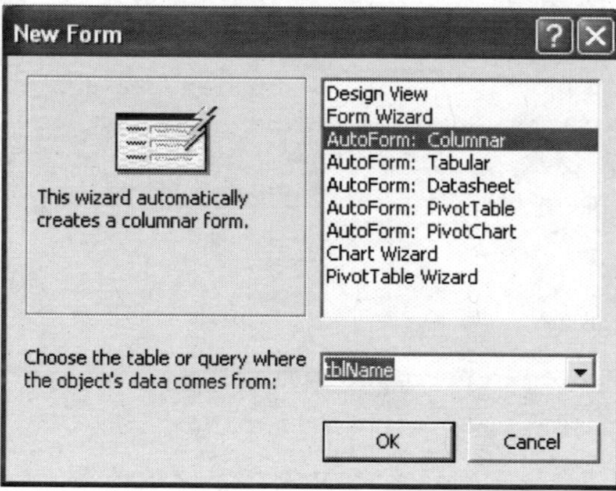

Figure 79 – Creating a New Form

2. Press OK to display the form in design view.
3. Maximize the design window by double-clicking the title bar showing frmName : Form. Next, double-click the title bar of the tblName popup form, which selects all fields. Now drag and drop all the fields to the gray detail area of the form and align them as shown in the sample form in Figure 80.

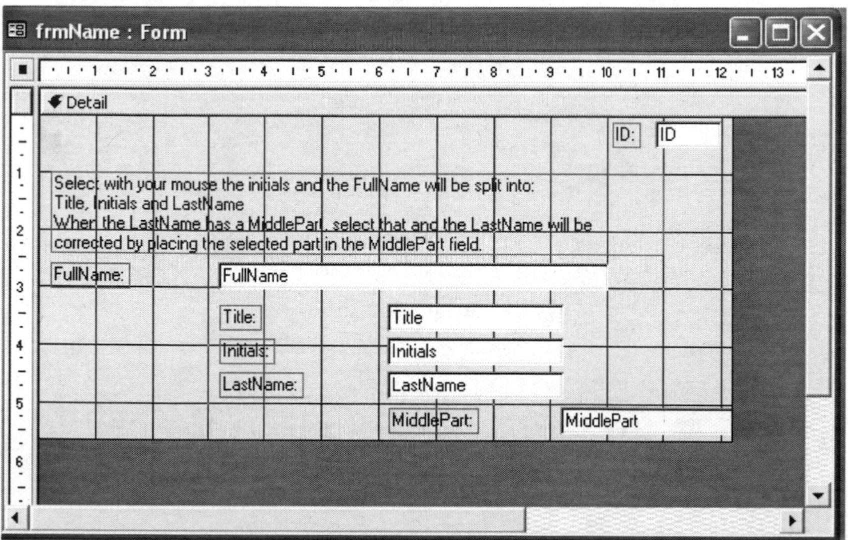

Figure 80 – Sample Form Layout

4. Now, you need to add the code to make things happen as described on the form.
   Select the FullName field with a single click. If the properties window is not present, right-click for its pop-up menu, then choose properties.

5. Go to the Events tab in the Properties window. Double-click the field after the Mouse up event to get the text Event Procedure and then press the [...] button to go to the code section.

   The cursor will be between the lines:

Acs

```
Private Sub FullName_MouseUp(Button As Integer, Shift As Integer, X As
Single, Y As Single)¶
'paste code here¶
End Sub¶
' * * * * *
Private Sub FullName_MouseUp(Button As Integer, Shift As Integer, X As
Single, Y As Single)¶
'First initialize all fields by filling them with space¶
'When the user has made a wrong selection there can be data in one of
the fields that should be empty¶
Me.Title = ¶
Me.Initials = ¶
Me.MiddlePart = ¶
Me.LastName = ¶
Me.MiddlePart = ¶
```

```
'Test if something has been selected¶
If Me.FullName.SelLength > 0 Then¶
   ' Move the initials¶
   Me.Initials = Trim(Mid(FullName, Me.FullName.SelStart + 1,
Me.FullName.SelLength + 1))¶
   ' Move the last name¶
Me.LastName = Trim(Mid(FullName, Me.FullName.SelStart +
Me.FullName.SelLength + 1))¶
   ' Test for name without title¶
   If Me.FullName.SelStart > 0 Then¶
      ' Skip filling title field¶
      Me.Title = Left(FullName, Me.FullName.SelStart - 1)¶
   End If¶
   ' Refresh the form to reflect changes¶
   Me.Refresh¶
End If¶
End Sub¶
```

The MID function hse three parameters representing string, start position, and length. Leaving out the length will capture all the characters until the end. For the Initials, just the selected part is needed.

The TRIM function removes leading and trailing spaces. Here, that makes the correction of the length and/or start position obsolete. One or more spaces between the different sections of the FullName are also not relevant because all strings are now separated by one space.

The real work is done based on the field properties SelLength and SelStart, which will hold the dynamically selected part of the field. A problem arises when FullName is without a title. This causes the Me.Title = Left(FullName, Me.FullName.SelStart – 1) to fail because a Left(string,–1) is impossible. Thus, an additional IF is placed in the code to skip the filling in case the selection starts at the beginning of the field.

6. Finally, you need to add the code shown below to the LastName text box.
   Double-click the field after the MouseUp event in the Properties window for the LastName text box to get the text Event Procedure. Press the button [...] to go to the code section.

7. Select the LastName option in the left drop-down of the VBE and then the MouseUp in the right drop-down to open the proper code window.

```
Private Sub LastName_MouseUp(Button As Integer, Shift As Integer, X As
Single, Y As Single)¶
'Initialize field¶
Me.MiddlePart = ¶
```

```
'Test if something has been selected¶
If Me.LastName.SelLength > 0 Then¶
   'Fill MiddlePart¶
   Me.MiddlePart = Trim(Mid(LastName, Me.LastName.SelStart + 1,
Me.LastName.SelLength + 1))¶
   'Correct LastName¶
   Me.LastName = Trim(Mid(LastName, Me.LastName.SelStart +
Me.LastName.SelLength + 1))¶
End If¶
End Sub¶
```

8. Save the form as frmName and start using it.

Designing Consistent Forms

Creating a sample “boilerplate” form, perhaps similar to the one shown below in Figure 81, is important to the consistency of the database interface. This procedure will help.

Scenario: When designing a full-blown application, there is more to consider than just straightforward forms creation. Easy form navigation is important, but so is keeping your application consistent throughout to keep from distracting users.

Example file:
A006.mdb with form frmMain

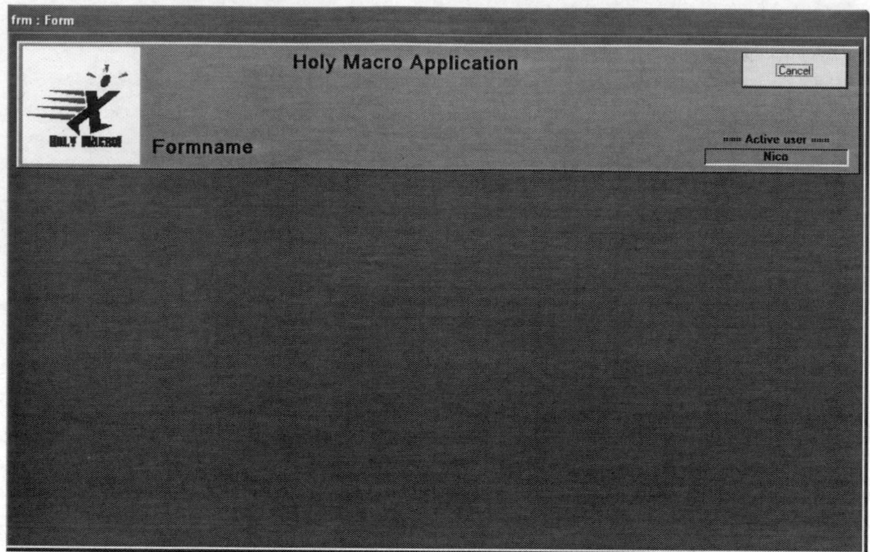

Figure 81 – Sample "Boilerplate" Form

Creating a boilerplate form should always be the first action. This ensures that the Cancel button and other similar buttons will always be in exactly the same place. This helps to keep the screen from flickering during a form change, too. Using a header with a logo, the application name, the form name, and the Cancel button, and displaying the active user makes the application look more professional.

This form can be used not only for the manipulation of individual records, but also as the frmMain with buttons that go to the different sections of the database by the click of a button. Most applications have a limited set of forms and reports, and this method avoids using the Access Switchboard manager under Tools | Database Utilities | Switchboard manager.

Generally, the form will consist of a main form called frmMain, with buttons for the main choices (such as Order, Client, and Reports), optionally followed by another form (such as one for all Reports), which will suffice 90% of the time.

A visual representation of this concept is presented in Figure 82:

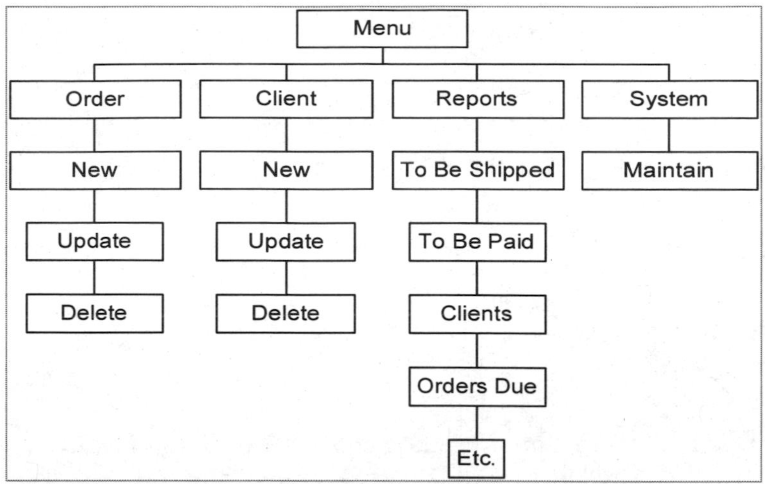

Figure 82 – Visual Sample of a Boilerplate Form

Each box in the diagram represents a form accessed by a button on the form at the top of each "stack". The Menu button has Order, Client, Reports, and System buttons that launch forms with the options listed underneath them, available as buttons to go to the next form.

Acs

This code is behind the main form:

```
Option Compare Database¶
Option Explicit¶
' * * * * *
Private Sub btnCancel_Click()¶
   ' Close form¶
   DoCmd.Close¶
End Sub¶
' * * * * *
Private Sub Form_Activate()¶
   ' Maximize form when it becomes active¶
   DoCmd.Maximize¶
End Sub¶
```

Open the VBE (Alt+F11). The preceding code can be displayed by choosing the btnCancel option in the left drop-down at the top of the code window. Selecting Form shows the other subroutine.

The Docmd.Close command closes the form and returns to the previously opened form. This way you get forms opening on top of one another in an "Internet Browser" kind of way. This is a nice, simple way for users to navigate a database, because most users are familiar with this functionality.

Finally the Docmd.Maximize in the Form_Activate event makes sure that the form always fills the whole Access screen when opened or when control returns, even after a user has resized the window.

Triggering a New Form Based on a Subform Selection

This procedure jumps to a record details form from a subform.

Scenario: On a datasheet subform with all available information, offer the user the possibility to update the data from a selected row on a separate form. Suppose you have a list of open invoices that contain company name and amount due. You can trigger the company information form to be created when you press the update button on the list of open invoices.

Example file: A007.mdb with forms frmNameSelect, frmNameUpdate

When the Update button is pressed on a form, show the frmNameUpdate for the selected row (here we are selecting row 1) as shown in Figure 83:

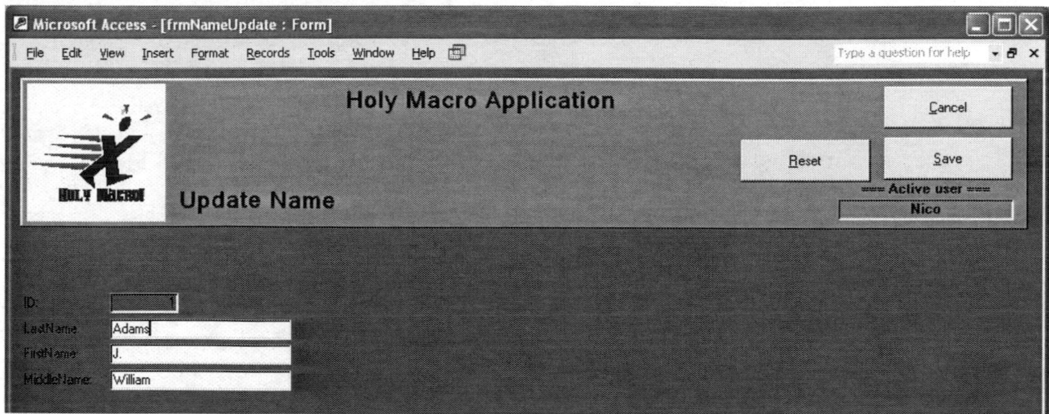

Figure 83 – Sample Update Form

These forms look familiar, even though the datasheet subform sfrmName is a new element. This is placed on the form by using the subform button from the toolbox in design mode. This launches a wizard that asks which table/query and which fields from the table/query are to be included.

Enter the form name and press Finish. A subform with the entered name is added to the Forms tab of the database window. Next, add the Update button and name that btnUpdate before opening the OnClick event in which to place the following code:

```
Private Sub btnUpdate_Click()¶
   ' Open form frmNameUpdate and pass the ID from¶
   ' the active row of the subform¶
   DoCmd.OpenForm frmNameUpdate, , , [ID]= & Me.sfrmName.Form.ID¶
End Sub¶
```


When typing the commas behind the frmNameUpdate, note that Access does show the appropriate parameter that needs to be entered. The one used here is called the WHERE condition. Pass a string that is a concatenation of the name of the field and the value it should have, such as:

```
[ID]=1
```

The same string could be used in a query to extract this row, such as:

```
SELECT * FROM tblName WHERE [ID]=1
```

The nice thing about this is the fact that the frmNameUpdate can be built without knowing which row to display, because Access uses this string to filter the data. When the Form View menu bar is active, note that the filter button appears to be pressed!

The extraction from the [ID] value is done with Me.sfrmName.Form.ID. Notice that an extra .Form is used before referring to the key field from the subform.

The frmNameUpdate is slightly different in the header because there are two new buttons: Reset and Save. The Reset button is used to undo changes when the record has been partially edited and the user needs to start over. The Cancel and Save buttons are self-explanatory.

The code used is as follows:

```
Option Compare Database¶
Option Explicit¶
' * * * * *
Private Sub btnCancel_Click()¶
   'Before the form is closed, reset the field values¶
   'if the user has changed something¶
   If Me.Dirty Then¶
      ' reset all fields to their old value¶
      Me.Undo¶
   End If¶
   DoCmd.Close¶
End Sub¶
' * * * * *
Private Sub btnReset_Click()¶
   ' reset all fields to the old value¶
   Me.Undo¶
   ' make sure they are displayed¶
   Me.Refresh¶
End Sub¶
' * * * * *
Private Sub btnSave_Click()¶
   ' Close form and Access will save the data¶
   DoCmd.Close¶
End Sub¶
' * * * * *
Private Sub Form_Activate()¶
   ' Maximize form when it becomes active¶
   DoCmd.Maximize¶
End Sub¶
```

Acs

The new items here are the Me.Undo and the Me.Dirty. When looking into the properties that Access expands after a field, note a property named OldValue, as shown in the following figure.

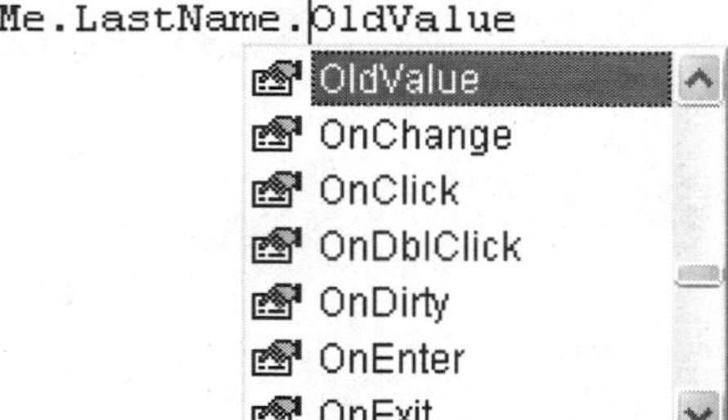

Figure 84 – Properties Drop-down

Using Me.Dirty triggers Access to check if all field values are the same as when the form was completed and the Me.Undo moves the OldValue into the current Value of the field.

Selecting and Filtering with Cascading Combo Boxes

Use this procedure to offer the user the ability to select the rows in two stages when displaying a subform with many rows of information.

Scenario: From a general selection form that has a datasheet subform with all available information, you can offer the user the possibility to filter first by all FirstNames and then with a combo box with all available LastNames.

There are two sets of combo boxes, both doing the same cascading and filtering. The first set (left) works with a query for LastName1 retrieving the information from the form's combo box cmbFirstName1. The second set (right) manipulates the query for LastName2 using code.

Example file:
A008.mdb with form frmNameSelect

Acs

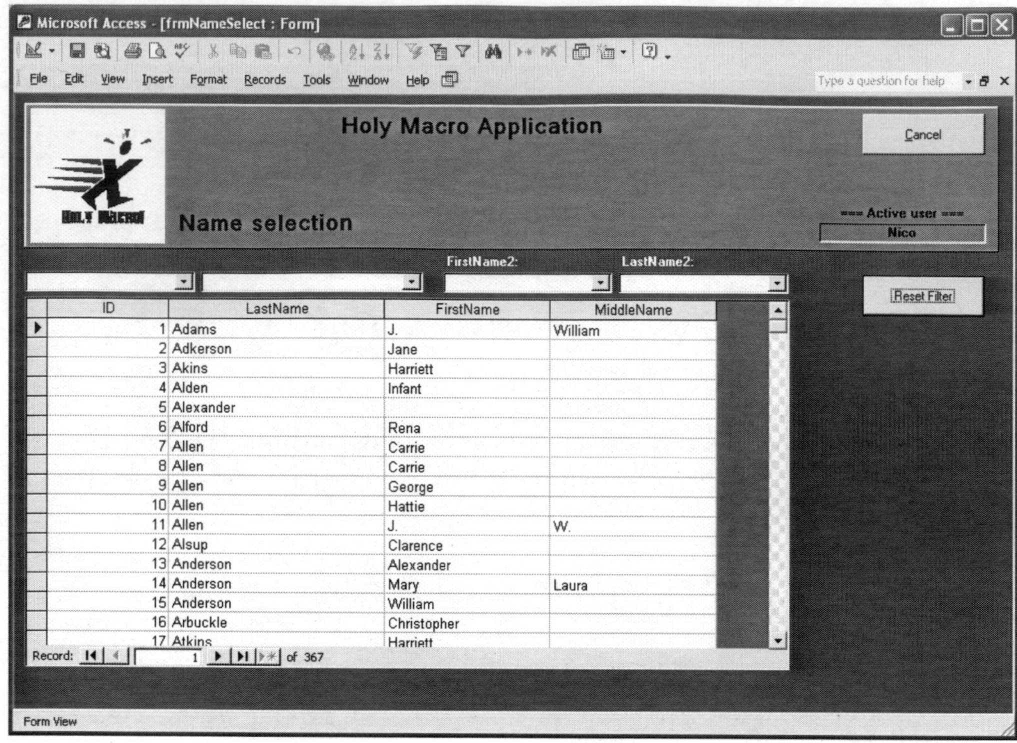

Figure 85 – Sample Cascading Drop-downs

Acs

Both sets work identically, except for the following:

Test the same combo boxes on frmNameSelection. For the LastName1 combo box, the popup displayed in Figure 86 appears:

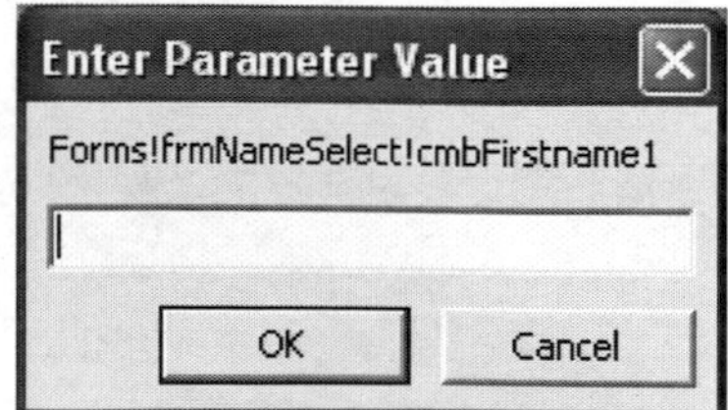

Figure 86 – Enter Parameter Value Popup

This is because the query used for the second combo box looks like the following:

```
SELECT tblName.LastName, Count(tblName.ID) AS CountOfID
FROM tblName GROUP BY tblName.LastName, tblName.FirstName
HAVING(((tblName.FirstName)=Forms!frmNameSelect!cmbFirstname1));
```

The variable Forms!frmNameSelect!cmbFirstname1 is a reference to the cmbFirstName1 from the form frmNameSelect, so a rename destroys the reference. Because the field is not found, Access thinks it is a parameter and asks for its value.

Construction of the first set of combo boxes is done by creating the queries in the Row Source property as follows:

1. After placing the combo boxes on the form, open the properties and change the Name under the Other tab into cmbFirstName.

2. Now, go to the Data tab and set the cursor in the field after the Row Source property to get the [...] button for designing the query. The cmbFirstName1 query simply gets the FirstName from tblName.

3. To ensure that no duplicates are returned, add the DISTINCT option. Do this manually after saving the query or press the Properties button in the query editor and set the Unique values property to Yes. The result will look like this:

```
SELECT DISTINCT tblName.FirstName FROM tblName;
```

Acs

The cmbLastName looks similar, but the reference to the combo box on the form must be added to filter only the selected value form cmbFirstName.

4. To do this, add the FirstName field and uncheck the checkbox in the Show row for this field. Now, right-click the criteria cell and select the Build option.

5. A form appears. Navigate to the open form and select the cmbFirstName1 field from the list by double-clicking it. This result in something like Figure 87:

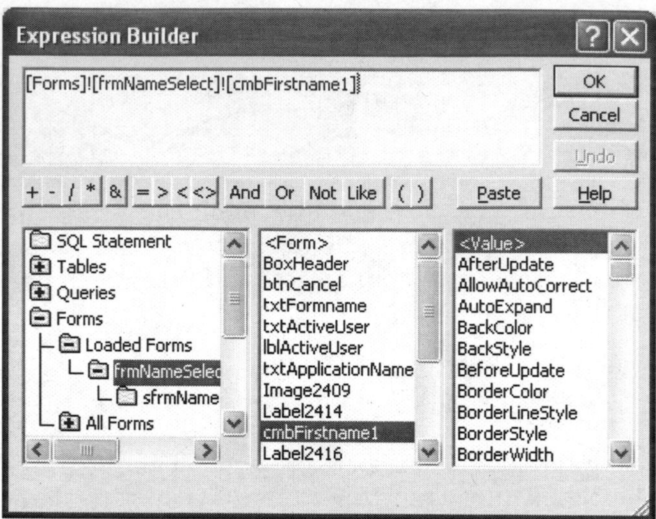

Figure 87 – Expression Builder

6. Press OK to place the build expression into the Row Source of the combo box, as shown in Figure 88.

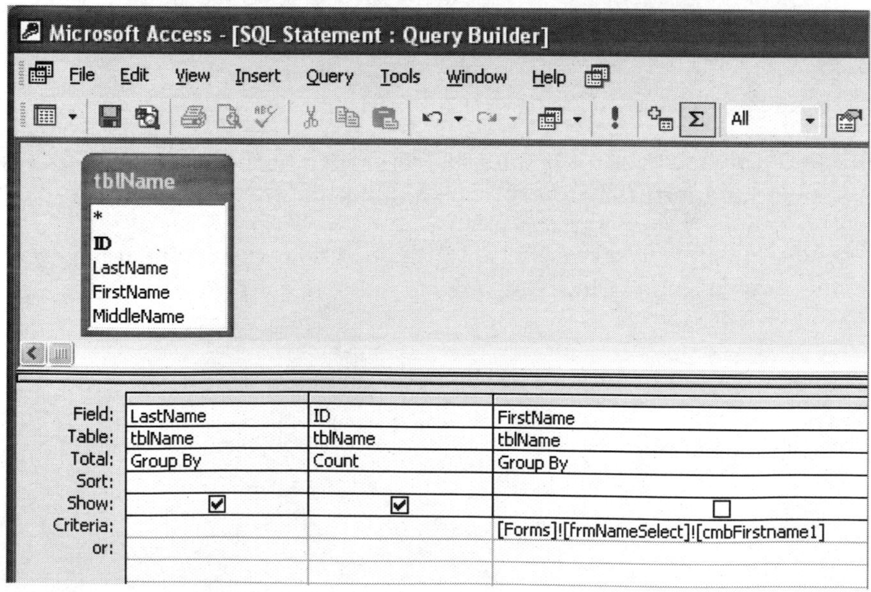

Figure 88 – SQL Statement Query Builder

Acs

7. Beside the unchecked Show checkbox and the reference to the form field, note that the GroupBy button has been pressed and that a Total row is now present. The GroupBy suppresses duplicate rows (the way Distinct did for us in the previous combo box), but also offers the possibility to perform statistics.

   It is a good idea to show the user how many LastNames there are. The field [ID] has been added and instead of grouping on this field, the Count option has been set. Now every name is unique, but there will also be a count showing the user how many rows are displayed when selected. Just try the combo box cmbFirstName1 for the name Carrie to see the result.

8. Finally, ensure that after selecting the LastName, the filtered row(s) are made visible in the datasheet subform. Use the After Update event of the cmbLastName. After every change, the following code is triggered:

```
' Now that First and lastname have been selected¶
' apply a filter to the subform to show them¶
' 1 - fill filter¶
Me.sfrmName.Form.Filter = [LastName]= & Chr(34) & Me.cmbLastName1 &
Chr(34) &  AND [FirstName]= & Chr(34) & Me.cmbFirstname1 & Chr(34)¶
' 2 - apply filter by making it active¶
Me.sfrmName.Form.FilterOn = True¶
```

The interesting part of this bit of code is the use of CHR(34). Using a string in a WHERE clause requires the embedding of it in single quotes. The problem with names, however, is that they can contain a single quote. When this happens, Access sees the string as complete, and sees the remainder of the name as a command. The CHR(34) is another way to create a double quote. Embedding the name within double quotes ensures that a single quote does not break up the created string.

Acs

Sample with single quote name in a query:

```
SELECT LastName FROM tblName WHERE FirstName = 'O'Conner'¶
```

Sample with the CHR(34) and the same name:

```
SELECT LastName FROM tblName WHERE FirstName = O'Conner¶
```

When using these combo boxes, there must be the option to reset the selection. This is done in the ResetFilter button's code:

```
' Reset filter¶
Me.sfrmName.Form.FilterOn = False¶
' Also reset the possibly filled comboboxes¶
Me.cmbFirstname1 = ¶
Me.cmbFirstname2 = ¶
Me.cmbLastName1 = ¶
Me.cmbLastName2 = ¶
```

Setting FilterOn to False is all that is needed to ensure that filtering is removed from the subform. The emptying of the combo boxes ensures that the user is not confused by inconsistent information on the form. The same mechanism is also used within the cmbLastName combo boxes to make clear that a new LastName needs to be chosen.

Finally the second method sets the Row Source of the cmbLastName2 to a query dynamically with a WHERE that is constructed in code:

```
' When a new FirstName2 has been chosen, the contents¶
' of the combo needs to be refreshed, but first a¶
' possible old selection is reset to space¶
Me.cmbLastName2 = ¶
Me.cmbLastName2.RowSource = SELECT Distinct LastName FROM tblName WHERE
Firstname= & Chr(34) & Me.cmbFirstname2 & Chr(34)¶
```

Acs

E-mailing a Selection

This procedure demonstrates how to e-mail data directly from a database.

Scenario: On a general selection form, have a datasheet subform with all available information. Offer the option to filter the rows and then e-mail the information to pre-selected recipient(s).

Example file:
A009.mdb with form frmNameSelect

A form has been added to show the current selections made, as shown in Figure 89.

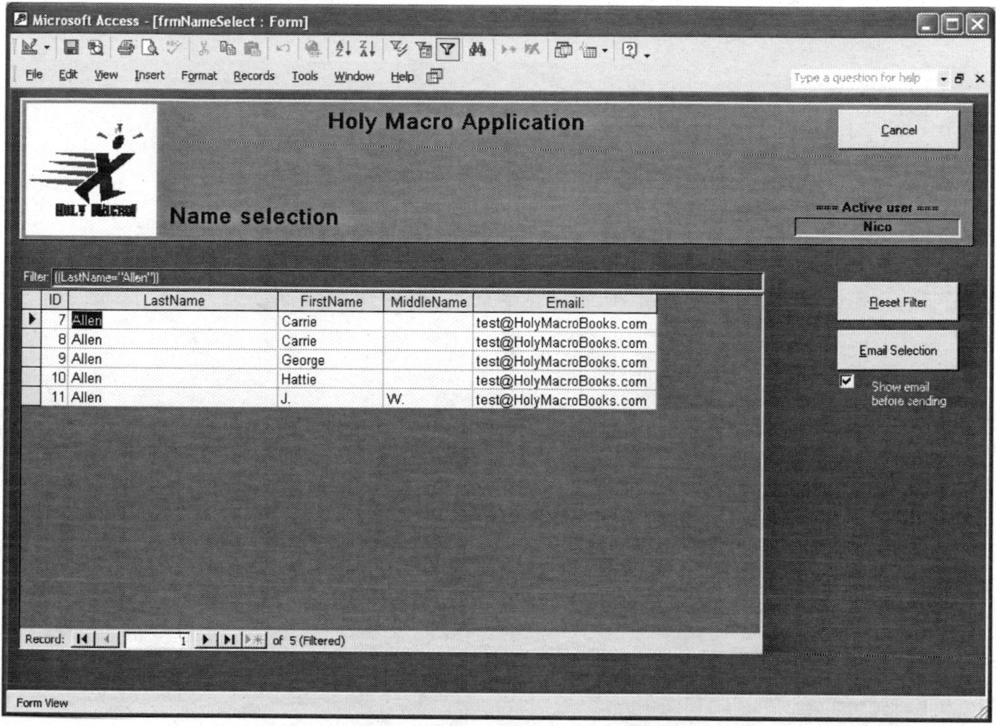

Figure 89 – Selecting Names

The selection for Allen is visible in the Filter field; pressing the Email Selection button triggers the generation of five e-mails. For testing purposes, an e-mail address, test@HolyMacroBooks.com, has been created that has a rule to respond when the e-mail has been received.

The e-mail command implements the possibility of allowing the user to change the e-mail before sending it. A checkbox has been defined so the user can decide (per session) to press the Send button after editing the standard text or to e-mail directly.

In the newer versions of Access, you may be prompted by the Operating System's security to determine if sending e-mail from this application is permitted.

To make the filter appear on the form, the following code needs to be added to the OnCurrent event of the subform:

```
' First test if the FilterOn is true to see if the filter has been
applied¶
If Me.FilterOn = True Then¶
   ' Move the filter to the txtFilter field of the parent form¶
   Parent.txtFilter = Me.Filter¶
Else¶
   ' Empty the txtFilter field of the parent form¶
   Parent.txtFilter = ¶
End If¶
```

Finally, code is added behind the Email Selection button to loop through all selected rows.

Follow these steps:

1. Ensure that the application is referencing the correct library. To be backward compatible, choose the older DAO library.

2. To make sure that the application works, open the Tools/References when in the VBA code window and select a reference to a Microsoft DAO version x.xx library. The version number is not relevant for our purposes.

Now for the code:

```
Private Sub btnEmail_Click()¶
Dim rs As DAO.Recordset ' object to hold the recordset¶
Dim strWhere As String ' variable to hold the needed WHERE clause¶
' Test if a selection has been made, when not¶
' first confirm that all persons need to be mailed.¶
If Len(Me.txtFilter) > 0 Then¶
   ' Create the WHERE clause for the email processing¶
   ' by concatenating WHERE with the build filter string¶
   strWhere =  WHERE  & Replace(Me.txtFilter, sfrmName., )¶
Else¶
   ' Ask for confirmation¶
   If MsgBox(, vbYesNo) = vbYes Then¶
      ' All means no WHERE clause needed¶
      strWhere = ¶
```

```
    Else¶
        ' skip processing¶
        GoTo exit_btnEmail_Click¶
    End If¶
End If¶
' Create a recordset for sequential processing¶
Set rs = CurrentDb.OpenRecordset(select * from tblName  & strWhere)¶
' Test if the recordset contains records¶
If rs.EOF And rs.BOF Then¶
    ' No records found¶
    MsgBox Your selection gave no rows, please try again¶
    GoTo exit_btnEmail_Click¶
End If¶
' position on the first row¶
rs.MoveFirst¶
' loop through all rows till the end of file¶
While Not rs.EOF¶
    ' send an email for the selected person and allow editing when¶
    ' the chkEmail has been set to true¶
    DoCmd.SendObject acSendNoObject, , , rs!Email, , , Multi mail test,
Dear  & rs!LastName & , & vbCrLf & This is a test, Me.chkEmail¶
    ' read the next record¶
    rs.MoveNext¶
Wend¶
exit_btnEmail_Click:¶
End Sub¶
```

That may seem like a lot of code, but there is just one line still needed for sending the e-mail – this one:

```
DoCmd.SendObject acSendNoObject, , , rs!Email, , , Multi mail test,
"Dear " & rs!LastName & , & vbCrLf & "This is a test", Me.chkEmail¶
```

Acs

There are many parameters available. To study them, use the F1 help key. The first, acSendNoObject, looks a bit odd, but implies that an object like a report is not going to be mailed. Access attaches it to the e-mail automatically. The rs!Email takes the e-mail address from the active row and place that in the To field. The Subject field is filled with a string, and so is the Message Text. The Message text shows how to use concatenation of strings to personalize the e-mail by inserting the LastName from the table. It shows how to create multiple lines by using the vbCRLF system variable.

The code basically consists of two sections: the verification and construction of the WHERE clause, and the processing of the records selected.

In the first section, the build string is used to create the WHERE string. Access invisibly adds the qualification string sfrmName. The REPLACE function corrects that. When selecting all records, the whole WHERE clause can be dropped.

The second section uses the standard record processing loop and starts with testing if there are records selected using IF rs.EOF AND rs.BOF THEN. The IF rs.EOF looks odd, perhaps, but it is short for IF rs.EOF = True. As both EOF (End Of File) and BOF (Beginning Of File) are Boolean values, they can only hold True or False.

Note: Testing to ensure that records are selected should always be coded so that there is at least one record to process in the loop. When there is no record, the rs.movefirst that is intended to set the cursor to the first record will fail. Within the WHILE / WEND loop, the last statement is rs.movenext to ensure that a new record is processed the next time. If this statement is omitted, the loop will run forever.

Making a Rolodex-type Selection List Box

This procedure demonstrates how to use a datasheet tabbed like a Rolodex using the first character of the names.

Scenario: A rather intuitive way of selecting names is to use a tabbed list to do the selection. There is a tabbed control in Access, but making 26 separate controls and controlling them requires a lot of code. It is possible to mimic such a control by using a list box and the selected letter to do the filtering.

Example file:
A010.mdb with a form frmNameSelect

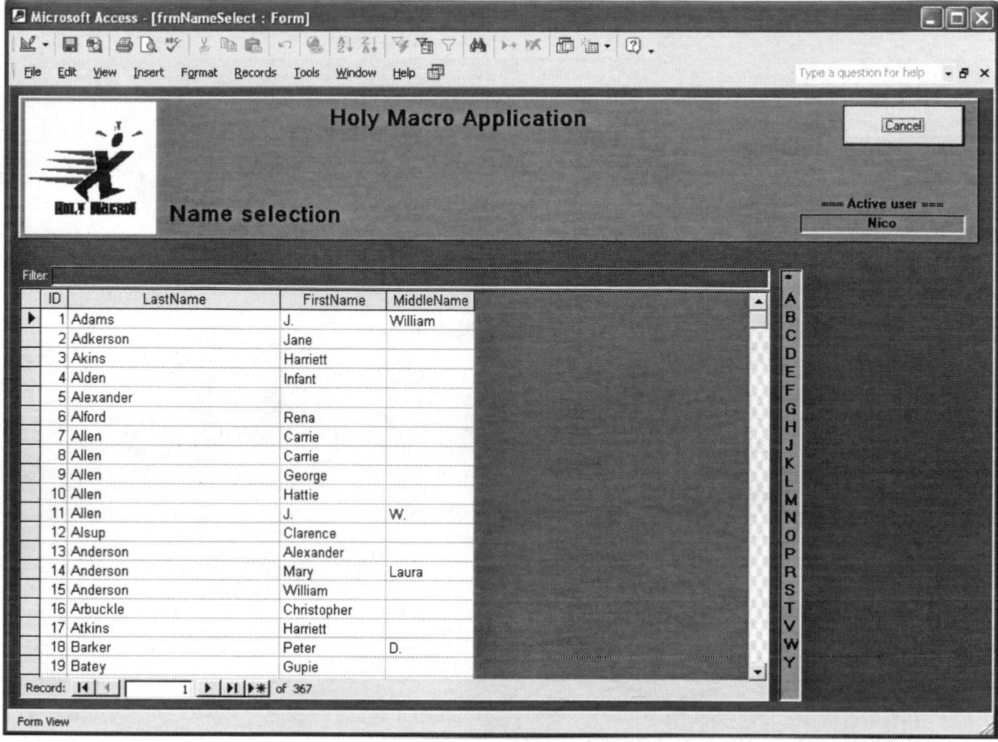

Figure 90 – Rolodex-style Selection

Looking closely at this form reveals that the >* button of the record navigation buttons at the bottom is activated. To test the dynamic nature of the datasheet and the changes in the added list box, the subforms data properties have been set to allow for the Insert, Update, and Deletion of records. Just click the subform twice and open the properties window, as shown in Figure 91.

Figure 91 – Form Properties Window

All of the Allow properties have been set to Yes; it is impossible to manipulate the data without doing this. For a test, go to the bottom of the list and enter a new last name, "Xtra". This triggers an insert when another line is chosen. The X will appear in the list box. Next, click on the left gray square in front of the [ID] field and press the Del button on the keyboard. This triggers a Delete, and Access requests confirmation. Press Yes; the row is removed and the X disappears from the list box.

Updating a row causes a change in the character list, too. Add the name "Xtra" again. After the X is added, change the name to Ixtra to see this occur.

To create the list box based on the first character of the first name, you need this simple query:

```
SELECT DISTINCT UCase(Left([LastName],1)) AS [Char] FROM tblName;
```

The Left([LastName],1) pulls the first character from the Lastname field and the UCase() function ensures that uppercase characters are returned. Because only unique characters are desired, there is the DISTINCT predicate to remove the duplicates. The query looks like Figure 92:

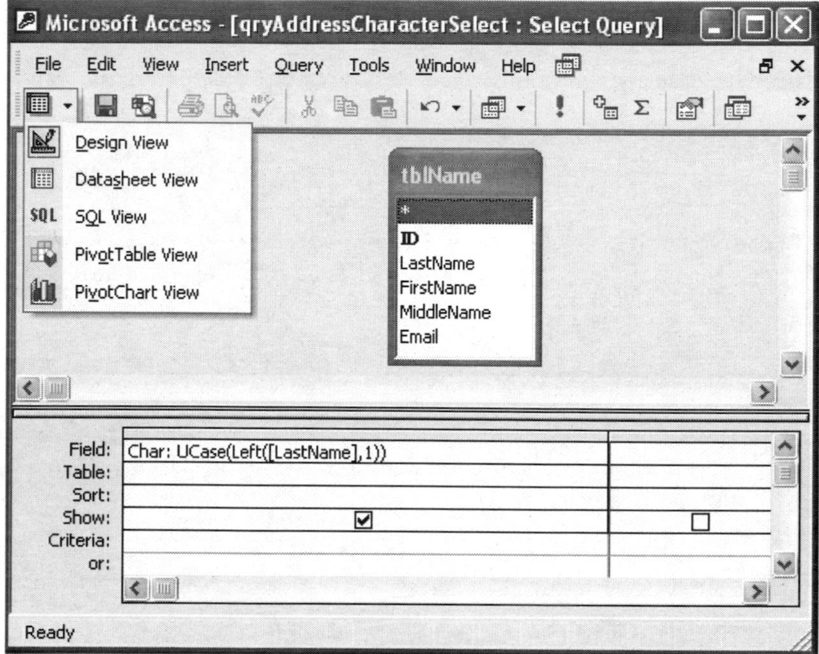

Figure 92 – Select Query

To have an extra character (*) do the reset of the filter, the following change is needed to add it in this query: Go into the SQL mode. Use the SQL View option from the drop-down list from the top left button to get to SQL mode, and add to the select statement a dummy select of the fixed value * as follows:

Acs

```
SELECT * as Chr from tblName
UNION
SELECT DISTINCT UCase(Left([LastName],1)) AS [Char] FROM tblName;
```

Note that the two SELECT statements have been combined by putting a UNION in between them. Using a UNION works only when both SELECT statements have the same number of rows and each row type (Text, Number, Date) corresponds.

Using a UNION has another advantage: The DISTINCT clause to remove the duplicates is dropped, as a UNION automatically sorts the field(s) and removes duplicate rows. To get all rows to appear, use the UNION ALL statement.

Place the following code in the On-Click event of the list box:

```
' Check for the special character * to show all rows¶
If Me.lstChar = * Then¶
    ' reset filter to show all¶
    ' by deactivating the FilterOn property¶
    Me.sfrmName.Form.FilterOn = False¶
Else¶
    ' set filter to show names that match the selected first character¶
    Me.sfrmName.Form.Filter = [Lastname] like ' & Me.lstChar & *'¶
    ' activate the filteron property¶
    Me.sfrmName.Form.FilterOn = True¶
End If¶
' Make sure changes will be displayed¶
Me.Refresh¶
```

The following code goes in each of the After Insert, After Delete Confirm, and After Update events of the subform:

```
' Refresh the listbox on the parent form¶
Parent.lstChar.Requery¶
```

Instead of moving a field to the parent form, simply requery the list box to ensure it reflects all current values.

Validating Data

Acs

Use this procedure to validate data entered into a form before saving a record.

Scenario: When users are entering or editing data, mistakes can occur. Before storing the data, you can test to ensure that mandatory fields have been completed. You can also check that related fields (like start and end dates) are logically correct (start date needs to be equal or less than the end date).

Select a row and press the Update button to see which error messages occur when editing the update form.

Example file:
A011.mdb with forms frmNameSelect and frmNameUpdate

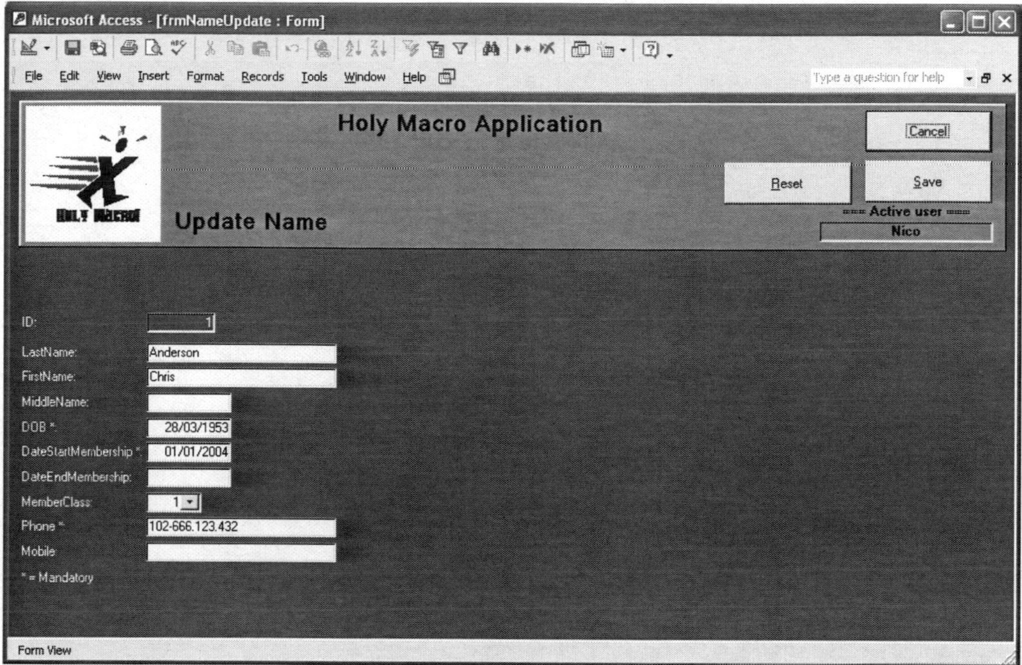

Figure 93 – Data Entry Form

The mandatory fields have been marked with an asterisk (*). Empty these fields to see the effect.

Many developers try to validate each field, but being forced to enter a value in a field before proceeding to another field can be frustrating for users, so all testing is done when the Save button is pressed, and all errors report to the user in a message box. To show which fields were in error, change the background color so that, even after the message box is closed, the user is aware of the error that must be corrected. Finally, we place the cursor in the first field that is wrong.

The code that provides this functionality is a follows:

```
Private Sub btnSave_Click()¶
Dim strMessage As String¶
   ' reset all backcolors in case errors have been reported previously¶
   Me.Phone.BackColor = vbWhite¶
   Me.DOB.BackColor = vbWhite¶
   Me.DateStartMembership.BackColor = vbWhite¶
   Me.DateStartMembership.BackColor = vbWhite¶
```

```
    ' Test fields from bottom to top so the last focus is¶
    ' set on the first¶
    If Not Len(Nz(Me.Phone)) > 0 Then¶
        ' No phonenumber¶
        strMessage = strMessage & vbCrLf & "Phone number is required"¶
        Me.Phone.BackColor = vbRed¶
        Me.Phone.SetFocus¶
    End If¶
    If Len(Nz(Me.DateStartMembership)) > 0 And
Len(Nz(Me.DateEndMembership)) > 0 Then¶
        If Me.DateEndMembership < Me.DateStartMembership Then¶
            ' Enddate before Startdate ? !¶
            strMessage = strMessage & vbCrLf & "End date needs to be
larger than start date"¶
            Me.DateEndMembership.BackColor = vbRed¶
            Me.DateEndMembership.SetFocus¶
        End If¶
    End If¶
    If Not Len(Nz(Me.DateStartMembership)) > 0 Then¶
        ' No DateStartMembership¶
        strMessage = strMessage & vbCrLf & "Date Start Membership is
required"¶
        Me.DateStartMembership.BackColor = vbRed¶
        Me.DateStartMembership.SetFocus¶
    End If¶
    If Not Len(Nz(Me.DOB)) > 0 Then¶
        ' No DOB¶
        strMessage = strMessage & vbCrLf & "Date of Birth is required"¶
        Me.DOB.BackColor = vbRed¶
        Me.DOB.SetFocus¶
    End If¶
    ' test if an error has been found¶
    If Len(strMessage) > 0 Then¶
        ' display message and don't close form¶
        MsgBox strMessage¶
    Else¶
        ' Close form and Access will save the data¶
        DoCmd.Close¶
    End If¶
End Sub¶
```

Acs

The strMessage field holds the concatenated error message(s). When this field is empty, the conclusion is that there are no errors.

Note: Backcolors need to be reset when starting the test, and also when the Reset button is selected.

Moving Rows Between List Boxes

Offer the user the ability to select multiple values from a list.

> **Scenario:** When the user needs to select multiple values, for instance, when producing reports for a selection of companies or divisions, we provide a method to select and store the selections. This is generally done by showing two list boxes and offering the user buttons that provide for moving items into a selection box. Most users are familiar with this setup.

Example file:
A012.mdb with form FrmMove

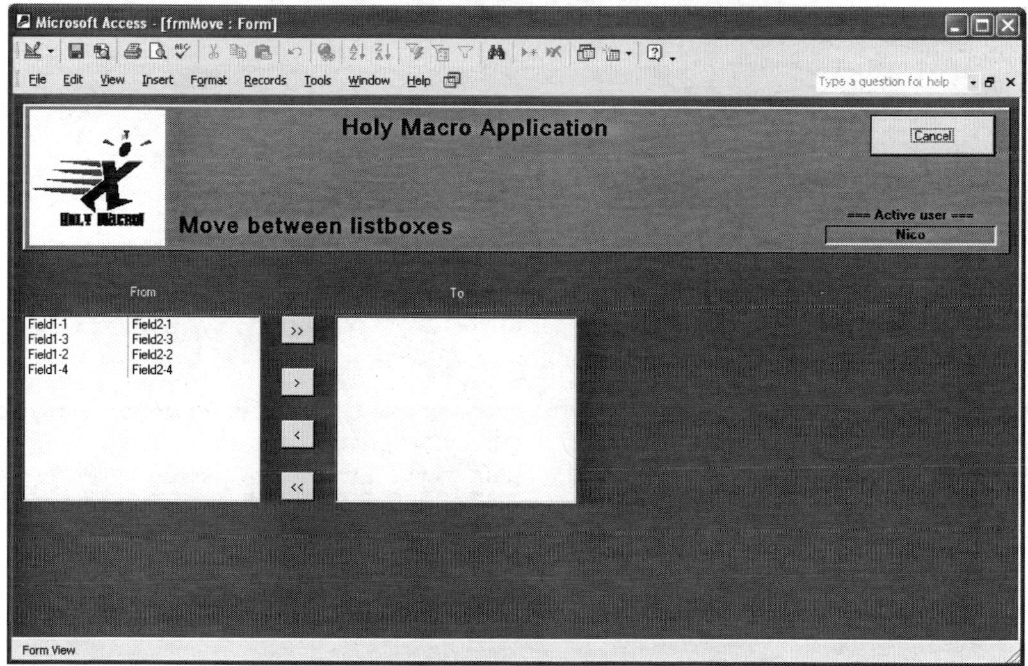

Figure 94 – Data Entry Form

You might expect this to require two tables, but it is much easier to use one with an additional Boolean (Yes/No) field.

Having a Boolean field requires setting only a True to False or False to True. All that is needed is to list only the False rows of the table in the From list box and only the True rows in the To list box.

The query for the From list box:

```
SELECT tblMove.Sequence, tblMove.Field1, tblMove.Field2
FROM tblMove
WHERE tblMove.LeftRight=False;
```

The move itself is established by an Update query in the code. For moving one row, use the behind > button:

```
Private Sub btnTo_Click()¶
' set the value of the LeftRight field to True for¶
' the selected row¶
If Me.lstFrom.ItemsSelected.Count > 0 Then¶
   CurrentDb.Execute (UPDATE tblMove SET LeftRight=true WHERE
[Sequence]= & Me.lstFrom)¶
   ' make changes visible¶
   Me.Refresh¶
Else¶
   ' No item selected¶
   MsgBox "Please select ""From"" item"¶
End If¶
End Sub¶
```

The Boolean field is named LeftRight, and the main statement is the UPDATE that sets the field to True for the selected row from the list box. We test for no items being selected so that a warning is displayed.

Acs

Note The double quote is used twice to get the warning message to display. Also, there is a me.refresh to make the changes visible.

The code for the Move All button is even easier. Simply update all fields to the required value. Testing for no selection is not even necessary!

```
Private Sub btnAllTo_Click()¶
' switch all values of the LeftRight to True¶
CurrentDb.Execute (UPDATE tblMove SET LeftRight=True)¶
' make changes visible¶
Me.Refresh¶
End Sub¶
```

For other buttons, just switch names and True to False.

Having manipulated the table this way, you can use it for such tasks as report selection. When this table is JOINED with the table or query for the report, all that you need to do is to test for the LeftRight field to be set to True to produce the report.

Moving Rows in List Boxes

This procedure offers the user the possibility to manipulate the sequence of a list.

Scenario: Items in a list may need to be reshuffled. Allow the user to set the priority / sequence of a list of items. Provide them with Up and Down buttons to accomplish this task.

Example file:
A013.mdb with form frmMoveUpDown

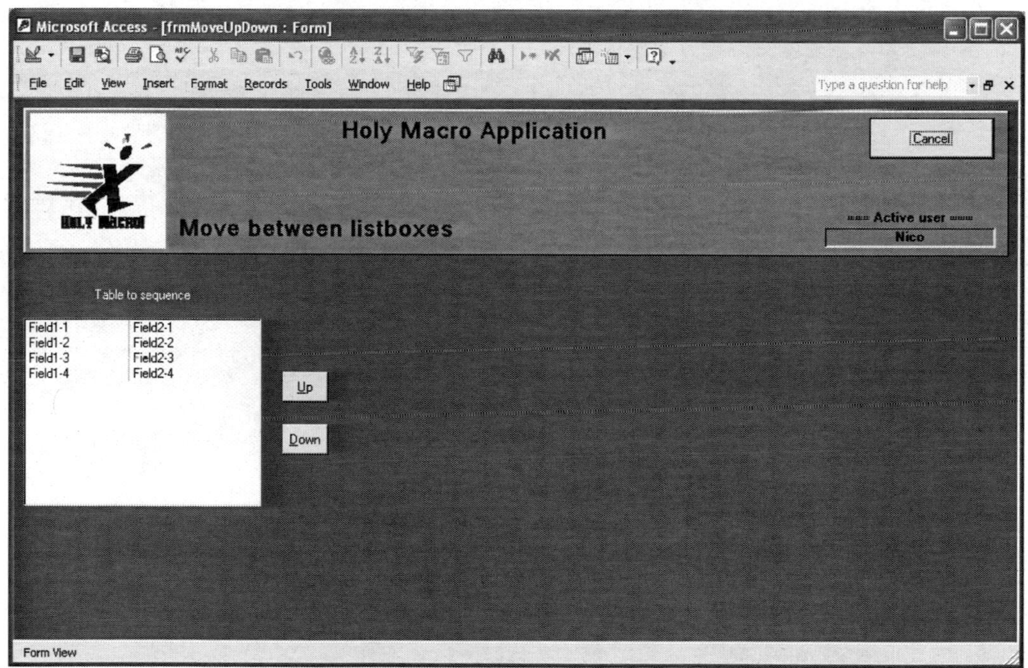

Figure 95 – Move In List Boxes

Acs

Although this looks simple, some problems arise when trying to code this process:

- The table needs to have a closed row of numbers, starting with 1 and no gaps.
- The straight forward update of a row with the new sequence number will cause a Duplicate key error.
- After a move, the selected row needs to move too; so the user can keep pressing up until a row is in the first location.
- Finally, take care that an Up on the first row or a Down on the last row is handled.

The following code does all this on click:

```
Private Sub btnDown_Click()¶
Dim intSaveIndex As Integer¶
'The click event is taking care that only valid moves can be made¶
'Check if an item before the last one is selected¶
If Me.lstMove.ItemsSelected.Count > 0 And Me.lstMove.ListIndex <
Me.lstMove.ListCount - 1 Then¶
    intSaveIndex = Me.lstMove.ListIndex¶
    dbKeyFrom = Me.lstMove.Column(0, Me.lstMove.ListIndex)¶
    dbKeyTo = Me.lstMove.Column(0, Me.lstMove.ListIndex + 1)¶
    ' Move¶
    Call subMove¶
    'Make change visible and move item selection with it¶
    Me.Refresh¶
    Me.lstMove.SetFocus¶
    Me.lstMove.Selected(intSaveIndex + 1) = True¶
    Me.lstMove.ListIndex = intSaveIndex + 1¶
Else¶
    If Me.lstMove.ListIndex < Me.lstMove.ListCount - 1 Then¶
       'No item selected¶
       MsgBox "First select an item from the list"¶
    Else¶
       'No action, already on last row...¶
    End If¶
End If¶
End Sub¶
' * * * * *
Private Sub subMove()¶
    ' Switch two records based on dbKeyFrom and dbKeyTo¶
    ' the 0 is used to park the first entry.¶
    ' Otherwise a duplicate key error will occur !¶
    CurrentDb.Execute UPDATE tblMove SET Sequence = 0 WHERE Sequence= &
dbKeyFrom & ;¶
```

Acs

```
    CurrentDb.Execute UPDATE tblMove SET Sequence =  & dbKeyFrom &
WHERE Sequence= & dbKeyTo & ;¶
    CurrentDb.Execute UPDATE tblMove SET Sequence =  & dbKeyTo &  WHERE
Sequence=0;¶
End Sub¶
```

Testing for selection must be performed, and testing for move possibilities has been added. The Up on the first row and the Down on the last row are just ignored. An error message displays only when no row has been selected.

The Me.refresh makes the changes visible when the table is updated. Because the index of the selected item will be lost, we must first save the index and fill the Key From and the Key To so that the sub performs the switch of the rows, which can be called as follows:

```
intSaveIndex = Me.lstMove.ListIndex¶
dbKeyFrom = Me.lstMove.Column(0, Me.lstMove.ListIndex)¶
dbKeyTo = Me.lstMove.Column(0, Me.lstMove.ListIndex + 1)¶
```

The switch in the general subMove is done with three UPDATE statements:

1. Neutralize the row to be moved by setting the key to zero (0).
2. Move the row that is on the location needed to the previous location of the selected row.
3. Update the Neutralized row to get the correct value.

Acs

Creating a Dynamic Crosstab Report

This procedure demonstrates a way to display crosstab query data dynamically in a report.

Scenario: When using a crosstab query for a report, notice not only that the field contents are transformed into fieldnames, but also that adding a new value in the Column field doesn't show on the report. Removing a value entirely causes the report to fail. Here, we make a report that handles all field values from a query.

Example file: A015.mdb with form frmCrossTable, query qryCrossTable, and report rptCrossTable.

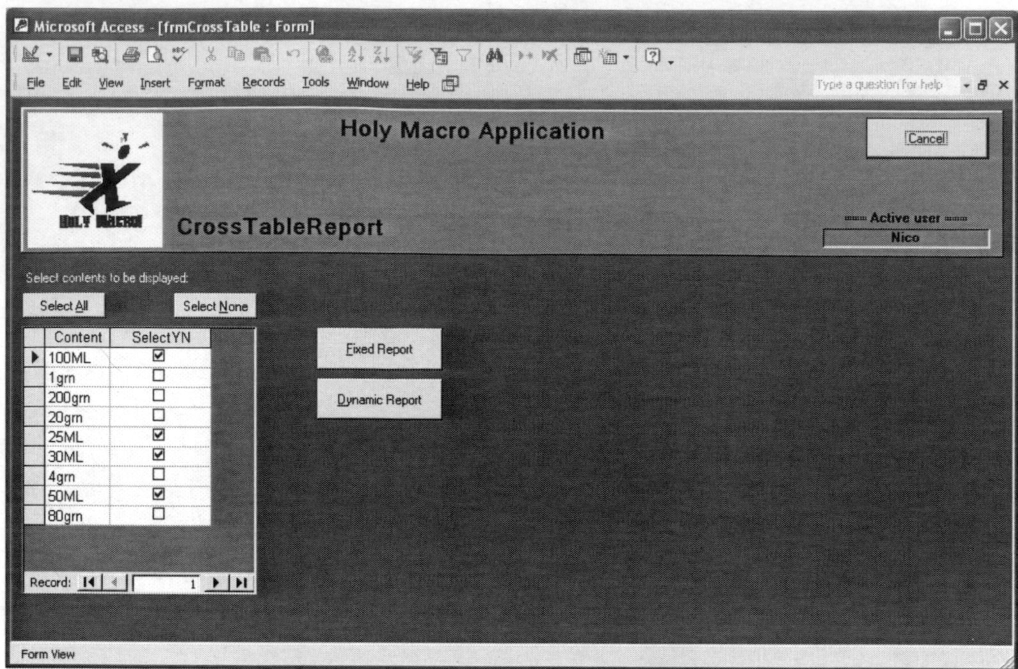

Figure 96 – Dynamic CrossTab Report

The two buttons allow the user to choose from a Fixed (static) report and a Dynamic report. The Fixed report only works when all fields are selected; the Dynamic report always works. The reports are based on a query that is working with a link to a table with the selection field filtered to be True, as described in the Moving Rows in List Boxes example found on page 355. The basic code for making the report dynamic is straightforward and based on the fact that the fields on the report are coded in VBA and that the .fields property of the recordset can be processed to be enumerated.

```
Private Sub Report_Open(Cancel As Integer)¶
Dim intI As Integer¶
Dim rs As DAO.Recordset¶
' Set the recordset to the Recordsource of the report¶
Set rs = CurrentDb.OpenRecordset(Me.RecordSource)¶
' By default all fields are set to invisible¶
'Place headers¶
For intI = 2 To rs.Fields.Count - 1¶
    ' use fieldname for column heading,¶
    ' but skip the part with the sequence number¶
    Me(lblCol & intI - 1).Caption = Mid(rs.Fields(intI).Name, 3)¶
    Me(lblCol & intI - 1).Visible = True¶
```

```
    ' Set controlsource to field¶
    Me(Col & intI - 1).ControlSource = rs.Fields(intI).Name¶
    Me(Col & intI - 1).Visible = True¶
    'Place Total field¶
    Me(ColTotal & intI - 1).ControlSource = =SUM([ &
rs.Fields(intI).Name & ])¶
    Me(ColTotal & intI - 1).Visible = True¶
Next intI¶
End Sub¶
```

All fields have been set to be invisible and are only made visible when a field is found. The coded names like Me(Col & intI - 1) are used to fill the fields from right to left, but also limit the working of the report to the maximum number of fields that are predefined.

Generating Periodic Reports

Using this procedure, you can total data by periods using grouped dates.

Scenario: Periodic reports may need to be generated by day, week, month, four grouped weeks, quarters, or years. In general, a query per period is created and one subform fills the period subform on-the-fly.

Example file:
A016.mdb with
form frmPeriods

Acs

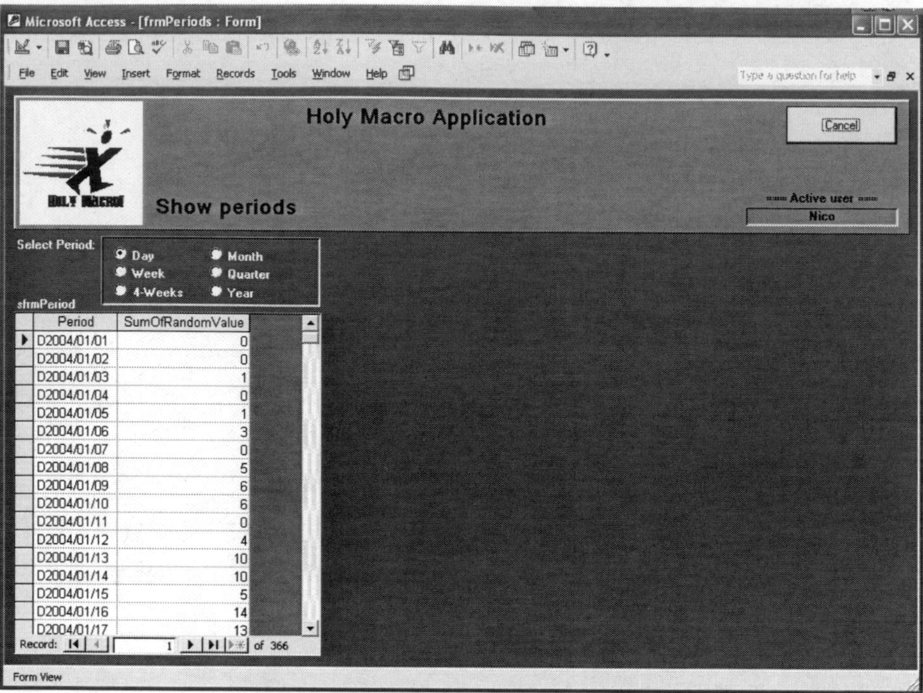

Figure 97 – Periodic Reports

To select the time period, a frame with radio buttons is used. A value from 1 to 6 is returned when a selection is clicked. In the AfterUpdate event of the frame, the query that fills the subform is set, depending on the choice.

This only works when each period has exactly the same fields to show. If this is not the case, a different subform needs to be created. In this case, we change the subform instead of changing the subform's record source.

The code is as follows:

```
Private Sub fraPeriod_AfterUpdate()¶
Select Case Me.fraPeriod¶
Case 1¶
   Me.sfrmPeriod.Form.RecordSource = qryDay¶
Case 2¶
   Me.sfrmPeriod.Form.RecordSource = qryWeek¶
Case 3¶
   Me.sfrmPeriod.Form.RecordSource = qry4weeks¶
Case 4¶
   Me.sfrmPeriod.Form.RecordSource = qryMonth¶
```

```
Case 5¶
   Me.sfrmPeriod.Form.RecordSource = qryQuarter¶
Case 6¶
   Me.sfrmPeriod.Form.RecordSource = qryYear¶
End Select¶
End Sub¶
```

The real work is done in the query. In general, using the FORMAT function provides formatting as desired.

The snag? When the fields should be sorted by date, the format does not force a prefix zero in front of the single-digit months, which causes a result with a sequence such as 20041, 200410, 200411, 200412, 20042.

To overcome this, the often-used RIGHT provides a prefixed zero: RIGHT(00&[Month],2).

This first places two zeroes (just to be sure) in front of the month and then takes the last two characters of the result to always show a two-digit month.

For readability, the abbreviation of the period has been added to the Period field in the subform.

Creating Controlled Numbers

This procedure creates ControlID numbers.

Scenario: When designing an order system, coded keys are often used. The problem is that they are not limitless. When an order number is defined, for instance, as the year + three digits, the maximum number of orders will be 999. When the system gets to 1,000 or more orders, you're in trouble. Using the AutoNumber is possible, but has some limitations. The moment the database is made replicatable for asynchronous use, the AutoNumber changes from the default +1 into a randomly created number.

Example file:
A017.mdb with form frmControlledNumbers

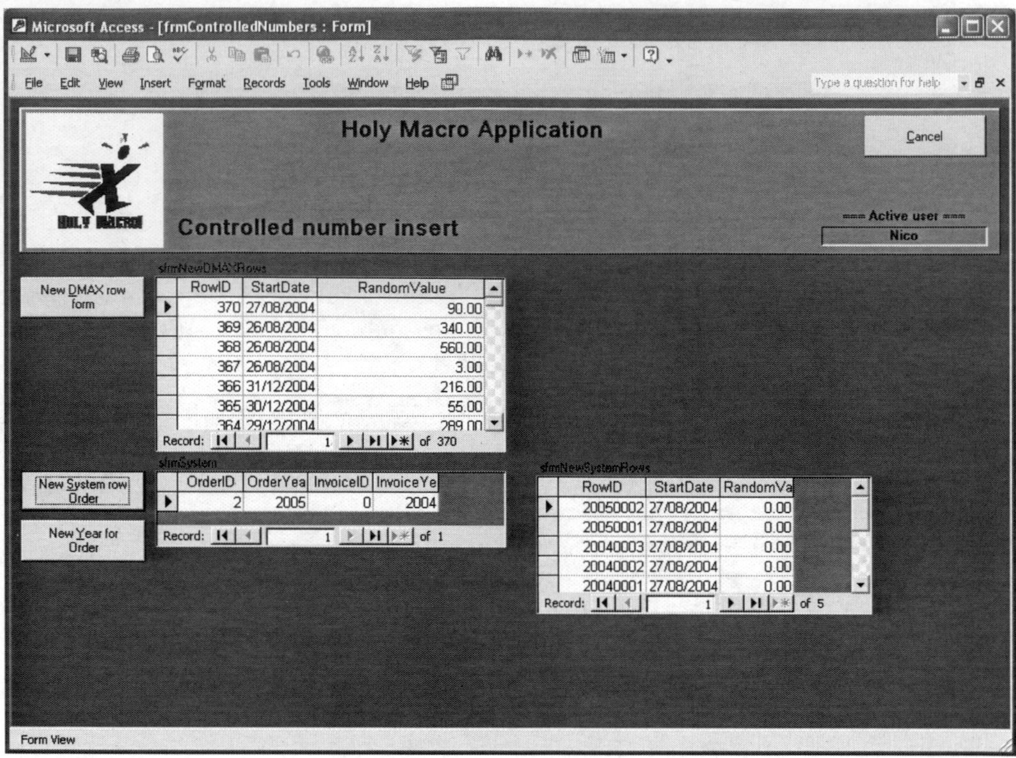

Figure 98 – Controlled Numbers

Acs

Two main options are available for controlling unique ID numbers: Using DMAX + 1 when inserting a new record, and using a system table with the last used number.

The DMAX function retrieves the maximum number from the table. In the OnInsert event of the form, the value is set. This event is triggered the moment the first field value is entered. Then the code executes, the number is set, the Save button is enabled, and the issued number appears in the key field. The Cancel button first executes the Me.Undo to ensure nothing is saved.

The DMAX function works, but using a table with the last used number offers a more flexible approach because it allows the user to change the highest number and/or year whenever necessary. We need only be concerned that the numbers are unique. Thus, a new number can only be a number higher than the previous one (within a given year). Two functions have been created in a module modOrderNumber.

The code is a simple update of the row in the tblSystem and the formatting of the number:

```
Function fncGetNewOrdernumber() As String¶
' Function to get a new ordernumber in the format yyyy9999¶
Dim rs As DAO.Recordset¶
' open tblSystem¶
Set rs = CurrentDb.OpenRecordset(tblSystem)¶
' make sure first (and only) row is available¶
rs.MoveFirst¶
' update row¶
rs.Edit¶
rs!orderid = rs!orderid + 1¶
' create ordernumber as string with four fixed digits¶
fncGetNewOrdernumber = rs!orderyear & Format(rs!orderid, 0000)¶
rs.Update¶
Set rs = Nothing¶
End Function¶
```

The year increment code is almost identical; only the rs.Edit is different:

```
rs.Edit¶
rs!orderyear = rs!orderyear + 1¶
rs!orderid = 1¶
' create ordernumber as string with four fixed digits¶
fncStartNewYearOrdernumber = rs!orderyear & Format(rs!orderid, 0000)¶
rs.Update¶
```

Making a Wizard with Tabbed Control

Acs

This procedure demonstrates how to force users to fill in fields in a predefined sequence.

Scenario: To direct the input of the user, you would normally use a wizard. In a previous example, we demonstrated how to check entered data when the user pressed the Save button. Sometimes, values to be displayed in a field are determined by previous field selections. In this instance, a wizard can be used to assist the user.

Example file:
A019.mdb with form frmWizard

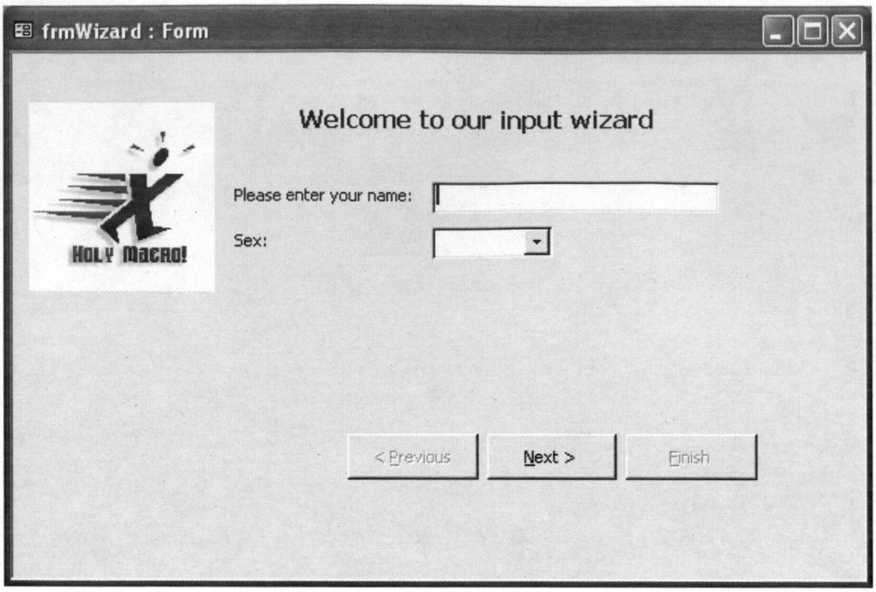

Figure 99 – Data Entry Wizard

When using the wizard, notice that the image and the buttons remain in the same location. They are not placed in the tabbed control, but above it. Editing the tab control is somewhat cumbersome. Making sure the correct object is selected is important. Placing an object on the tabbed control requires that the page be selected. This is indicated by a dotted line around the pagename on the tab. This is especially critical when using copy/paste; otherwise, the object is placed above the tabbed control.

To create the control, start with a regular tabbed control and add as many new pages as needed. The tabs can be switched off. (That will be done when all is tested.) Next, place the stable elements above the tabbed control. Finally, fill the specific pages. A third page that only appears when a radio button is pressed has been chosen for the wizard. This demonstrates how to navigate conditionally through the pages.

The buttons are page-specific. A special procedure is used to activate them when needed. The button handling is also page-specific; for the btnPrev, we use a trick to go back one page and to skip the conditional page.

Lets start with the btnNext:

```
Private Sub btnNext_Click()¶¶
' As the button is above the tabbed pages,¶
' the page value can be tested to detect what action is necessary¶
Select Case Me.tabWizard¶
Case 0¶
    Me.tabWizard.Pages(1).SetFocus¶
Case 1¶
    ' test if the extra page needs to be displayed¶
    If Me.fraExplain = 1 Then¶
       Me.tabWizard.Pages(2).SetFocus¶
    Else¶
       Me.tabWizard.Pages(3).SetFocus¶
    End If¶
Case 2¶
    Me.tabWizard.Pages(3).SetFocus¶
End Select¶
' Set the buttons fitting to the page¶
Call SetButtons¶
End Sub¶
```

A simple SELECT CASE is used to determine the page in focus, and to set the focus to the next page. Because the radio button does interfere, an extra IF is needed. Finally the enabling of the buttons is moved to a procedure because it saves duplication of work when doing the btnPrev code.

This is the btnPrev code:

```
Private Sub btnPrev_Click()¶
   ' Previous always activates the previous page, except¶
   ' when no explanation was requested¶
   Me.tabWizard.Pages(Me.tabWizard - 1).SetFocus¶
   If Me.tabWizard > 0 And Me.fraExplain <> 1 Then¶
      ' subtract again to skip the explanation page¶
      Me.tabWizard.Pages(Me.tabWizard - 1).SetFocus¶
   End If¶
   Call SetButtons¶
End Sub¶
```

Acs

Normally, lowering the page number by one is sufficient. If the explanation radio button is pressed, then one additional subtraction must be made. The btnPrev is disabled on the first page so it is not possible to move before the first page. Please keep in mind that the pages are zero-base numbered; in other words, the first page is number 0, the second is number 1, and so on.

Finally the procedure sets the buttons as needed per page:

```
Private Sub SetButtons()¶
Select Case Me.tabWizard¶
Case 0¶
    Me.btnPrev.Enabled = False¶
    Me.btnNext.Enabled = True¶
    Me.btnFinish.Enabled = False¶
Case 1¶
    Me.btnPrev.Enabled = True¶
    Me.btnNext.Enabled = True¶
    Me.btnFinish.Enabled = False¶
Case 2¶
    Me.btnPrev.Enabled = True¶
    Me.btnNext.Enabled = True¶
    Me.btnFinish.Enabled = False¶
Case 3¶
    Me.btnPrev.Enabled = True¶
    Me.btnNext.Enabled = False¶
    Me.btnFinish.Enabled = True¶
End Select¶
End Sub¶
```

The tabbed control has a property Style on the Format tab that has these options: Tabs, Buttons, or None. For the wizard, use None to hide the tabs and to have full control over which page is displayed. The fact that the buttons are placed above the control makes it necessary to use the Select Case, but saves a lot of positioning and buttons that scatter the code over multiple events. In general, it is best to get the navigation done in as few procedures as possible for easy maintenance.

Combined Procedures

The following procedures involve code that directs tasks to more than one application.

Transferring Charts From Excel to PowerPoint

by Suat Ozgur

This code demonstrates how to transfer Excel Charts in worksheets and to create a new PowerPoint presentation file that includes a slide for each chart.

Scenario: Presenting the charts in an Excel workbook using a PowerPoint presentation is a time consuming task when done by the traditional manual cut and paste. Now, you can create that presentation easily using VBA.

Example file:
O011.xls

View the Appendix to learn how to store this procedure in a Standard module (in Excel).

```
Option Explicit¶
' * * * * *¶
Public Sub TransferToPPT()¶
'Excel Application objects declaration¶
Dim objSheet       As Worksheet¶
Dim objChartObject As ChartObject¶
Dim objChart       As Chart¶
'Powerpoint Application objects declaration¶
Dim pptApp As Object 'PowerPoint.Application¶
Dim pptPre As Object 'PowerPoint.Presentation¶
Dim pptSld As Object 'PowerPoint.Slide¶
  'Create a new Powerpoint session¶
  Set pptApp = CreateObject("PowerPoint.Application")¶
  'Create a new presentation¶
  Set pptPre = pptApp.Presentations.Add¶
  'Loop through each worksheet¶
  For Each objSheet In ActiveWorkbook.Worksheets¶
    'Verify if there is a chart object to transfer¶
    If objSheet.ChartObjects.Count > 0 Then¶
      'Loop through each chart object in worksheet¶
      For Each objChartObject In objSheet.ChartObjects¶
        'Set chart object¶
        Set objChart = objChartObject.Chart¶
```

Cmb

```
        'Create new slide for the chart¶
        'ppLayoutBlank = 12¶
        Set pptSld = pptPre.Slides.Add(pptPre.Slides.Count + 1, 12)¶
        With objChart¶
         'Copy chart object as picture¶
          objChart.CopyPicture xlScreen, xlBitmap, xlScreen¶
          'Paste copied chart picture into new slide¶
          pptSld.Shapes.Paste¶
        End With¶
      Next objChartObject¶
    End If¶
  Next objSheet¶
  'Activate PowerPoint application¶
  pptApp.Visible = True¶
  pptApp.Activate¶
End Sub¶
```

Saving Word Form Data to an Excel Spreadsheet

by Cindy Meister

This procedure transfers information from Word to Excel using automation.

Example file: W024

> **Scenario:** Word's online forms are a comfortable way to distribute a form and get information back from numerous sources. The question remains, however, how to most efficiently use the data coming back in the forms documents.
>
> While Word does provide the option to "Save data only for forms", this only saves the form input as a comma-delimited text file. Any use requires additional steps to import or append this to an Excel or database table, one data set at a time.

The example file contains the code for the preceding “Forms: Placing a Picture in a Protected Form” entry on page 193 because adding a picture to the Word file is an option. The picture is not saved in the Excel file, but the caption for the picture is.

This macro opens the target Excel workbook and writes a new record to the table. It takes the data from form fields with names matching the column headers in the Excel table.

View the Appendix to learn how to store this procedure in a Standard module (in Word).

```
Option explicit¶
' * * * * *¶
Const xlWorkbook As String = _¶
    "C:\SaveFormData.xls"¶
' * * * * *¶
Sub SendDataToExcel()¶
    'Variable declaration¶
    Dim objXL As Excel.Application¶
    Dim wb As Excel.Workbook¶
    Dim rng As Excel.Range¶
    Dim rngNewRecord As Excel.Range¶
    Dim trackVal As Long¶
    Dim rowIndex As Long¶
    Dim nrFields As Long¶
    Dim fieldName As String¶
    Dim counter As Long¶
    'Opens the workbook and Excel if necessary¶
    Set objXL = New Excel.Application¶
    Set wb = objXL.Workbooks.Open(FileName:=xlWorkbook)¶
    'Start in the first cell of the table¶
    'May be any cell in the worksheet as long¶
    'as it is named "Start"¶
    Set rng = wb.Sheets(1).Range("Start")¶
    'Find the last cell with content¶
    trackVal = rng.End(xlDown).Value¶
    'Get the number of columns in the table¶
    nrFields = rng.End(xlToRight).Column¶
    'Get the next empty row¶
    If trackVal = 0 Then¶
        Set rngNewRecord = rng.Offset(1, 0)¶
    Else¶
        Set rngNewRecord = rng.End(xlDown).Offset(1, 0)¶
    End If¶
    'Calculate the next tracking number¶
    'for the left column¶
    rngNewRecord.Value = trackVal + 1¶
    'Get the new record's row number¶
    rowIndex = rngNewRecord.Row¶
    'Cycle through all the fields in the table¶
    For counter = 2 To nrFields¶
        'Get the field name (column header)¶
        fieldName = _¶
            rng.Worksheet.Cells(1, counter).End(xlUp).Value¶
        'Insert the data from the matching form field¶
        'Ignore fields with no match in the form¶
```

Cmb

```
        'Continue when error occurs¶
        On Error Resume Next¶
        rng.Worksheet.Cells(rowIndex, counter).Value _¶
            = ActiveDocument.FormFields(fieldName).Result¶
        On Error GoTo 0¶
    Next¶
    'Save the workbook with the new record¶
    wb.Save¶
    'Bring Excel to the front¶
    objXL.Visible = True¶
    objXL.Quit¶
    'Clear memory¶
    Set ObjExcel = Nothing¶
    Set wb = Nothing¶
End Sub¶
```

Follow these steps:

1. Enter the complete path to the workbook as the value for the constant xlWorkbook.

Note: The macro runs from a toolbar that displays when a document is created using the template.

2. Create a table in an Excel worksheet. The first column is reserved for an incremental record tracking number. Give it an appropriate heading name, such as “Record”.
3. Select the column heading. Go to Insert | Names | Define and give it the range name: Start. All positions in the table are calculated from this point. It need not be cell A1, and it need not be the first worksheet.
4. For the remaining column headings, enter the same names used for the form fields in the Word form. Be careful to use the exact same spelling as in the Word form.

Tip: Double-click a form field to see its name in the Options dialog box.

5. Save the Excel workbook. Run the macro.

Filling a Word Combo Box with Data from Excel

by Cindy Meister

This macro expands on the Entering Data Easily Using a Custom Dialog Box procedure found on page 254 by using an Excel workbook to fill the combo box from which data can be selected to go into the State field.

> **Scenario:** When entries should be limited to a certain selection, it is often easier to present them to the user in a list or drop-down. This is often a time-saver for the user, as well.

Example file:
W037

This tool builds on the example presented in the previously noted entry. The text box for the State information has been replaced with a drop-down list. The values to fill the list come from an Excel workbook.

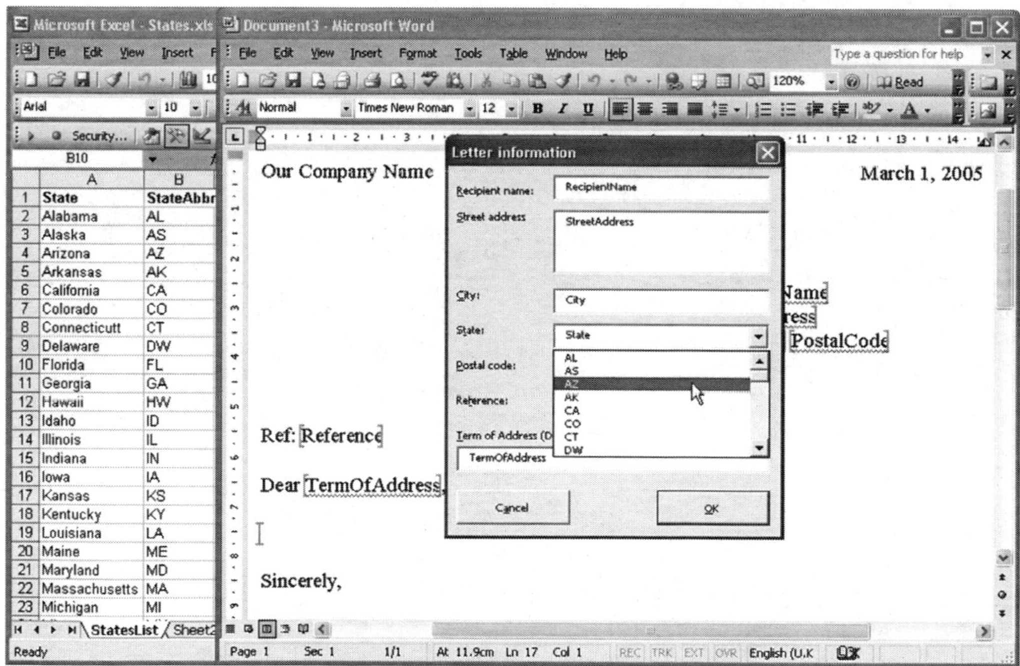

Figure 100 – Choosing Data from Excel

View the Appendix to learn how to store this procedure in a Standard module (Word template).

```
Option explicit¶
' * * * * *¶
Sub AutoNew()¶
    GetUserInput¶
End Sub¶
' * * * * *¶
Sub GetUserInput()¶
    'Variable declaration¶
    Dim frm As frmUserInput¶
    Dim doc As Word.Document¶
    Set doc = ActiveDocument¶
    If doc.Bookmarks.Count < 1 Then¶
        MsgBox "Invalide document. " & _¶
        "No bookmarks could be found.", _¶
        vbCritical + vbOKOnly¶
        Exit Sub¶
    End If¶
    Set frm = New frmUserInput¶
    GetDataFromDocument frm, doc¶
    '!Substitute the correct combo box name!¶
    FillStateList frm.cboState¶
    '!Substitute the correct combo box¶
    'and text box names below!¶
    frm.cboState.Text = frm.txtState.Text¶
    frm.Show¶
    If frm.Tag = "OK" Then¶
        '!Substitute the correct combo box¶
        'and text box names below!¶
        frm.txtState.Text = frm.cboState.Text¶
        PutDataIntoDocument frm, doc¶
    End If¶
    Unload frm¶
    If doc.Bookmarks.Exists("txtStartBody") Then¶
    doc.Bookmarks("txtStartBody").Range.Select¶
    End If¶
End Sub¶
' * * * * *¶
Sub GetDataFromDocument(frm As UserForm, doc As Word.Document)¶
    'Variable declaration¶
    Dim ctl As MSForms.Control¶
    Dim firstControl As Boolean¶
    For Each ctl In frm.Controls¶
        If doc.Bookmarks.Exists(ctl.Name) Then¶
            ctl.Text = doc.Bookmarks(ctl.Name).Range.Text¶
            If Not firstControl Then¶
                ctl.SelStart = 0¶
                ctl.SelLength = Len(ctl.Text)¶
                firstControl = True¶
```

nb

```
            End If¶
        End If¶
    Next¶
End Sub¶
' * * * * *¶
Sub PutDataIntoDocument(frm As UserForm, doc As Word.Document)¶
    'Variable declaration¶
    Dim ctl As MSForms.Control¶
    Dim rng As Word.Range¶
    For Each ctl In frm.Controls¶
        If doc.Bookmarks.Exists(ctl.Name) Then¶
            Set rng = doc.Bookmarks(ctl.Name).Range¶
            rng.Text = ctl.Text¶
            doc.Bookmarks.Add Name:=ctl.Name, Range:=rng¶
        End If¶
    Next¶
End Sub¶
' * * * * *¶
Sub FillStateList(cbo As MSForms.ComboBox)¶
    '!Remember to set reference to ADO library!¶
    'Variable declaration¶
    Dim conn As ADODB.Connection¶
    Dim rs As ADODB.Recordset¶
    Dim SQL As String¶
    Dim wbPath As String¶
    Dim wbName As String¶
    Dim sheetName As String¶
    Dim fieldName As String¶
    'The relevant information for the Excel file¶
    wbName = "States.xls"¶
    wbPath = "C:\test\" & wbName¶
    sheetName = "StatesList"¶
    fieldName = "StateAbbr" 'column heading¶
    SQL = "Select [" & fieldName & _¶
      "] FROM [" & sheetName & "$]"¶
    Set conn = New ADODB.Connection¶
    conn.Open "Provider=Microsoft.Jet.OLEDB.4.0;" & _¶
          "Data Source=" & wbPath & ";" & _¶
          "Extended Properties=""Excel 8.0;HDR=Yes"""¶
    Set rs = New ADODB.Recordset¶
    rs.Open SQL, conn, , adCmdText¶
    Do While Not rs.EOF¶
        cbo.AddItem rs.Fields("StateAbbr").Value¶
        rs.MoveNext¶
    Loop¶
    rs.Close¶
    conn.Close¶
    'Free memory¶
    Set rs = Nothing¶
    Set conn = Nothing¶
End Sub¶
```

Cmb

Follow these steps:

1. Copy the macro code to the correspondence template's VBA project.
2. Transfer the UserForm frmUserInput to the same project using either the Organizer, or by dragging it in the Visual Basic Editor (VBE) to the template's project. The code for this UserForm module is as follows.

View the Appendix to learn how to store this procedure in a UserForm (in Word).

```
Option explicit¶
' * * * * *¶
Private Sub btnCancel_Click()¶
     Me.Hide¶
    Me.Tag = "Cancel"¶
End Sub¶
' * * * * *¶
Private Sub btnOK_Click()¶
     Me.Hide¶
    Me.Tag = "OK"¶
End Sub¶
```

The code in the example file also includes the module 'basCreateBookmark', which is utilized in the Creating a Bookmark from a Selection entry on page 260. It is included below for reference.

```
Option explicit¶
' * * * * *¶
Const varName As String = "BookmarkCounter"¶
Const varDuplicateName As String _¶
= "DuplicateBookmarkCounter"¶
' * * * * *¶
Sub CreateBookmark()¶
'Variable declaration¶
Dim rng As Word.Range¶
Dim BookmarkName As String¶
Dim var As Word.Variable¶
'Check whether the document variable that stores¶
'a counter for bookmarks without content exists¶
If varExists(ActiveDocument, varName) = False Then¶
    'If not, create it and assign it the value 1¶
    ActiveDocument.Variables.Add _¶
    Name:=varName, Value:="1"¶
End If¶
Set var = ActiveDocument.Variables(varName)¶
Set rng = Selection.Range¶
If Selection.Type = wdSelectionIP Then¶
```

```
    'The user didn't select any text; a bookmark without¶
    'content will be inserted with¶
    'an incremented name txt#¶
    'Calculate that name¶
    BookmarkName = "txt" & var.Value¶
    var.Value = CStr(CLng(var.Value) + 1)¶
    'Alternately, a prompt can be displayed¶
    'to ask the user for the name¶
    'Uncomment the next two lines to use that method¶
    'BookmarkName = InputBox( _¶
    'No text is selected. Type in a bookmark name.")¶
Else¶
    'Get the bookmark name based on the selected text¶
    BookmarkName = ProcessBookmarkName(rng.Text)¶
End If¶
'Check if the bookmark name already exists;¶
'if it does it will be incremented with a counter¶
BookmarkName = "txt" & CheckIfDuplicateName( _¶
ActiveDocument, BookmarkName)¶
'Insert the bookmark¶
ActiveDocument.Bookmarks.Add _¶
Name:=BookmarkName, Range:=rng¶
End Sub¶
' * * * * *¶
Function ProcessBookmarkName(s As String) As String¶
'Variable declaration¶
Dim i As Long¶
'Maximum length of a bookmark name is 40 characters¶
'Because txt will be added to the beginning¶
'therefore cut off at 37¶
If Len(s) > 37 Then s = Left(s, 37)¶
    'Replace all spaces with underline characters¶
    s = Replace(s, " ", "_")¶
    'Remove any numbers at the beginning¶
    Do While IsNumeric(Left(s, 1)) = True¶
        s = Mid(s, 2)¶
        Debug.Print s¶
    Loop¶
    'Remove invalid characters¶
    '(following list is not comprehensive)¶
    For i = 1 To Len(s)¶
        Select Case Mid(s, i, 1)¶
            Case "§", "°", "+", "¦", "@", Chr$(34), "*", _¶
            "#", "%", "&", "", "/", "|", "(", "¢", ")", _¶
            "=", "?", "'", "´", "^", "`", "~", "[", "]", _¶
            "¨", "!", "{", "}", "$", "£", "<", ">", "<", _¶
            ".", ",", ":", ";", "-"¶
            s = Left(s, i - 1) & Mid(s, i + 1)¶
        Case Else¶
```

Cmb

```
            'Otherwise, do nothing¶
        End Select¶
    Next i¶
ProcessBookmarkName = s¶
End Function¶
' * * * * *¶
Function CheckIfDuplicateName(doc As Word.Document, _¶
BookmarkName As String) As String¶
'Variable declaration¶
Dim var As Word.Variable¶
If varExists(doc, varDuplicateName) = False Then¶
    ActiveDocument.Variables.Add _¶
    Name:=varDuplicateName, Value:="1"¶
End If¶
Set var = ActiveDocument.Variables(varDuplicateName)¶
If doc.Bookmarks.Exists(BookmarkName) Then¶
    'Calculate incremented name¶
    BookmarkName = Left(BookmarkName, _¶
    Len(BookmarkName) - Len(var.Value)) & var.Value¶
    var.Value = CStr(CLng(var.Value) + 1)¶
End If¶
CheckIfDuplicateName = BookmarkName¶
End Function¶
' * * * * *¶
Function varExists(doc As Word.Document, _¶
s As String) As Boolean¶
'Variable declaration¶
Dim var As Word.Variable¶
varExists = False¶
'Loop through the list of document variables¶
'and check whether it already exists by¶
'comparing the name¶
For Each var In doc.Variables¶
    If var.Name = s Then¶
        varExists = True¶
        Exit For¶
    End If¶
Next var¶
End Function¶
```

3. Create bookmarks in the template where the data items in the UserForm should be inserted (select the location, then Insert | Bookmark). The bookmark names should match the names of the text boxes in the form. In the sample, some of these are: txtRecipient, txtStreetAddress, and txtCity.

Tip: See the Creating a Bookmark from a Selection entry on page 260 for a tool to quickly create bookmarks from text selections.

---

4. To see and change the text box names in the Visual Basic Editor (VBE), click on a text box, and then look at the Name information in the Properties window (it will usually be the first entry listed). Type the correct name in the box if changes need to be made.
5. Insert a bookmark named txtStartBody in the location where the user should start typing once the macro has finished.
Deciding not to use a bookmark means that the macro will simply skip selecting the location if a bookmark isn't present.
6. Feel free to change the form to fit various requirements. Deleting and adding labels and text boxes will not affect the macro tool. Just be careful not to delete the buttons.
7. In the Visual Basic Editor (VBE), go to Tools | References and activate the checkbox next to one of the Microsoft ActiveX Data Object library entries. (As the code is very simple, the version of ADO is not significant. The sample document references the oldest version, 2.0.)
8. ADO connections are application-specific. If an Access table is used instead of an Excel workbook, a different connection ('conn' in the procedure 'FillStateList') is needed. Find the code for an Access connection in the tool in Mail Merge: Creating a One-to-Many List on page 205. For other database types, see the information on ADO OLE DB connections at http://www.able-consulting.com/tech.htm. If the data is in a Word table, see the code for generating an MS Graph chart in the Mail Merge: Merging with a Chart entry on page 215.
9. Set the .Visible property of the text box being replaced in the UserForm with the combo box to False. The text box is still needed on the UserForm so that Word can process the data to and from the corresponding bookmark.
10. Insert a combo box from the Forms toolbox. Position and size it. Give it a name; in the example, it is named 'cboState' and the corresponding text box is named 'txtState'.
11. In the procedure 'GetUserInput', substitute the names that were given to the combo boxes and text boxes in the lines following comments starting with !Substitute (three places).
12. In the procedure 'FillStateList', enter the information for the workbook in the four lines below the comment 'The relevant information for the Excel file.

13. The macro tool contains an 'AutoNew' procedure so that the UserForm appears whenever the user creates a new document from the template. Comment out the procedure if this is not wanted.
14. To make it easy to edit the input at a later time, assign the procedure 'GetUserInput' to a toolbar button. The macro automatically picks up the bookmarked content when it displays the UserForm. See Running a Macro from a Toolbar Button on page 418 for help in assigning a macro to a toolbar button.

Transferring Data from E-mail Attachments to Excel

By Suat Ozgur

This macro shows how to handle incoming e-mail messages in Outlook. It also illustrates how to read and write data between Excel workbooks.

Scenario: A workbook template is sent to all department heads. They are to fill in required information and then return the workbook. Now, you need an efficient way to retrieve the data and compile it.

This application tracks the e-mail messages. When the returned file meets the criteria in a received e-mail message (it is returned as the template file name in this sample code), then the application transfers the data in the returned file to a main data storage file.

Example file:
O006.xls and O006-1.xls

The code uses the Application_Startup event procedure to start tracking and creates an Items object to identify folder items for new e-mail messages. The assumptions in the sample code are listed below the code sections. These can be customized to implement the solution for special needs in a Class module declaration section.

Place the following code in the ThisOutlookSection class module (accessed by double-clicking the ThisOutlookSection title in the Project Explorer window (top left):

View the Appendix to learn how to store this procedure in a ThisOutlookSession Class module (in Outlook).

```
Option Explicit¶
' * * * * *¶
'Variable declaration¶
Dim myFolderEventsClass As clsFolderEvents¶
 ' * * * * *¶
Public Sub Application_Startup()¶
  'Create class object for handling received email items¶
  Set myFolderEventsClass = New clsFolderEvents¶
End Sub¶
```

Place the following code in a new Class module (Insert | Class Module from the menu bar). After creating it, rename it as clsFolderEvents by typing the name in the name box of the Properties window (bottom left):

```
Option Explicit¶
' * * * * *¶
Public WithEvents myOlItems As Outlook.Items¶
'Expected Attachment file name¶
'Distributed file to collect information¶
Const strFileName   As String = "0006-1.xls"¶
'Target file to write into¶
'Main workbook to collect received data in¶
Const strTargetFile As String = "C:\0006.xls"¶
 ' * * * * *¶
Private Sub Class_Initialize()¶
   Set myOlItems = Outlook.Session _¶
                  .GetDefaultFolder(olFolderInbox).Items¶
End Sub¶
' * * * * *¶
Private Sub myOlItems_ItemAdd(ByVal Item As Object)¶
'Outlook objects declaration¶
Dim objMail    As MailItem¶
Dim objAttachment  As Attachment¶
  'Verify if item is a MailItem¶
  If TypeName(Item) = "MailItem" Then¶
    'Set mail object¶
    Set objMail = Item¶
    'Loop in attachments to see if requested¶
    'file exists¶
    For Each objAttachment In objMail.Attachments¶
      If objAttachment.FileName = strFileName Then¶
        'Found requested attachment¶
        'Start process¶
        Call ExtractDataFile(objAttachment)¶
        'No need to continue since required¶
        'data has been transferred¶
        Exit Sub¶
      End If¶
    Next objAttachment¶
  End If¶
End Sub¶
```

```
' * * * * *¶
Private Sub ExtractDataFile(objAttachment As Attachment)¶
'This procedure reads the source file¶
'Adds/Updates data in main data workbook¶
'Saves attachment into temporary folder¶
'FileSystemObject Objects declaration¶
Dim fso         As Object¶
Dim strTempPath As String¶
Dim strFileName As String¶
  'Create File System Object¶
  'to retrieve temporary folder path¶
  Set fso = CreateObject("Scripting.FileSystemObject")¶
  ' = 2 Temporary Folder¶
  strTempPath = fso.GetSpecialFolder(2)¶
  Set fso = Nothing¶
  'Save attachment in temporary folder¶
  'by using a unique filename in Temp folder¶
  strFileName = strTempPath & "\" & _¶
                Format(Now, "ddmmyyhhmm") & ".xls"¶
  objAttachment.SaveAsFile strFileName¶
  'Call Read/Write module¶
  Call TransferData(strFileName)¶
End Sub¶
' * * * * *¶
Private Sub TransferData(strSourceFile As String)¶
'This module opens source and target workbooks¶
'and transfers requested data¶
'No need for an Excel Object Library reference¶
'since Late Binding is used¶
'Excel Application Object declarations¶
Dim xlsApp       As Object 'Excel Application¶
Dim wrkSource    As Object 'Source Workbook Object¶
Dim wrkTarget    As Object 'Target Workbook Object¶
Dim shtSource    As Object 'Source Worksheet Object¶
Dim shtTarget    As Object 'Target Worksheet Object¶
Dim rngSource    As Object 'Source Range Object¶
Dim rngTarget    As Object 'Target Cell Object¶
Dim cll          As Object 'Worksheet Cell object¶
  On Error GoTo ErrorHandler¶
  'Create new Excel Application¶
  Set xlsApp = CreateObject("Excel.Application")¶
  'Set source workbook¶
  Set wrkSource = xlsApp.workbooks.Open(strSourceFile)¶
  'Set source worksheet¶
  'It is supposed to be only one worksheet¶
  'So using index 1¶
  Set shtSource = wrkSource.Worksheets(1)¶
  'Set target workbook¶
  Set wrkTarget = xlsApp.workbooks.Open(strTargetFile)¶
```

```
    'Set target worksheet¶
    'It is supposed to be the first worksheet¶
    'So using index 1¶
    Set shtTarget = wrkTarget.Worksheets(1)¶
    'Source data is supposed to be in column B¶
    'B1:B5 range in sample workbook¶
    Set rngSource = shtSource.Range("$B$1:$B$5")¶
    'Target cell is the next empty cell¶
    'in target worksheet's column A¶
    'xlUp = -4162¶
    Set rngTarget = shtTarget.Cells(65536, 1) _¶
                    .End(-4162).Offset(1)¶
    'Loop through source data cells¶
    For Each cll In rngSource.Cells¶
      With rngTarget¶
        'Transfer data into corresponding column¶
        'Data order is trasposed version of source range¶
        .Cells(1, cll.Row).Value = cll.Value¶
      End With¶
    Next cll¶
    'Close workbook objects and free memory¶
    wrkSource.Close False¶
    wrkTarget.Close True¶
    'Delete temporary source workbook¶
    Kill strSourceFile¶
ExitSub:¶
    'Quit Excel Application that has been¶
    'created in this code¶
    If Not xlsApp Is Nothing Then¶
      xlsApp.Quit¶
    End If¶
    Exit Sub¶
ErrorHandler:¶
    'Critical error¶
    MsgBox Err.Number & "-" & Err.Description, _¶
           vbOKOnly + vbExclamation, "Error"¶
    GoTo ExitSub¶
End Sub¶
```

Cmb

The first code section goes in the class module ThisOutlookSession. The second code section goes in the class module clsFolderEvents.

Note: The strTargetFile: "C:\O006.xls" and the strFileName: "O006-1.xls" should be changed to the desired path and name of the Excel file that stores the data.

This macro runs automatically.

To test this sample code, follow these steps:

1. Copy the O006.xls file into the C:\ folder and send the O006-1.xls file (with some data in it) as an attachment to yourself.

2. Quit Outlook to stop the write access to the O006.xls file before opening it to enter data. Alternatively, a copy of this file can be used for reporting. To disable the functionality of this macro, delete the Application_Startup event procedure code and restart the Outlook application.

Creating Word Labels from an Excel Recipient List

By Suat Ozgur

This is a sample application that shows processing an Excel data range and creating a mailing label document for the requested number of labels by using selected label product. It also demonstrates a progress bar application.

Example file:
O013.xls

The sample code requires the following data sheet column structure.

	A	B	C	D	E	F	G
1	**Name**	**Address**	**City**	**State**	**Zip**	**Country**	**Label Qty**
2	Name1 LastName1	Address1	City1	State1	10000-01	Country1	60
3	Name2 LastName2	Address2	City2	State2	10000-02	Country2	30
4	Name3 LastName3	Address3	City3	State3	10000-03	Country3	21
5	Name4 LastName4	Address4	City4	State4	10000-04	Country4	15
6	Name5 LastName5	Address5	City5	State5	10000-05	Country5	10
7	Name6 LastName6	Address6	City6	State6	10000-06	Country6	0
8	Name7 LastName7	Address7	City7	State7	10000-07	Country7	11
9	Name8 LastName8	Address8	City8	State8	10000-08	Country8	25
10							
11							
12							
13							

Figure 101 – Setting up the Label Maker

Place the following code in a standard module in the Excel file that contains the data.

View the Appendix to learn how to store this procedure in a Standard module (Excel)

```
Option Explicit¶
' * * * * *¶
Public blnUserCancel As Boolean¶
Sub ShowForm()¶
  'Show UserForm¶
  blnUserCancel = False¶
  frmMain.Show¶
End Sub¶
```

Place the following code in the form module of the form that will use it. Access this module by double-clicking the form in the Visual Basic Editor (VBE) code window, or right-clicking the name of the form in the Project window (top left) of the VBE. To display the form in the VBE code window, double-click the form's name in the Project window (top left).

```
Option Explicit¶
' * * * * *¶
Private Sub UserForm_Initialize()¶
  'Reset Progress Bar label width¶
  Me.lblProgressBar.Width = 0¶
End Sub¶
' * * * * *¶
Private Sub cmdStart_Click()¶
  'Disable command button¶
  Me.cmdStart.Enabled = False¶
  'Call main routine¶
  Call StartLabelPrint¶
  'It's done. Quit application.¶
  Unload Me¶
End Sub¶
' * * * * * *¶
Sub StartLabelPrint()¶
'Word objects declaration¶
Dim objApp    As Word.Application¶
Dim objDoc    As Word.Document¶
Dim objDefDoc As Word.Document¶
'Excel objects declaration¶
Dim objSht As Excel.Worksheet¶
Dim objRng As Excel.Range¶
Dim objRow As Excel.Range¶
'variable declaration¶
Dim lngQTY       As Single  'Total label count¶
Dim lngPage      As Single  'Word Page count¶
Dim intLabelRow As Integer 'Label row indicator¶
Dim i As Long          'Counter¶
Dim j As Long          'Counter¶
'Variable declarations for progress bar¶
Dim lngJobCount   As Long   'Total job count¶
Dim sngUnitWidth  As Single 'Unit width for progress bar¶
```

Cmb

```
'Variable declaration for labels¶
Dim intCols     As Integer¶
Dim intRows     As Integer¶
Dim totCols     As Integer¶
Dim totRows     As Integer¶
Dim sngMaxDim   As Single¶
Dim sngMinDim   As Single¶
Dim tblIndex    As Integer¶
  On Error GoTo ErrHandler¶
  'Working in active worksheet¶
  Set objSht = Excel.ActiveSheet¶
  'Set Data Range¶
  With objSht¶
    Set objRng = .Range(.Cells(2, 1), _¶
      .Cells(65536, 1).End(xlUp))¶
  End With¶
  'Calculate total label count¶
  lngQTY = Application.WorksheetFunction.Sum(objRng. _¶
     Offset(, 6))¶
  'Total job count to do (for progress bar)¶
    'Opening Word Application            = 1¶
    'Preparing document                  = 1¶
    'Creating empty labels               = 1¶
    'Writing into labels                 = lngQty¶
  lngJobCount = lngQTY + 1 + 1 + 3¶
  'Progress unit width on progress bar¶
  'Completed width of progress bar is equal to¶
  'background frame width¶
  sngUnitWidth = Me.fraProgressBack.Width / lngJobCount¶
  'Create Word application object¶
  Set objApp = New Word.Application¶
  'Update progress bar and status message¶
  Call UpdateProgressBar("Creating Word Application", _¶
    1 * sngUnitWidth)¶
  'Start working in Word Application¶
  With objApp¶
    Call UpdateProgressBar("Preparing Word Document", _¶
      2 * sngUnitWidth)¶
    'Create new document in Word¶
    'This is a temporary document object that¶
    'we are using to create the new mailing label document¶
    Set objDefDoc = .Documents.Add¶
    'Create mailing label document¶
    With .MailingLabel¶
      .DefaultPrintBarCode = False¶
      'wdPrinterManualFeed = 4¶
      Set objDoc = .CreateNewDocument(Me.txtProduct.Text _¶
        , "", "", 4)¶
      'Close the temporary document¶
      objDefDoc.Close False¶
    End With¶
```

```
Call UpdateProgressBar("Creating Empty Labels", _¶
  3 * sngUnitWidth)¶
'Calculating the actual number of labels in a single page¶
'This is accomplished by comparing column widths and row¶
'heights.  If there are differences of widths or heights¶
'then it means there is a distance between two labels¶
  With objDoc.Tables(1)¶
  intCols = .Columns.Count¶
  For i = 1 To intCols¶
    If .Columns(i).Width < sngMaxDim Then¶
      sngMinDim = .Columns(i).Width¶
    Else¶
      sngMaxDim = .Columns(i).Width¶
    End If¶
  Next i¶
  If sngMaxDim = sngMinDim Or intCols = 1 _¶
    Or sngMinDim = 0 Then¶
    'If column widths are same or there is only one column¶
    'then there are actual number of columns for labels¶
    totCols = intCols¶
  Else¶
    'There is distance between two labels¶
    totCols = (intCols + 1) / 2¶
  End If¶
  'Same comparison using Rows¶
  sngMinDim = 0: sngMaxDim = 0¶
  intRows = .Rows.Count¶
  For i = 1 To intRows¶
    If .Rows(i).Height < sngMaxDim Then¶
      sngMinDim = .Rows(i).Height¶
    Else¶
      sngMaxDim = .Rows(i).Height¶
    End If¶
  Next i¶
  If sngMaxDim = sngMinDim Or intRows = 1 _¶
    Or sngMinDim = 0 Then¶
    totRows = intRows¶
  Else¶
    totRows = (intRows + 1) / 2¶
  End If¶
End With¶
'Total necessary page count determined by total label count¶
lngPage = lngQTY / (totCols * totRows)¶
'Round the page count if necessary¶
If Int(lngPage) < lngPage Then¶
  lngPage = Int(lngPage) + 1¶
Else¶
  lngPage = Int(lngPage)¶
End If¶
```

```
        'Only one page is created so far.¶
        'Now, copy the same page¶
        '(with label structure in it) the necessary¶
        'number of times for page count calculated above.¶
        With .Selection¶
          .WholeStory¶
          .Copy¶
          For i = 1 To lngPage - 1¶
              'wdStory = 6¶
              .HomeKey 6¶
              .InsertBreak 7¶
              .HomeKey 6¶
              .Paste¶
          Next i¶
        End With¶
      End With¶
      'Processed job count so far¶
      j = 3¶
      i = 0¶
      intLabelRow = 1¶
      tblIndex = 1¶
      'Loop through Excel data range¶
      For Each objRow In objRng.Rows¶
        DoEvents¶
        'Increment processed job count¶
        j = j + 1¶
        Call UpdateProgressBar("Printing labels for : " & _¶
          objRow.Cells(1, 1).Value, j * sngUnitWidth)¶
        'Validate if quantity cell doesn't include a numeric value¶
        If IsNumeric(objRow.Offset(, 6)) Then¶
          'Fill necessary number of selected row in data range¶
          'column 6 - column G shows the total necessary label count¶
          'to print for the corresponding name in the sample code¶
          For i = i To objRow.Offset(, 6) - 1 + i¶
            'Check if user closed the form¶
            'and exit application if requested¶
            'otherwise continue until all¶
            'labels are created even if form is closed¶
            If blnUserCancel Then¶
              With objApp¶
                .Selection.HomeKey 6¶
                .Visible = True¶
              End With¶
              Exit Sub¶
            End If¶
            j = j + 1¶
            Call UpdateProgressBar("", j * sngUnitWidth)¶
```

```
        'Fill in the label with data¶
        'Following code line in this section¶
        'determines if there are empty columns between labels¶
        '***i Mod totCols) * (1 - (intCols <> intRows)) + 1***¶
        objDoc.Tables(tblIndex).Cell(intLabelRow, _¶
            (i Mod totCols) * (1 - (intCols <> intRows)) + 1) _¶
            .Range.Text = objRow.Cells(1, 1).Value & vbCrLf & _¶
            objRow.Cells(1, 2).Value & ", " & _¶
            objRow.Cells(1, 3).Value & " " & _¶
            objRow.Cells(1, 4).Value & vbCrLf & _¶
            objRow.Cells(1, 5).Value & vbCrLf & _¶
            objRow.Cells(1, 6).Value¶
        If ((i + 1) Mod totCols) = 0 Then¶
          'If there is no space between labels (vertically)¶
          'then just increment 1 row¶
          'Following comparison determines this in code line¶
          '*** (intRows = totRows) ***¶
          intLabelRow = intLabelRow + 1 - (intRows <> totRows)¶
          If intLabelRow > objDoc.Tables(tblIndex).Rows.Count Then¶
            tblIndex = tblIndex + 1¶
            intLabelRow = 1¶
          End If¶
        End If¶
      Next i¶
    End If¶
    'Decrease job count¶
    j = j - 1¶
  Next objRow¶
  'Labels have been created¶
  With objApp¶
    'Goto top of the label document¶
    .Selection.HomeKey 6¶
    'Show Word application¶
    .Visible = True¶
  End With¶
  'Inform user about completition¶
  Me.lblStatus.Caption = "Done!"¶
ErrHandler:¶
  If Err Then¶
    'This error means that user entered a label product name¶
    'that does not exist in Word's label products¶
    If Err.Number = 5843 Then¶
      MsgBox "Selected label product does not exist.", _¶
                vbOKOnly + vbExclamation, "Error"¶
    Else¶
      'Other error¶
      MsgBox "There is something wrong." & vbCrLf & _¶
              Err.Number & "-" & Err.Description, _¶
              vbOKOnly + vbExclamation, "Error"¶
    End If¶
```

Cmb

```
    'If this section has been reached by error¶
    'The Word application should be quit¶
    'it is not visible yet.¶
    'otherwise there will be an invisible Word session¶
    'listed in Task Manager¶
    If Not objApp Is Nothing Then¶
      objApp.Quit False¶
    End If¶
  End If¶
End Sub¶
' * * * * *¶
Private Sub UpdateProgressBar(strStatus As String, _¶
                                currWidth As Single)¶
  With Me¶
    'Increase progress bar width¶
    .lblProgressBar.Width = currWidth¶
    'Change caption of progress bar¶
    .lblProgressBar.Caption = Format(currWidth / _¶
                    .fraProgressBack.Width, "0%")¶
    'Change status text if it is requested¶
    If Not strStatus = "" Then¶
      .lblStatus.Caption = strStatus¶
    End If¶
    .Repaint¶
  End With¶
End Sub¶
' * * * * *¶
Private Sub UserForm_QueryClose(Cancel As Integer, CloseMode As Integer)¶
  blnUserCancel = True¶
End Sub¶
```

Place the first section of code in a standard module of the Excel spreadsheet that has the label information and the second section of code in the form module of the 'frmMain'.

Note: This sample requires a reference to the Microsoft Word Object Library to be set (because early binding is used). If Office has been custom-installed, this may need to be set in the Visual Basic Editor under Tools | References | Microsoft Word x.x Object Library.

Creating Custom Mail Merge Using Data in Excel Worksheet

By Suat Ozgur

This code shows how to create a custom mail merge instead of using Word's internal Mail Merge feature. A new document is created to include more than one mail merge document with related records.

Scenario: To use this method in a document, create bookmarks in the appropriate Word documents. Use field names that correspond with Excel column headers. The code simply searches for the bookmark names in the Excel columns. Then the code uses the column header to return the data for the related record. Finally, the code creates a continuous document even though multiple merge documents are being used.

Example file:
O014.xls
Code/data workbook/sheet for mail merge;
O014-1.doc
Word Template;
O014-2.doc
Word Template

The following code goes in a standard module of the Microsoft Excel worksheet that houses the merge data. Access the Visual Basic Editor by pressing Alt + F11, by using the Tools | Macro | Visual Basic Editor menu option, or by right-clicking the worksheet tab and selecting View Code from the pop up menu. Once the VBE is open, select Insert | Module from the menu bar. In the window in the top right side, place the following code (either type it in or cut and paste it).

Note: The example file already has the code in place.

Cmb

```
Option Explicit¶
' * * * * *¶
Public Sub MailMerge()¶
'Word application objects declaration¶
Dim wrdApp      As Object 'Word.Application¶
Dim objDoc      As Object 'Word.Document¶
Dim objTemplate As Object 'Word.Document¶
Dim objBookMark As Object 'Word.Bookmark¶
'Excel application objects declaration¶
Dim sht As Excel.Worksheet¶
Dim rng As Excel.Range¶
Dim cll As Excel.Range¶
Dim fnd As Excel.Range¶
Dim strFileName As String¶
```

```
  'Using activesheet¶
  Set sht = ActiveSheet¶
  'Set data range¶
  Set rng = sht.Range(sht.Cells(2, 1), sht.Cells(65536, 1).End(xlUp))¶
  'Create new word application¶
  Set wrdApp = CreateObject("Word.Application")¶
  'Create new document¶
  Set objDoc = wrdApp.Documents.Add¶
  'Loop in data range¶
  For Each cll In rng.Cells¶
    'Retrieve file name - 6 columns from the first column¶
    strFileName = cll.Offset(, 6).Value¶
    'If file name doesn't include path information¶
    'then use this workbook's path by assuming the merge files¶
    'are saved in this folder¶
    If InStr(strFileName, "\") = 0 Then¶
      strFileName = ThisWorkbook.Path & "\" & strFileName¶
    End If¶
    'Insert requested file into the main document¶
    wrdApp.Selection.InsertFile strFileName¶
    'Find all bookmarks and put the corresponding values¶
    'for these bookmarks¶
    For Each objBookMark In objDoc.Bookmarks¶
      'Corresponding header found in first row ?¶
      Set fnd = sht.Rows(1).Find(objBookMark.Name, LookIn:=xlValues, _¶
        LookAt:=xlWhole)¶
      If Not fnd Is Nothing Then¶
        'Data column is found. Put date instead bookmark¶
        'this action also removes bookmark¶
        'so new inserted document's bookmark will be the¶
        'unique bookmark¶
        objBookMark.Range.Text = cll.Offset(, fnd.Column - 1).Value¶
      End If¶
    Next objBookMark¶
    'Goto next page¶
    'wdPageBreak = 7¶
    wrdApp.Selection.InsertBreak 7¶
  Next cll¶
  wrdApp.Selection.TypeBackspace¶
  'wdStory = 6¶
  'Goto begining of the document¶
  wrdApp.Selection.HomeKey 6¶
  'Display word document¶
  wrdApp.Visible = True¶
  wrdApp.Activate¶
End Sub¶
```

Create Word documents with bookmarks for the fields that will be merged.

Using Calendar Control for Office Applications

By Suat Ozgur

This sample code shows a custom calendar that would make it easy for a user to select a date from it.

> **Scenario:** When using Excel or Word it is handy to have a calendar you can use to place a date in the worksheet or document you are working in.

Example file:
O015.doc and
O015.xls

To use this control in applications, transfer the clsCalendar, frmCalendar, and basCalendar objects from the sample documents into the worksheet or document in which it will be used.

Place the following code in the basCalendar module. This is a Standard module that has been renamed basCalendar using the name box in the properties window (bottom left) of the Visual Basic Editor (VBE). This can be imported and exported for use in other projects.

```
Option Explicit¶
' * * * * *¶
Public Sub ShowForm()¶
  With frmCalendar¶
    .Show¶
  End With¶
End Sub¶
```

Insert the following code in the UserForm module of UserForm frmCalendar.

```
Option Explicit¶
'forces variable declaration¶
Private cvarValue    As Date¶
Private cVarCDay     As Byte      'Day¶
Private cVarCMonth   As Byte      'Month¶
Private cVarCYear    As Integer   'Year¶
Private cVarDayBackColor   As Long  'Day backcolor¶
Private cVarDayForeColor   As Long  'Day forecolor¶
Private cVarSelBackColor   As Long  'Selected backcolor¶
Private cVarSelForeColor   As Long  'Selected forecolor¶
Private cVarSelBackToday   As Long  'Today backcolor¶
Private cVarSelForeToday   As Long  'Today forecolor¶
Private cVarDisForeColor   As Long  'Disabled forecolor¶
Private cVarBackColor      As Long  'Calendar backcolor¶
Private cVarForeColor      As Long  'Calendar forecolor¶
```

Cmb

```
'An object array is needed to handle every¶
'day controls' events¶
Dim dayArray()  As clsCalendar¶
' * * * * *¶
Private Sub SetDefaults()¶
'Day cells¶
'Create Controls class object to create new controls on the fly¶
Dim objControl As New clsCalendar¶
Dim objDays     As clsCalendar¶
Dim lbl         As MSForms.Label¶
'Counter variables¶
Dim i As Integer¶
Dim j As Integer¶
  With Me¶
    'There are 6 rows and 7 columns for a month view¶
    For i = 1 To 6¶
      For j = 1 To 7¶
        ReDim Preserve dayArray((j - 1) + ((i - 1) * 7))¶
        Set objDays = New clsCalendar¶
        Set lbl = .fraBack.Controls.Add("Forms.Label.1", _¶
            "day" & Trim(Str((j - 1) + ((i - 1) * 7))), True)¶
        With lbl¶
          .Width = 17¶
          .Height = 11.25¶
          .Left = (j - 1) * .Width¶
          .Top = 16 + (i - 1) * (.Height + 3)¶
          .Caption = i & j¶
          .FontSize = 8¶
          .TextAlign = 2¶
        End With¶
        'Set the Controls object's day control as¶
        'the one that has been created above¶
        Set objDays.DayCell = lbl¶
        'Put it into array control¶
        Set dayArray(UBound(dayArray)) = objDays¶
      Next j¶
    Next i¶
    'Add month names into the drop-down box¶
    For i = 1 To 12¶
      .cmbMonth.AddItem MonthName(i)¶
    Next i¶
    'Spinbutton limits¶
    With .spnYear¶
      .Max = 2099¶
      .Min = 1980¶
    End With¶
  End With¶
End Sub¶
' * * * * *¶
Public Sub ChangeDay(DayCell As MSForms.Label)¶
```

mb

```
'This is the event that is triggered by¶
'clicking day control¶
  'If selected day is after the max year¶
  'of this application then do not let it execute¶
  If Year(CLng(DayCell.Tag)) > Me.spnYear.Max _¶
      Or Year(CLng(DayCell.Tag)) < Me.spnYear.Min _¶
      Then Exit Sub¶
  'Set calendar value as selected day¶
  'Remember day controls' tag has been set¶
  'as the long value of the related date¶
  Me.Value = CLng(DayCell.Tag)¶
  If DayCell.ForeColor = cVarDisForeColor Then¶
    'If clicked day control belongs to previous or next¶
    'month then month view should be redrawn¶
    'This is handled by verifying if clicked control's¶
    'forecolor is the disabled day forecolor¶
    Call SelectDate¶
  Else¶
    'Changing in same month¶
    'Just change the selected date on view¶
    Call MarkDate(DayCell)¶
  End If¶
End Sub¶
' * * * * *¶
Public Sub SelectDate()¶
'Variable declaration¶
Dim cnt   As MSForms.Label¶
Dim selStart  As Long¶
Dim selEnd    As Long¶
Dim disStart  As Long¶
Dim disEnd    As Long¶
'Counter variables¶
Dim i As Long¶
Dim j As Long¶
  'The first day of the selected month¶
  selStart = DateSerial(cVarCYear, cVarCMonth, 1)¶
  'The last day of the selected month¶
  selEnd = DateSerial(cVarCYear, cVarCMonth + 1, 0)¶
  'Find which date shows for the previous month as disabled¶
  disStart = selStart - Weekday(selStart) + 1¶
  disEnd = DateSerial(cVarCYear, cVarCMonth, 0)¶
  With Me¶
    'Loop each control on UserForm¶
     For Each cnt In .fraBack.Controls¶
      'If control is not a day caption then reset¶
      'back and fore colors¶
      If cnt.Tag <> "caption" Then¶
        cnt.BackColor = cVarDayBackColor¶
        cnt.ForeColor = cVarDayForeColor¶
      End If¶
    Next cnt¶
```

Cmb

```
'Start from the previous month¶
'Show disabled the previos month's days¶
For i = disEnd - disStart To 0 Step -1¶
  With .fraBack.Controls("day" & Trim(i))¶
    .ForeColor = cVarDisForeColor¶
    .Caption = Day(disEnd - (disEnd - disStart - i))¶
    .Tag = disEnd - (disEnd - disStart - i)¶
  End With¶
Next i¶
'Show selected month's days¶
'i variable is the long value of the¶
'related day¶
For i = selStart To selEnd¶
  With .fraBack.Controls("day" & _¶
    Trim(Weekday(selStart) - 1 + i - selStart))¶
    .Caption = Day(i)¶
    'Store this day's long value in Tag property¶
    'to know which day is assigned for this control¶
    .Tag = i¶
    'If i meets the selected date of calendar¶
    'then set back and fore colors of this control¶
    If i = cvarValue Then¶
        If i = Date Then¶
          'If selected date is today, then use special colors¶
          'assigned for Today¶
          .BackColor = cVarSelBackToday¶
          .ForeColor = cVarSelForeToday¶
        Else¶
          'Use selected day colors¶
          .BackColor = cVarSelBackColor¶
          .ForeColor = cVarSelForeColor¶
        End If¶
    End If¶
  End With¶
Next i¶
'Continue with next month¶
'Show disabled the next month's days¶
For i = Weekday(selStart) + selEnd - selStart To 41¶
  j = j + 1¶
  With .fraBack.Controls("day" & Trim(i))¶
    .ForeColor = cVarDisForeColor¶
    .Caption = j¶
    .Tag = CLng(DateSerial(cVarCYear, cVarCMonth + 1, j))¶
  End With¶
Next i¶
'Set selected month value in drop-down control¶
.cmbMonth.ListIndex = cVarCMonth - 1¶
'Set spin button value as selected year¶
.spnYear.Value = Year(cvarValue)¶
```

```
      'Change caption of UserForm to show the selected day¶
      .Caption = Format(cvarValue, "mmmm dd, yyyy")¶
    End With¶
End Sub¶
' * * * * *¶
Private Sub MarkDate(DayCell As MSForms.Label)¶
'If day is changing but month is not¶
'then this procedure will simply mark the¶
'selected day on UserForm¶
'No need to change month or year controls¶
'and also no need to change month view since¶
'same month is still needed¶
Dim cnt As MSForms.Label¶
  With Me¶
    'Set day back and fore colors as default to not selected¶
    For Each cnt In .fraBack.Controls¶
      If cnt.Tag <> "caption" Then¶
        If cnt.BackColor <> cVarDayBackColor Then¶
          cnt.BackColor = cVarDayBackColor¶
          cnt.ForeColor = cVarDayForeColor¶
        End If¶
      End If¶
    Next cnt¶
    'Set selected days (Value) back and fore color¶
    If cvarValue = Date Then¶
      'If selected date is today, then use special colors¶
      'assigned for Today¶
      DayCell.BackColor = cVarSelBackToday¶
      DayCell.ForeColor = cVarSelForeToday¶
    Else¶
      'Use selected day colors¶
      DayCell.BackColor = cVarSelBackColor¶
      DayCell.ForeColor = cVarSelForeColor¶
    End If¶
    'Change caption of UserForm to show the selected day¶
    .Caption = Format(cvarValue, "mmmm dd, yyyy")¶
  End With¶
End Sub¶
' * * * * *¶
Private Sub cmbMonth_Click()¶
'This is the event that is triggered by¶
'changing the month drop-down control¶
  With Me¶
    'If the selected day is in the range of the newly¶
    'selected month then there is no problem¶
    'However if selected day is 31 and the next month¶
    'has only 30 days then this should be handled¶
    If Month(DateSerial(cVarCYear, .cmbMonth.ListIndex + 1, _¶
      cVarCDay)) <> .cmbMonth.ListIndex + 1 Then¶
```

Cmb

```
      'Selected day is not existing in newly selected month¶
      'Set the last day of month¶
      Me.Value = CLng(DateSerial(cVarCYear, _¶
       .cmbMonth.ListIndex + 2, 0))¶
    Else¶
      'We can use the same day number¶
      'It is in range of the next month¶
      Me.Value = CLng(DateSerial(cVarCYear, _¶
              .cmbMonth.ListIndex + 1, cVarCDay))¶
    End If¶
    'Change month view¶
    Call SelectDate¶
  End With¶
End Sub¶
' * * * * *¶
Private Sub cmdOK_Click()¶
  'Close calendar¶
  Unload Me¶
End Sub¶
' * * * * *¶
Private Sub cmdToday_Click()¶
  'Set calendar value as today¶
  'and repaint calendar by using selected date¶
  Me.Value = Date¶
  Call SelectDate¶
End Sub¶
' * * * * *¶
Private Sub spnYear_Change()¶
'This is the event that is triggered by¶
'clicking the year spin control¶
  With Me¶
    'Set year textbox value¶
    .txtYear.Value = .spnYear.Value¶
    'If the selected day is in the range of the newly¶
    'selected month then there is no problem¶
    'However if selected day is 31 and the next month¶
    'has only 30 days then this should be handled¶
    If cVarCMonth <> .cmbMonth.ListIndex + 1 Then¶
      'Selected day does not exist in newly selected month¶
      'Set to the last day of month¶
      Me.Value = CLng(DateSerial(.spnYear.Value, _¶
        .cmbMonth.ListIndex + 2, 0))¶
    Else¶
      'Use the same day number¶
      'It is in range of the next month¶
      Me.Value = CLng(DateSerial(.spnYear.Value, _¶
        .cmbMonth.ListIndex + 1, cVarCDay))¶
    End If¶
    'Change month view¶
    Call SelectDate¶
  End With¶
```

```
End Sub¶
' * * * * *¶
Private Sub UserForm_Activate()¶
  If Me.cmbMonth.ListIndex = -1 Then¶
    Call SelectDate¶
  End If¶
End Sub¶
' * * * * *¶
Private Sub UserForm_Initialize()¶
  Me.Value = CLng(Date)¶
  'Set default colors for objects¶
  cVarDayBackColor = &HFFFFFF¶
  cVarDayForeColor = &H80000012¶
  cVarSelBackColor = &H8000000D¶
  cVarSelForeColor = &HFFFFFF¶
  cVarSelBackToday = &HFF&¶
  cVarSelForeToday = &HFFFFFF¶
  cVarDisForeColor = &H80000010¶
  cVarBackColor = &HFFFFFF¶
  cVarForeColor = &H80000012¶
  Call SetDefaults¶
End Sub¶
' * * * * *¶
Public Property Let Value(ByVal vNewValue As Date)¶
  'Set calendar value and¶
  'assign related day, month and year variables¶
  'by using current value of calendar¶
  cvarValue = vNewValue¶
  cVarCYear = Year(cvarValue)¶
  cVarCMonth = Month(cvarValue)¶
  cVarCDay = Day(cvarValue)¶
End Property¶
' * * * * *¶
Public Property Get Value() As Date¶
  'Return form's Value property¶
  Value = cvarValue¶
End Property¶
' * * * * *¶
Private Sub UserForm_QueryClose(Cancel As Integer, CloseMode As Integer)¶
'variable declaration¶
Dim selcell As Object¶
  If CloseMode = 0 Then Exit Sub¶
  'Continue when error occurs¶
  On Error Resume Next¶
  'Different actions for Excel and Word¶
  If Application.Name = "Microsoft Excel" Then¶
    Set selcell = Selection¶
    selcell.Cells(1, 1).Value = Me.Value¶
  ElseIf Application.Name = "Microsoft Word" Then¶
    Selection.typetext Me.Value¶
```

```
  Else¶
    MsgBox Me.Value¶
  End If¶
End Sub¶
' * * * * *¶
Public Sub CloseForm()¶
  'Close calendar¶
  Unload Me¶
End Sub¶
```

Place the following code in a class module. Tools | Insert | Class Module from the menu bar will insert a class module in the selected VBAProject. Rename the class module using the name box in the Properties window (lower left) of the VBE. The new name should be clsControls.

```
Option Explicit¶
' * * * * *¶
'Form control to handle day clicks¶
'These controls are created on the fly¶
Public WithEvents DayCell   As MSForms.Label¶
' * * * * *¶
Private Sub DayCell_Click()¶
  'Day is changed¶
  'Call parent's related procedure to change¶
  'the selected day¶
  Call DayCell.Parent.Parent.ChangeDay(DayCell)¶
End Sub¶
' * * * * *¶
Private Sub DayCell_DblClick(ByVal Cancel As _¶
  MSForms.ReturnBoolean)¶
  'Double-click means select and quit calendar¶
  'Call parent's related procedure to change¶
  'the selected day and quit calendar¶
  'If it is a day out of selected month range then¶
  'it will not execute double-click since the month¶
  'view will be changed and second click will be¶
  'finalized on the new month view¶
  Call DayCell.Parent.Parent.ChangeDay(DayCell)¶
  Call DayCell.Parent.Parent.CloseForm¶
End Sub¶
```

If you are using Excel, place the following code in the ThisWorkbook module. Access this module by double-clicking the ThisWorkbook title in the Project Explorer window (top left) or right-clicking the ThisWorkbook title and selecting View Code from the drop-down menu. If you are using Word, see the following page.

```
Option Explicit¶
' * * * * *¶
Public Sub CreateCommandBar()¶
'Variable declaration¶
Dim cmdBar As CommandBar¶
Dim cmdButton As CommandBarButton¶
  Call RemoveCommandBar¶
  Set cmdBar = Application.CommandBars.Add("Calendar", Temporary:=True)¶
  Set cmdButton = cmdBar.Controls.Add(msoControlButton)¶
  With cmdButton¶
    'Caption to display on button¶
    .Caption = "Calendar"¶
    'Procedure name to run when button is clicked¶
    .OnAction = "ShowForm"¶
    'Style of new command bar button¶
    .Style = msoButtonCaption¶
    'Show new button¶
    .Visible = True¶
  End With¶
  cmdBar.Visible = True¶
End Sub¶
' * * * * *¶
Public Sub RemoveCommandBar()¶
  'Continue when error occurs¶
  On Error Resume Next¶
  'Remove custom control button¶
  Application.CommandBars("Calendar").Delete¶
End Sub¶
' * * * * *¶
Private Sub Workbook_BeforeClose(Cancel As Boolean)¶
  Call RemoveCommandBar¶
End Sub¶
' * * * * *¶
Private Sub Workbook_Open()¶
  Call CreateCommandBar¶
End Sub¶
```

Cmb

If you are using Word, place the following code in the ThisDocument module. Access this module by double-clicking the ThisDocument title in the Project Explorer window (top left) or right-clicking the ThisDocument title and selecting View Code from the drop-down menu.

```
Option Explicit¶
' * * * * *¶
Public Sub CreateCommandBar()¶
'Variable declaration¶
Dim cmdBar As CommandBar¶
```

```
Dim cmdButton As CommandBarButton¶
  Call RemoveCommandBar¶
  Set cmdBar = Application.CommandBars.Add("Calendar", Temporary:=True)¶
  Set cmdButton = cmdBar.Controls.Add(msoControlButton)¶
  With cmdButton¶
    'Caption to display on button¶
    .Caption = "Calendar"¶
    'Procedure name to run when button is clicked¶
    .OnAction = "ShowForm"¶
    'Style of new command bar button¶
    .Style = msoButtonCaption¶
    'Show new button¶
    .Visible = True¶
  End With¶
  cmdBar.Visible = True¶
End Sub¶
' * * * * *¶
Public Sub RemoveCommandBar()¶
  'Error handler if control is not existing¶
  On Error Resume Next¶
  'Remove custom control button¶
  Application.CommandBars("Calendar").Delete¶
End Sub¶
' * * * * *¶
Private Sub Document_Close()¶
  Call RemoveCommandBar¶
End Sub¶
' * * * * *¶
Private Sub Document_Open()¶
  Call CreateCommandBar¶
End Sub¶
```

The code for this application has four sections. Each must be placed in a specific place.

1. The first section of code goes in a bas module called basCalendar. The code shows the UserForm when the calendar needs to be displayed.
2. The second section of code goes in the calendar form called frmCalendar. This code allows the form to be dynamic in nature (allowing the selection of dates from months within the range defined in the code – 1980 to 2099).
3. The third section of code goes in a class module called clsCalendar. This code is where the class controls required to use the calendar reside.
4. The fourth section of code goes in the ThisX module (where X is either Workbook or Document, depending on the application) of the project.

This code creates and removes the menu with a button that launches the calendar.

To run the macro, click the button on the custom menu.

Note: This calendar is NOT the ActiveX calendar control that can be programmed via VBA. That calendar requires a reference to be set in order to work properly. This causes problems with users who operate older versions of Office. This calendar should avoid that difficulty.

nb

Appendix A

Opening and Using the Visual Basic Editor

You can open the Visual Basic Editor (VBE) from within any Microsoft application by either of two methods. You can either go to the Tools menu and chose Macro | Visual Basic Editor, (as shown below,) or just use the keyboard shortcut: Alt+F11.

Note: Some keyboards have F-Lock keys. On reboot, you must hit this key to turn that feature off, so that Alt+F11 and other keyboard shortcuts using Function keys work properly.

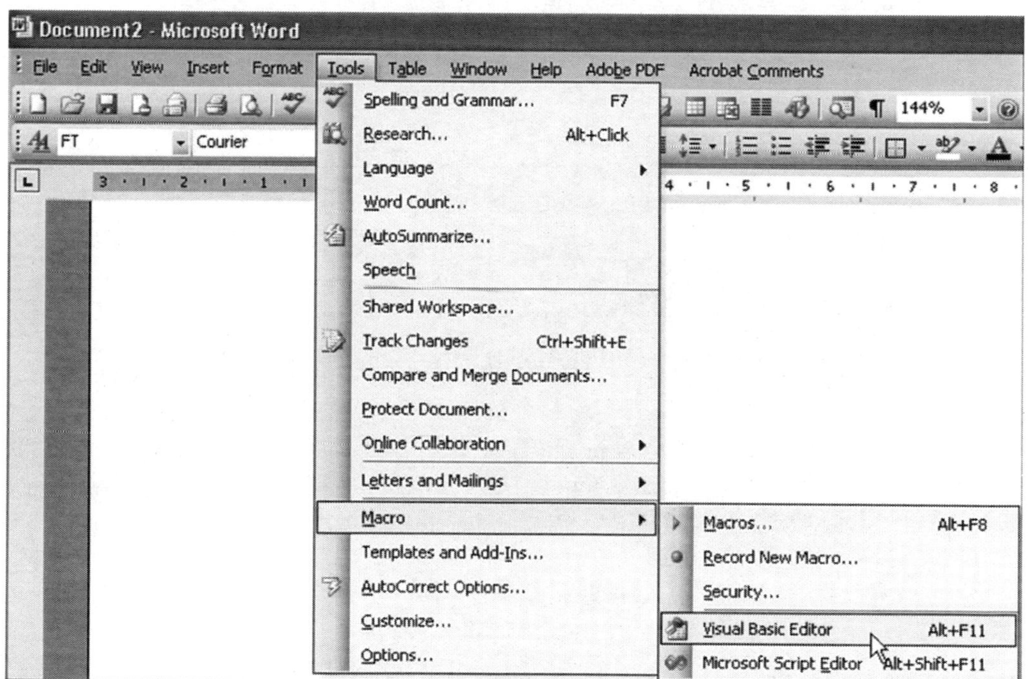

Figure 102 – Opening Visual Basic Editor

Once you have opened the VBE, you will see a screen similar to the one on the following page. If you do not see the Project Explorer—the window shown on the left side—press Ctrl+R to open it.

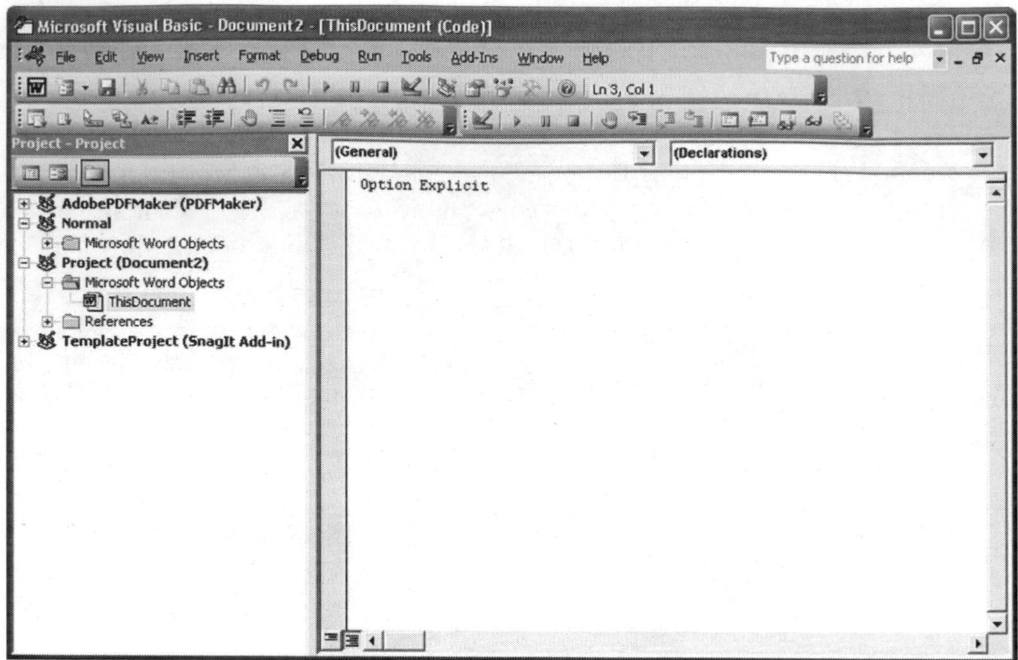

Figure 103 – VBE with Project Explorer

Locating the Code Object

Open the VBE by hitting Alt+F11. Refer to the Project Explorer window at the left.

The Project Explorer works very much like Windows Explorer. Locate the project (file) you are working on. By clicking once on the little + signs, you can drill down to locate the module or UserForm you need.

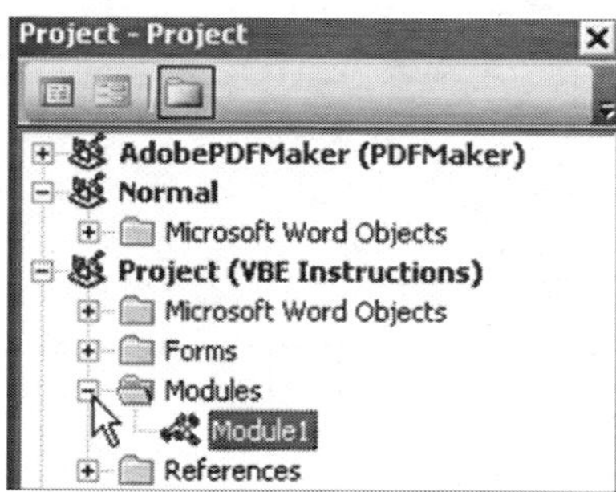

Figure 104 – Using Project Explorer to open a Module

Once you've found the object in which you will store your code, right-click it and choose View Code. The appropriate code window opens in the right-hand pane, and your cursor is ready for you to type or paste your code.

Note: If you have done as directed in the Accessing Visual Basic Editor (VBE) section on page 8, the words "Option Explicit" appear automatically at the top of the code window.

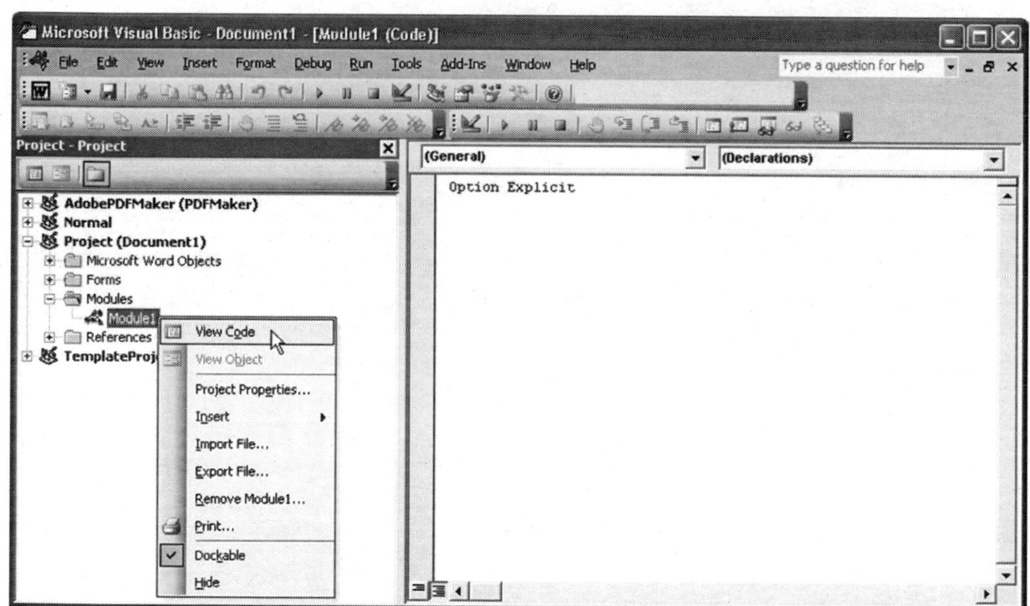

Figure 105 – Viewing the Code

Apx

If you do not find a folder for the object, it means that no objects of that category have been created. Continue reading to learn how to create them.

Inserting a Module

Open the VBE by hitting Alt+F11.

Note: A "Standard module" is often referred to as just "module". Other module types are preceded by their description, such as "Class module" or "UserForm".

In the Project Explorer, locate the project (file) to which you want to add your code. When you find it, right-click on its name and choose Insert | Module (or Class Module, if directed). In the example on the following page, we are adding a new Standard module to Document2.

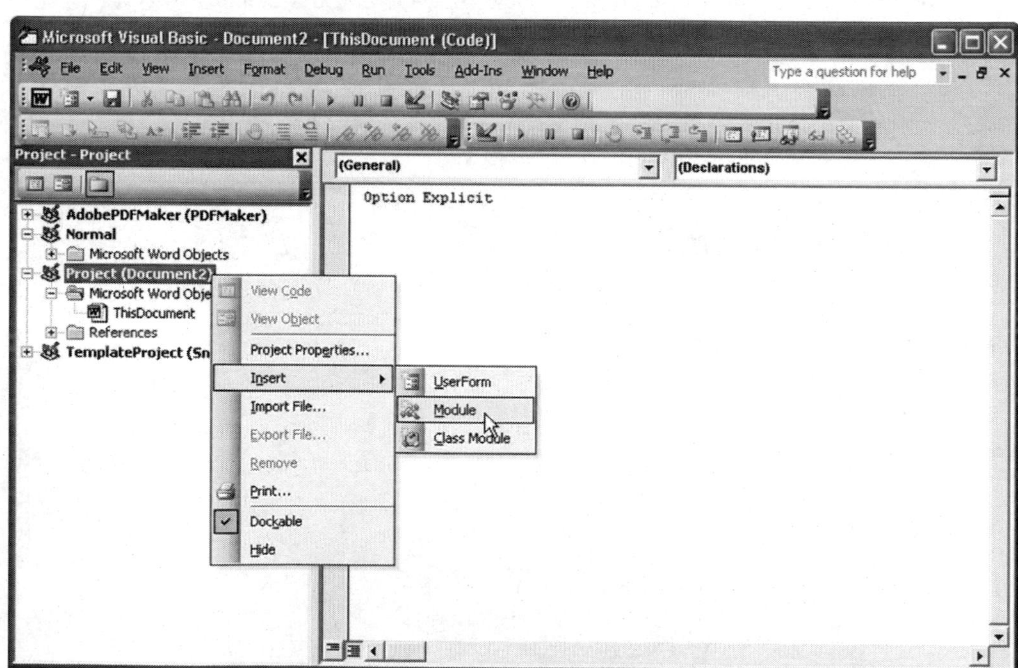

Figure 106 – Inserting a New Module

Apx

As shown in the following example, your Project Explorer will display your new code module in the Modules container. The cursor will also be flashing in the code screen on the right, waiting for you to enter some VBA code.

Notice that the name of the active module is displayed in the application's title bar.

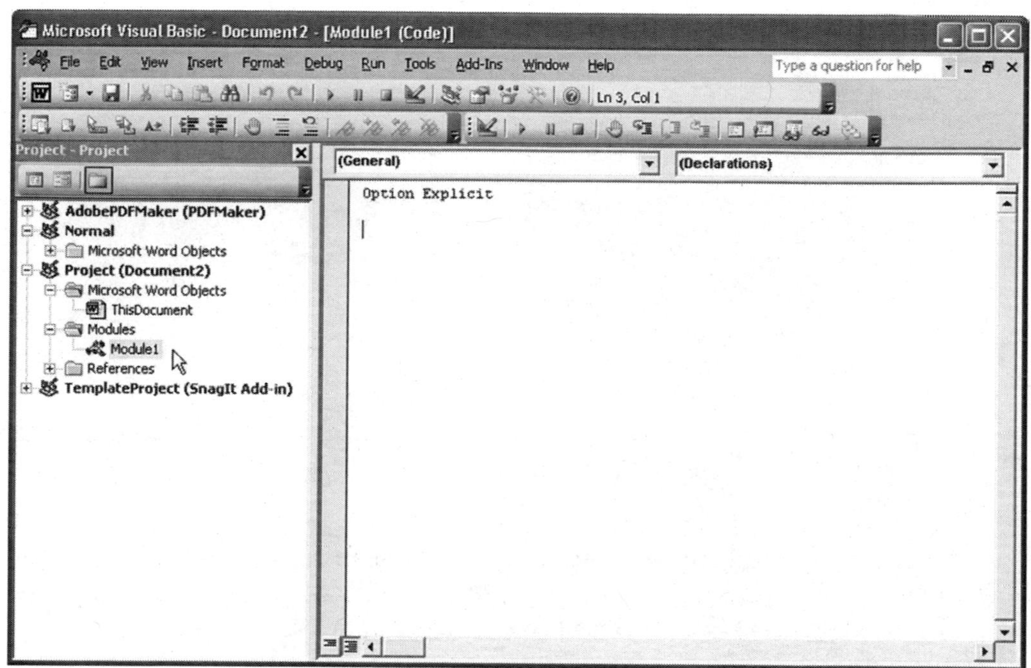

Figure 107 – New Module Name Shown in Title Bar

Inserting a UserForm

Open the VBE by hitting Alt+F11.

In the Project Explorer, locate the project (file) to which you want to add your UserForm. When found, right-click its name and choose Insert | UserForm. In the example below, we are adding a new UserForm to Document2.

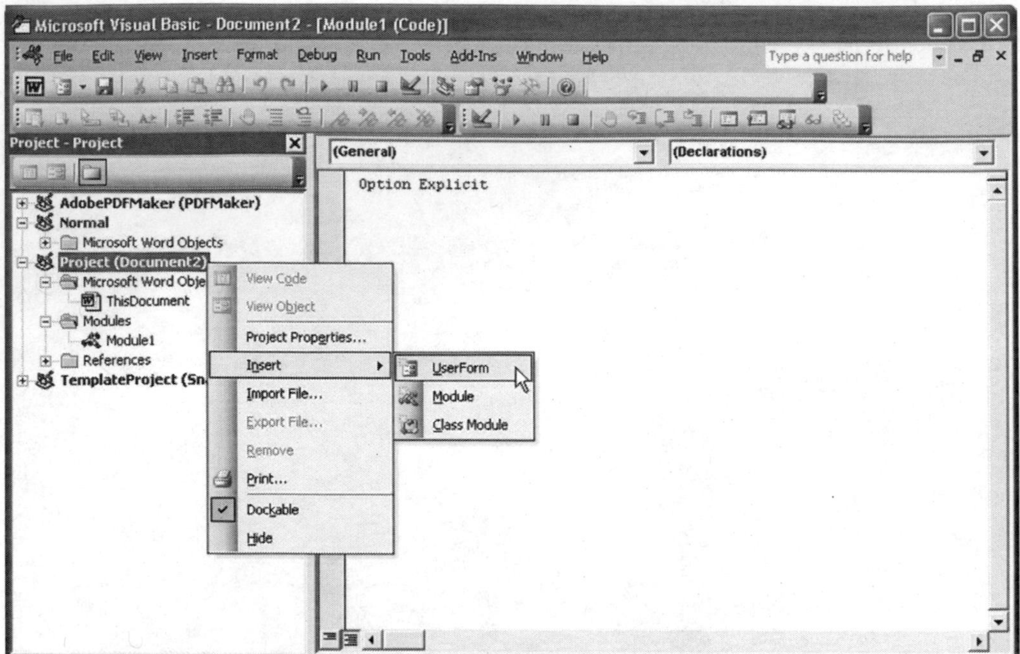

Figure 108 – Inserting a New UserForm

As shown in the example on the following page, your Project Explorer will now show your new UserForm in the Forms container. You will also notice that the name of the active UserForm is displayed in the application's title bar.

Apx

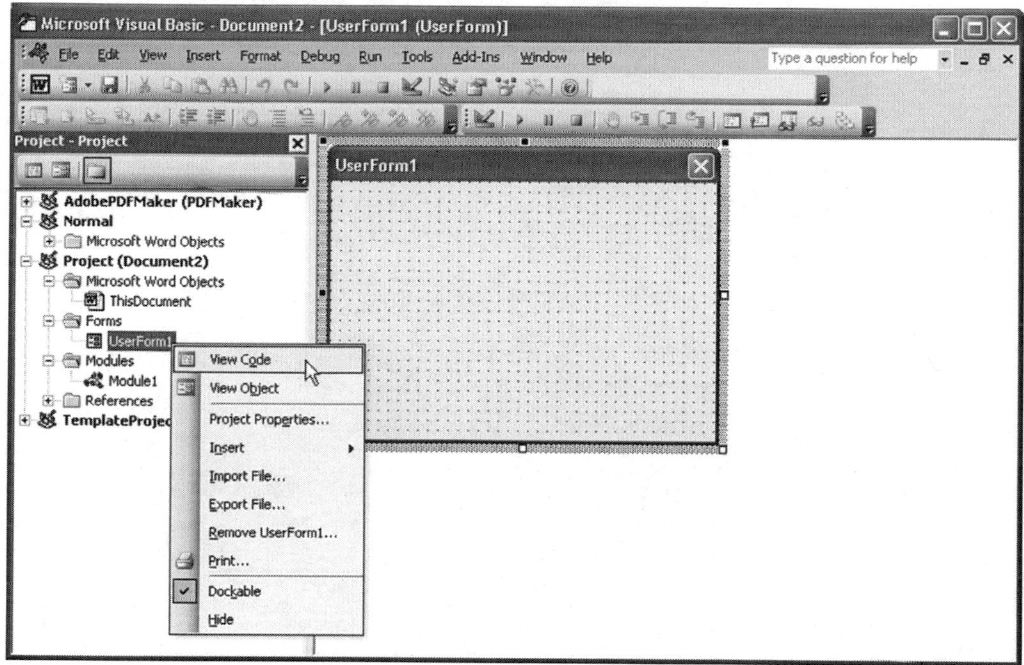

Figure 109 – View Code on a UserForm

By default, a UserForm always displays the design screen when you access it in the Project Explorer. To view the code of a UserForm, either right click its name and choose View Code, or double-click on it. You can then view the code screen in the right-hand pane, where the cursor will be flashing, waiting for you to type or paste some VBA code.

Apx

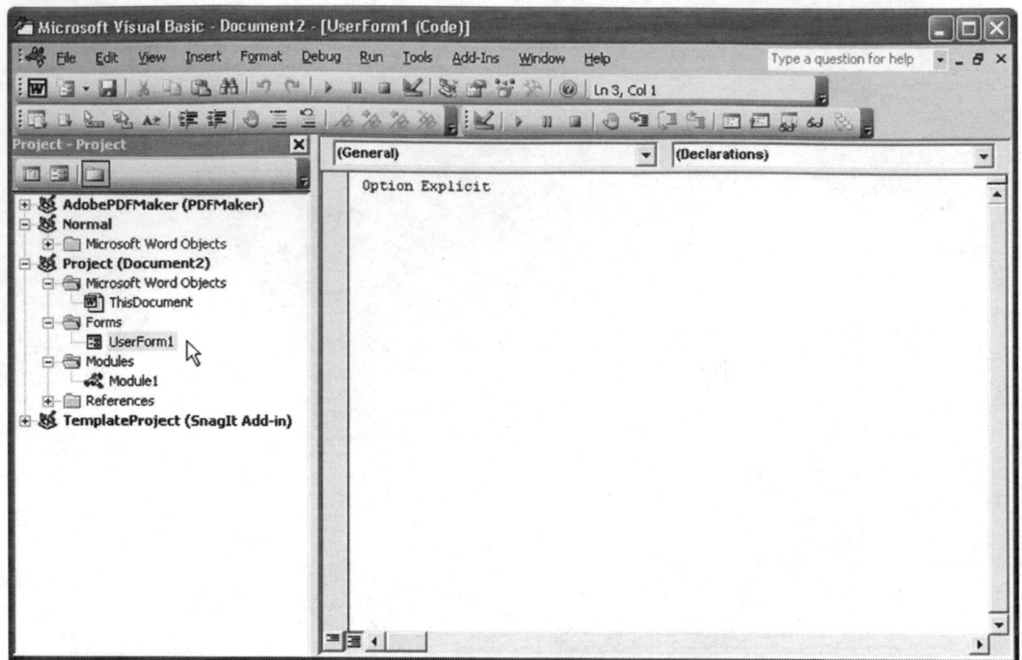

Figure 110 – Default UserForm Window

Opening Worksheet Objects (Excel)

Open the VBE by hitting Alt+F11.

Using the Project Explorer, locate the project (file) you are working on. By clicking the little + signs, drill down into the folder called Microsoft Excel Objects.

Apx

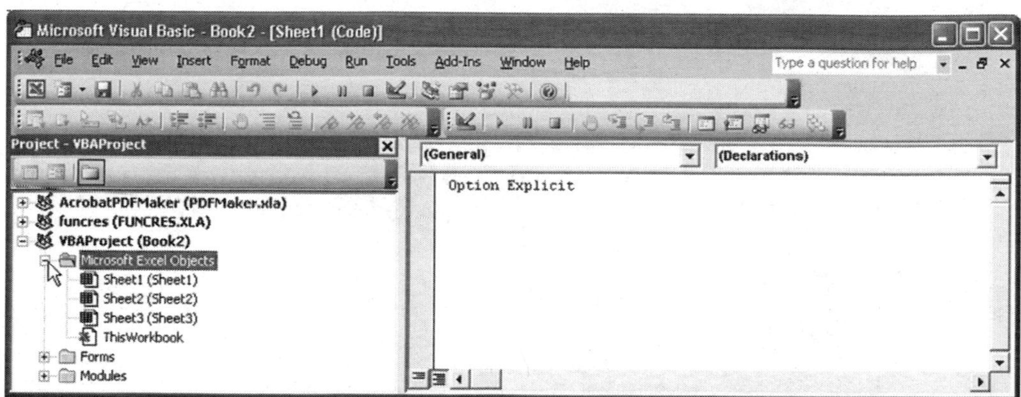

Figure 111 – Opening Excel Worksheet Object

You will be presented with a list of all the sheets in the workbook, as shown below. To activate the code pane of a specific sheet, either right-click it and choose View Code from the menu, or double-click the sheet.

Tip: If you are in the main Excel screen, you can open up the Visual Basic Editor at the correct sheet module by right-clicking the sheet tab and choosing View Code from the menu!

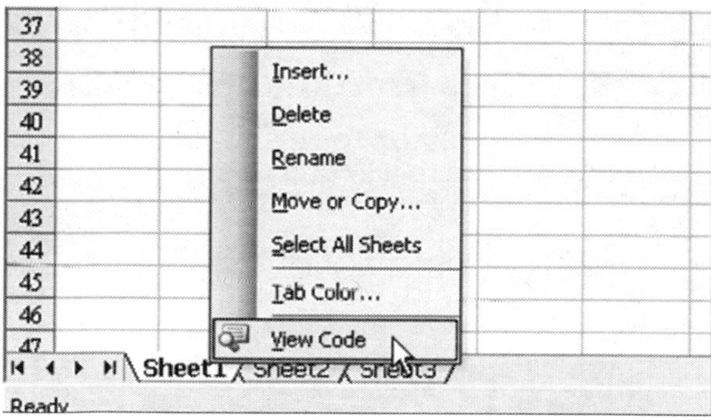

Figure 112 – Viewing Worksheet Code

Apx

Opening ThisWorkbook Object (Excel)

Open the VBE by hitting Alt+F11.

Using the Project Explorer, locate the project (file) you are working on. Click the little + signs to drill down into the folder called Microsoft Excel Objects.

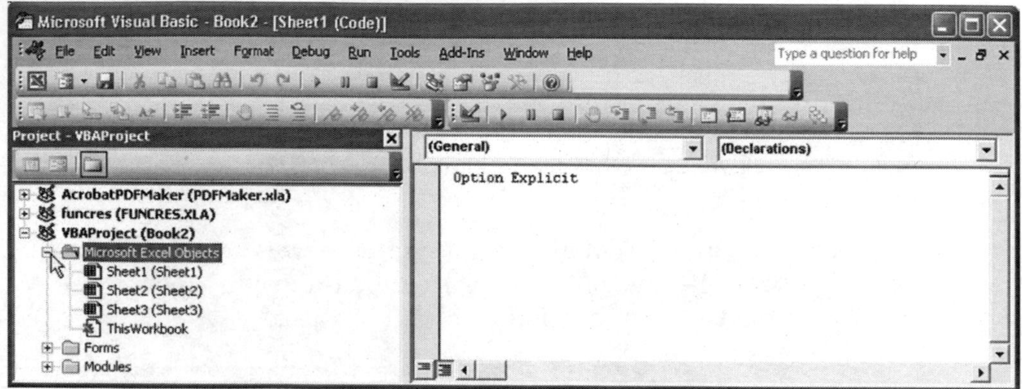

Figure 113 – Opening Excel ThisWorkbook Object

As shown in the example, you will be presented with a list of all the sheets in the workbook. To activate the code pane for the ThisWorkbook object, either right-click it and choose View Code from the menu, or double-click it.

Opening ThisDocument Objects (Word)

Open the VBE by hitting Alt+F11.

Using the Project Explorer, locate the project (file) on which you are working. By clicking the little + signs, drill down into the folder called Microsoft Word Objects.

Apx

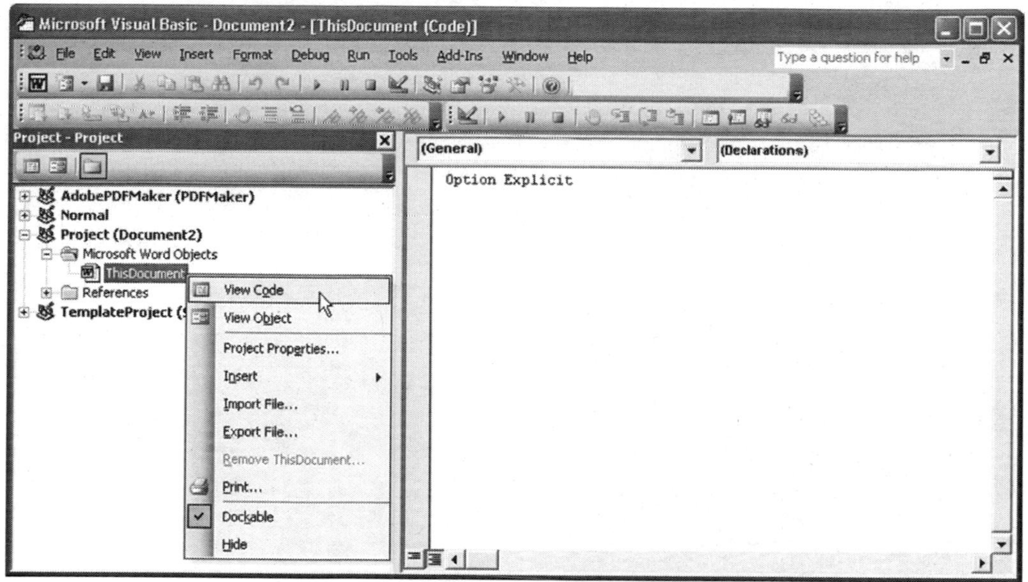

Figure 114 – Opening Word ThisDocument Object

As shown in the example, you will see the ThisDocument module in the Microsoft Word Objects folder. To activate the code pane for the ThisDocument object, either right-click it and choose View Code from the menu, or double-click it.

Opening ThisOutlookSession Objects (Outlook)

Open the VBE by hitting Alt+F11.

Using the Project Explorer, click the little + signs to drill down into the folder called Microsoft Outlook Objects.

Apx

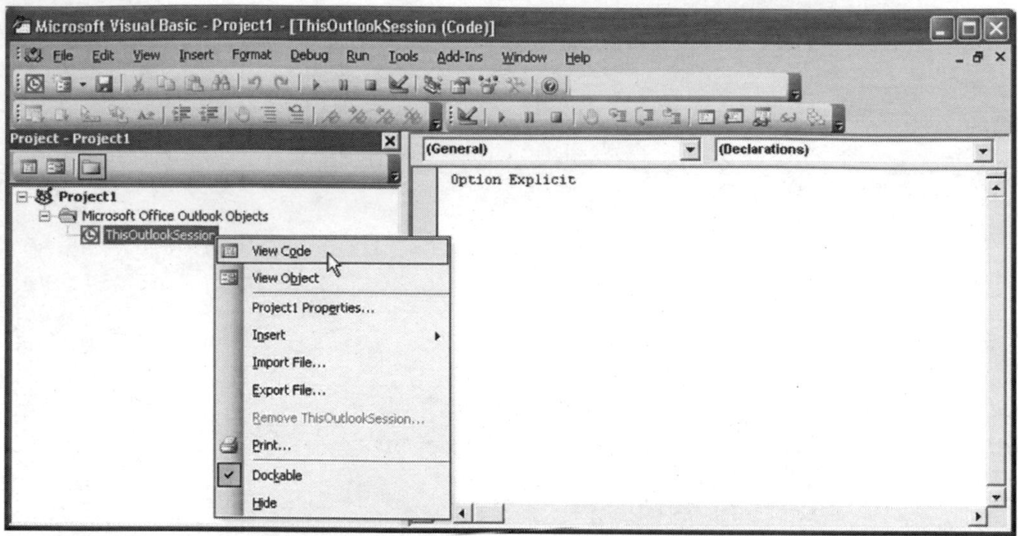

Figure 115 – Opening Outlook ThisOutlookSession Object

As shown in the example, the ThisOutlookSession object resides in the Microsoft Office Outlook Objects folder. To activate the code pane for the ThisOutlookSession object, either right-click it and choose View Code from the menu, or double-click it.

Opening Slide Objects (Powerpoint)

Open the Visual Basic Editor by hitting Alt+F11.

Using the Project Explorer click the little + signs to drill down into the folder called Microsoft Powerpoint Objects.

Apx

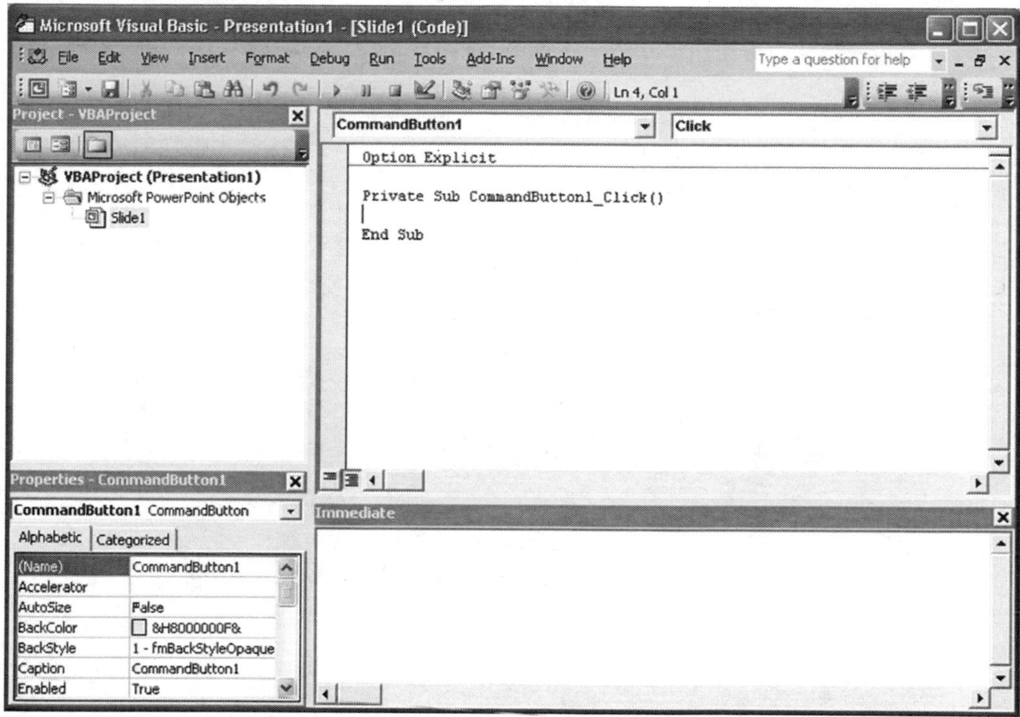

Figure 116 - Opening PowerPoint Slide Object

As shown in the example, Slide objects reside in the Microsoft PowerPoint Objects folder. To activate the code pane for the Slide object, either right-click it and choose View Code from the menu, or double-click the desired slide.

If the slide does not already exist, you will need to place an ActiveX control on the Slide (using the Control Toolbox in the main Powerpoint interface). The Slide module will run just like a module-based macro, but will be attached to the slide. If the slide is copied, so is the macro; if a slide is deleted, so is the macro.

Apx

Access Objects

Access VBA is somewhat different than programming done in the other applications. Many database programmers have never touched a Word document, and many Word programmers have never touched a database. Simply follow the instructions by our Access Code Developer to learn where to place the code provided.

Appendix B

Running a Macro

There are many ways to run a macro; some run automatically when a specified event occurs, while others require execution.

Running a Macro Automatically

An event in VBA is the same as anywhere else; it's something that occurs. Event procedures are procedures that are designed to run when an event occurs. Events include the opening of an Excel workbook (Workbook_Open), a change on an Excel worksheet (Worksheet_Change), or the creation of a new Word document from a template (Document_New). There are other events that occur on UserForms, such as On_Click of a button.

Most Microsoft Access macros are event procedures.

For a complete list of events in the Microsoft Office Applications, see http://www.mugrs.org/etc/MSDNRef.htm.

Running a Macro Manually

There are also many other macros in this book, however, that need to be run either manually or with a keyboard shortcut or toolbar button. Fortunately, this is very easy to do.

From the main program interface, there are three ways for you to choose which macro you wish to run:

1. From the menu, choose Tools | Macro | Macros.
2. Click the Run icon on the Visual Basic toolbar.
3. Press Alt+F8.

Choosing any of the methods above will open the macro dialog box. A copy of Excel's macro dialog box is shown on the following page:

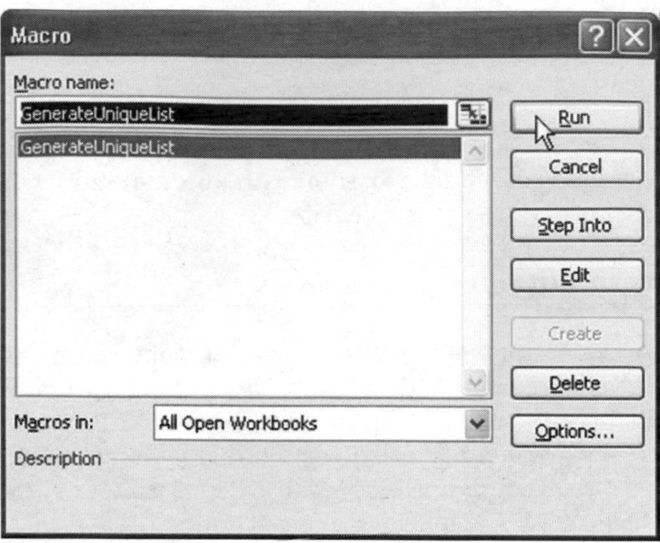

Figure 117 - Manually Running a Macro

To run your code, select the macro in the list, and click "Run", or double-click the macro's name.

You can also run your macro while still in the Visual Basic Editor. Just locate the procedure, click somewhere in the code, and choose one of the following methods to run it:

1. Press F5.
2. Choose "Run Sub/UserForm" from the Run Menu.
3. Click the Run icon on either the Standard or Debug toolbars.

If your cursor is not placed within the macro code, or the macro requires an argument to run, the macro dialog box (as illustrated above) launches, allowing you to choose a procedure.

Running a Macro from a Toolbar Button

Toolbar buttons can be added to your toolbar via the Tools | Customize menu. Choose the Commands tab and then choose the Macros Category; a toolbar button appears on the right-hand side of the dialog. Drag the toolbar button up onto your toolbar.

In Excel, you must then click the button once, and you're then provided with a list of macros from which you can choose one to assign. Using those steps in the other applications immediately assigns the specific macro to the button. (The button you drag up has a macro already assigned to it.)

Running a Macro Using Shortcut Keys

The exact procedure top assign a shortcut to a macro varies, depending on the application.

- In Excel and PowerPoint, just choose Tools | Macro | Macros and select your macro, then choose the Options button. Assign a shortcut key to your macro there.
- In Word and Access, choose Tools | Customize and click the Commands tab.

Tip: Check the Help files for "assign a macro" in your specific version.

Apx

This page intentionally left blank.

Index

A

Access Objects, 13, 415
Access Tables
  Fill Combo Box, 377
Action Setting-Triggered Macros, 310–316
ActiveX Data Object libraries. See ADO, 214
Add-ins, 7, 13
ADO Connections, 214, 373, 377
AllowPrint Variable, 49, 50
Apostrophe ('). See Commented code, 3, 24, 29, 34, 36, 72, 98, 263
Append Variable, 23
Application Environment, 7
Applications, Custom, 56
Ascending Variable, 27
Asterisk (*), 3
Attachments
  Rename, 271
  Save, 271
  Send per Schedule, 287
  Send to Specific Recipients, 287
  Transfer Data to Workbooks, 378
AutoFilter, 30
Auto-Incremented Version Numbers, Attachment Names, 271
AutoNumber Field, 79
AutoNumbered Text, Convert to Plain Text, 144
AutoText Entries, 130, 188

B

Background Color, 37, 351
  Criteria for Calculations, 38, 39
Backups, 5, 93
Boilerplate Forms, 331, 332
Bookmarks, 136, 224, 225, 258–264, 375–377
  Create from Selection, 260
  Highlight, 264
  Names, 136, 224, 225, 258–264, 375–377
  Names, Place in Comments, 264
Highlight, 264
Boolean Fields, 354
Borders, Frames, 169
Buttons
  Break, 10
  Design Mode, 10
  Insert, 9, 14, 130
  Project Explorer Window, 10
  Properties Window, 10
  Reset, 10
  Run, 10
  View Microsoft Office, 9

C

Calculate Event, 47
Calendar Form, 42–45, 401
Calendar Wizard, 157, 163, 164
Calendars, 42–45, 163, 164, 391, 401
  Format, 163, 164
  Generate, 157, 163, 164
  Input Dates from, 42–45, 401
Calendars for Excel or Word, 391
Captions, 164, 168, 169
  Wrap-around, 164
Cascading Combo Boxes, Filtering, 337
Cascading Combo Boxes, Selecting, 337
Case, Change, 62
Cell Color
  Criteria for Calculations, 38
Cells
  Dependent, 47
  Entry, Delete, 83
  Upon Change, Log Actions, 113
  Upon Change, Run Macro, 47
Change Events, 41, 47, 51, 118
Charts, Mail Merge, 215
Charts, Transfer to PPT Slides, 367
CHR(34), 341
Class Modules, 14
Code, 7, 16
  Comment, 3, 7
  VBE Window, 312, 405
    Open, 405
  View, 405, 409
Code Object, Locate, 404
Color
  Background, 37, 351
  Change, 25, 306
  Criteria for Calculations, 38, 39
Column Variable, 33, 34
Columns, Compare, 80
Combo Boxes, 337, 339
  Fill from Access Table, 377
  Fill from Workbook, 371
Combo Boxes, Cascading, 337
Commands, Menu, 4, 202
Commented Code, 3, 7
Commented Text, Highlighting, 127

Concatenate Strings, 345
Concatenated Error Messages, 352
Condition Variable, 33, 34
Conditional Formats, 24, 25, 40, 42
    Multiple, 40, 42
Consistent Forms, 331, 332
Contacts, 96, 98, 274
    Create from Database, 274
    Criteria, 96, 98
    Import, 96, 98, 274
Control Buttons
    Create with VBA, 269, 270
Controlled Numbers, 361
COUNT by Color, 37
Criteria, 33, 34, 38, 39, 378
    Color for Calculations, 38, 39
    Compare Columns, 80
    Delete Records, 31, 32, 34
    Delete Rows, 31, 32, 34
    Import Contacts, 96, 98
    Transfer E-Mail Messages, 378
Crosstab Reports, Dynamic, 357
Custom
    Applications, 56
    Calendars, 391
    Control Buttons, 269, 270
    Dictionaries, Change, 245
    Mail Merge, 389
    Print Procedure, Force Use, 49, 50
    Toolbars, 56

D

DAO Library, 344
Data
    Access Table Transferred to Combo Box, 377
    Attachment to Workbook, 378
    Convert to Tabular Format, 76
    Filtered by Strings, 336
    Mail Merge from Worksheet, 389
    Validate, 350
    Word Form Transferred to Spreadsheet, 368
    Worksheet Transferred to Combo Box, 371
Data Entry, 1, 254
    Dialog Box, 254
    Tabbed Control, 363
Data Entry Form, 351, 353
Data Range
    Create Word Labels, 382
Data Source, 195–199, 201, 206, 225, 295
    Link Dynamically for Mail Merge, 195, 196
Database
    Consistent Design Interface, 331, 332
    Create from Contacts, 274
    Create Task Items for Records, 294
    Mail Merge, 197, 214, 215, 377
    Send E-Mail, 342
Database Form Events, 294
DateFormat Variable, 22
Dates
    Enter from Calendar, 42, 44, 45, 401
    Format, 23
    Grouped, 359
Dependent Cells, 47
Design Mode Macro, 310, 318, 321
Dialog Box, 254
Dictator Applications, 85
Dictionaries, Change Custom, 245
Directory, List of Files, 69
Documents
    Find and Replace in Multiple, 122
    Find and Replace Throughout, 122
    Format New, 225, 226, 229
    Generate with VBA, 265
    Open with Macros, 267
    Protect File as Word Form, 267
    Split into Multiple Files, 230
Drop-down Lists
    Data from Access Tables, 377
    Data from Worksheets, 371
Drop-down Menus, 236
Duplicate Entries, Find, 23
Duplicates, Highlight, 23
Dynamic
    Crosstab Reports, 357
    Links, 195, 196
    Queries, 357

E

E-mail, 99
E-Mail, 301, 342, 378
E-Mail Attachments, 271, 378
    Rename, 271
    Save, 271
    Transfer Data to Workbooks, 378
E-Mail Directly from Database, 342
E-Mail Messages
    Include Web Page, 279
    Send per Schedule, 287
    Send Reply to Specific, 301
    Send to Multiple Recipients, 282
    Send to Specific Recipients, 287
E-Mail Worksheet or Workbook, 99
Empty Rows, Insert, 54
Enter Key, Disable, 175
Entries
    AutoText, 130

X

Find Duplicate, 23
List Unique, 27
Entry Cells, 83
Delete, 83
Error Handling, 178
Error Messages
Concatenated, 352
Event Macros, 47, 51, 313, 322
Event Procedures, 417
Event/Procedure List Drop-down, 17
Events, 41, 46, 47, 51, 118, 350, 362, 417
Database Form, 294
Excel Objects, 13, 410, 412
Expression Builder, 340

F

Field Codes
Copy Nested as Text, 141
Fields
Boolean, 354
Create AutoNumber, 79
Fill in Predefined Sequence, 363
Insert, 266
Mandatory, 351
Update, 131, 354
File Name Format, 22
Files
Check if Exists, 35
Find, 35
Insert, 236
List all in Directory, 69
Names, 22, 23
Print, 19
Save, 22, 66, 72
Select, 236
Send as Attachment, 287
Split Documents into Multiple, 230
Filter
Remove from Subform, 342
Find and Replace, 75, 126
Documents, Multiple, 122
Documents, Through all parts, 122
Strings, 75
Folders
Display Contents, 236
Tree Menus, 236
Folders Button, Toggle, 14
Folders View, 15
Font Color, Criteria for Calculations, 39
Form Event Procedures, 294
Form Properties, 348
Formats, 24, 25, 40, 42, 76, 119–121, 266
Apply, 266
Conditional, 24, 25, 40, 42
Convert Data to Tabular, 76
Multiple Conditional, 40, 42
New Documents, 225, 226, 229
Spelling Errors, 249
Transferred Selections, 225, 226, 229
Forms, 175, 178, 183, 189, 193, 368
Create When Triggered by Subform, 334
Data Transferred to Spreadsheet, 368
Design Consistent, 331, 332
Fields, 175, 178, 182
Format Text, 178, 182
Password Protection, 182, 187, 192, 194
Suppress New Lines, 175
Protected, 183, 188
Insert Picture, 193
Table Rows
Insert, 183, 188
Forms Container, 408
Forms, Calendar, 42–45, 401
Formulas, Copy in Tables, 151, 153, 156
Frames, Border, 169
Functions, User-defined, 2

G

Graph, Automate at Mail Merge Event, 215
Graph, Insert, 224
Graphics, 164, 168–170, 193
Insert, 168, 170
Insert in Protected Form, 193
Insert with Caption, 164, 169
Link, 168, 170
Link to Page, 170
Move Around Screen in Presentation, 310
Grouped Dates, 359

H

Highlight
Commented Text, 127
Remove, 129
Selection, 126–128
History Constant, 95
Hyperlinked Index, 132
Hyperlinks, 36, 132
Remove, 36

I

ID Numbers, 361
Immediate Window, 17
Index, 60, 132
Create, 60

Hyperlinks, 132
Intellisense, 253, 306
Interior.ColorIndex Variable, 25

K

Key Field, 300, 336, 362
Keyboard Shortcuts
Alt+F11, 8, 334, 403–414
Alt+H, 127
Ctrl+Alt+F9, 40
Ctrl+R, 12, 403
F4, 16
F5, 418
F7, 17
F9, 40
KeyPress Event, 46, 47

L

Labels
Create from Excel Data Range, 382
Links
Data Source for Mail Merge, 195, 196
Graphics, 168, 170
Insert, 266
Pictures, 168, 170
Links to Worksheet, 60
List Boxes, 346, 347, 353, 355
After Delete Confirm Event, 350
After Insert Event, 350
After Update Event, 350
Create, 348
Move Rows Between, 353
Move Rows in, 355
On-Click Event, 350
Rolodex Replacement, 346, 347
List Sequence, Manipulate, 355
Lists, Unique, 27
Locals Window, 17
LookInSubFolders Variable, 66, 72

M

Macros, 47, 263, 267, 313-322, 378, 417– 419
Action Setting-Triggered in Presentations, 310
Design Mode, 310, 318, 321
Event, 47, 51, 313, 322
Force to Enable, 73, 265, 267
VBA, 265
Names, 120
Presentation Mode, 313–316, 322
Record, a, 108, 119–121, 126, 182, 196, 197
Run, 47, 263, 378, 417–419
Automatically, 417
Manually, 417
Shortcut Keys, 263, 419
Toolbar Button, 263, 378, 418
Security, Adjust While Executing, 267
Toolbars, Assign to Button, 119–121
Mail Merge, 195–205, 215, 377, 389
Chart, 215
Create Using Worksheet Data, 389
Data Source, 205, 377
Database, 197, 214, 215, 377
Display, 198, 199, 202
Display Toolbar/Tqskpane, 198, 199, 202
Dynamic Link to Data Source, 195, 196
Events, 215
Fields, Display List, 200, 202
Link to Relational Database, 205, 377
OLE Database, 197, 214, 377
One-to-Many List, 205, 377
Results in WordArt, 203
VBA Code, 207
Mail Merge Toolbar/Taskpane, 198, 199, 202
Mailing Labels, 382
Main Code Window, 16, 17
Mandatory Fields, 351
Master Documents, 230
Menu Commands, 4, 202
Menus, Drop-down, 236
Menus, Tree, 236
Merge Fields, 200, 202, 203, 205
Convert to WordArt, 203, 205
Message, Sent as Reply to Selected Messages, 301
Message, Sent to Multiple Recipients, 282
Millions, Display as Text, 138
Modules, 7, 14, 17, 406
Class, 14
Code, 16
Group Procedures, 14
Insert, 14, 406
Menus, 17
Name, 15, 16, 407
Open, 17
Standard, 14
Modules Container, 407
MS Graph
Automate at Mail Merge Event, 215
Insert, 224
Multiple Documents, Find and Replace, 122
Multiple Files
Split Documents into, 230
Multiple Recipients, Same E-Mail Message, 282

X

N

Named Ranges, Delete Reference Errors, 111
Names
    Splitting Parts into Separate Fields, 327
Nested Field Codes, Copy as Text, 141
Normal Project, 13
Normal Text, Converting AutoNumbers to, 144
Normal.dot. See Templates, Default, 13
Notes, Import Outline Text to PPT, 316
Number Format, 119–121
Number in Reverse Order, 144, 145
Numbers, 138, 361
    Converting AutoNumbers to Plain Text, 144
    Extracting, 109
    Format in Table, 149
Numbers as Text, Display Millions, 138
Numeric Entry, 45

O

Object List Drop-down, 17
Objects
    Access, 13, 415
    Code, Locate, 404
    Excel, 13, 410, 412
    Outlook, 13, 413
    PowerPoint, 414
    Redemption, 300–304
    Word, 13, 246, 248, 267, 399, 412, 413
ODBC Connections, 197
OLE Database Connections, 197, 214, 377
OLE Database, Mail Merge, 197, 214, 377
On-Click Event, 350
OnInsert Event, 362
Outline Text, Export to Notes in PPT, 316
Outlines, 30, 31
Outlook Objects, 13, 413
Outlook Security, 300

P

Page Fields, 88, 116
    Synchronize, 116
Paragraph Returns, 4
Parameter Values, 338
Parameters, 345
Password Protection, 31, 181, 182, 187, 192, 194
Path Variable, 22, 36, 66, 72, 93, 196
Path, List Files in, 69
Periodic Reports, 359
Personalized Presentations, 322, 324
Photo Album, Create, 64
Pictures, 164, 168–170, 193
    Insert, 170
    Insert in Protected Form, 193
    Insert with Caption, 164, 168, 169
    Link to Page, 170
    Links, 168, 170
    Move Around Screen in Presentation, 310
Pivot Charts, 88–91
Pivot Tables, 116
    Synchronize, 116
Placecards, 203
Placeholder Shapes, 319
Plain Text, Converting AutoNumbers to, 144
PowerPoint Objects, 414
PowerPoint Presentation Based on Pivot Chart, 88
Predefined Range, 29
Presentation Mode Macro, 313, 314, 316, 322
Presentations
    Action Setting-Triggered Macros, 310
    Based on Pivot Chart, 88
    Creating, 324
    Import Outline Text to Notes, 316
    Insert Slides, 305
    Jump to Random Slide, 313
    Move Shapes/Pictures Around Screen, 310
    Personalize, 322, 324
    Random Changes to Objects, 315
    Save Show Point, 321
    Shapes, Change Color, 306
    Slides from Excel Charts, 367
    Text, Export from Shape/Text box, 308
    Wrap Text to Next Slide, 319
Print Procedures, Custom, 49, 50
Print Spelling Errors, 249
Procedures, 3, 4, 7, 14
    Components, 4
Programming Environment, 7, 8, 12
Project Explorer, 12, 13, 16, 17, 378, 398–414
Projects
    Protect, 18
Properties Window, 15, 16, 259, 303, 329, 330, 377, 379, 398
    View, 15
Properties, Import from Outlook, 98
Protected Forms, 193
Protected Worksheets, Filter, 30

Q

Queries, 337, 339, 340, 354, 357
Query Builder, 340

R

Random Changes to Presentation Objects, 315
Random Slides, Jump to, 313
Range of Interest, 48
Range Variable, 24–39, 62–68, 84, 109, 110
Ranges, 23, 24, 29, 36, 48, 54, 67, 284
Currently Selected, 24, 29, 67, 284
Delete Reference Errors, 111
Duplicates, Highlight, 23
Extract Numbers, 109
Index, Set Hyperlinks, 132
Input by User, 29
Insert Rows, 54
Remove Hyperlinks, 36
Records
Delete Based on Criteria, 31–34
Duplicates, 23
Unique, 27
Recurring Task Entry, 287
Redemption, 300–304
Relational Database, Link to Mail Merge, 205, 377
Reminders, Create Automatically, 290
Reports
Periodic, 359
Restricted Area in Worksheet, 50, 51
Reverse Order, Numbering, 144, 145
Rolodex, Simulate, 346, 347
Rows, 54
Conditional, 32
Delete Based on Criteria, 31–34
Delete from Table, 189
Insert in a Range, 54
Move Between Text Boxes, 353
Move in Text Boxes, 355

S

Scripts, Malicious, 300
Scroll Area, 51
Security, 2, 52, 53, 268
SELECT Statements, 349
Selection
Create Bookmark, 260
Selection List Box, 346, 347
Selection, Transfer to New Document, 225, 226, 229
Setup Formatting, 225, 226, 229
Shapes
Change Color in Presentation, 306
Move Around Screen in Presentation, 310
Placeholders, 319
Shift+Enter Key, Disable, 175
Shortcut Keys
Alt+F11, 8, 334, 403–414
Alt+F8, 417
Alt+H, 127
Ctrl+Alt+F9, 40
Ctrl+R, 12, 403
F4, 16
F5, 418
F7, 17
F9, 40
Shift+Enter, 176–178
Show Point, Save, 321
Slide Objects, Open, 414
Slide Show, Resume, 321
Slides
Add Specified Number, 305
Excel Charts, Transfer from, 367
Insert in Presentation, 305
Jump to Random, 313
Resume Where Left Off, 321
Wrap Text to Next, 319
Spelling Errors, 249
Spreadsheet Data from Word Form, 368
SQL Mode, 349
SQL Statement Query Builder, 340
Standard Modules, 14
Static Text, 137, 146
strFileName Variable, 279
Strings, 75, 109, 336, 341, 345
Concatenate, 345
Filter Data, 336
Find and Replace, 75
strReplyMessage Variable, 302
Subdocuments, 230
Subfolders, 19, 21, 64, 66, 69–72
Subforms, 337, 342, 347
Data Properties, 347
Display, 337
Remove Filter, 342
Trigger New Forms, 334
SUM by Color, 37
Survey, Transfer Data to Spreadsheet, 368

T

Tabbed Control, 363, 364
Editing, 364
Table of Contents, Create, 60
Table Rows, Insert in form, 183, 188
Tables, 146–156, 189
Calendar, Generate, 157, 163, 164
Format Numbers, 149
Formulas, Copy, 151, 153, 156
Row, Delete in Protected Form, 189

Tab
Change Direction, 146
Suppress New Row, 148
Tabs
Change Direction In Tables, 146
Suppress New Row in Tables, 148
Task Items
Create Automatically, 290, 294
tblName Variable, 279
Templates, Default, 13
Text, 62, 126, 127, 137, 138, 146, 178, 182
Case, Change, 62
Copy Nested Field Codes as, 141
Display Numbers in Millions, 138
Export from Presentation Shape/Text box, 308
Export to Notes in PPT, 316
Format in Form Fields, 178, 182
Highlight Selected, 126, 127
Insert, 266
Label per Slide/Shape from Which Imported, 308
Static, 137, 146
Wrap to Next Slide, 319
Text Boxes, 45, 255, 259, 372, 377
Change Name, 255, 259, 372, 377
Entry Restricted to Numbers, 45
Text Files
Exported from Presentation, 308
Format, 105, 108
Import, 105, 108
Place in Workbook, 105, 108
Text Format, 119–121
Text Strings, 75, 109
Extract Numbers, 109
ThisDocument Objects, 13, 246, 248, 267, 399, 413
Open, 412
ThisOutlookSession Objects, 13, 280, 288, 303, 378, 381, 414
Open, 413
ThisWorkbook Objects, 13, 21, 30, 50, 52, 73, 74, 95, 115, 118, 287, 390, 398, 412
Open, 412
Time Period, Select, 360
Today's Date, Name Workbook as, 21
Toolbars, 56, 85
Create, 56
Customized, 56, 85
Hide, 85
Macro, Assign to Button, 119–121
Mail Merge, Display Automatically, 198–202
VBE, 9–17, 130
Tree Menus, 236

U

Unblocked Cells, Delete, 83
UNION, 349
Unique Entries, List, 27
Update Fields, 131, 354
User-defined Functions, 2
UserForms, 1, 102, 104, 407, 409
Insert, 104, 407
Print, 102
View Code, 409

V

Validate Data, 350
Variables, 25, 27, 29, 34, 36, 49, 50, 93, 196, 279, 302, 345
VB, 1
VBA, 1, 2, 7, 11, 269, 344
Code Window, 344
Generate Documents, 265
VBA Code
Control Buttons, 269
Remove, 52
VBA Projects, 13, 14, 18, 52
Protect, 18
VBA Training, 11
vbCRLF Variable, 345
VBE, 4, 7, 8, 13, 156, 175, 225, 253, 257, 259, 312, 325, 374, 377, 383, 391, 403, 405
Open, 4, 403
Options, 11
Toolbars, 9, 10, 14, 130
Window, 9, 312, 325
View Code, 8, 10, 17, 405, 409–415
UserForm, 409
Visual Basic Editor. See VBE, 13
Visual Basic for Applications. See VBA, 1, 7
Visual Basic. See VB, 1

W

Watch Window, 17
Web Page, Include in E-Mail Message, 279
Wizard, Tabbed Control, 363
Word Form, Protect with Password, 267
Word Objects, 13, 412, 413
Word, Print UserForms, 102
WordArt, 203
Words, Highlight, 126
Workbooks
Backups, 93
Copy, 52
E-mail, 99

Fill Combo Xox, 371
Find and Replace String, 75
Hyperlinks, Remove, 36
Index, 60
Links to Worksheets, 60
Log Action Upon Cell Change, 113
Macros, Enable to Run, 73
Names, 21
Today's Date, 21
Pivot Tables, 116
Print, 19
Table of Contents, 60
Track Changes, 113
VBA Code, Remove, 52
Worksheets, Sort, 25
Worksheet Objects, Open, 410
Worksheets
Area Restriction, 50, 51
Charts, Transfer to PPT Slides, 367
E-mail, 99
Hyperlinks, Remove, 36
Pivot Tables, 116
Protect, 30, 31
AutoFilter, 30, 31
Sort, 25
Workbook, Links to, 60

HOLY MACRO! BOOKS QUICK ORDER FORM

Fax Orders: (707)-220-4510. Send this form.
E-Mail Orders: store@MrExcel.com - Online: http://www.MrExcel.com
Postal Orders: MrExcel, 13386 Judy Ave NW, PO Box 82, Uniontown OH 44685

Quantity	Title	Price	Total
	Office VBA Macros You Can Use Today	$29.95	
	Learn Excel from Mr Excel	$39.95	
	Excel for Teachers	$24.95	
	Excel for Marketing Managers	$24.95	
	Excel for Scientists	$24.95	
	Holy Macro! It's 2,200 Excel VBA Examples (CD-ROM)	$89.00	
	Slide Your Way Through Excel VBA (CD-ROM)	$99.00	
	Join the Excellers League (CD-ROM)	$99.00	
	Excel for Scientists (CD-ROM)	$75.00	
	Guerilla Data Analysis Using Microsoft Excel	$19.95	
	The Spreadsheet at 25	$19.95	
	Grover Park George On Access	$29.95	
	Your Access to the World (CD-ROM)	$99.00	
	Access VBA Made Accessible (CD-ROM)	$99.00	
	DreamBoat On Word	$19.95	
	Kathy Jacobs On PowerPoint	$29.95	
	Unleash the Power of Outlook 2003	$19.95	
	Unleash the Power of OneNote	$19.95	
	VBA and Macros for Microsoft Excel	$39.95	
	Pivot Table Data Crunching	$29.95	

Name: ______________________________
Address: ____________________________
City, State, Zip: ______________________
E-Mail: _____________________________

Sales Tax: Ohio residents add 6% sales tax
Shipping by Air: **US** $4 for first book, $2 per additional book. $1 per CD.
International: $9 for first book, $5 per additional book. $2 per CD
FedEx available on request at actual shipping cost.
Payment: Check or Money order to "MrExcel" or pay with VISA/MC/Discover/AmEx:
Card #:______________________ Exp.:__________
Name on Card: __________________________
Bulk Orders: Ordering enough for the entire staff? Save 40% when you order 6 or more of any one title.